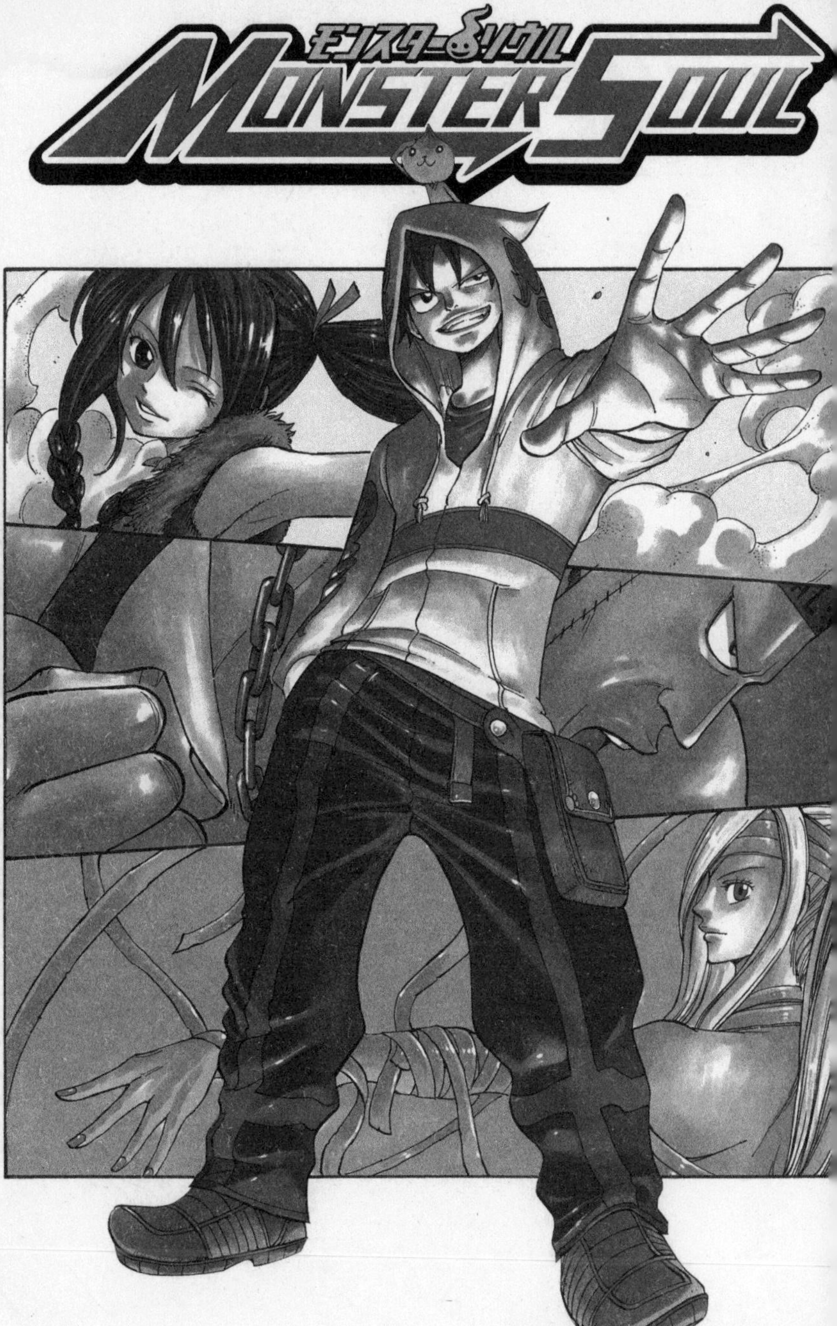
モンスター ソウル
MONSTER SOUL

ave arrived!!

MONSTER SOUL

モンスター・ソウル

Character Introduction

Who decided monsters have to be evil? This is a story of the monsters who work to overturn that stereotype and bring peace to the world.

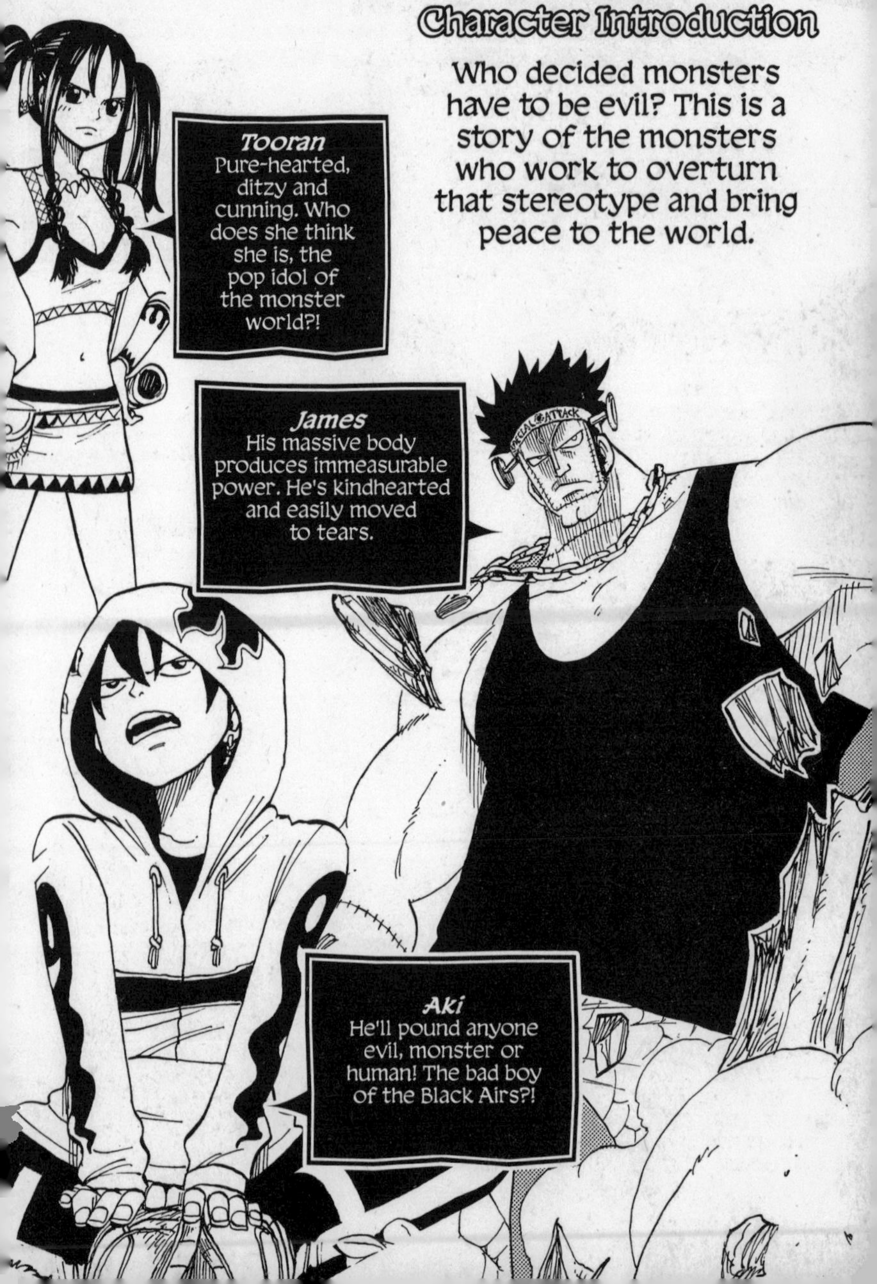
Tooran
Pure-hearted, ditzy and cunning. Who does she think she is, the pop idol of the monster world?!
James
His massive body produces immeasurable power. He's kindhearted and easily moved to tears.
Aki
He'll pound anyone evil, monster or human! The bad boy of the Black Airs?!

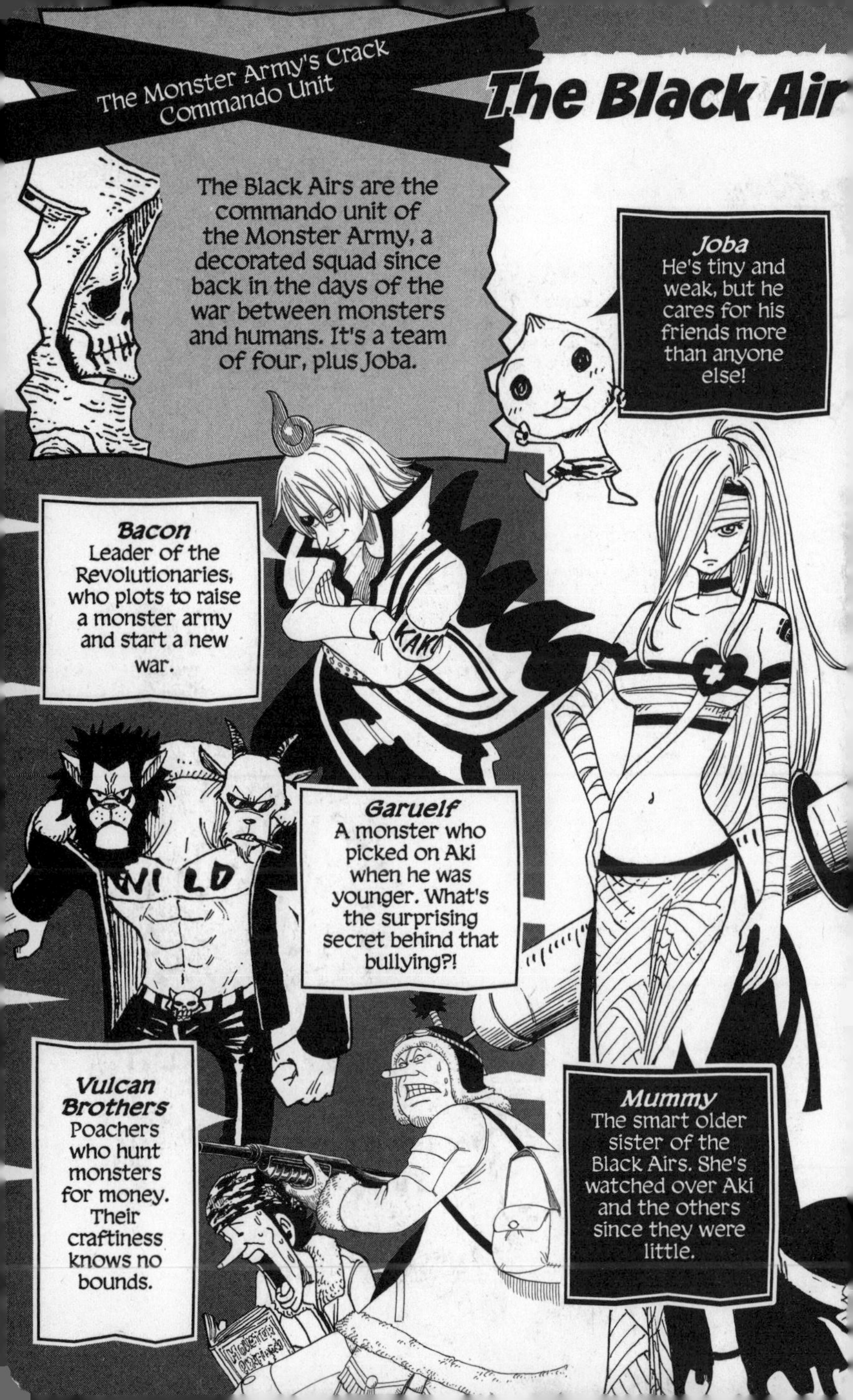
The Monster Army's Crack Commando Unit
The Black Air
The Black Airs are the commando unit of the Monster Army, a decorated squad since back in the days of the war between monsters and humans. It's a team of four, plus Joba.
Joba He's tiny and weak, but he cares for his friends more than anyone else!
Bacon Leader of the Revolutionaries, who plots to raise a monster army and start a new war.
KAKI
Garuelf A monster who picked on Aki when he was younger. What's the surprising secret behind that bullying?!
WILD
Mummy The smart older sister of the Black Airs. She's watched over Aki and the others since they were little.
Vulcan Brothers Poachers who hunt monsters for money. Their craftiness knows no bounds.

MONSTER SOUL

✖ ✖ ✖ ✖ ✖

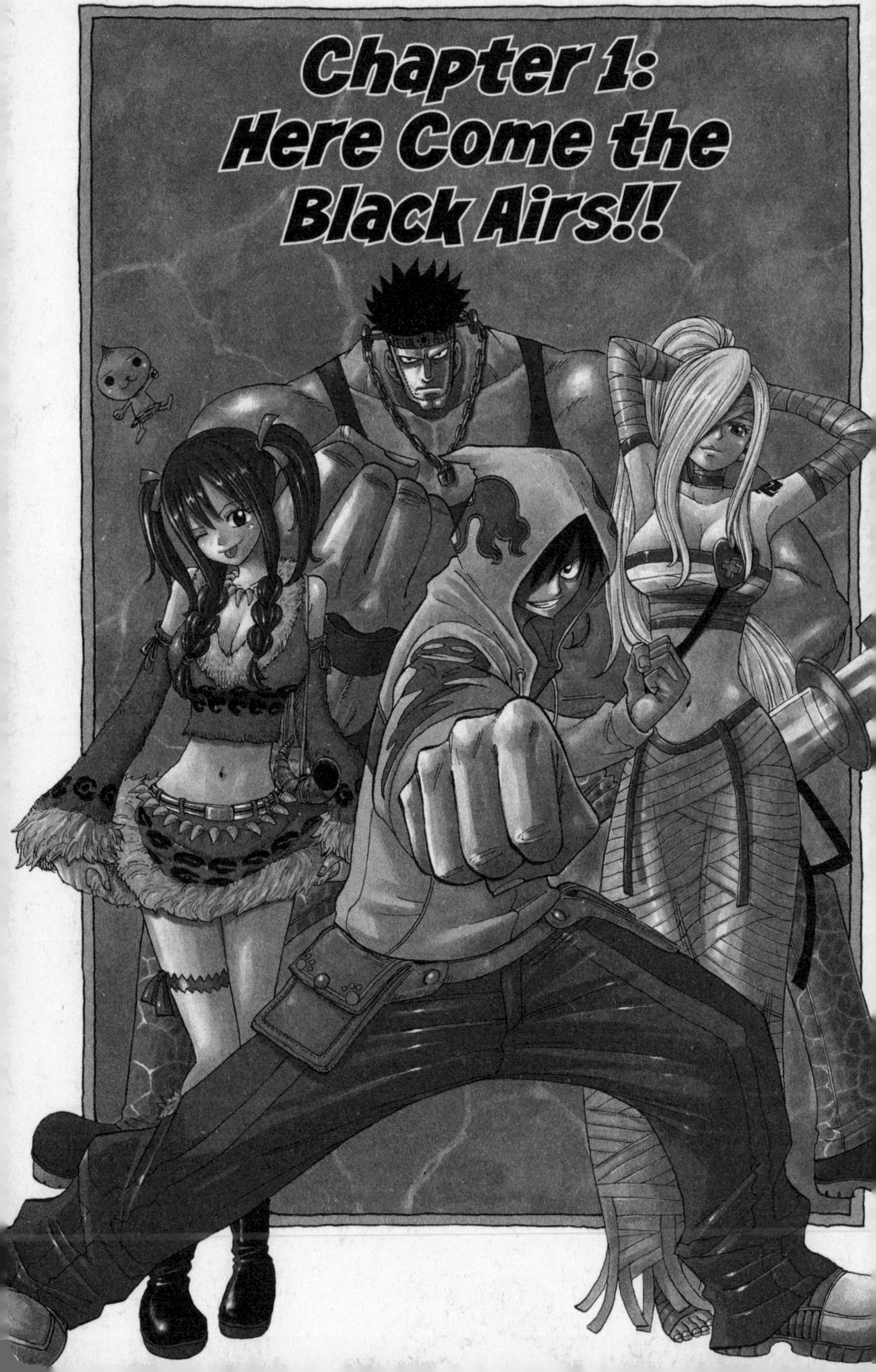
Chapter 1:
Here Come the
Black Airs!!

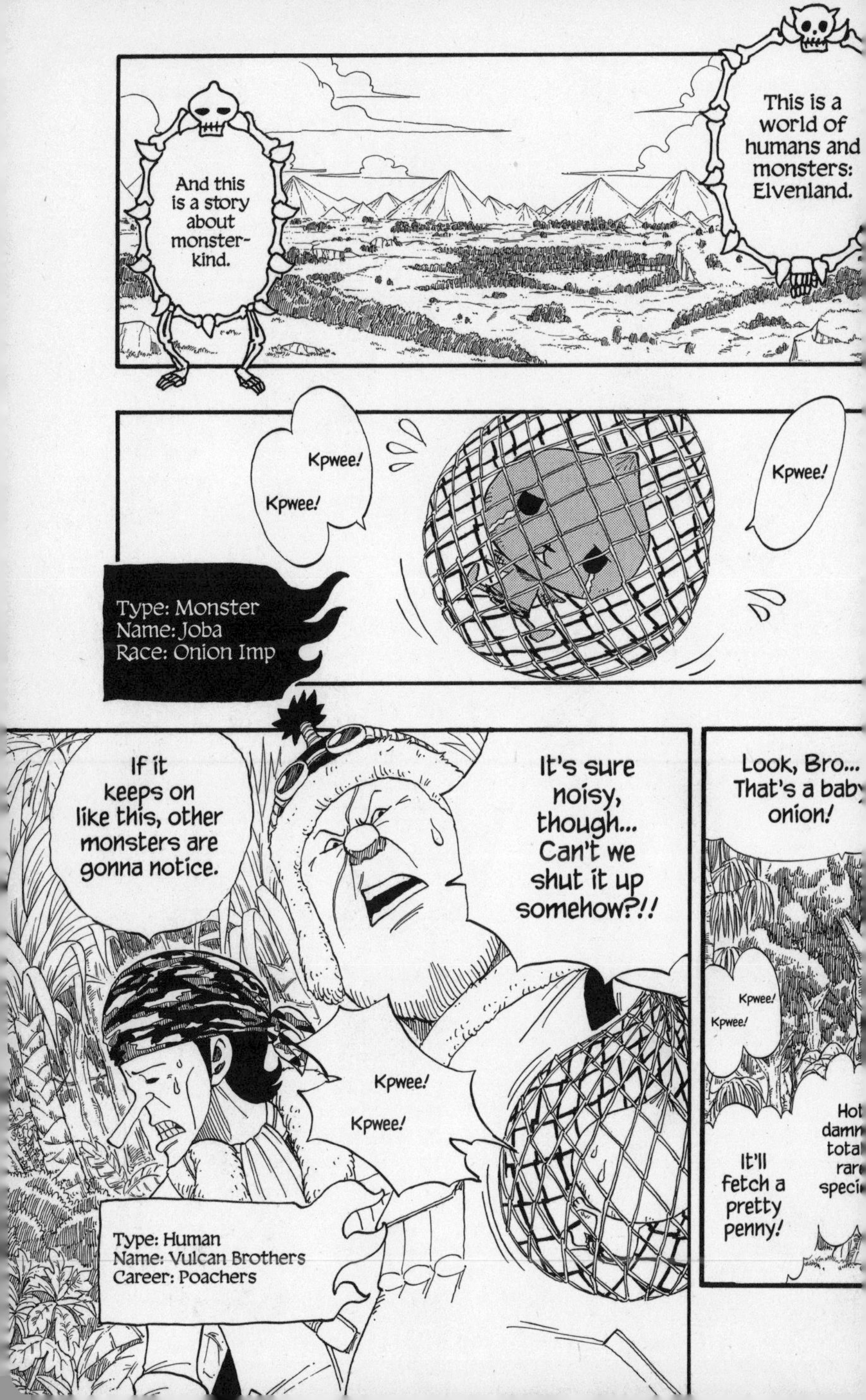
This is a world of humans and monsters: Elvenland.
And this is a story about monster-kind.
Kpwee!
Kpwee!
Kpwee!
Type: Monster
Name: Joba
Race: Onion Imp
Look, Bro... That's a bab
onion!
Kpwee!
Kpwee!
Hot damn
tota
rar
speci
It'll fetch a pretty penny!
It's sure noisy, though... Can't we shut it up somehow?!!
If it keeps on like this, other monsters are gonna notice.
Kpwee!
Kpwee!
Type: Human
Name: Vulcan Brothers
Career: Poachers

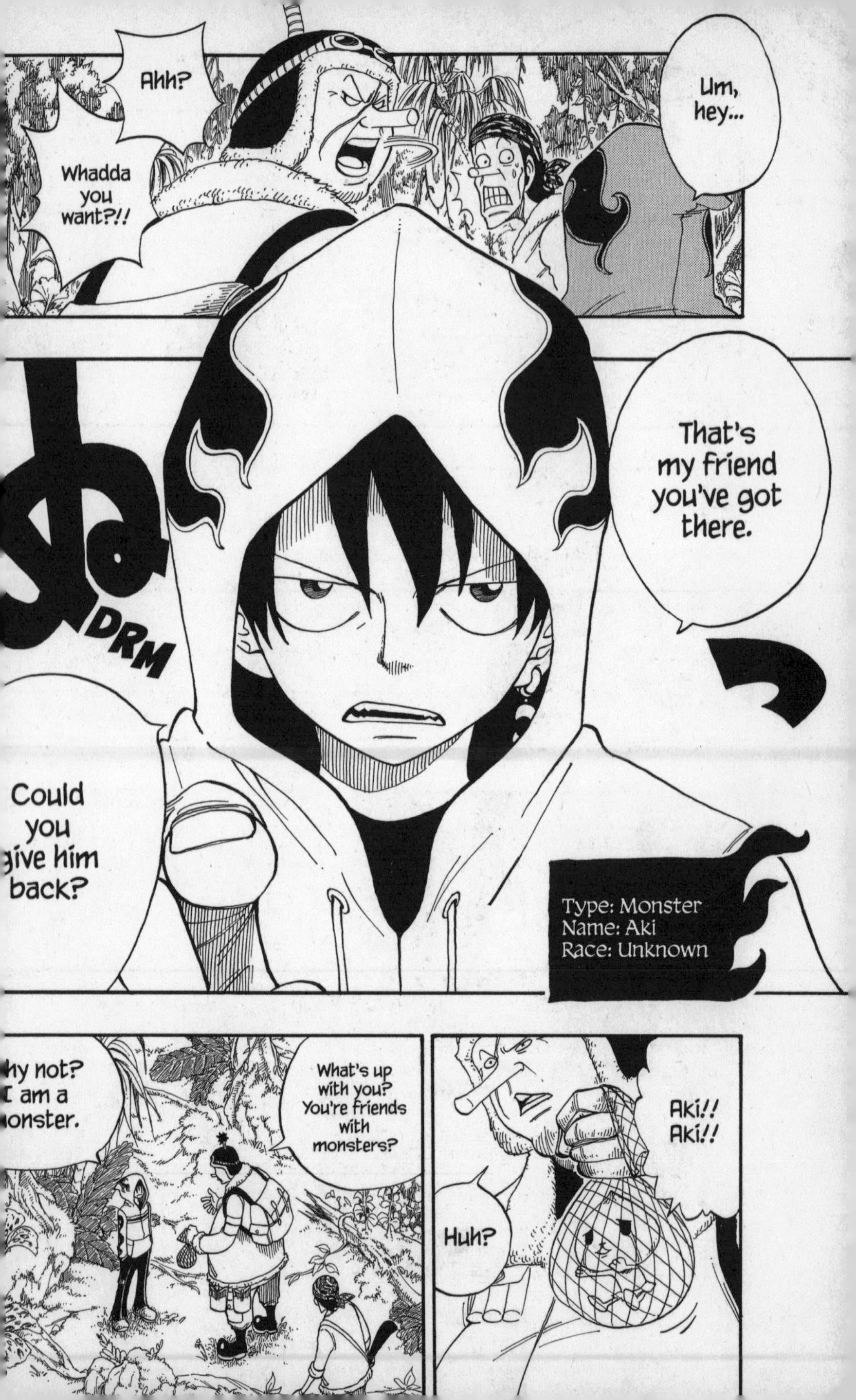
Um, hey...
Ahh?
Whadda you want?!!
That's my friend you've got there.
DRM
Could you give him back?
Type: Monster
Name: Aki
Race: Unknown
Aki!! Aki!!
Huh?
What's up with you? You're friends with monsters?
hy not? I am a onster.

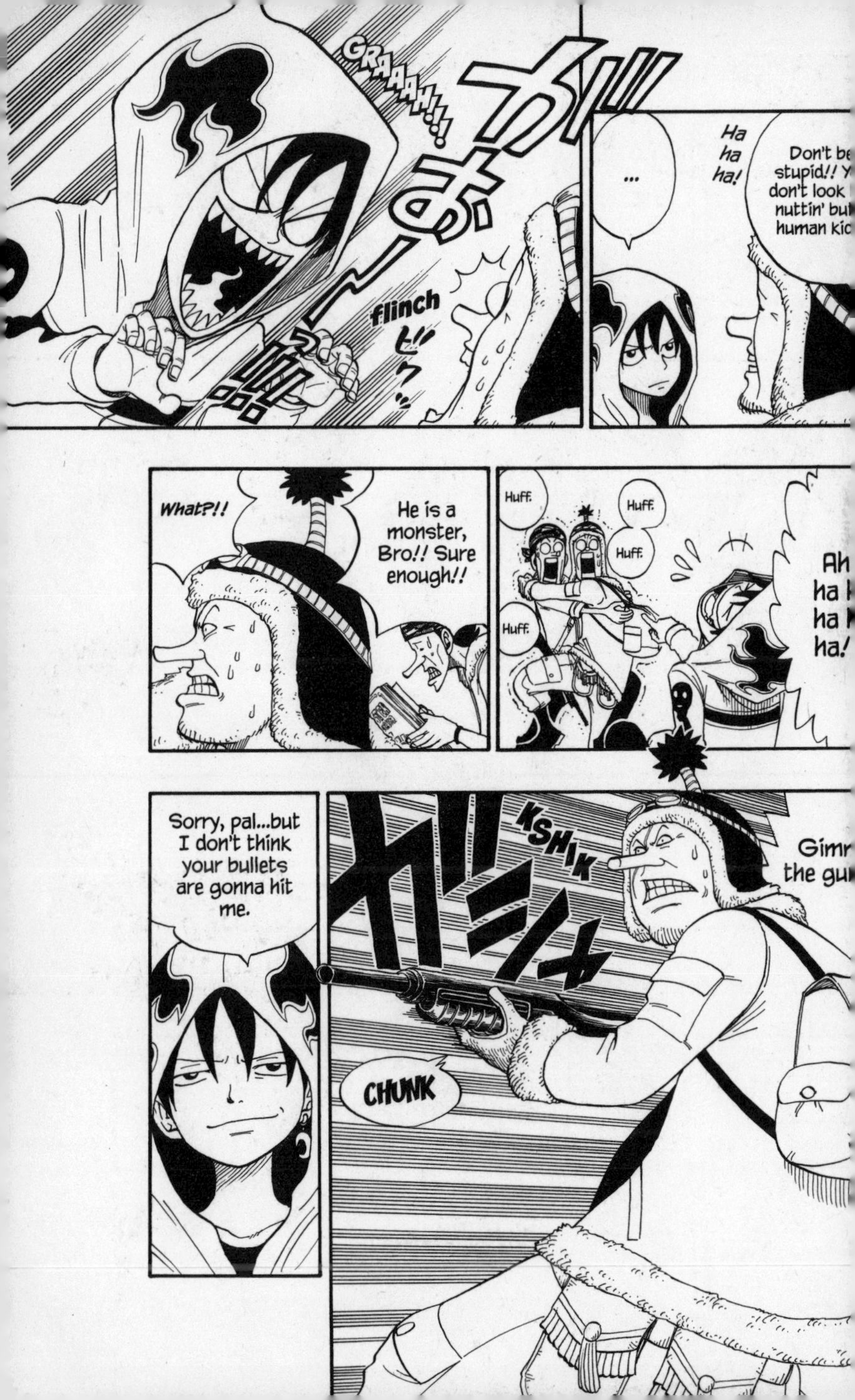
Don't be stupid!! Y don't look nuttin' bu human kic
Ha ha ha!
...
GRAAAAH!!!
flinch
Ah ha h ha h ha!
Huff.
Huff.
Huff.
Huff.
He is a monster, Bro!! Sure enough!!
What?!!
Gimr the gu
KSHIK
CHUNK
Sorry, pal...but I don't think your bullets are gonna hit me.

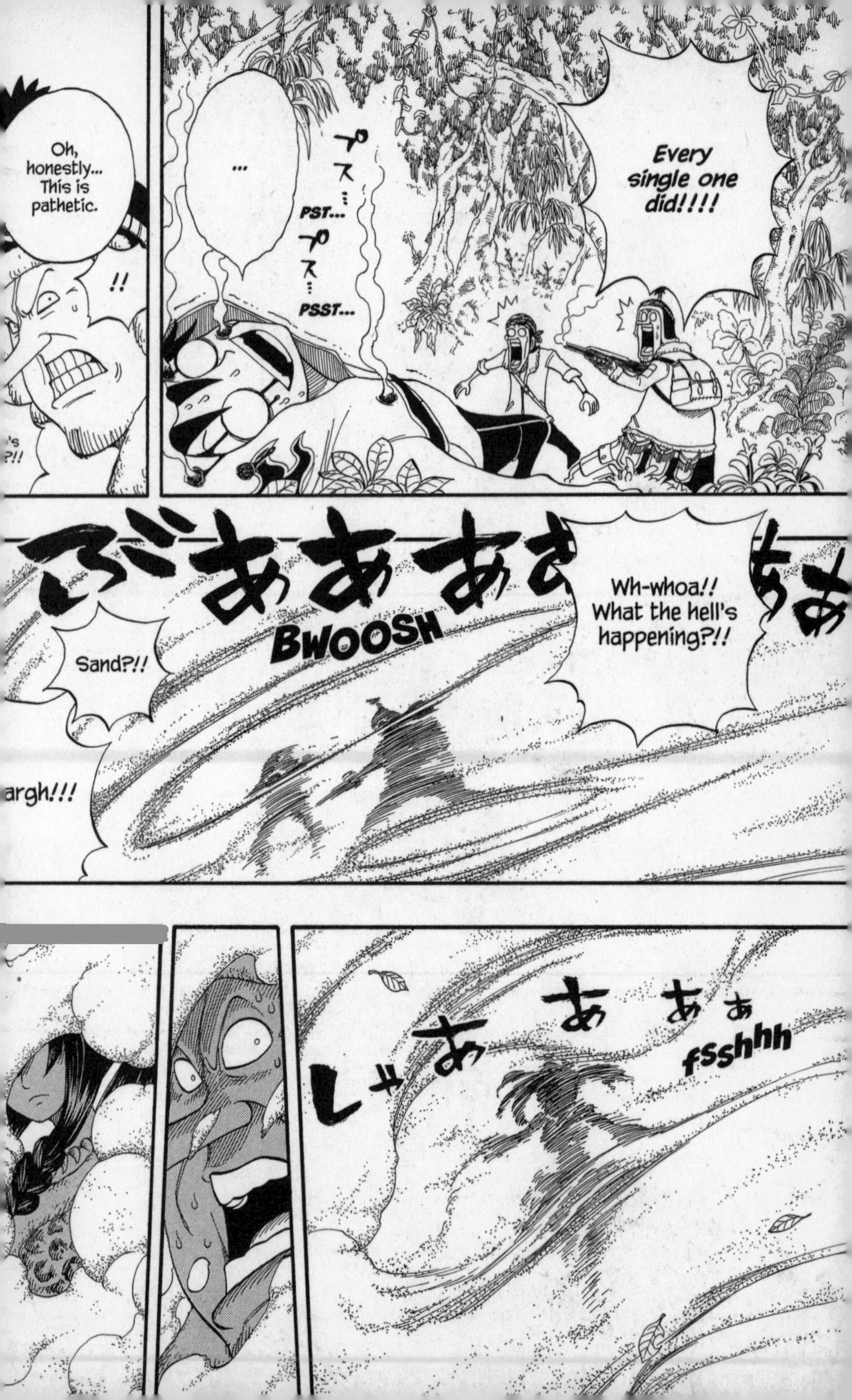

Every single one did!!!!
...
プス…
PST...
プス…
PSST...
Oh, honestly... This is pathetic.
!!
Wh-whoa!! What the hell's happening?!!
BWOOSH
Sand?!!
argh!!!
しゃあああぁ
fsshhh

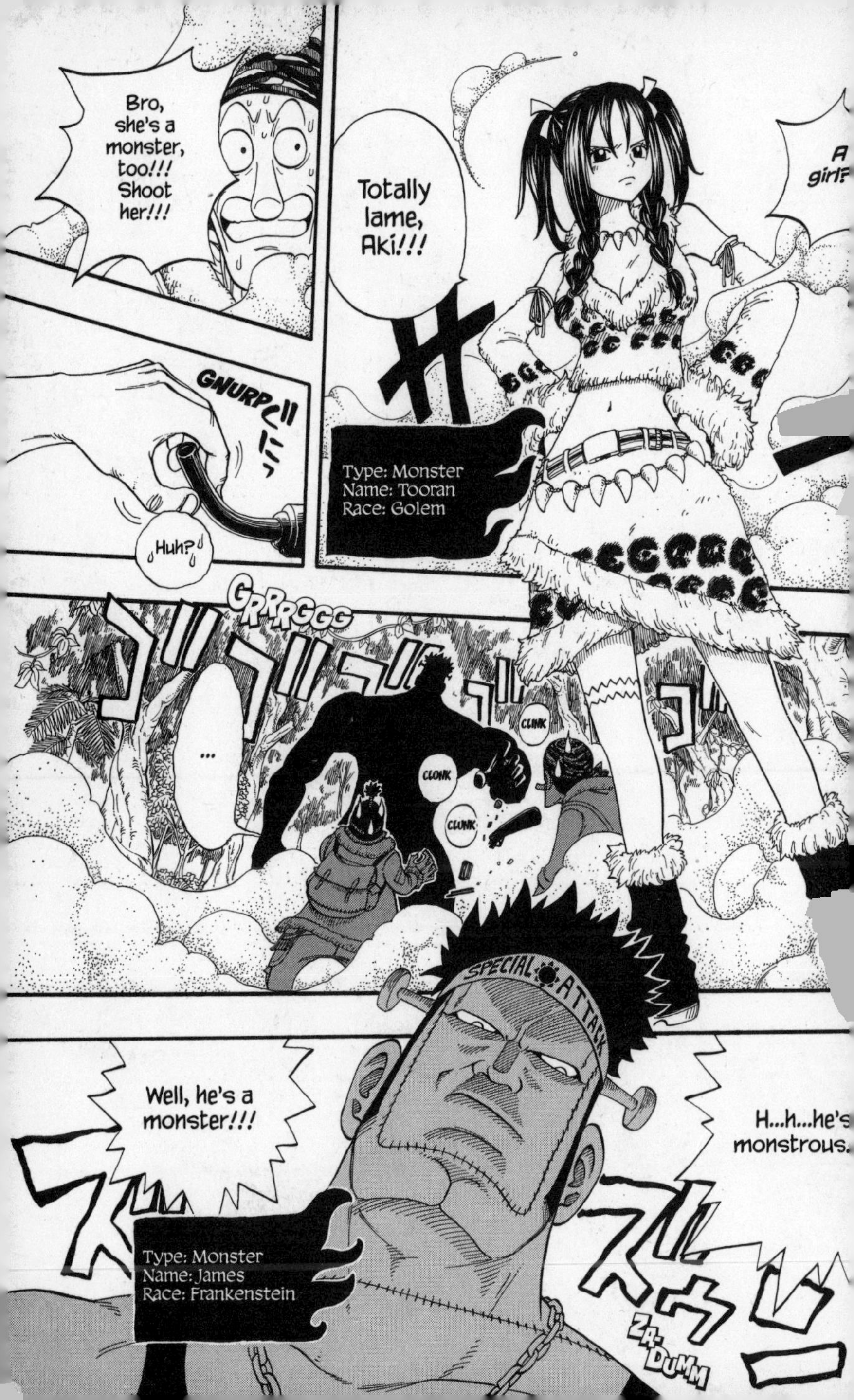
A girl?
Totally lame, Aki!!!
Type: Monster
Name: Tooran
Race: Golem
Bro, she's a monster, too!!! Shoot her!!!
GNURP
Huh?
GRRRGGG
CLINK
CLONK
CLUNK
...
H...h...he's monstrous.
Well, he's a monster!!!
SPECIAL ATTACK
Type: Monster
Name: James
Race: Frankenstein
ZA-DUMM

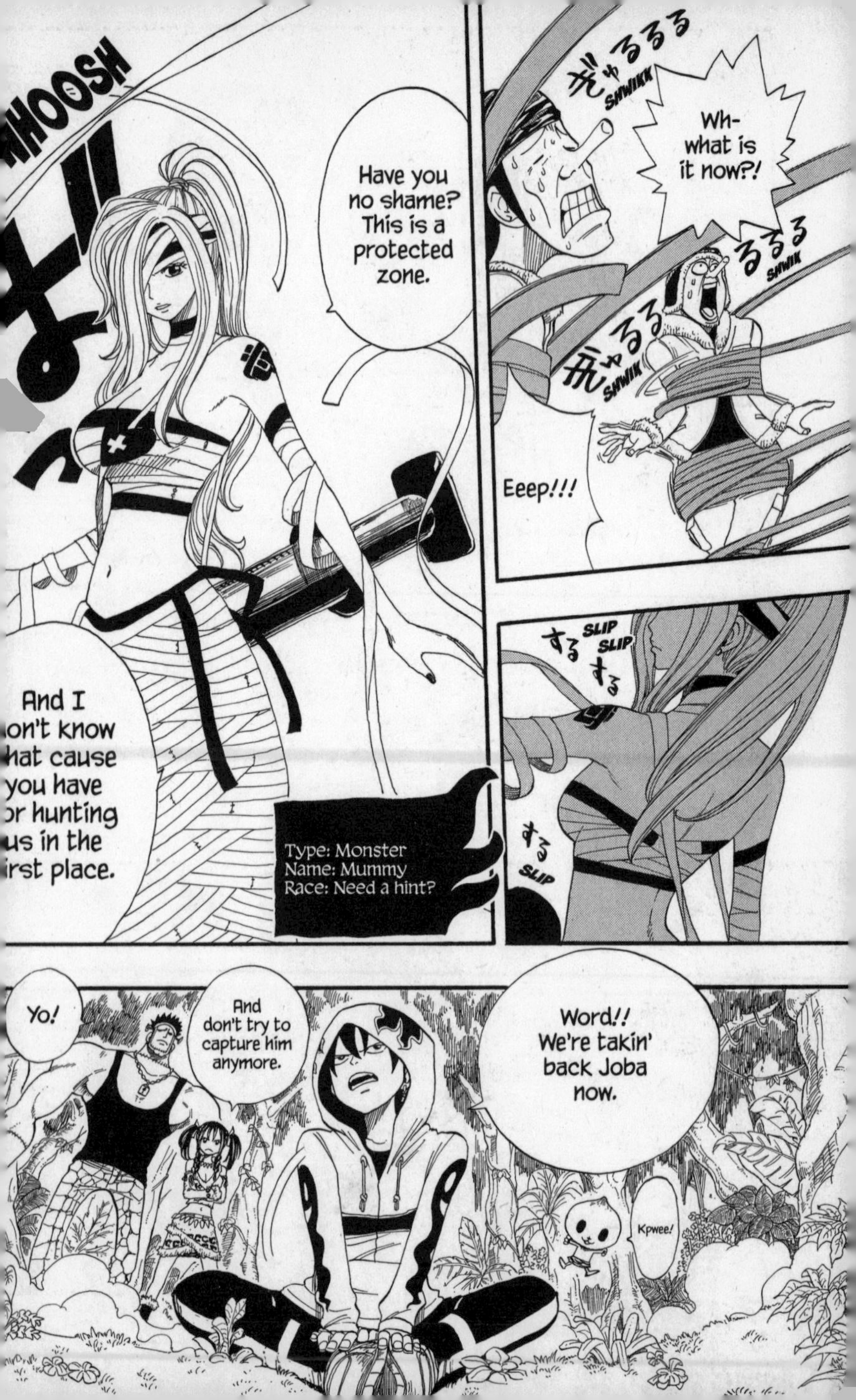
SHWIKK
Wh- what is it now?!
SHWIK
SHWIK
Eeep!!!
SLIP SLIP
SLIP
HOOSH
Have you no shame? This is a protected zone.
And I on't know hat cause you have or hunting us in the irst place.
Type: Monster
Name: Mummy
Race: Need a hint?
Word!! We're takin' back Joba now.
Kpwee!
And don't try to capture him anymore.
Yo!

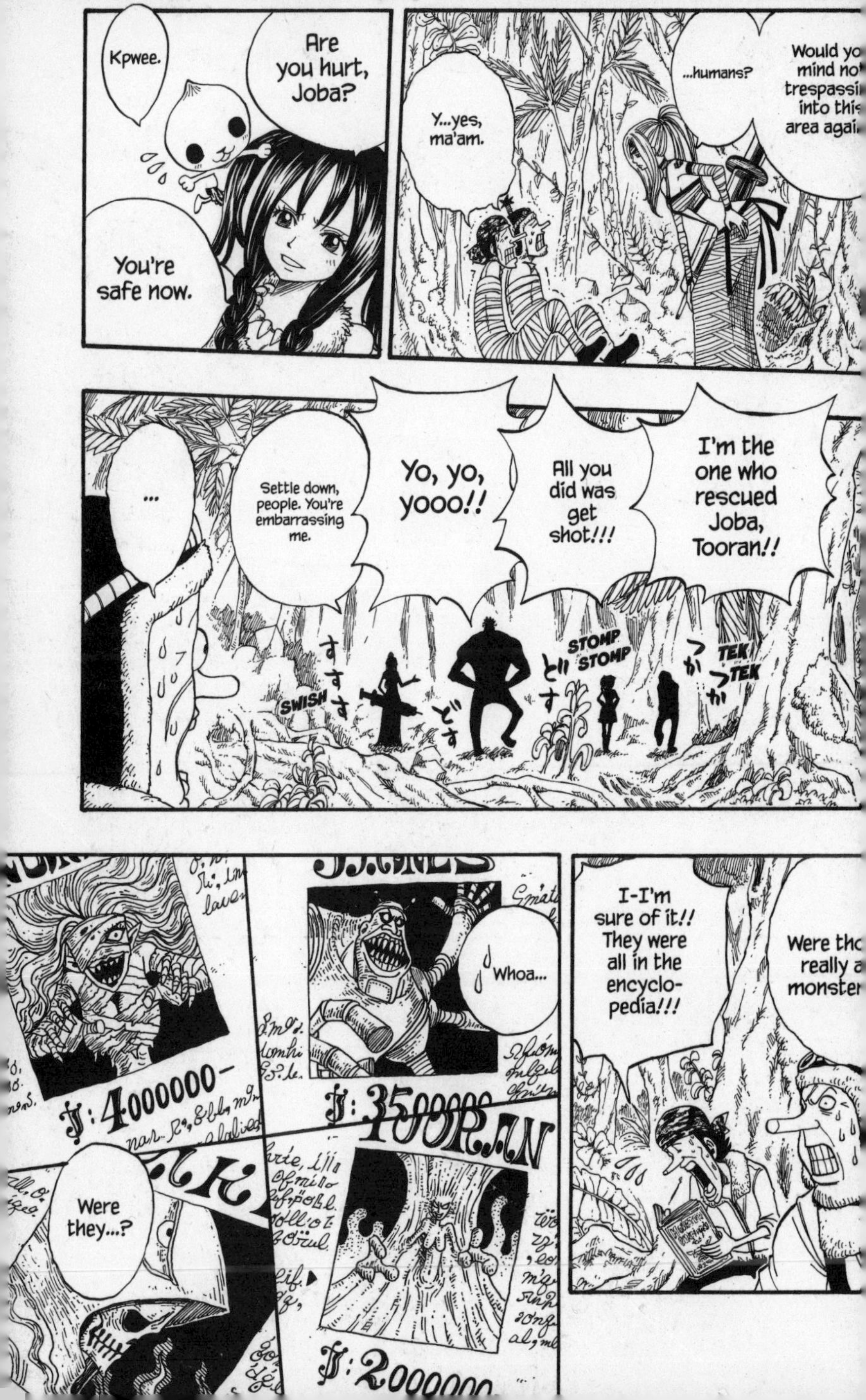

...humans?
Y...yes, ma'am.
Are you hurt, Joba?
Kpwee.
You're safe now.
I'm the one who rescued Joba, Tooran!!
All you did was get shot!!!
Yo, yo, yooo!!
Settle down, people. You're embarrassing me.
...
つかつか
TEK TEK
どすどす
STOMP STOMP
すすす
SWISH
I-I'm sure of it!! They were all in the encyclopedia!!!
Whoa...
TOORAN
Were they...?

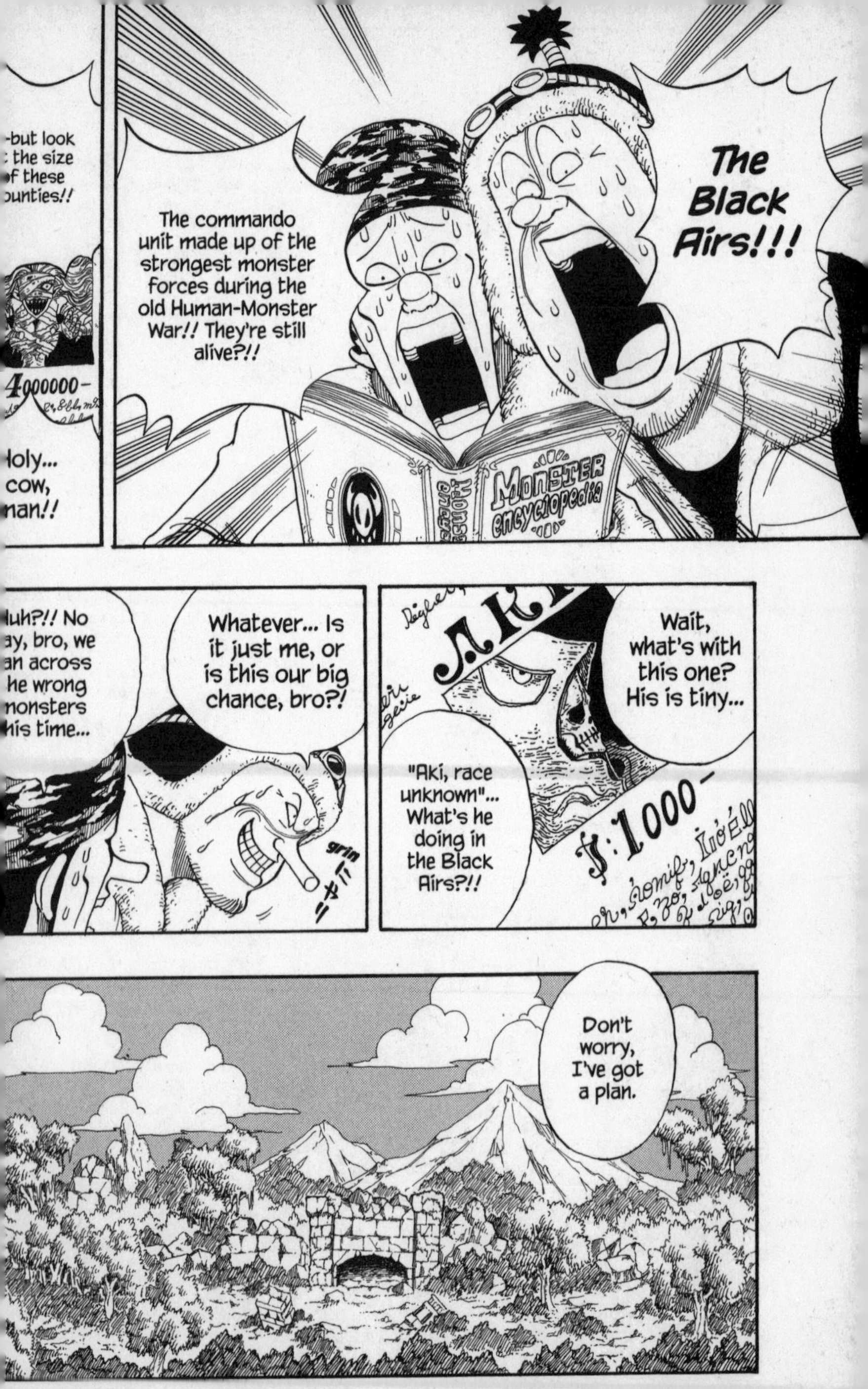
The Black Airs!!!
The commando unit made up of the strongest monster forces during the old Human-Monster War!! They're still alive?!!
MONSTER encyclopedia
-but look
the size
of these
ounties!!
4000000-
Holy...
cow,
man!!
Wait, what's with this one? His is tiny...
"Aki, race unknown"... What's he doing in the Black Airs?!!
$:1000-
uh?!! No
ay, bro, we
an across
he wrong
monsters
his time...
Whatever... Is it just me, or is this our big chance, bro?!
grin
Don't worry, I've got a plan.

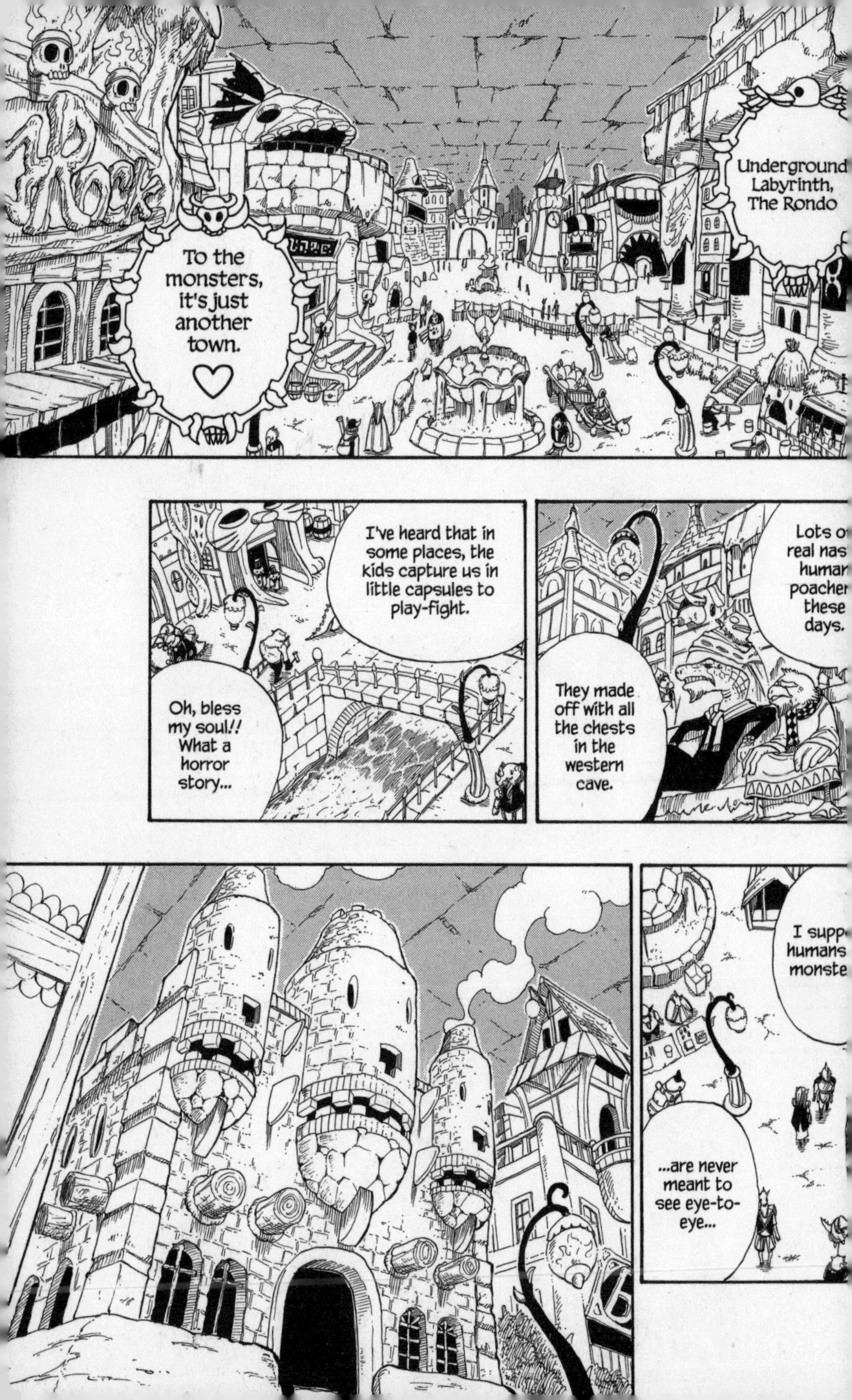
Underground Labyrinth, The Rondo
Rock
To the monsters, it's just another town. ♥
Lots o real nas human poacher these days.
They made off with all the chests in the western cave.
I've heard that in some places, the kids capture us in little capsules to play-fight.
Oh, bless my soul!! What a horror story...
I supp humans monste
...are never meant to see eye-to-eye...

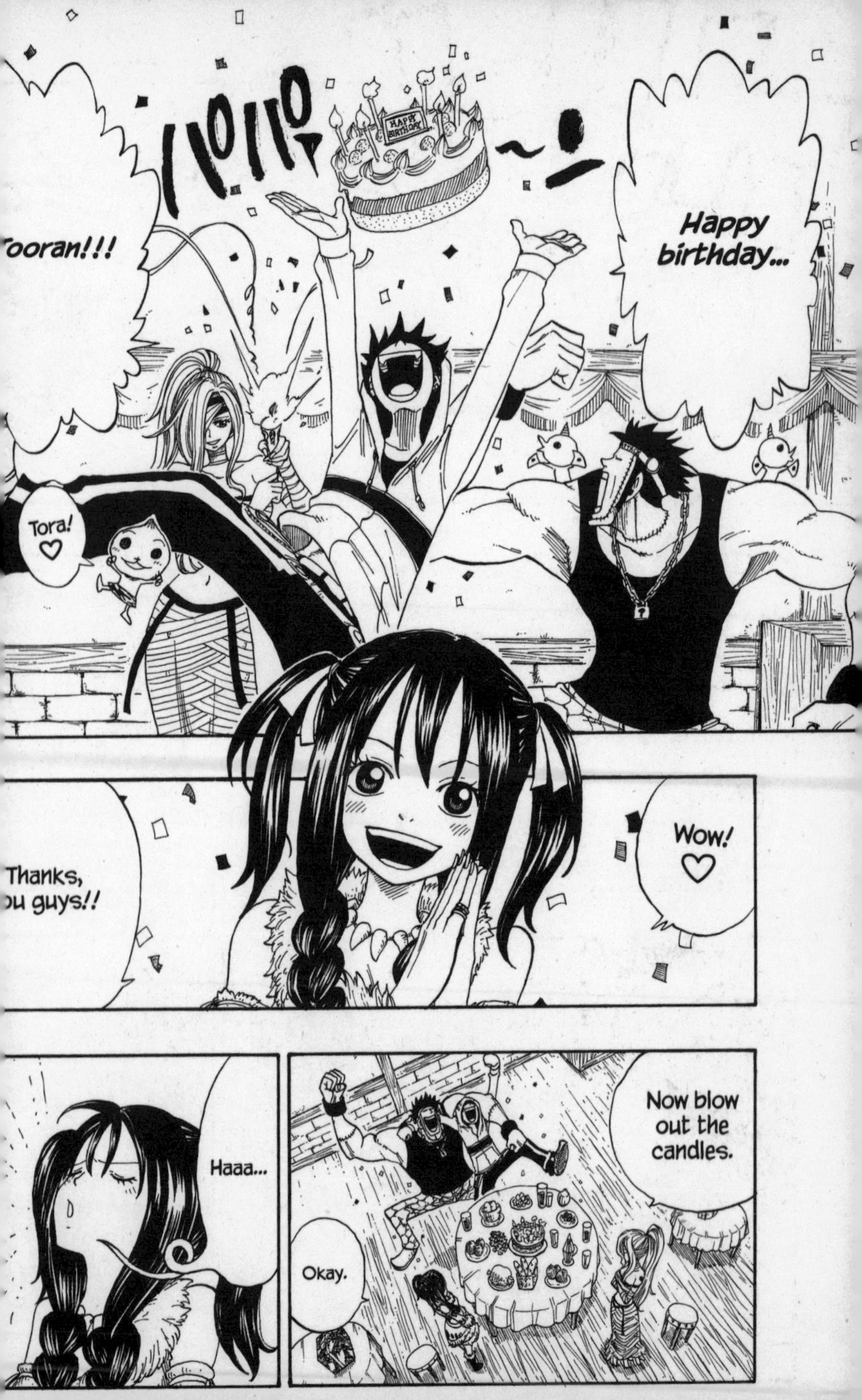
Happy birthday...
Tooran!!!
Tora! ♡
Wow! ♡
Thanks, ou guys!!
Now blow out the candles.
Okay.
Haaa...

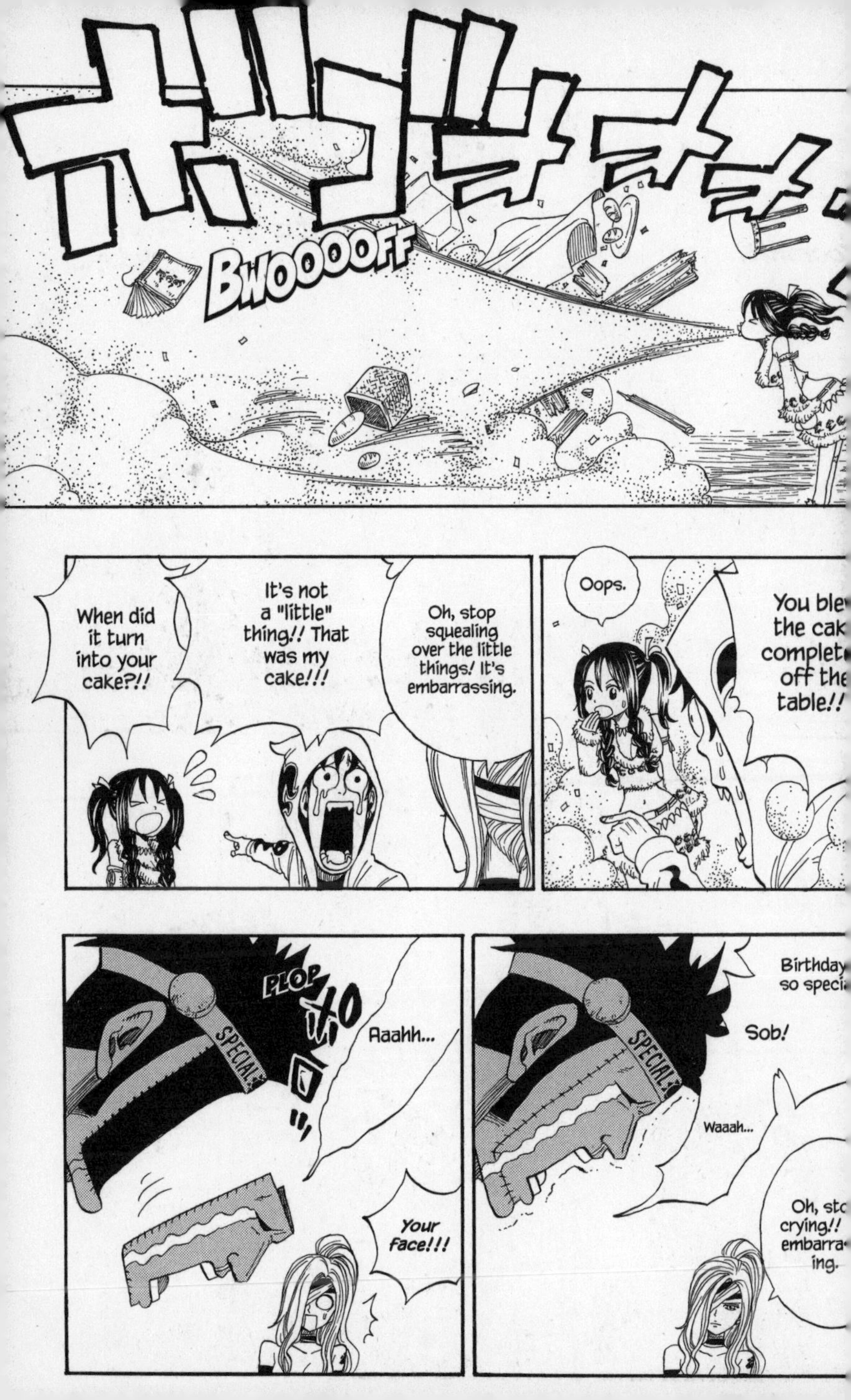

BWOOOOFF
Oops.
You ble the cak complet off the table!!
Oh, stop squealing over the little things! It's embarrassing.
It's not a "little" thing!! That was my cake!!!
When did it turn into your cake?!!
Birthday so speci
Sob!
Waaah...
Oh, sto crying!! embarra- ing.
PLOP
Aaahh...
Your face!!!

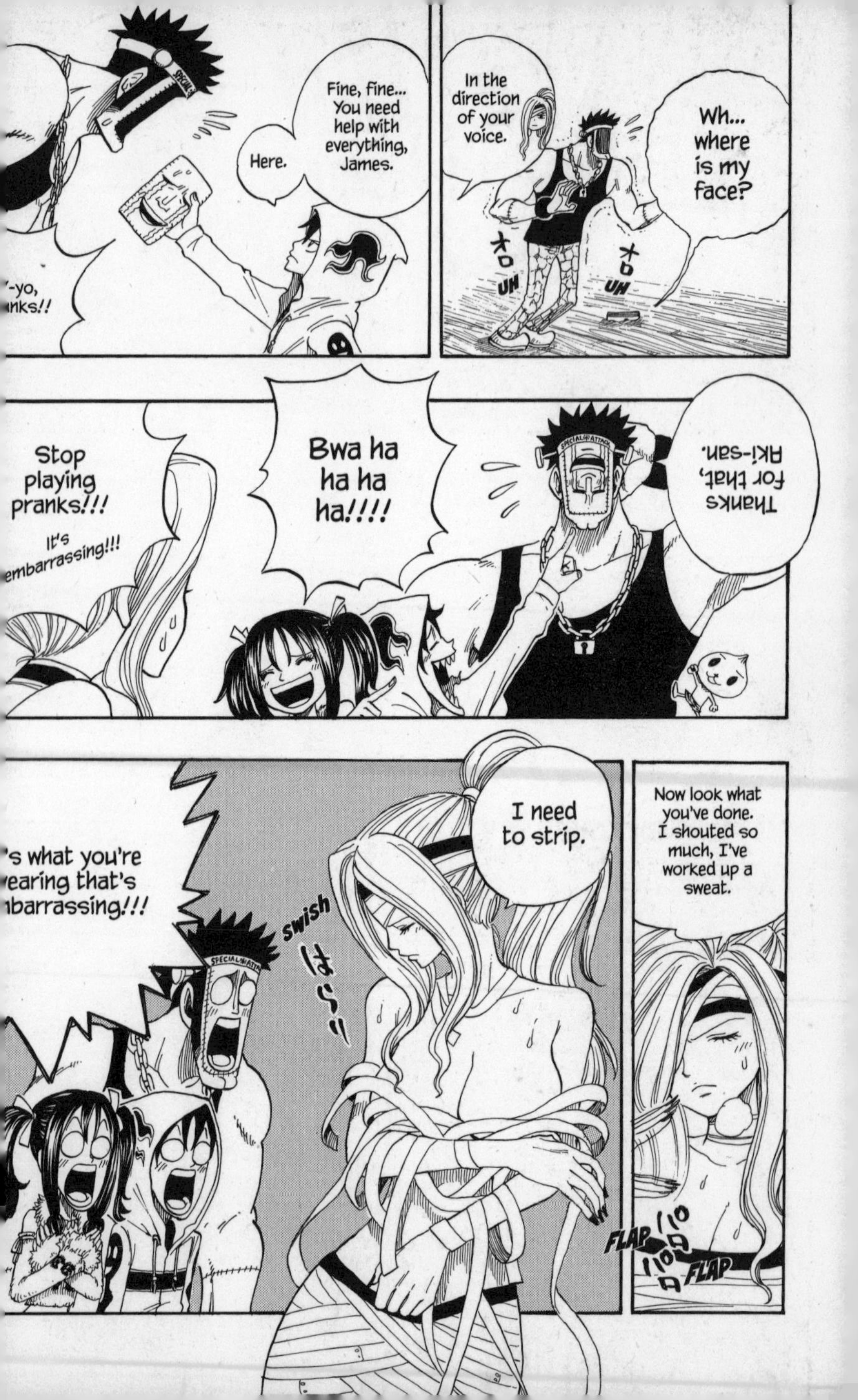
Wh... where is my face?
UH
UH
In the direction of your voice.
Fine, fine... You need help with everything, James.
Here.
'-yo,
nks!!
Thanks for that, Aki-san.
Bwa ha ha ha ha!!!!
Stop playing pranks!!!
It's embarrassing!!!
Now look what you've done. I shouted so much, I've worked up a sweat.
FLAP
FLAP
I need to strip.
swish
's what you're
earing that's
nbarrassing!!!

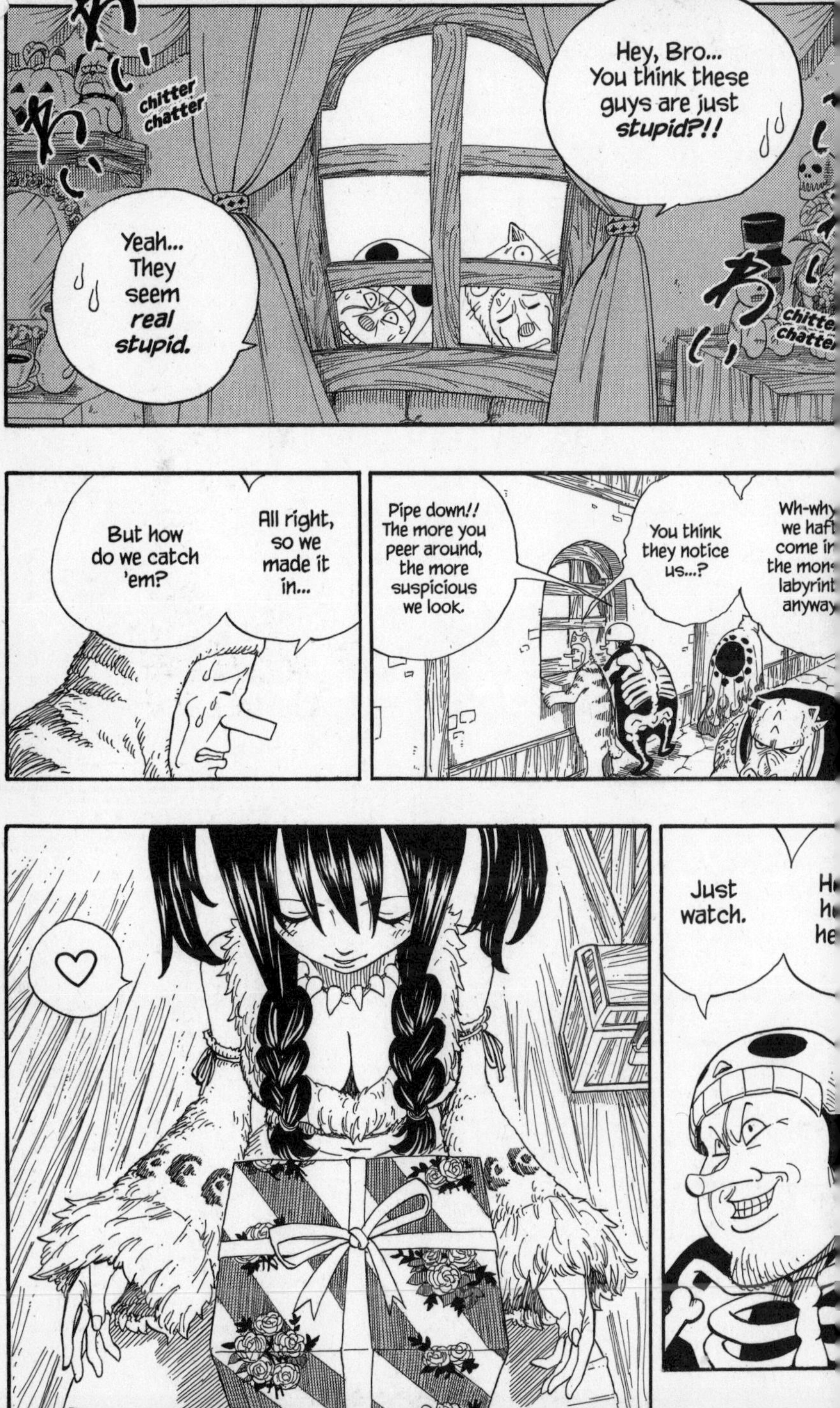
Hey, Bro... You think these guys are just stupid?!!
Yeah... They seem real stupid.
わいわい
chitter chatter
You think they notice us...?
Pipe down!! The more you peer around, the more suspicious we look.
All right, so we made it in...
But how do we catch 'em?
Just watch.
♡

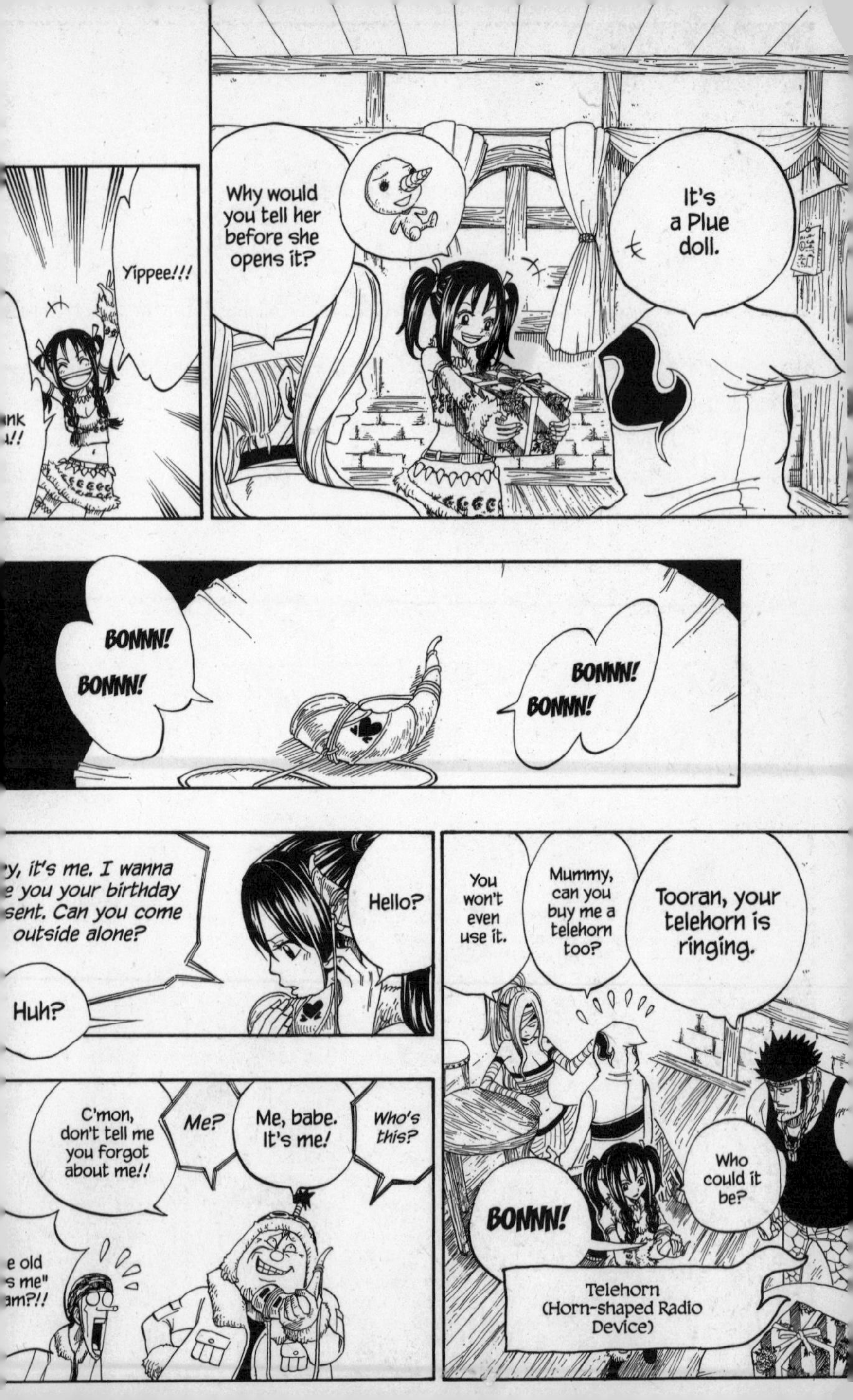
It's a Plue doll.
Why would you tell her before she opens it?
Yippee!!!
nk
u!!
BONNN! BONNN!
BONNN! BONNN!
Tooran, your telehorn is ringing.
Mummy, can you buy me a telehorn too?
You won't even use it.
Who could it be?
BONNN!
Telehorn (Horn-shaped Radio Device)
Hello?
y, it's me. I wanna
e you your birthday
sent. Can you come outside alone?
Huh?
Who's this?
Me, babe. It's me!
Me?
C'mon, don't tell me you forgot about me!!
e old
s me"
am?!!

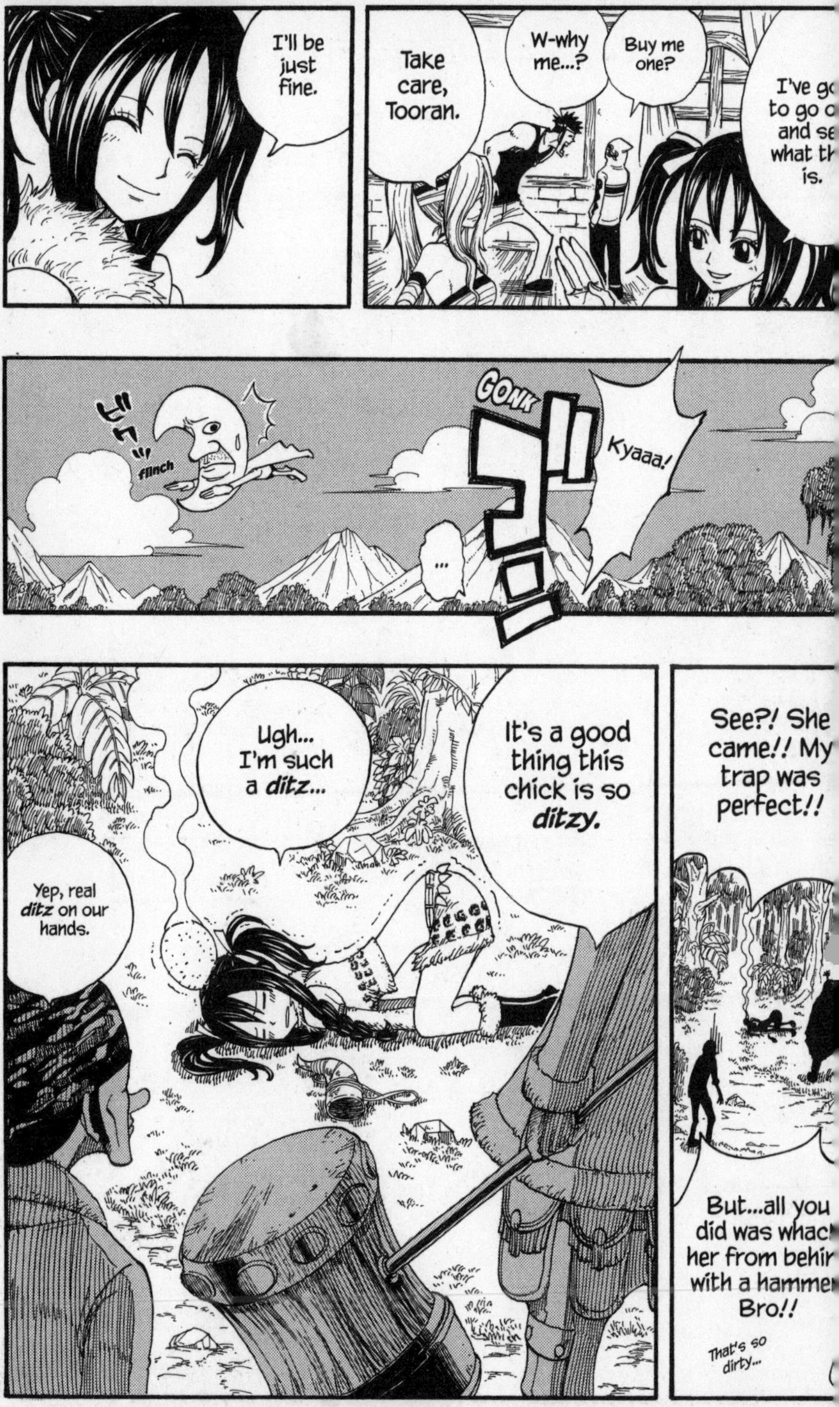
I've go
to go o
and se
what th
is.
Buy me one?
W-why me...?
Take care, Tooran.
I'll be just fine.
Kyaaa!
GONK
...
flinch
See?! She came!! My trap was perfect!!
But...all you did was whac
her from behi
with a hamme
Bro!!
That's so dirty...
It's a good thing this chick is so *ditzy.*
Ugh... I'm such a *ditz*...
Yep, real *ditz* on our hands.

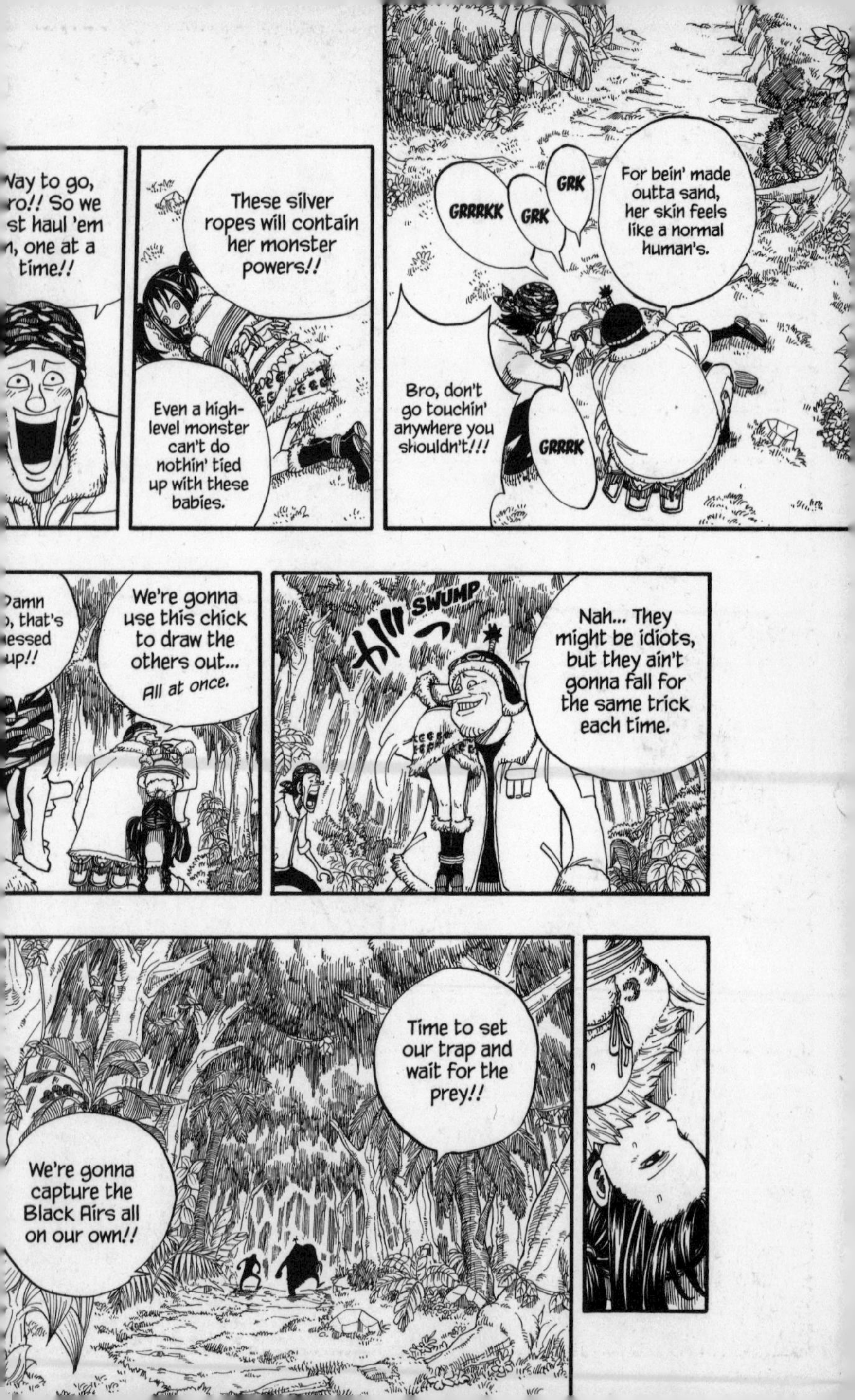
For bein' made outta sand, her skin feels like a normal human's.
GRK
GRK
GRRRKK
Bro, don't go touchin' anywhere you shouldn't!!!
GRRRK
These silver ropes will contain her monster powers!!
Even a high-level monster can't do nothin' tied up with these babies.
Way to go, ro!! So we st haul 'em n, one at a time!!
SWUMP
Nah... They might be idiots, but they ain't gonna fall for the same trick each time.
We're gonna use this chick to draw the others out... All at once.
amn o, that's essed up!!
Time to set our trap and wait for the prey!!
We're gonna capture the Black Airs all on our own!!

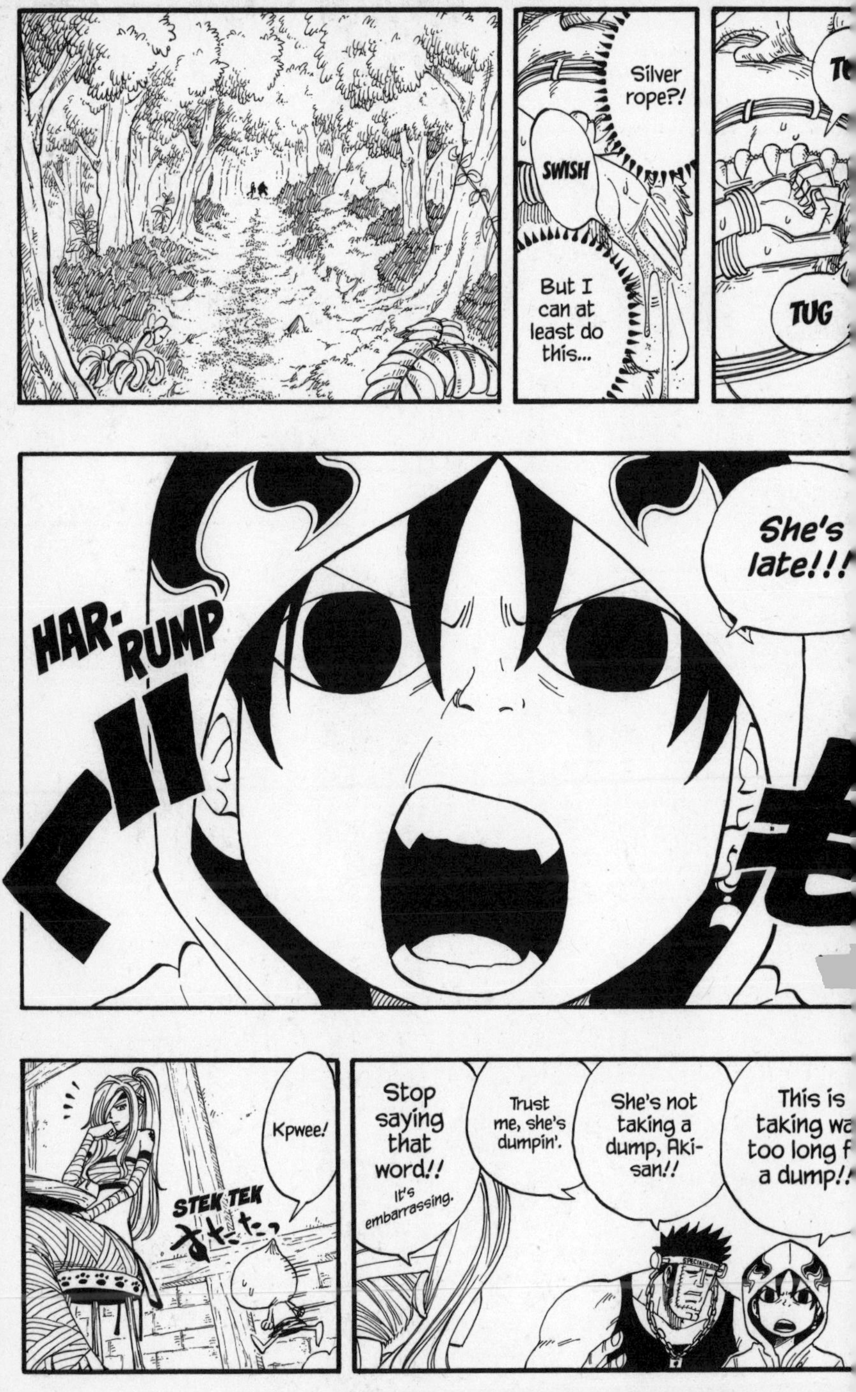

TUG
Silver rope?!
SWISH
But I can at least do this...
She's late!!!
HAR-RUMP
This is taking wa too long f a dump!!
She's not taking a dump, Aki-san!!
Trust me, she's dumpin'.
Stop saying that word!!
It's embarrassing.
Kpwee!
STEK TEK

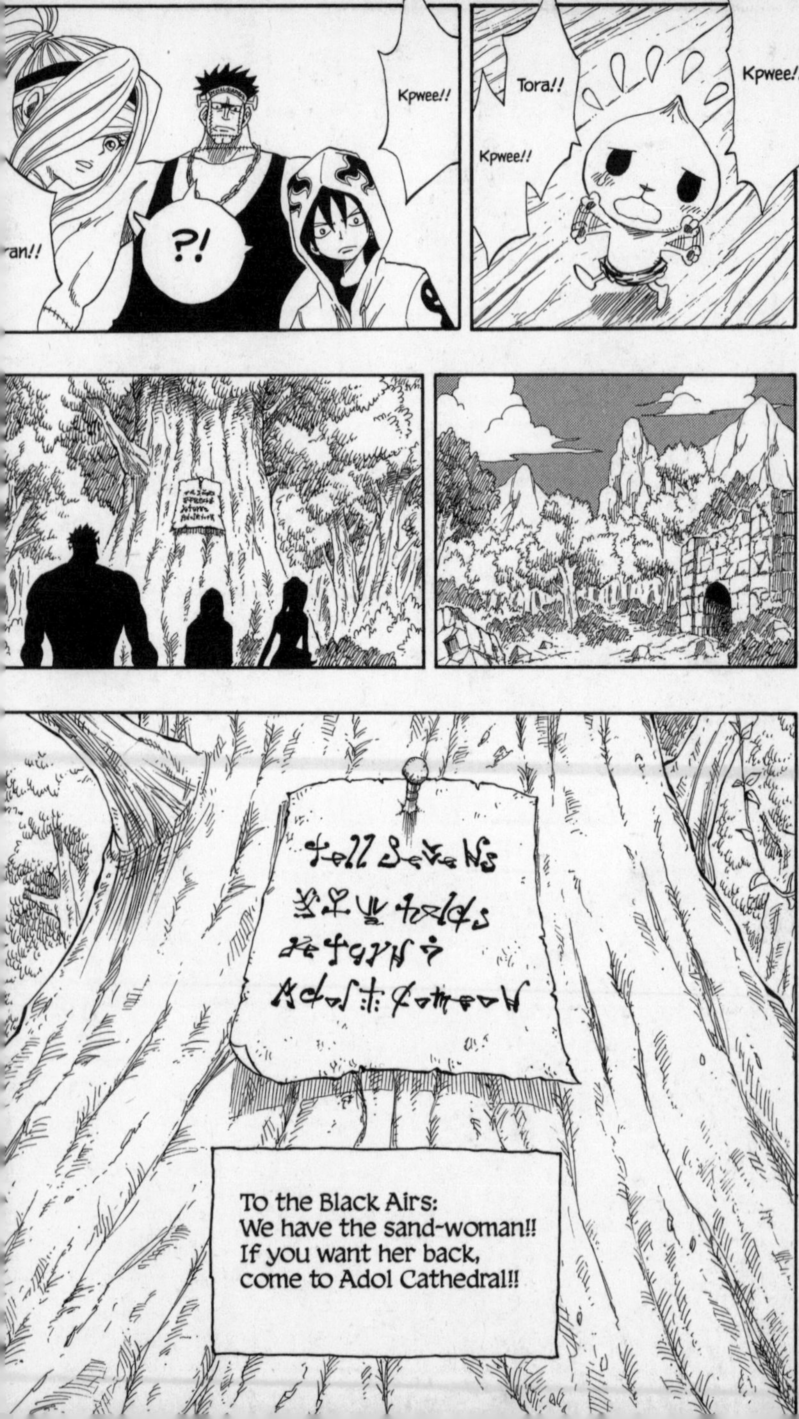
Kpwee!!
Tora!!
Kpwee!!
Kpwee!!
?!
To the Black Airs:
We have the sand-woman!!
If you want her back,
come to Adol Cathedral!!

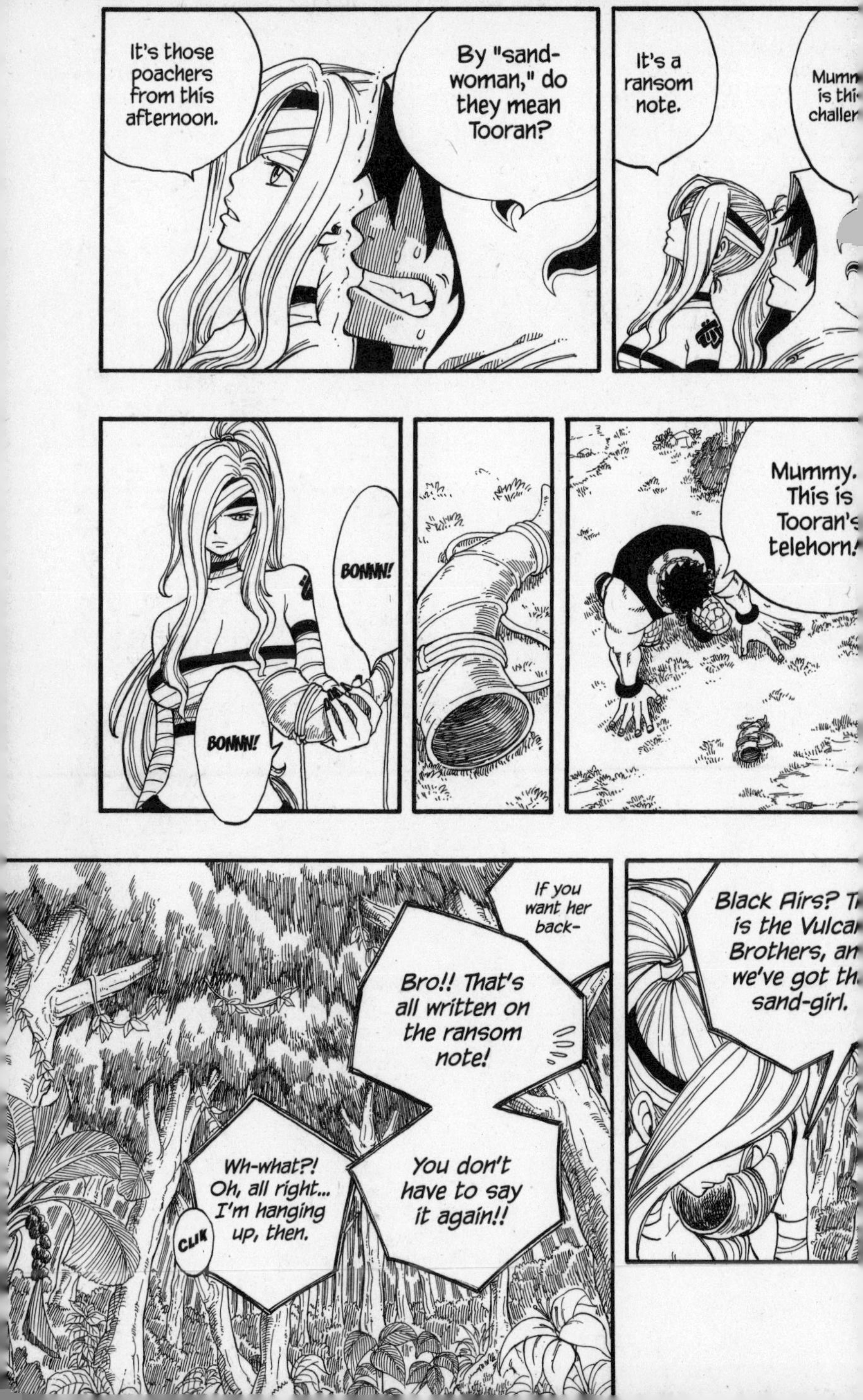
Mumm
is thi
challer
It's a ransom note.
By "sand-woman," do they mean Tooran?
It's those poachers from this afternoon.
Mummy. This is Tooran's telehorn!
BONNN!
BONNN!
Black Airs? T
is the Vulca
Brothers, an
we've got th
sand-girl.
If you want her back-
Bro!! That's all written on the ransom note!
You don't have to say it again!!
Wh-what?! Oh, all right... I'm hanging up, then.
CLIK

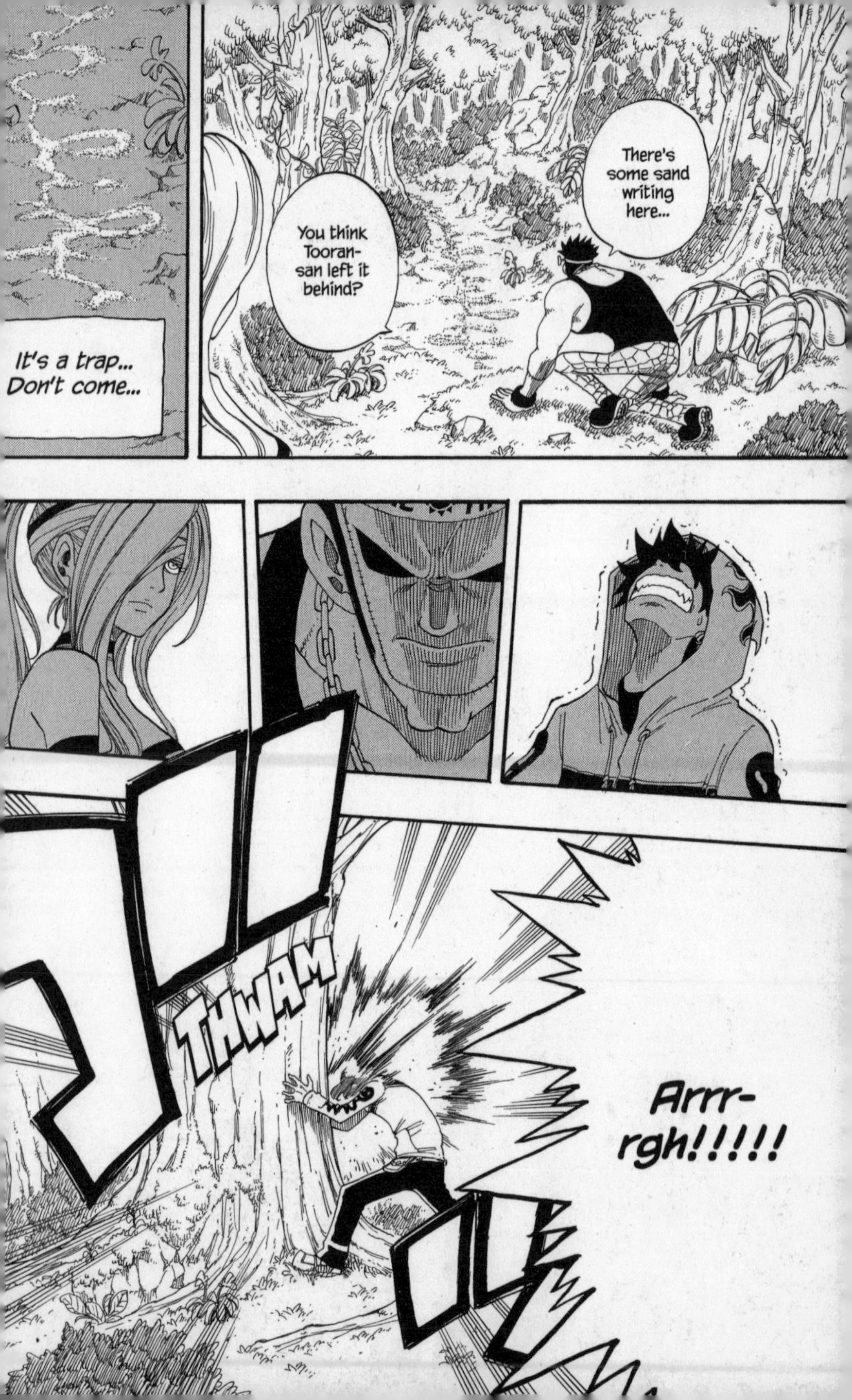
There's some sand writing here...
You think Tooran-san left it behind?
It's a trap... Don't come...
THWAM
Arrr-rgh!!!!!

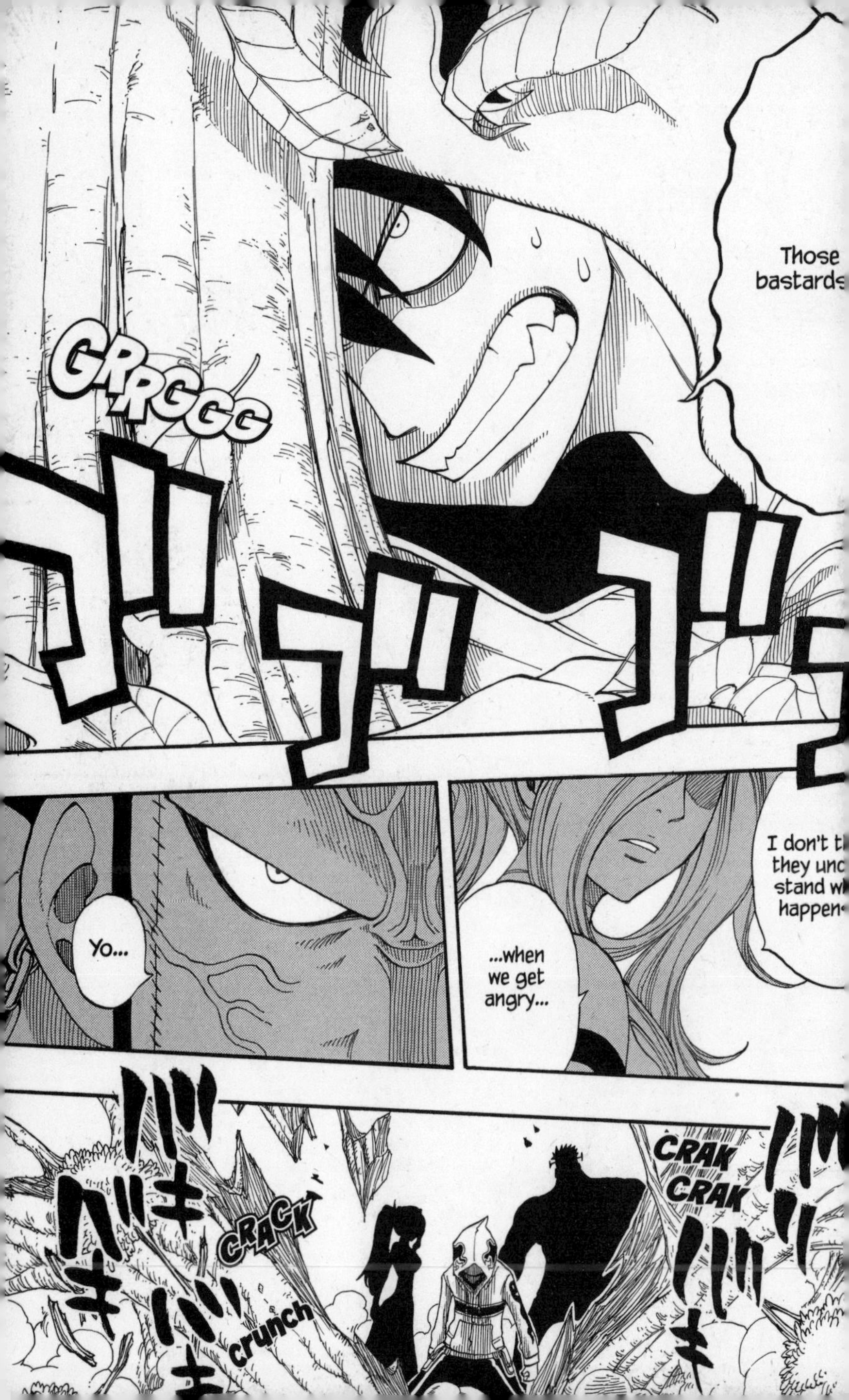
Those bastards
GRRGGG
I don't t they und stand wh happen
...when we get angry...
Yo...
CRAK CRAK
CRACK
crunch

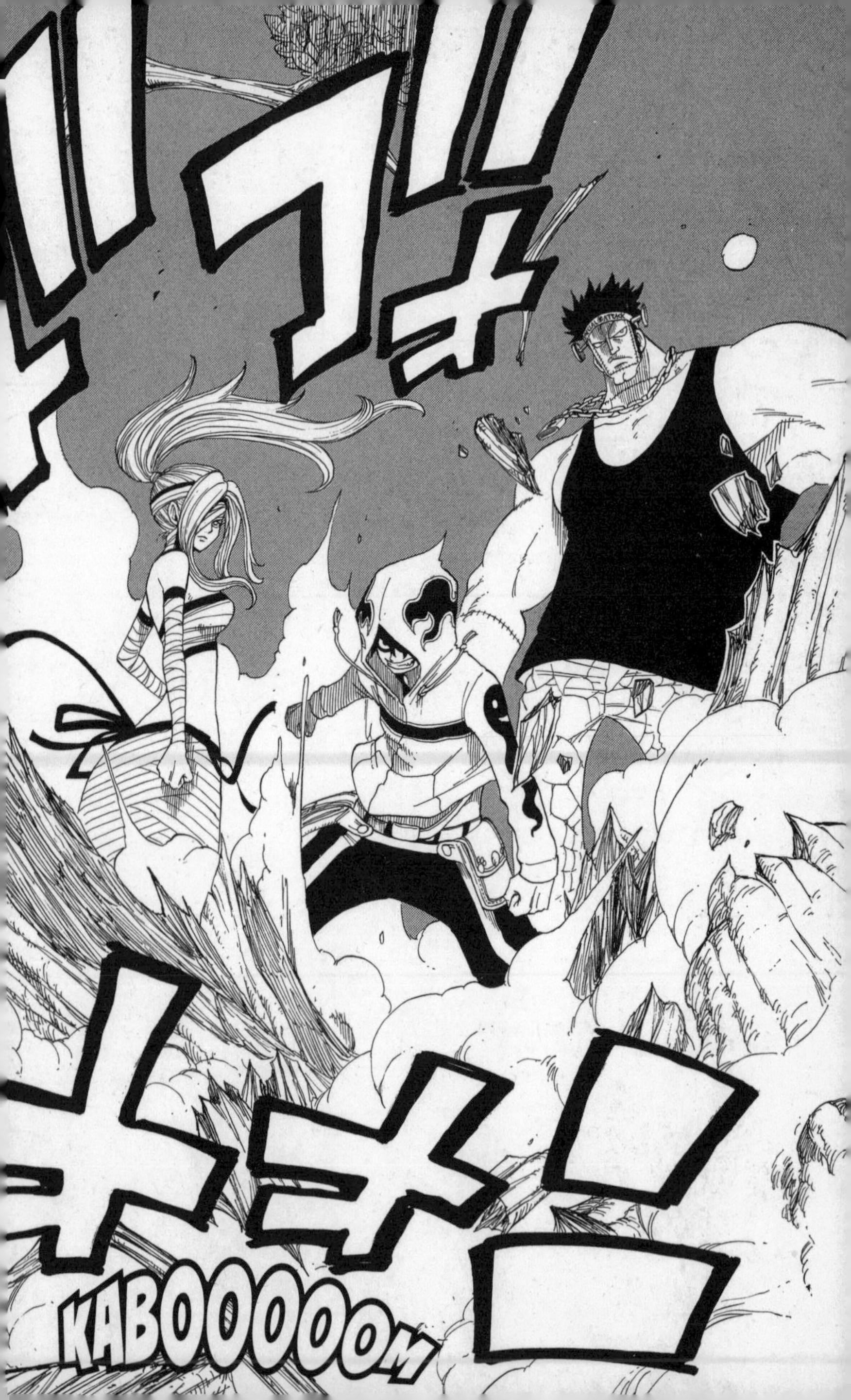
KABOOOOOOM

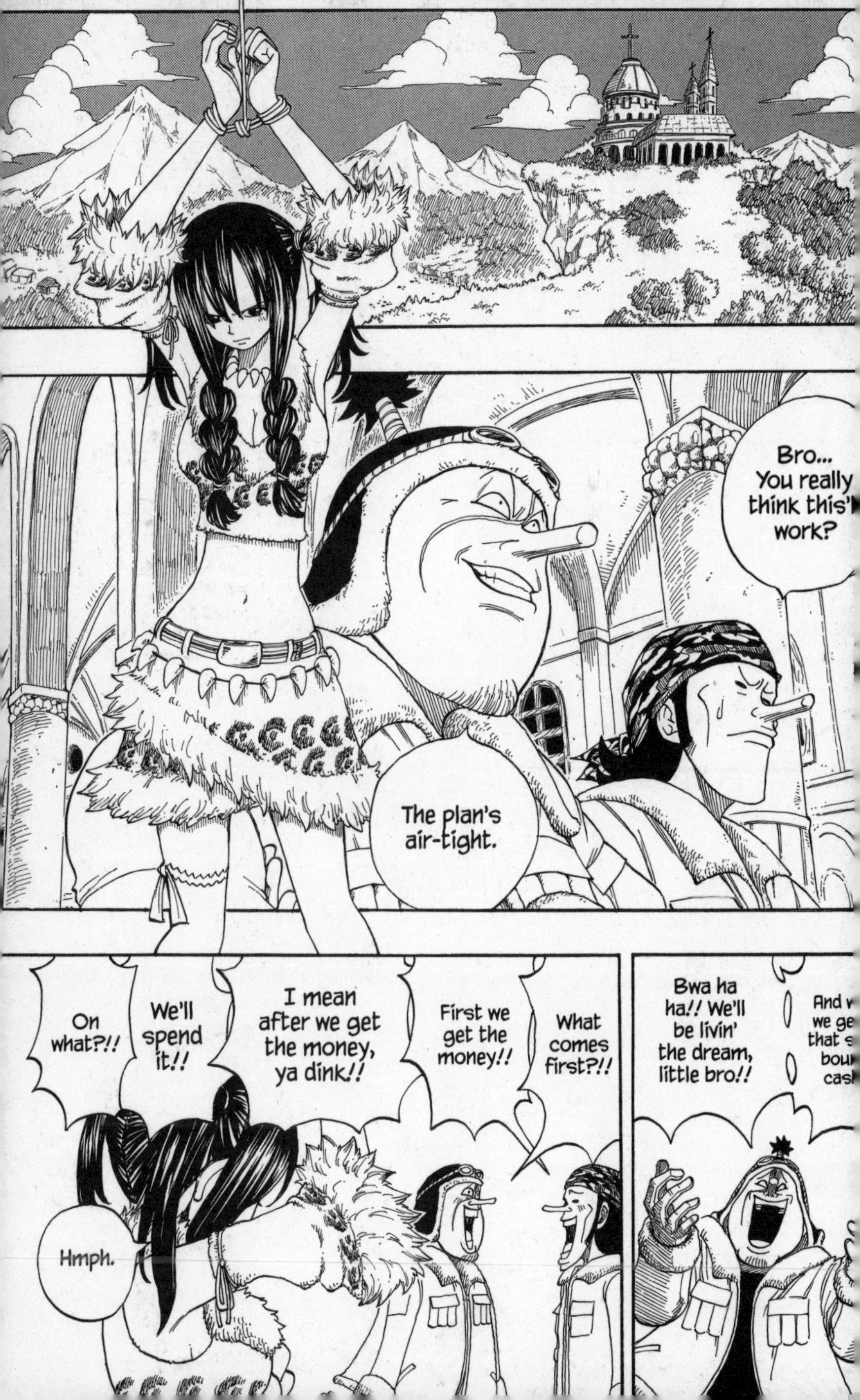
Bro... You really think this'
work?
The plan's air-tight.
Bwa ha ha!! We'll be livin' the dream, little bro!!
What comes first?!!
First we get the money!!
I mean after we get the money, ya dink!!
We'll spend it!!
On what?!!
Hmph.

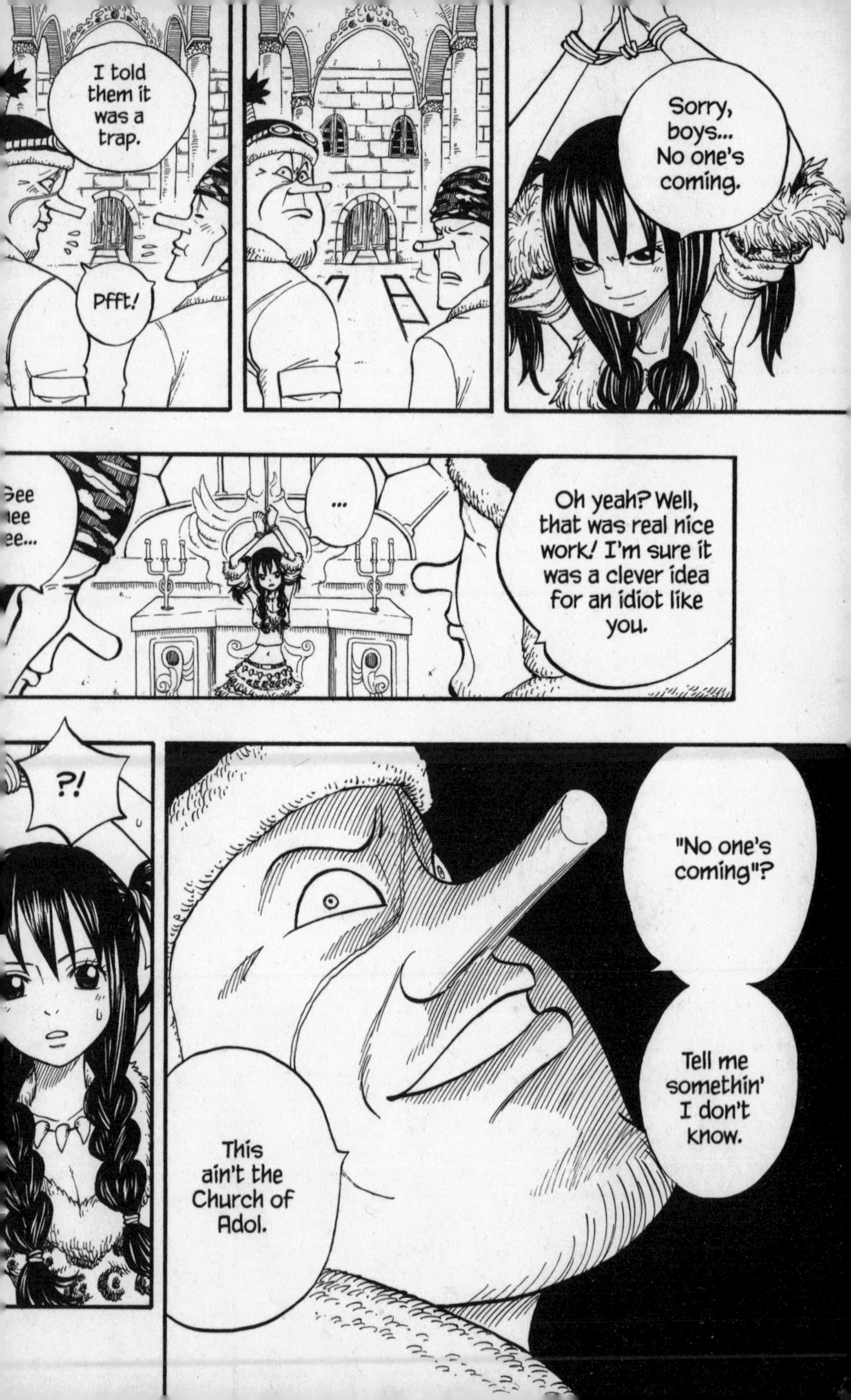
Sorry, boys... No one's coming.
I told them it was a trap.
Pfft!
Oh yeah? Well, that was real nice work! I'm sure it was a clever idea for an idiot like you.
...
Gee ee ee...
"No one's coming"?
Tell me somethin' I don't know.
This ain't the Church of Adol.
?!

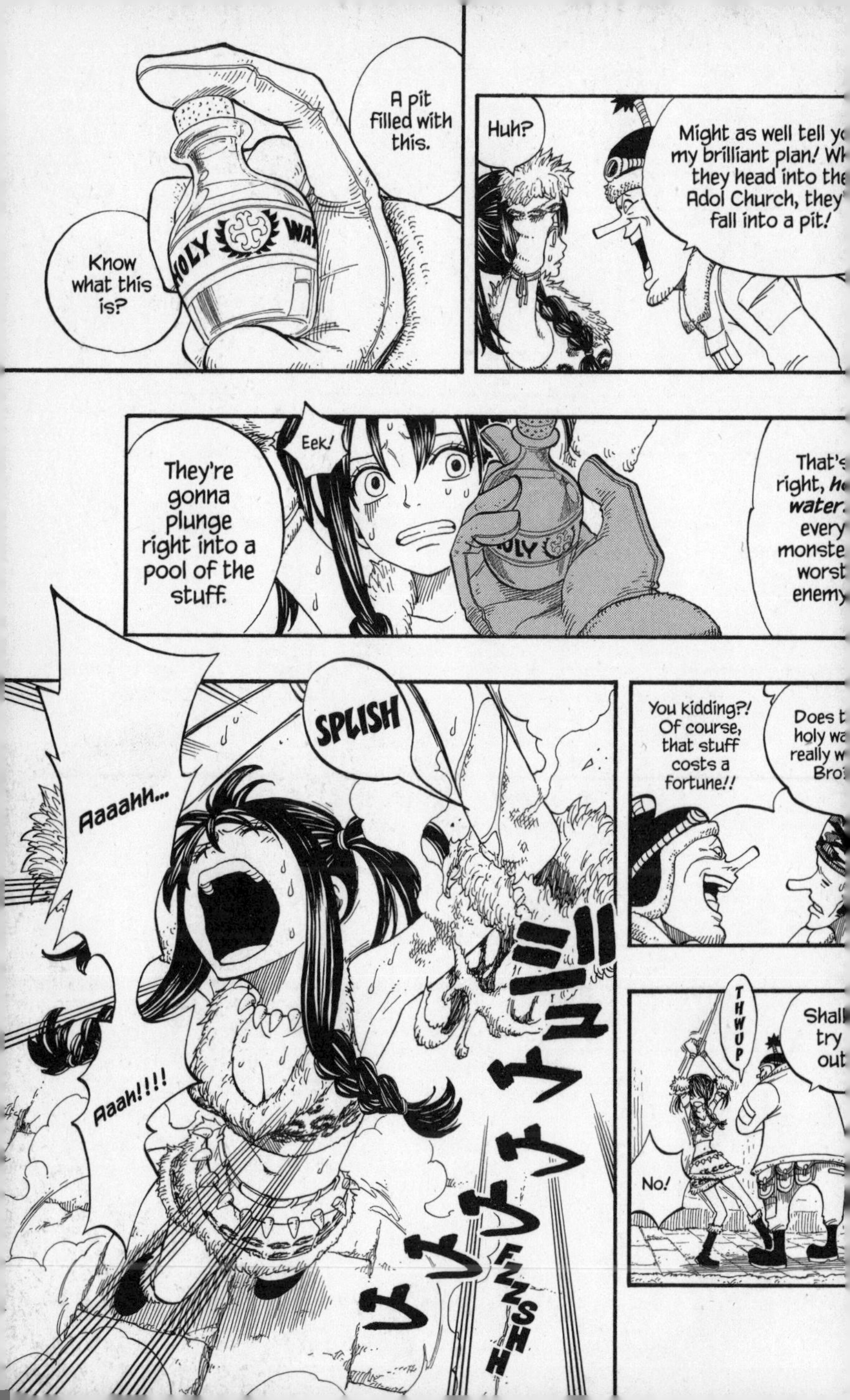

Might as well tell yo my brilliant plan! Wh they head into the Adol Church, they fall into a pit!
Huh?
A pit filled with this.
Know what this is?
HOLY WA
That's right, ho water. every monste worst enemy
Eek!
They're gonna plunge right into a pool of the stuff.
HOLY
Does t holy wa really w Bro
You kidding?! Of course, that stuff costs a fortune!!
Shall try out
THWUP
No!
SPLISH
Aaaahh...
Aaah!!!!
FZZSHH

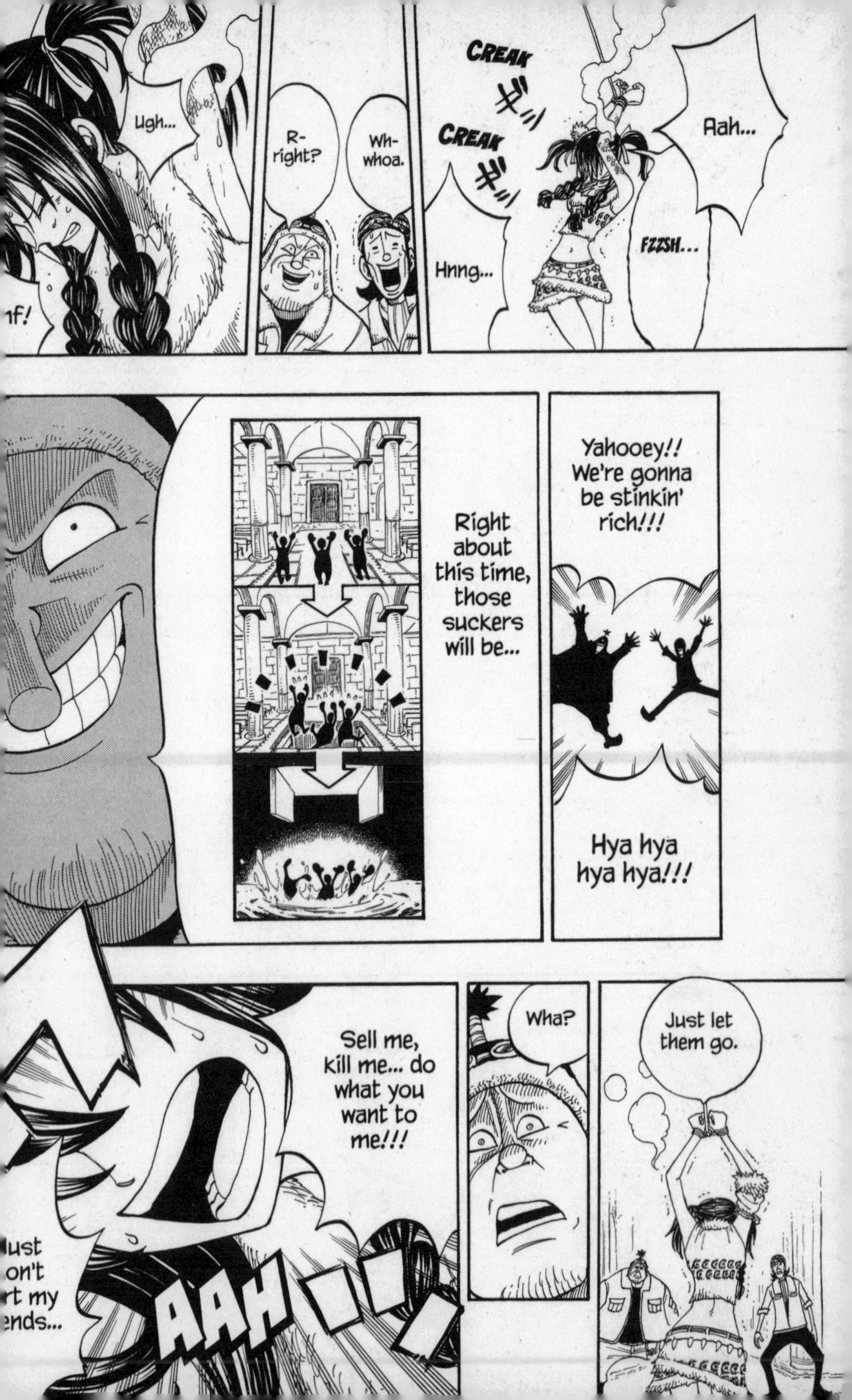

Aah...
CREAK
CREAK
FZZSH...
Hnng...
Wh- whoa.
R- right?
Ugh...
Yahooey!! We're gonna be stinkin' rich!!!
Hya hya hya hya!!!
Right about this time, those suckers will be...
Just let them go.
Wha?
Sell me, kill me... do what you want to me!!!
AAH...

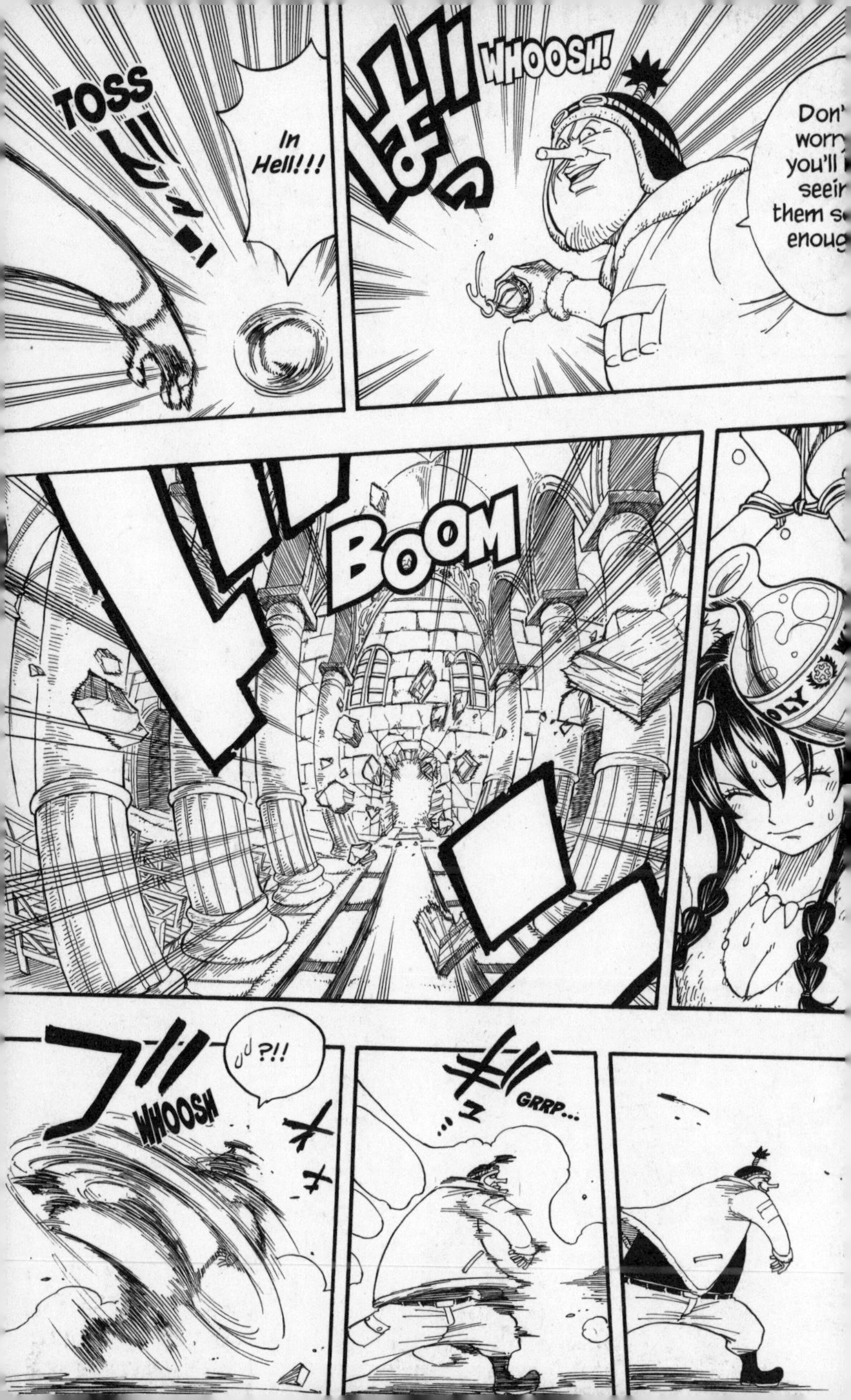
WHOOSH!
Don' worr you'll seeir them s enoug
TOSS
In Hell!!!
BOOM
GRRP...
WHOOSH
?!!

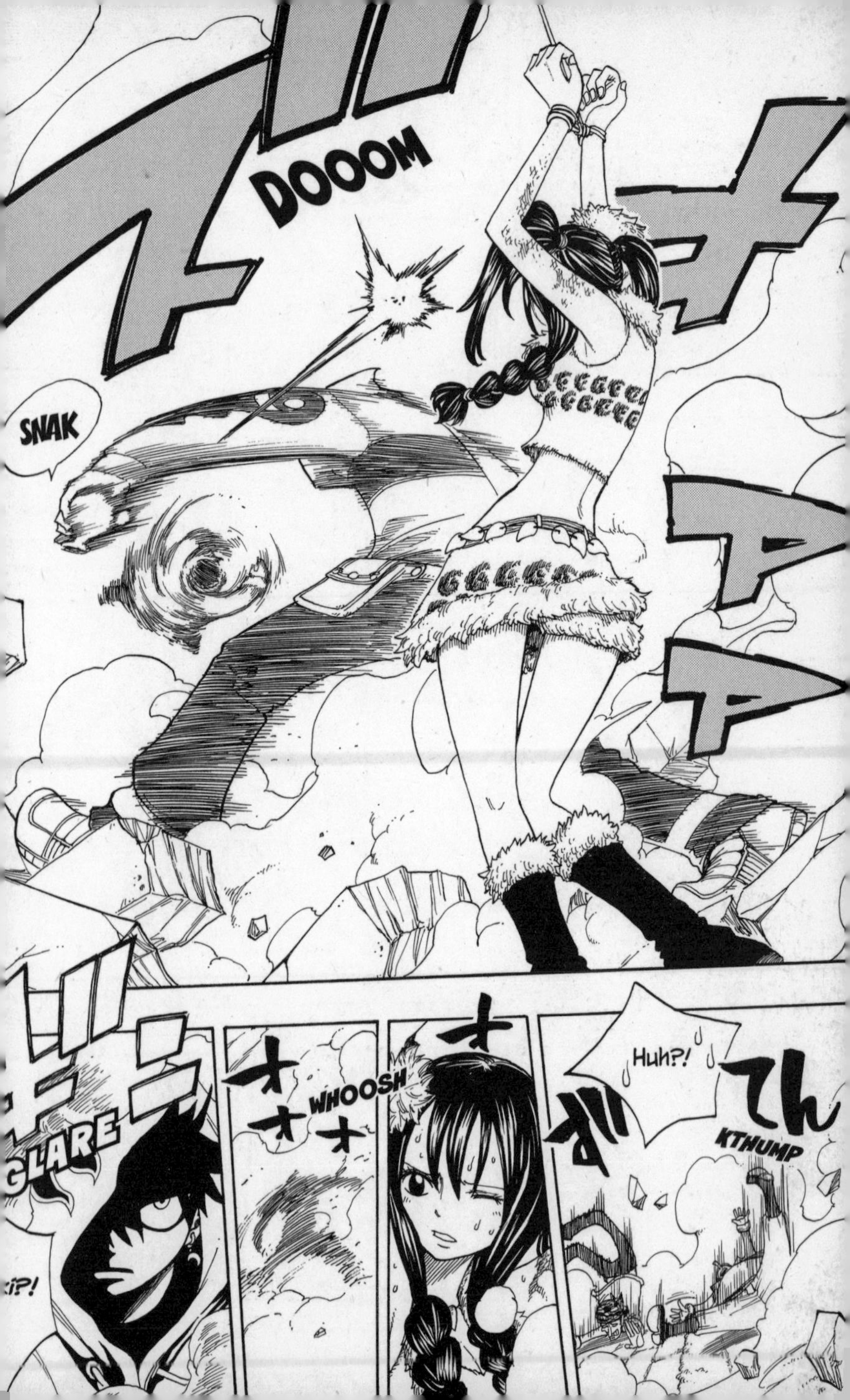
DOOOM
SNAK
Huh?!
てん
KTHUMP
WHOOSH
GLARE

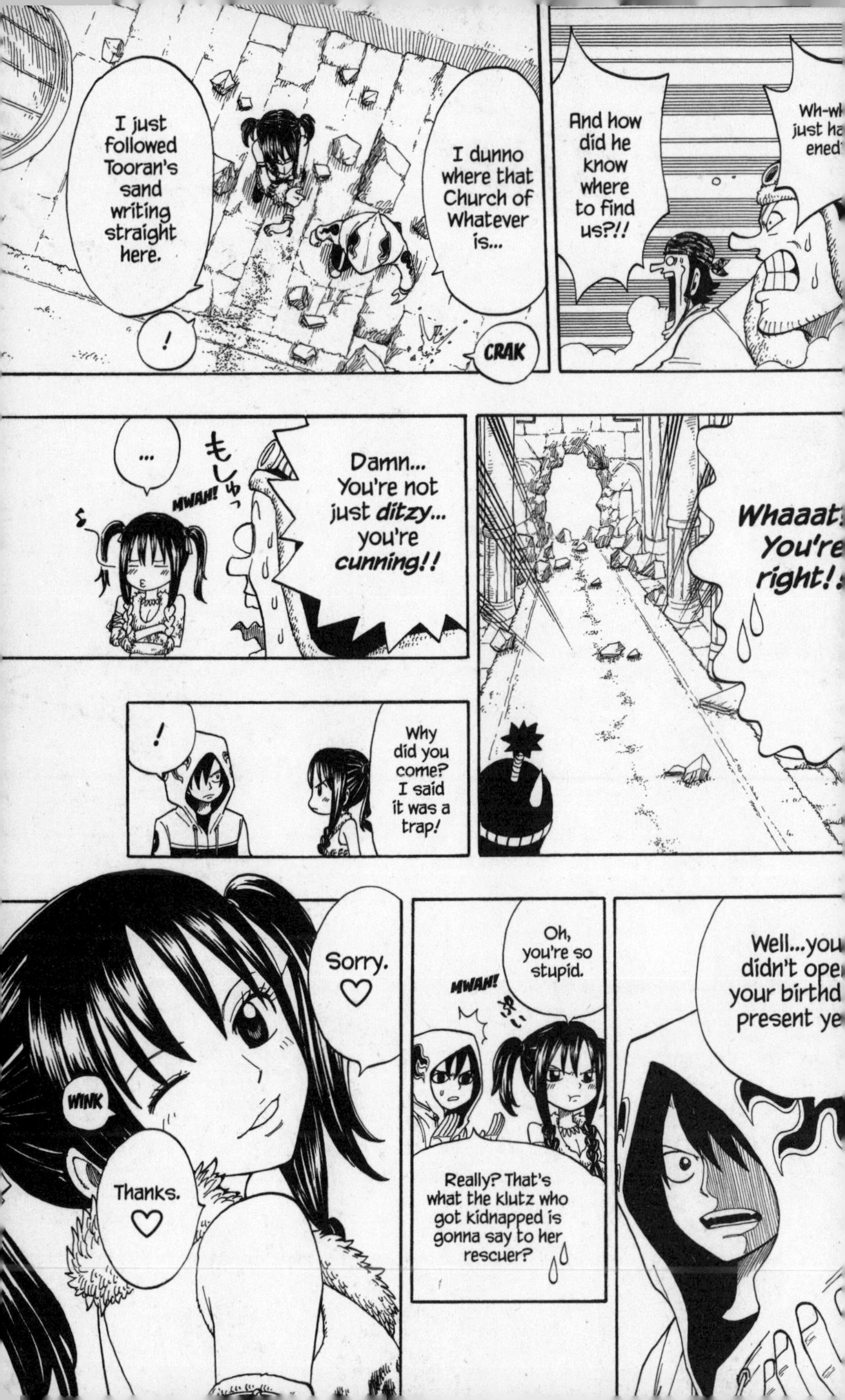
Wh-wh just ha ened
And how did he know where to find us?!!
I dunno where that Church of Whatever is...
CRAK
I just followed Tooran's sand writing straight here.
!
Whaaat! You're right!!
Damn... You're not just *ditzy*... you're *cunning!!*
もしゅっ
MWAH!
...
Why did you come? I said it was a trap!
!
Well...you didn't ope your birthd present ye
Oh, you're so stupid.
MWAH!
Really? That's what the klutz who got kidnapped is gonna say to her rescuer?
Sorry. ♡
WINK
Thanks. ♡

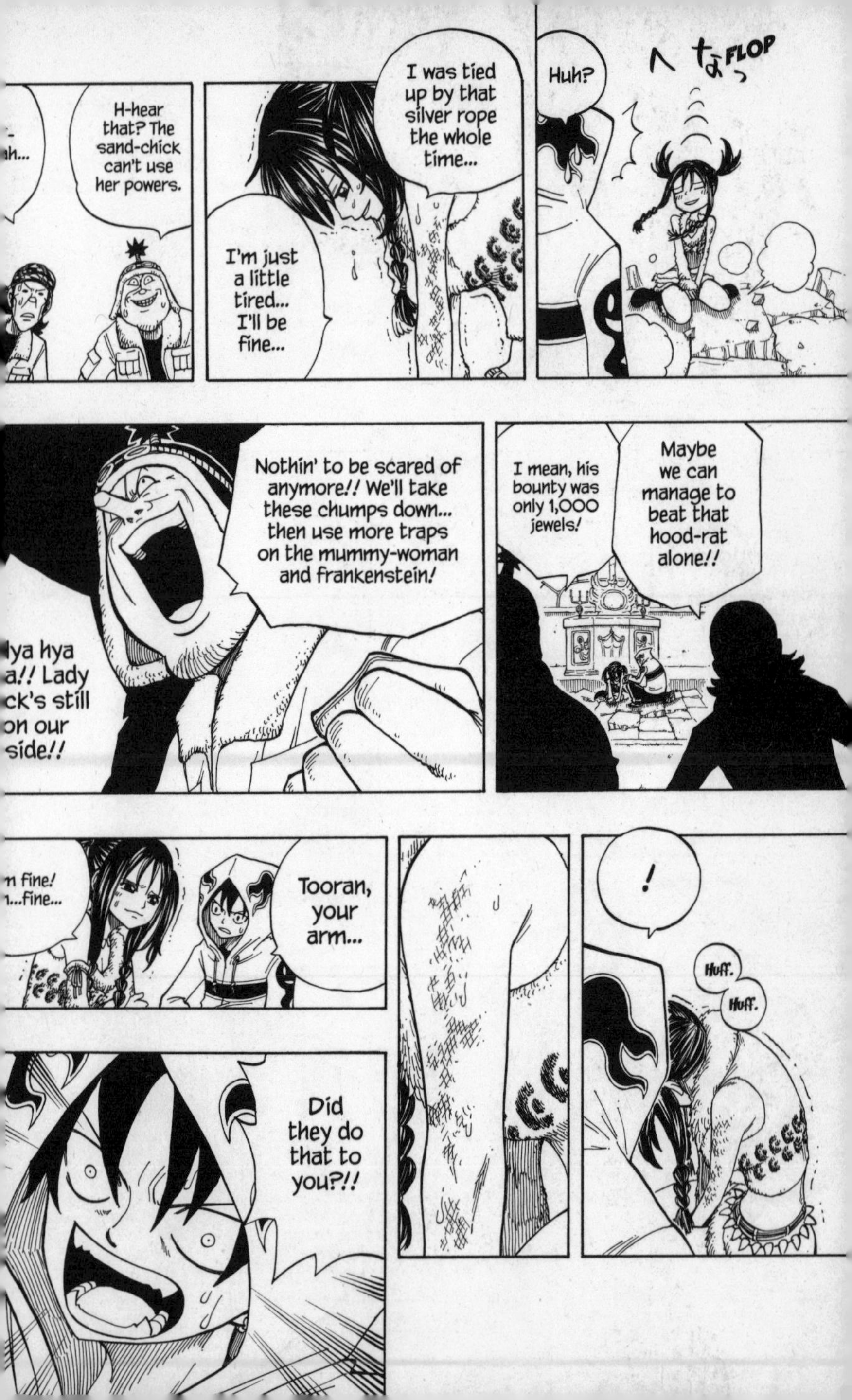
へなっ FLOP
Huh?
I was tied up by that silver rope the whole time...
I'm just a little tired... I'll be fine...
H-hear that? The sand-chick can't use her powers.
ah...
Maybe we can manage to beat that hood-rat alone!!
I mean, his bounty was only 1,000 jewels!
Nothin' to be scared of anymore!! We'll take these chumps down... then use more traps on the mummy-woman and frankenstein!
ya hya a!! Lady ck's still on our side!!
!
Huff.
Huff.
Tooran, your arm...
n fine! ...fine...
Did they do that to you?!!

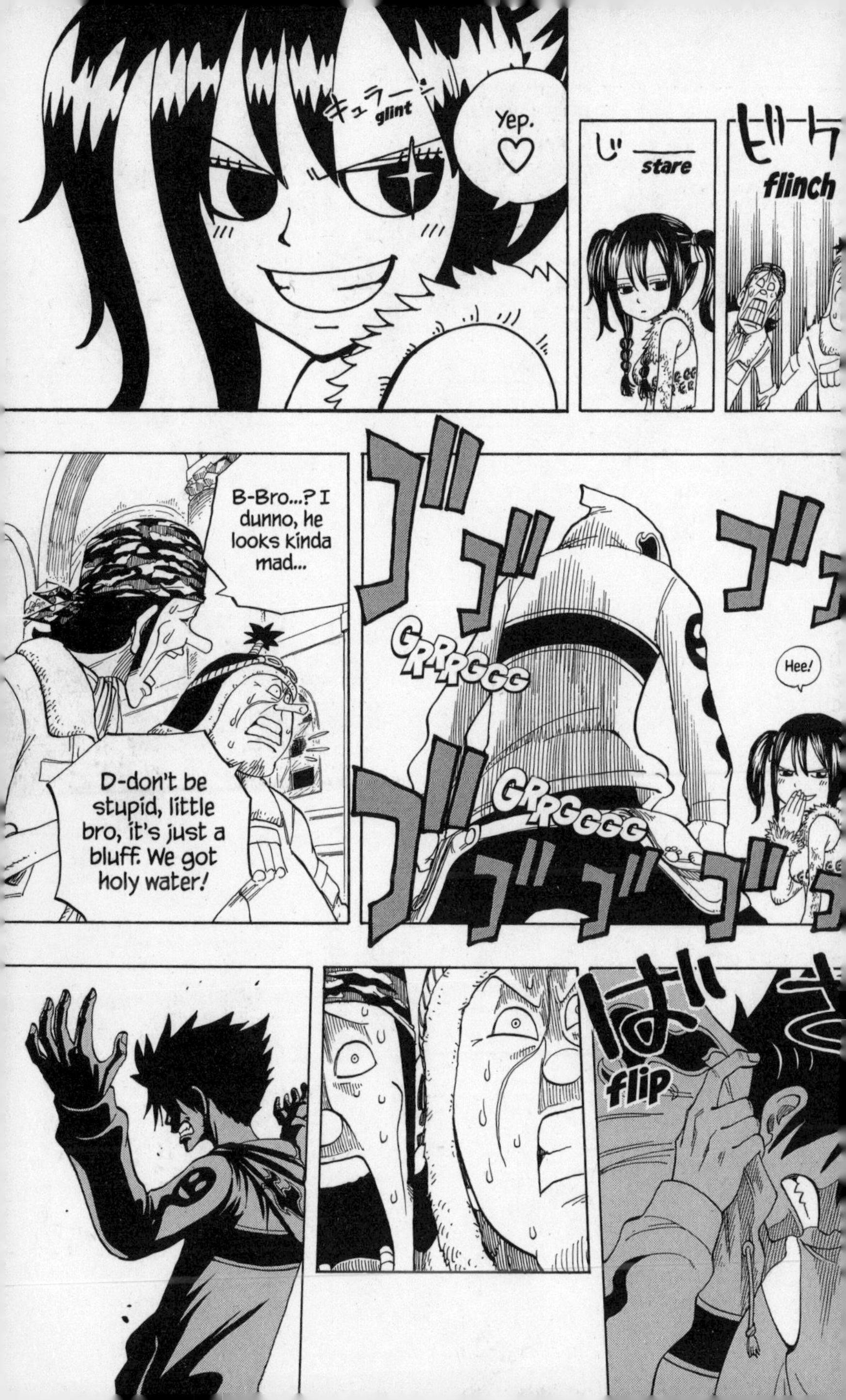
flinch
stare
glint
Yep. ♥
GRRRGGG
GRRGGGG
Hee!
B-Bro...? I dunno, he looks kinda mad...
D-don't be stupid, little bro, it's just a bluff. We got holy water!
flip

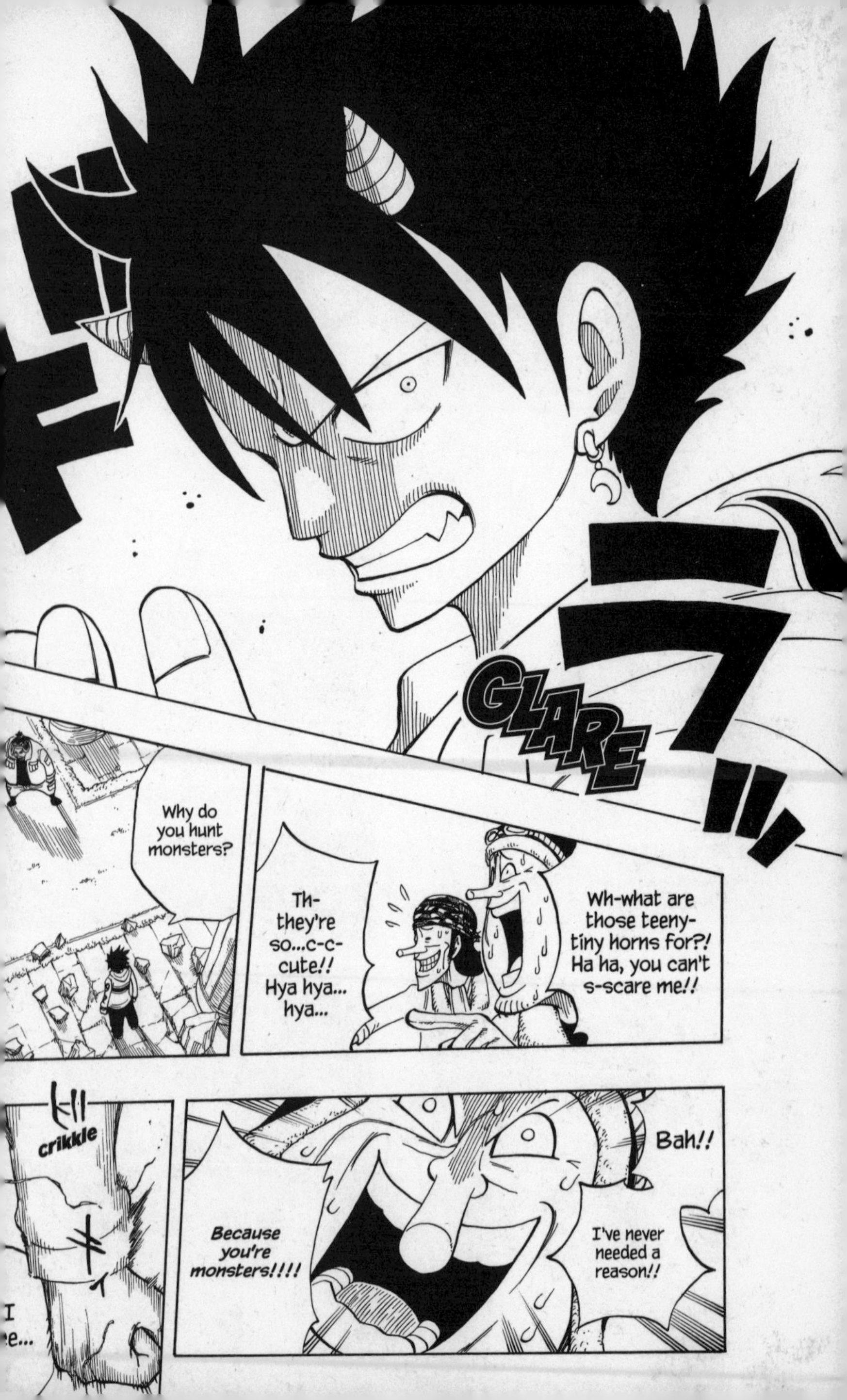
GLARE
Wh-what are those teeny-tiny horns for?! Ha ha, you can't s-scare me!!
Th- they're so...c-c-cute!! Hya hya... hya...
Why do you hunt monsters?
Bah!!
I've never needed a reason!!
Because you're monsters!!!!
crikkle

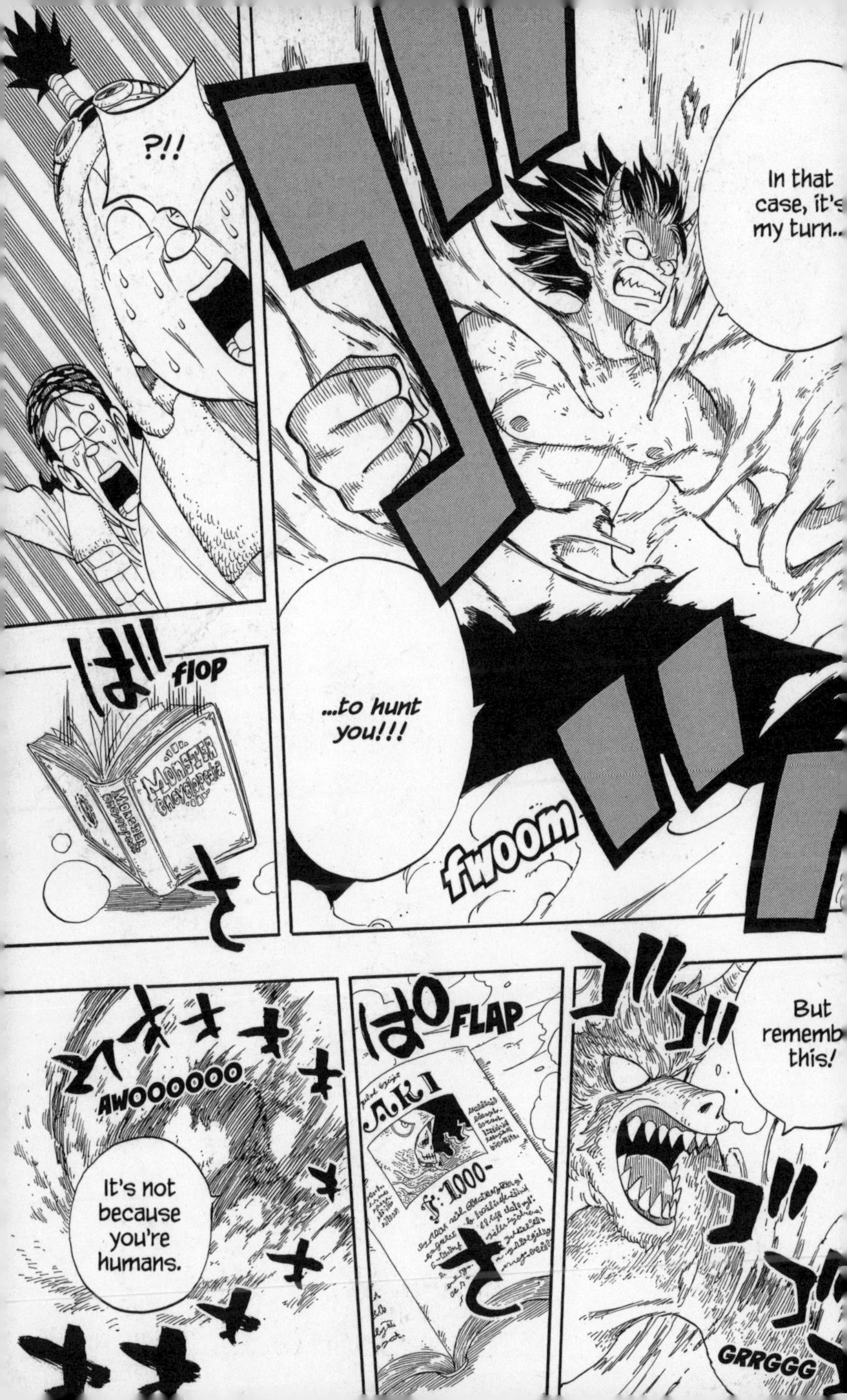

In that case, it's my turn...
...to hunt you!!!
fwoom
?!!
flop
Monster Encyclopedia
But rememb this!
GRRGGG
FLAP
AKI
1000-
AWOOOOOO
It's not because you're humans.

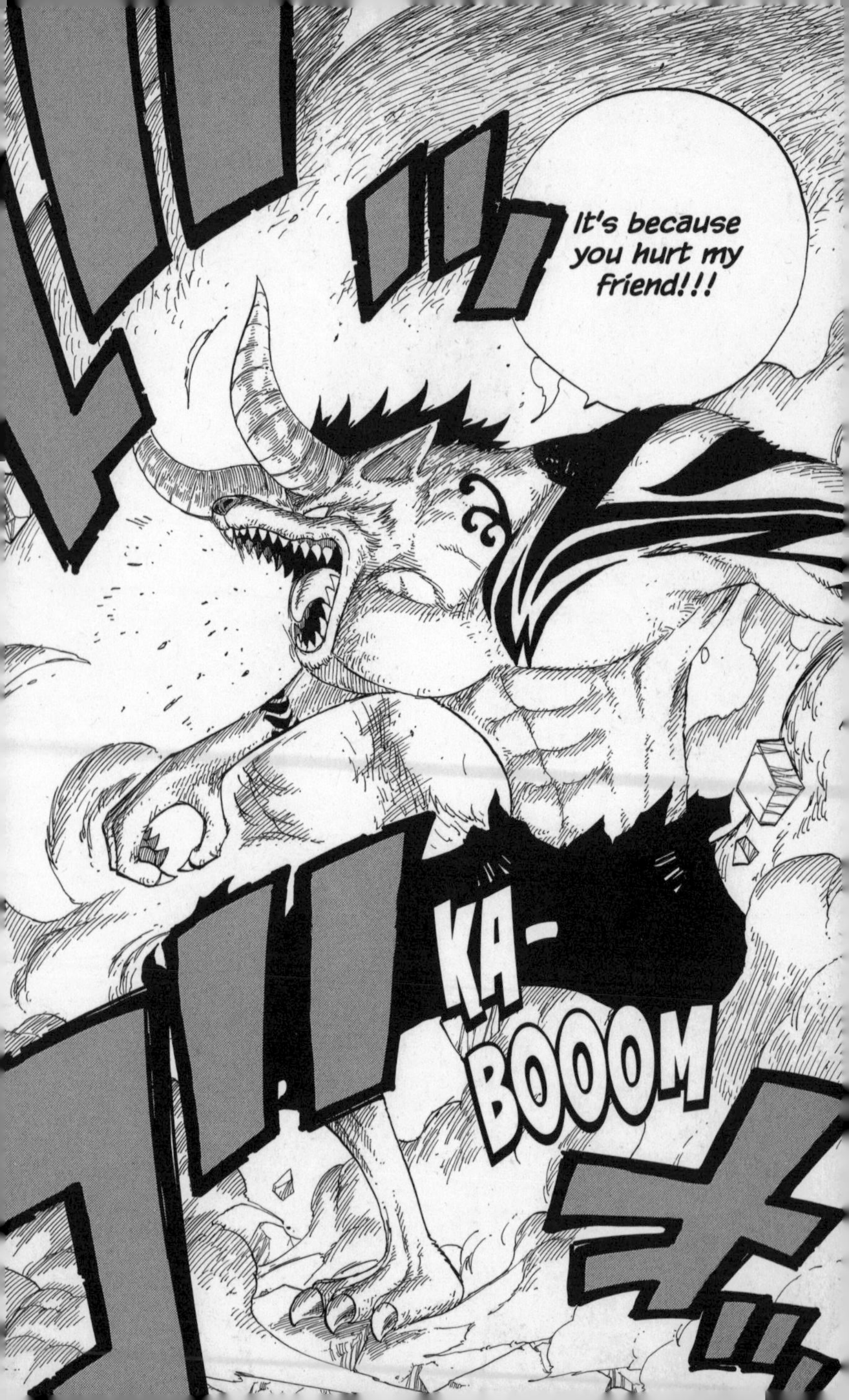
It's because you hurt my friend!!!
KA-BOOOM

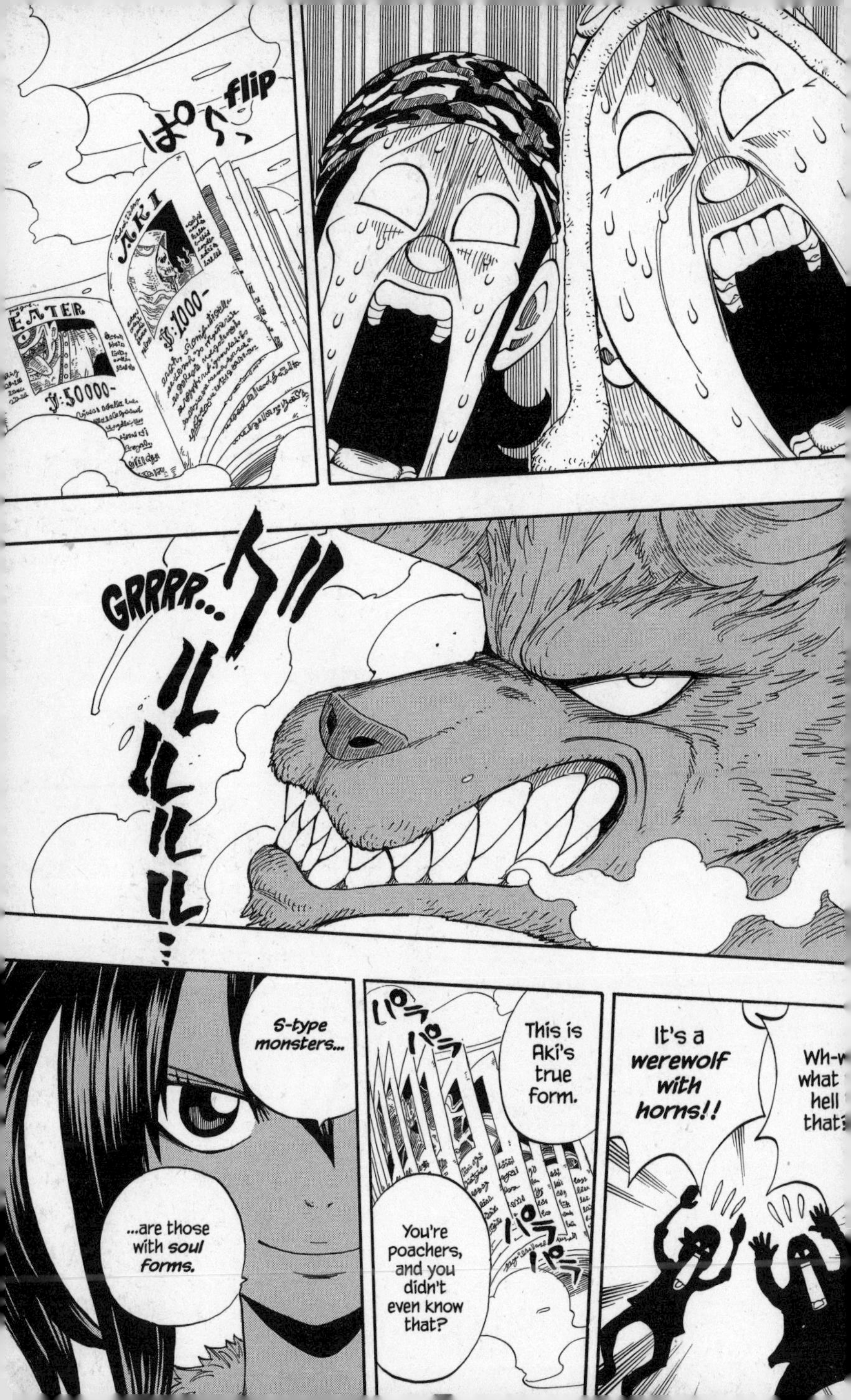
flip
GRRRR...
Wh-w what hell that
It's a *werewolf with horns!!*
This is Aki's true form.
You're poachers, and you didn't even know that?
S-type monsters...
...are those with *soul forms.*

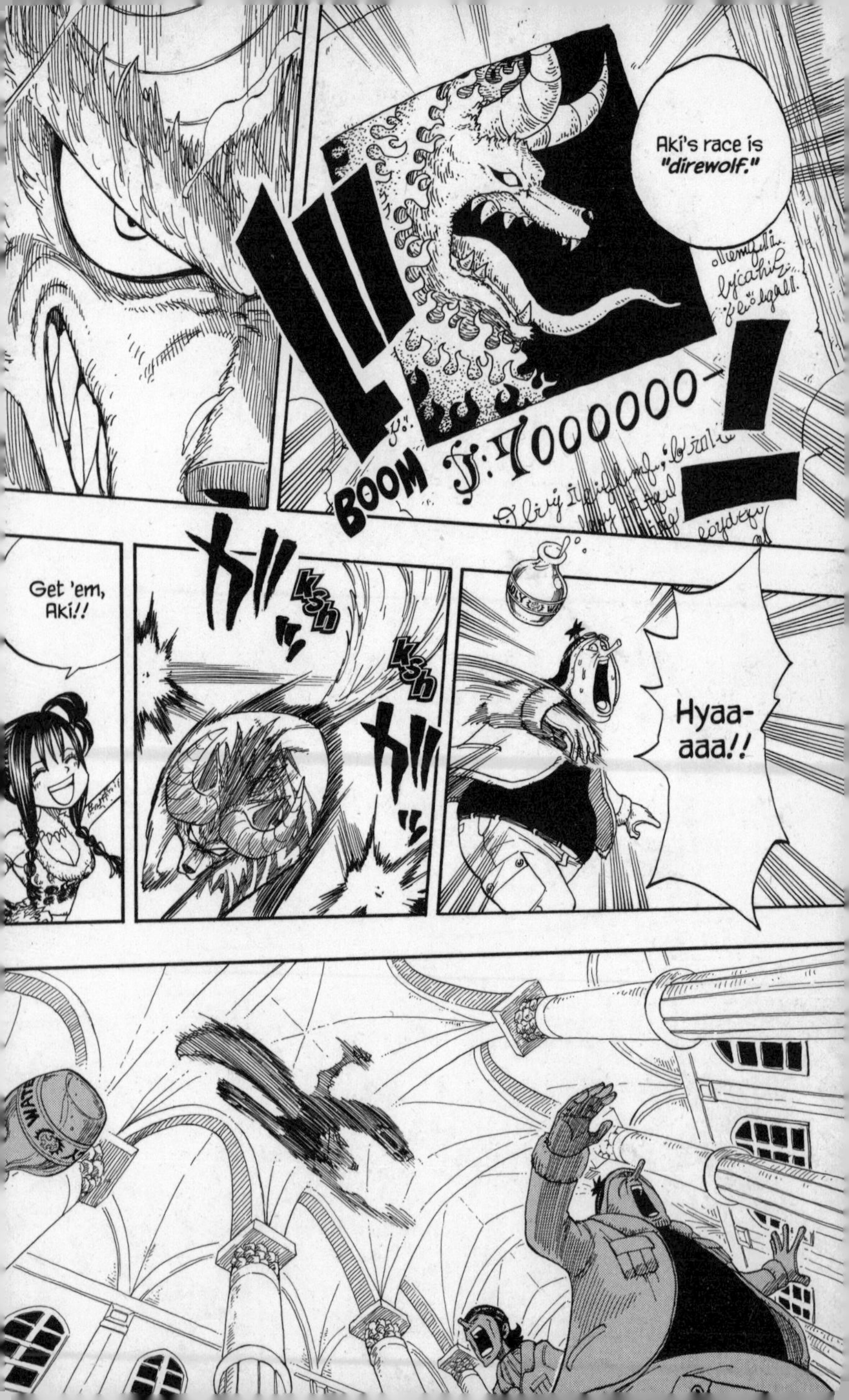
Aki's race is "direwolf."
BOOM
Get 'em, Aki!!
ksh
ksh
Hyaa-aaa!!

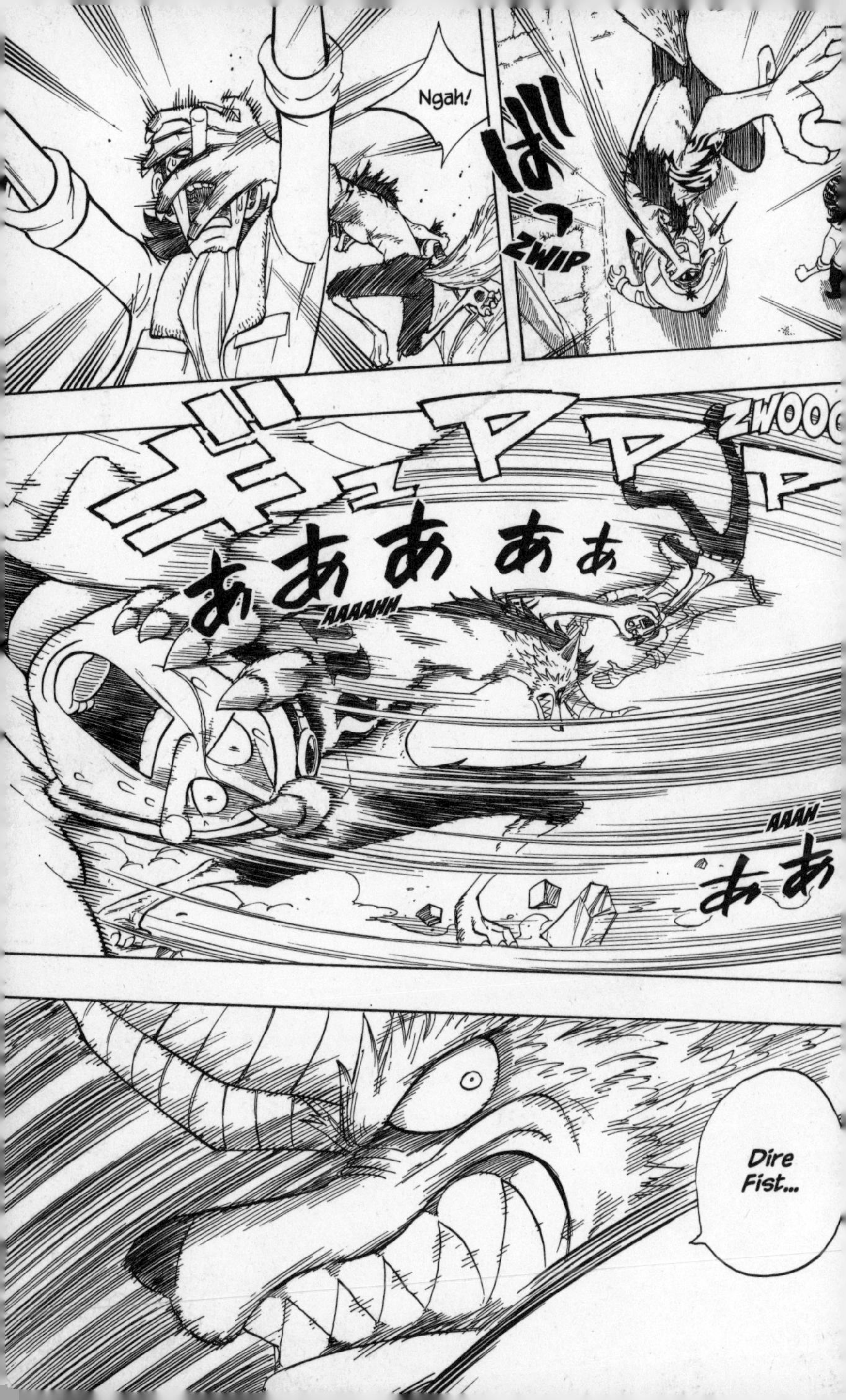
ばっ
ZWIP
Ngah!
ギュアアァ
ZWOOO
ああああぁ
AAAAHH
ああ
AAAH
Dire Fist...

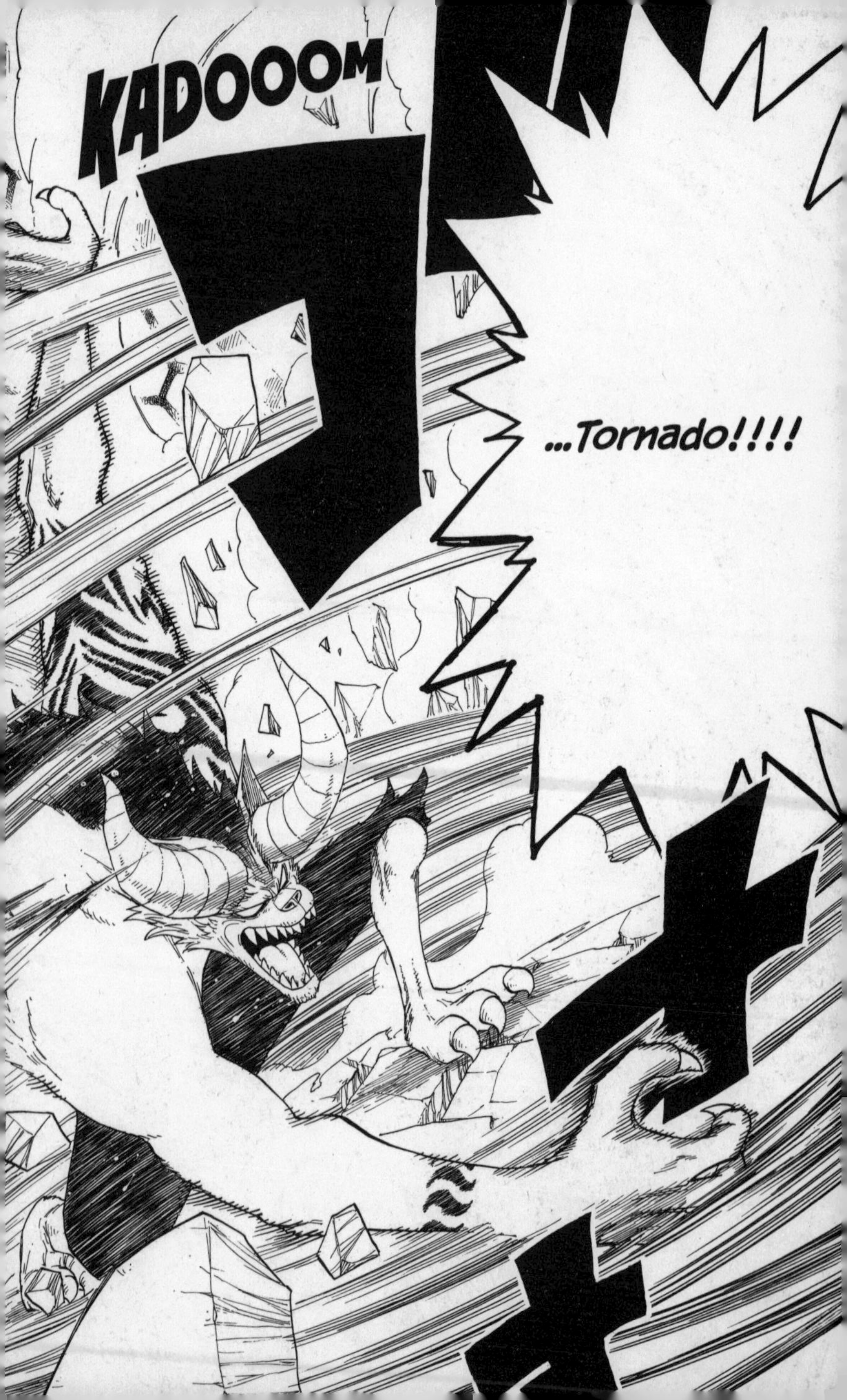
...Tornado!!!!
KADOOOM

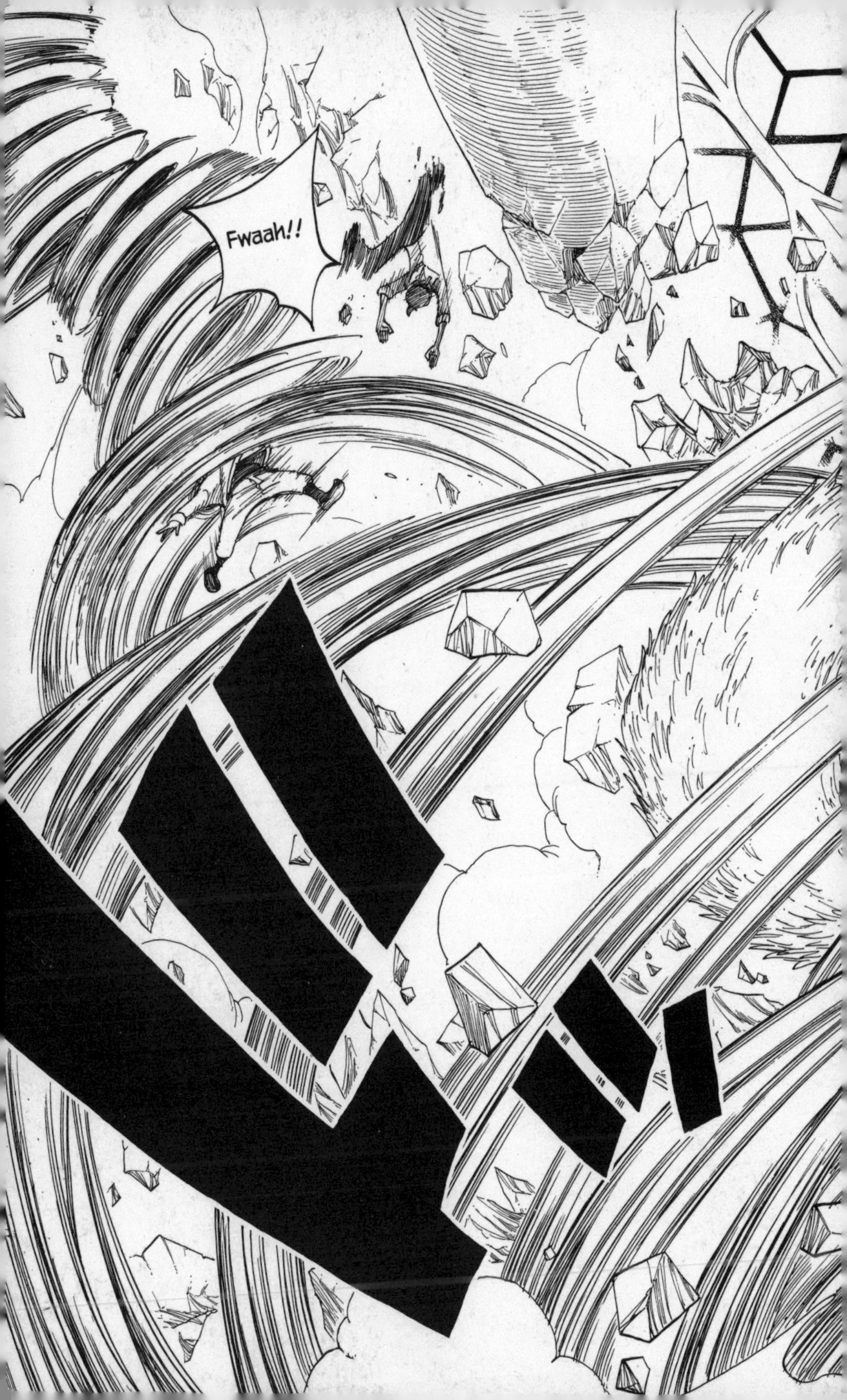
Fwaah!!

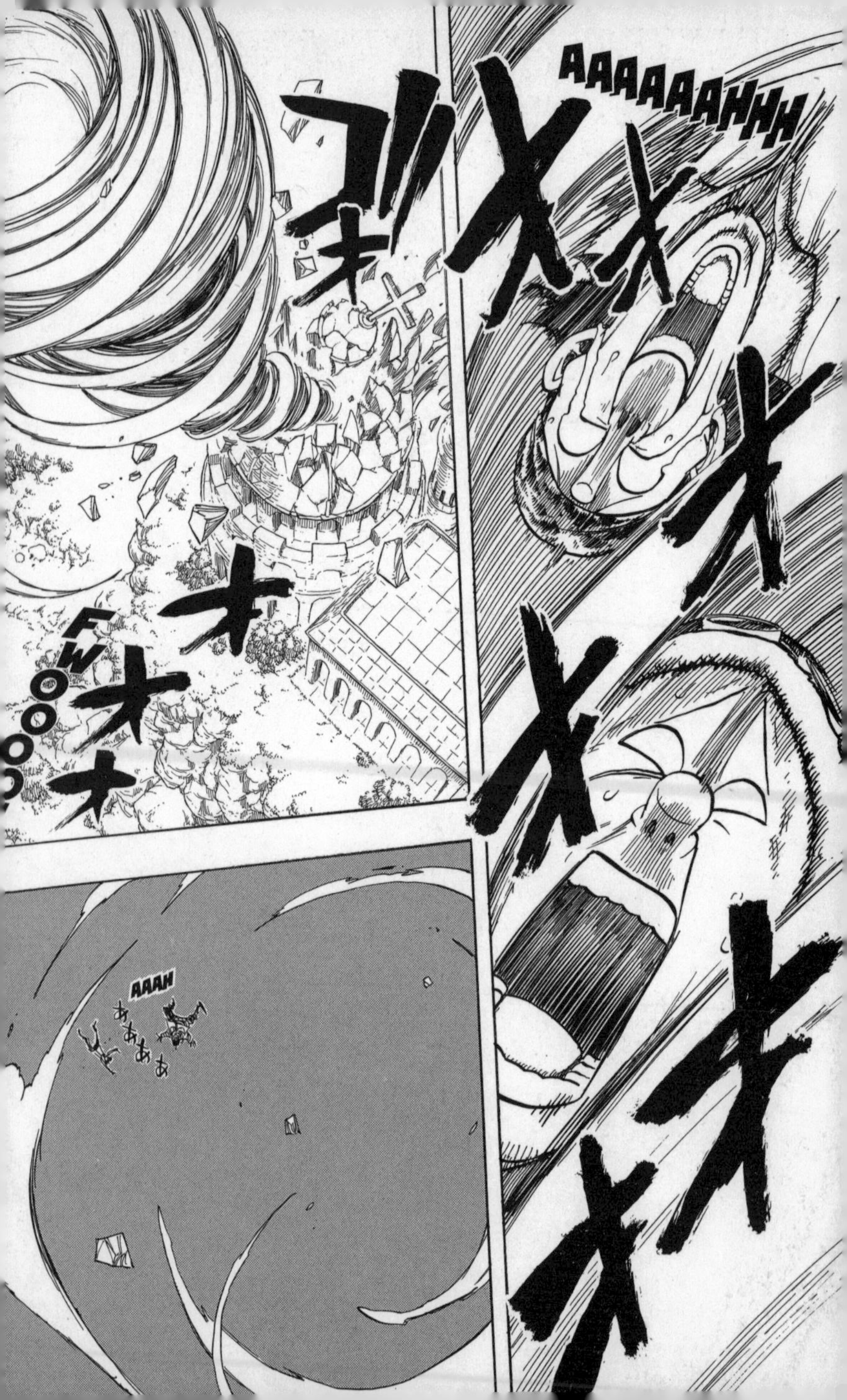
AAAAAAAHHH
FWOOOO
AAAH
ああああ

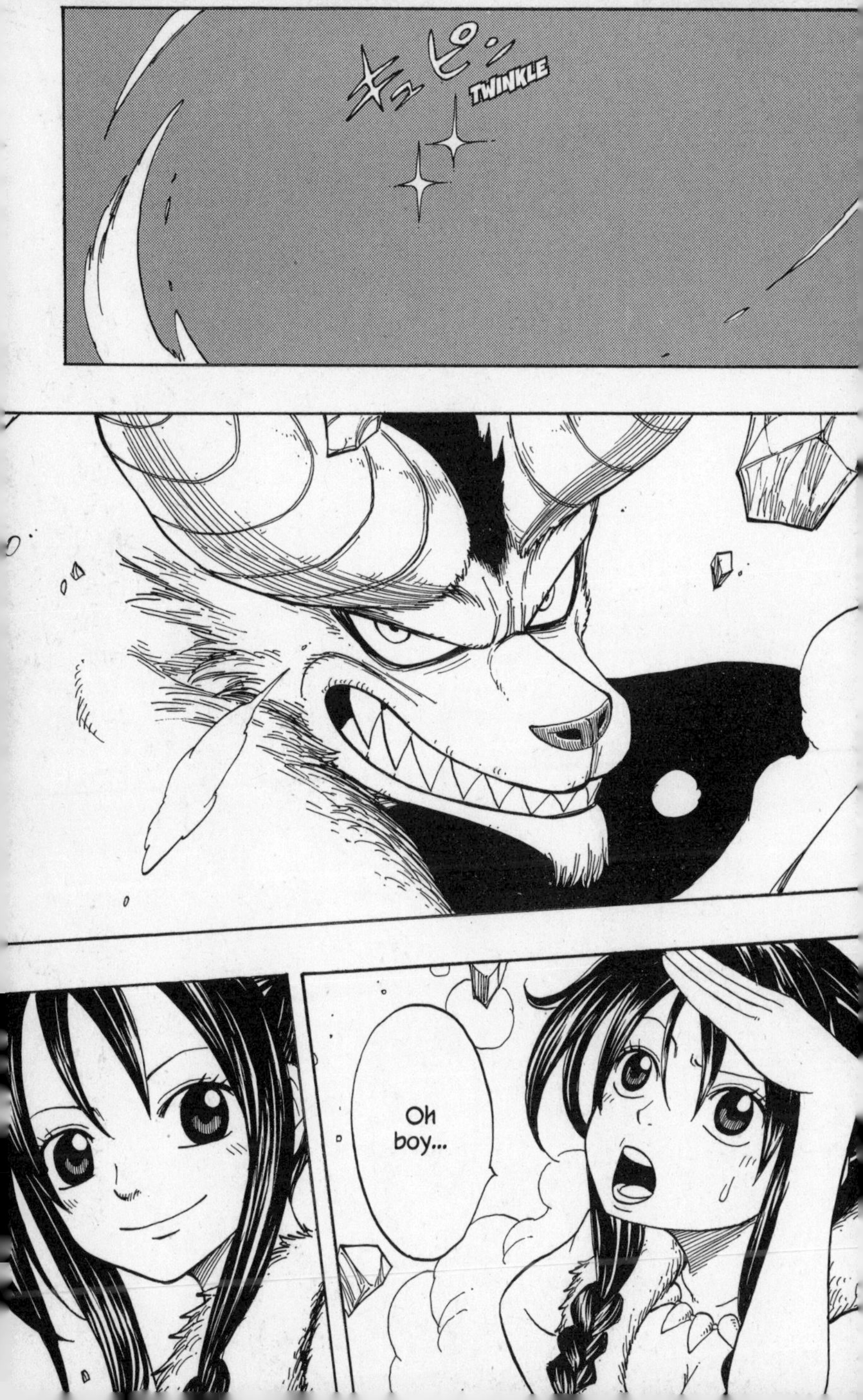
キュピン
TWINKLE
Oh boy...

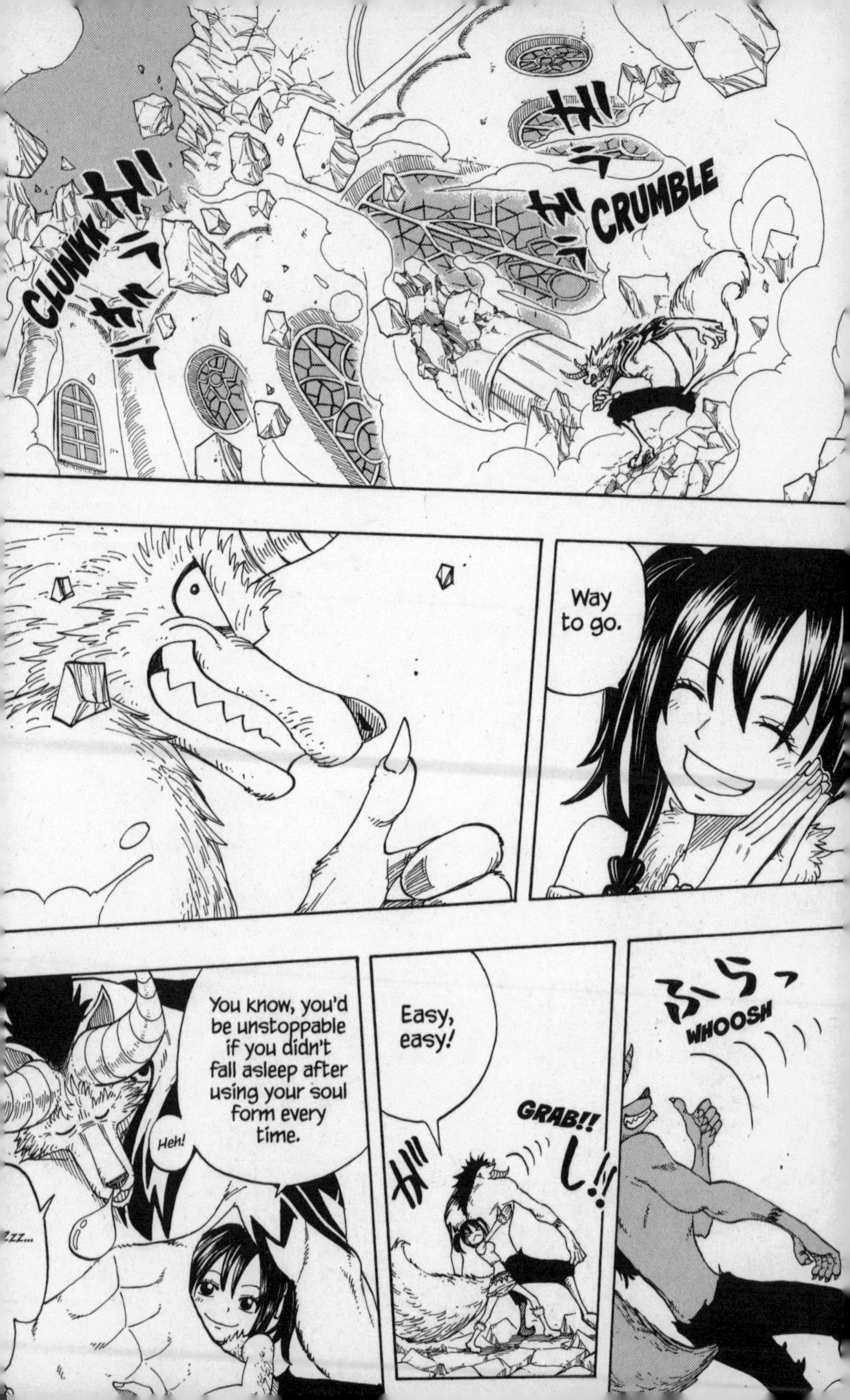
CRUMBLE
CLUNKK
Way to go.
ふらっ
WHOOSH
Easy, easy!
GRAB!!
You know, you'd be unstoppable if you didn't fall asleep after using your soul form every time.
Heh!
zzz...

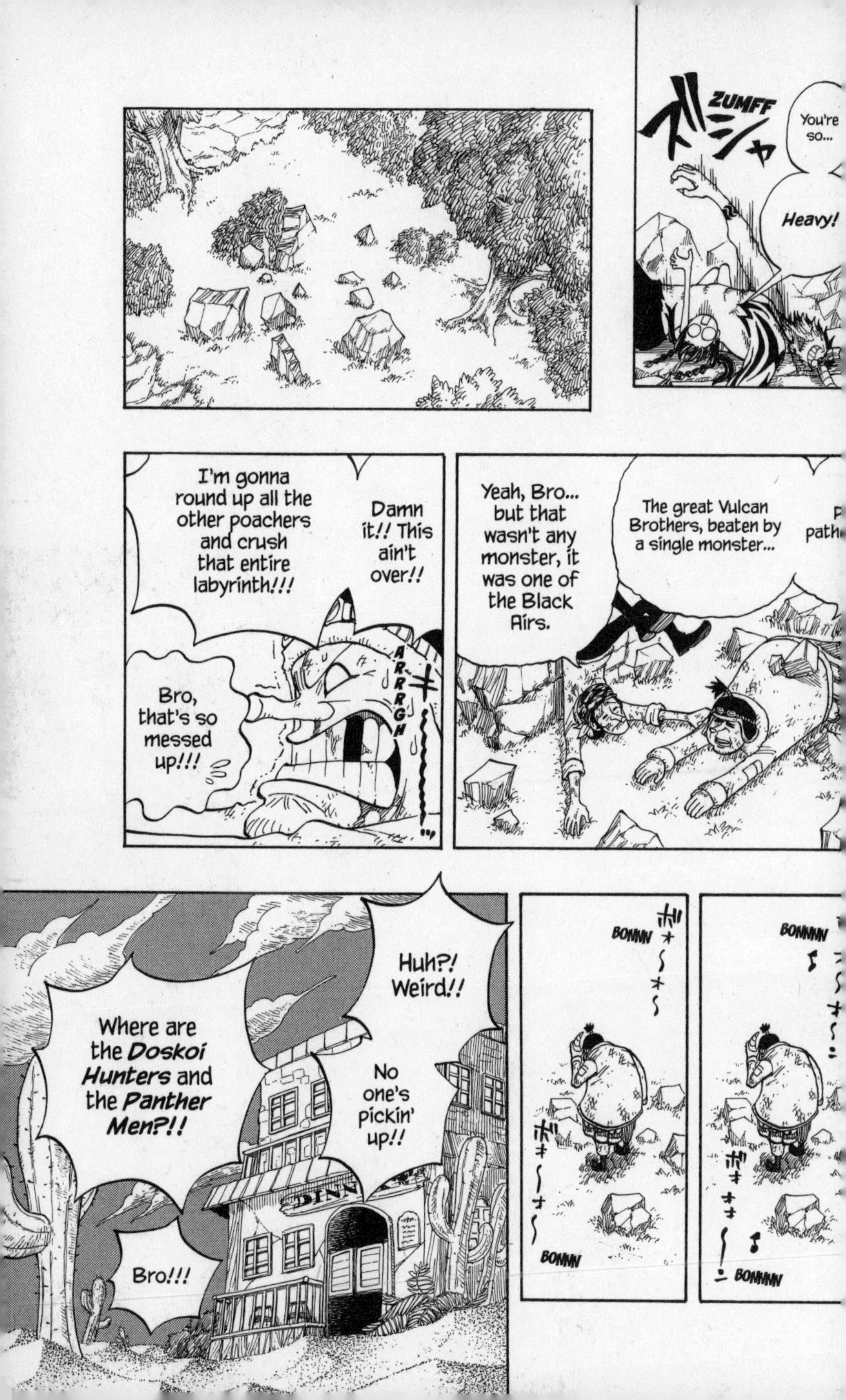
ZUMFF
You're so...
Heavy!
The great Vulcan Brothers, beaten by a single monster...
Yeah, Bro... but that wasn't any monster, it was one of the Black Airs.
Damn it!! This ain't over!!
I'm gonna round up all the other poachers and crush that entire labyrinth!!!
ARRRGH
Bro, that's so messed up!!!
BONNNN
BONNNN
BONNN
BONNN
Huh?! Weird!!
No one's pickin' up!!
Where are the Doskoi Hunters and the Panther Men?!!
Bro!!!

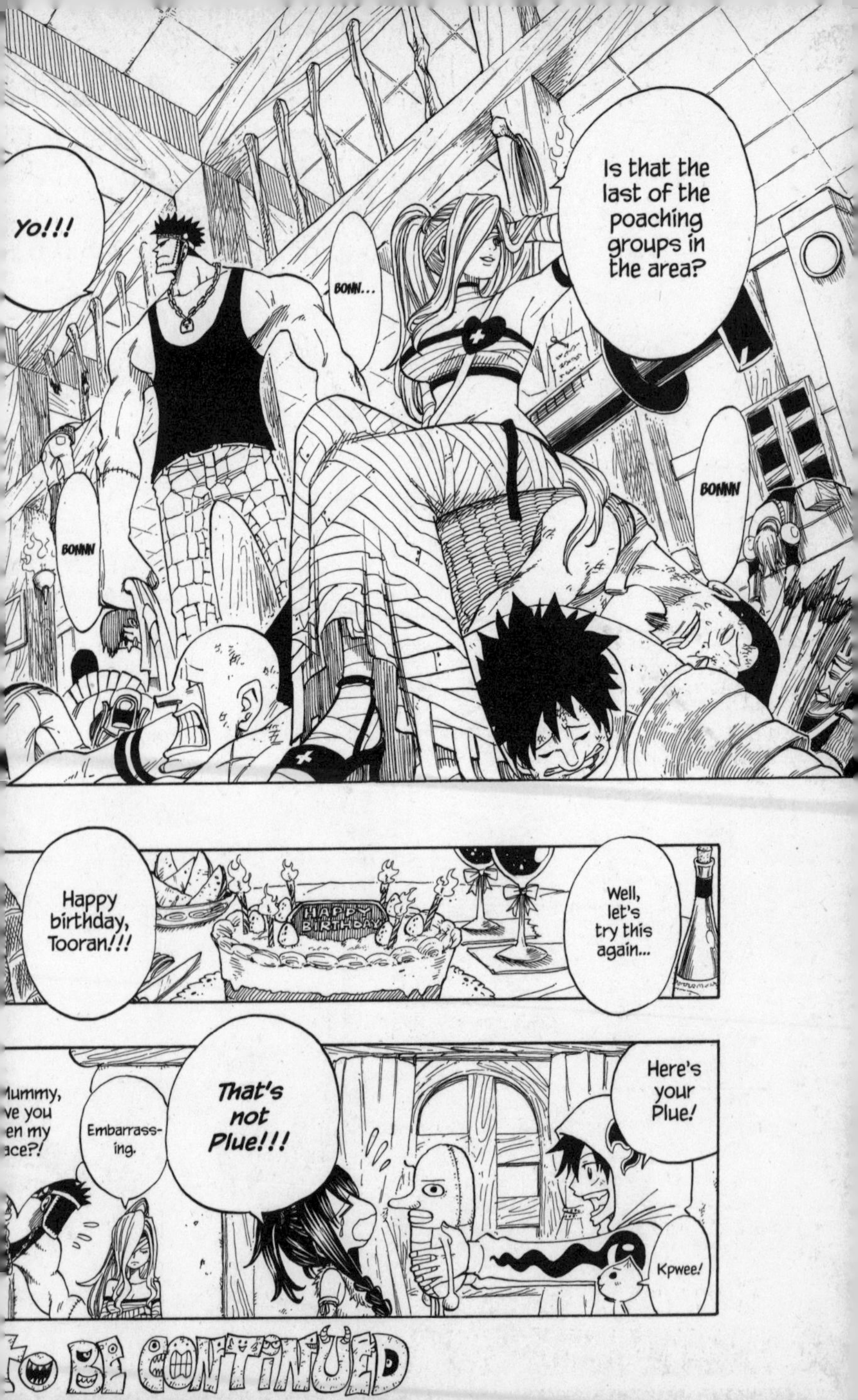
Is that the last of the poaching groups in the area?
BONNN
BONN...
Yo!!!
BONNN
Well, let's try this again...
Happy birthday, Tooran!!!
HAPPY BIRTHDAY
Here's your Plue!
Kpwee!
That's not Plue!!!
Embarrass-ing.
TO BE CONTINUED

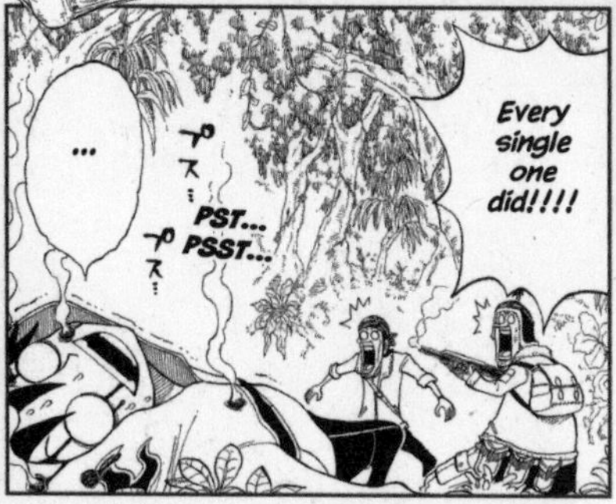
Every single one did!!!!
プス…
PST...
プス…
PSST...
...

Faster than the human eye can follow, but he's not quite experienced enough to make it count sometimes. His weakness is his tendency to act without thinking. Cheerful by nature, but you don't want to make him mad.

Bounty: 1000

Danger Lvl: ★☆☆☆☆☆

Aki

Race: ? Type: Monster

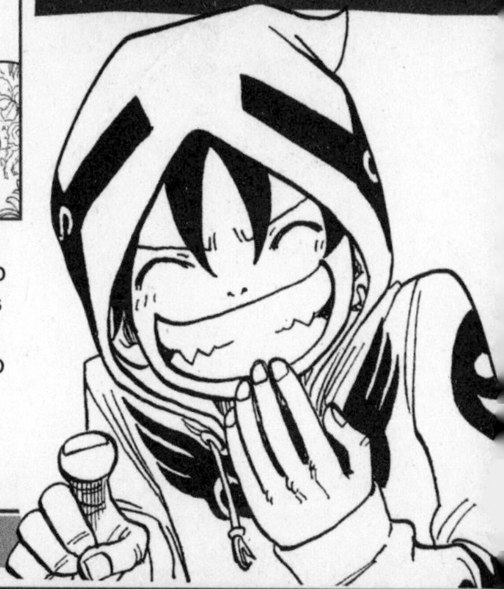

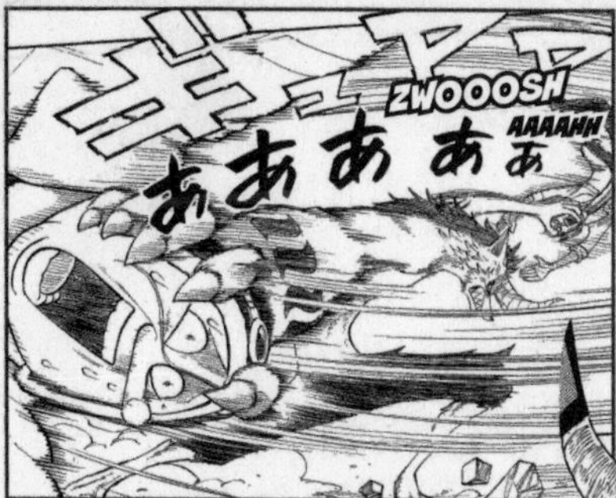
ZWOOOSH
AAAAHH
ああああぁ

When Aki's rage explodes, he turns into a direwolf, his soul form. His power and speed are vastly higher, but he does fall asleep immediately after battle. He's a master of the Dire Fist, a type of fighting that makes use of his powerful body. Got a few secret attacks, too.

Bounty: 7000000

Danger Lvl: Immeasurable

Aki (Soul Form)

Race: Direwolf Type: S-Type Monster

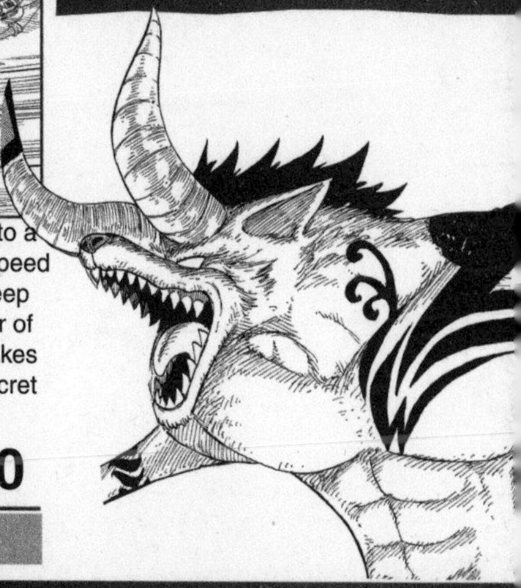

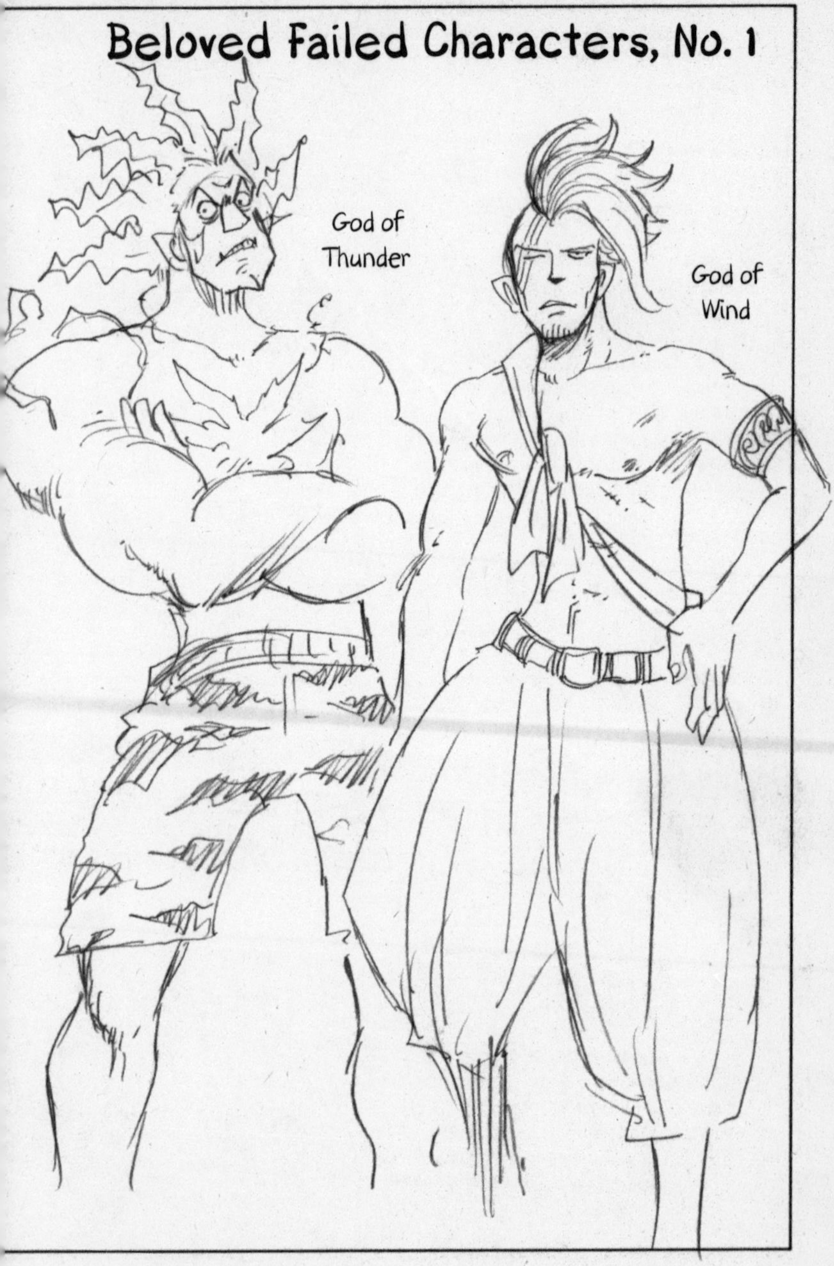
Beloved Failed Characters, No. 1
God of Thunder
God of Wind

Monster Soul

Woodman

Yeti

Rock Eater

Minotaur

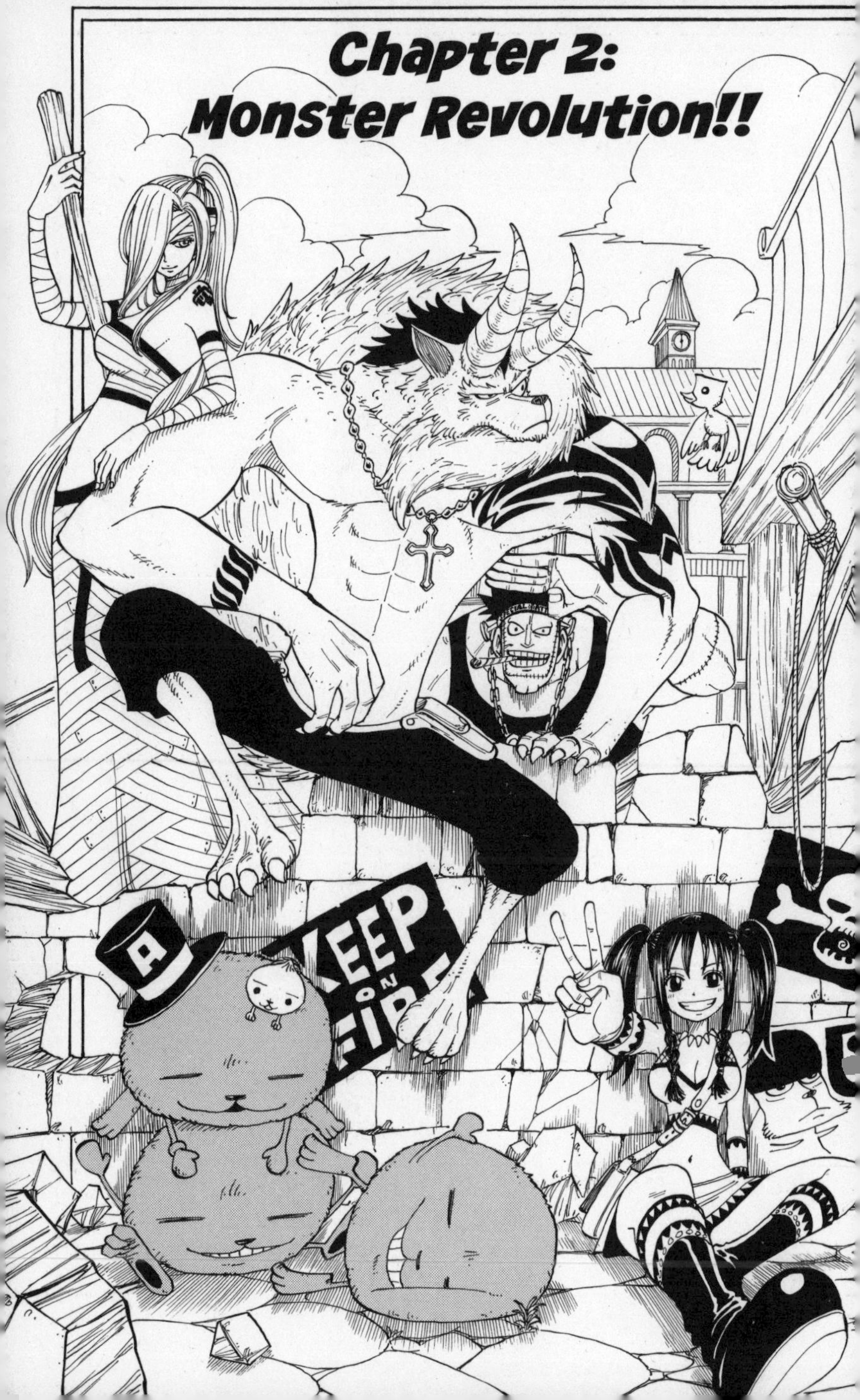
Chapter 2:
Monster Revolution!!
KEEP
ON

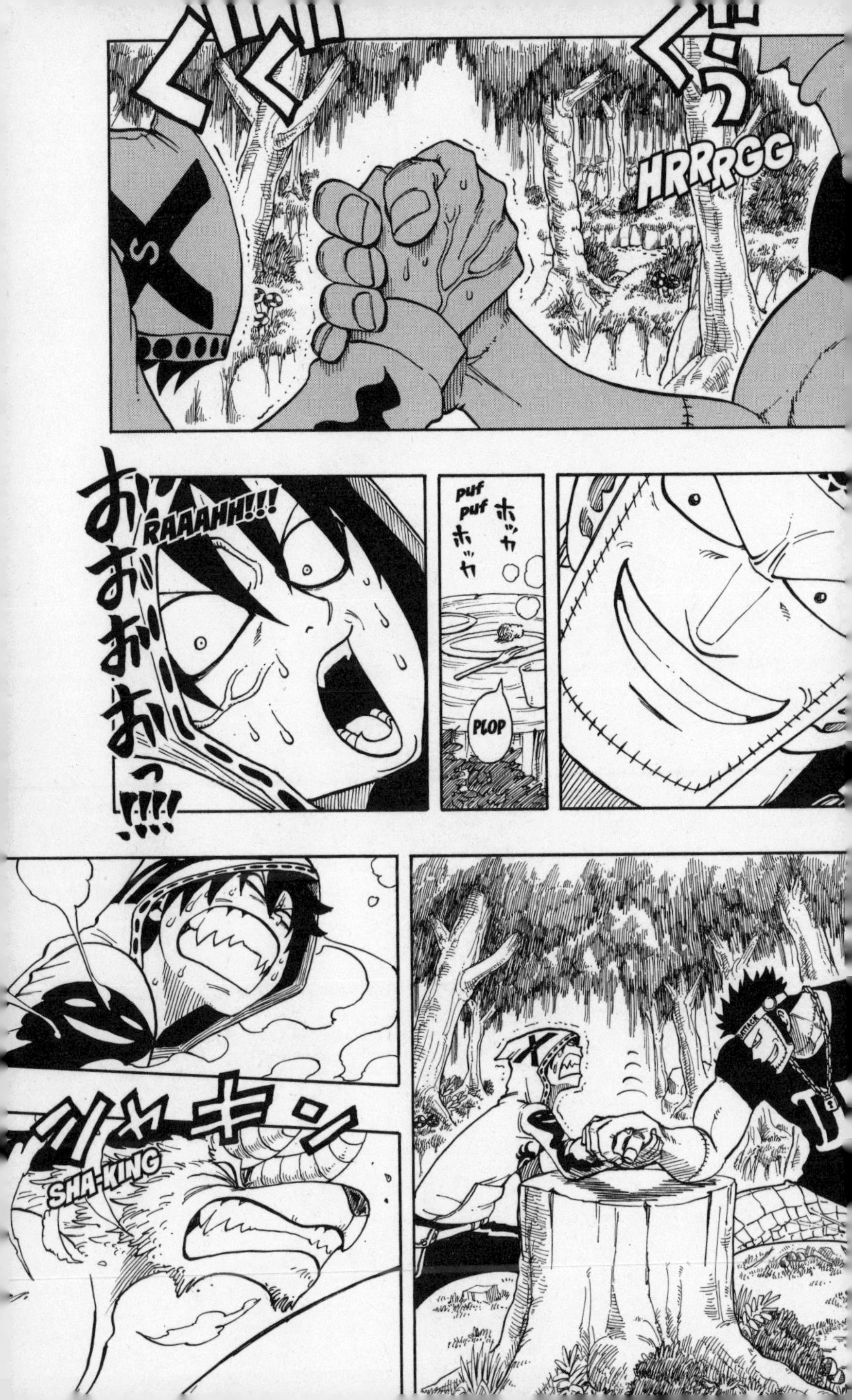
ぐっ
HRRRGG
ぐぐ
ホッカ ホッカ
puf puf
PLOP
おおおおっ!!!!
RAAAHH!!!
シャキーン
SHA-KING

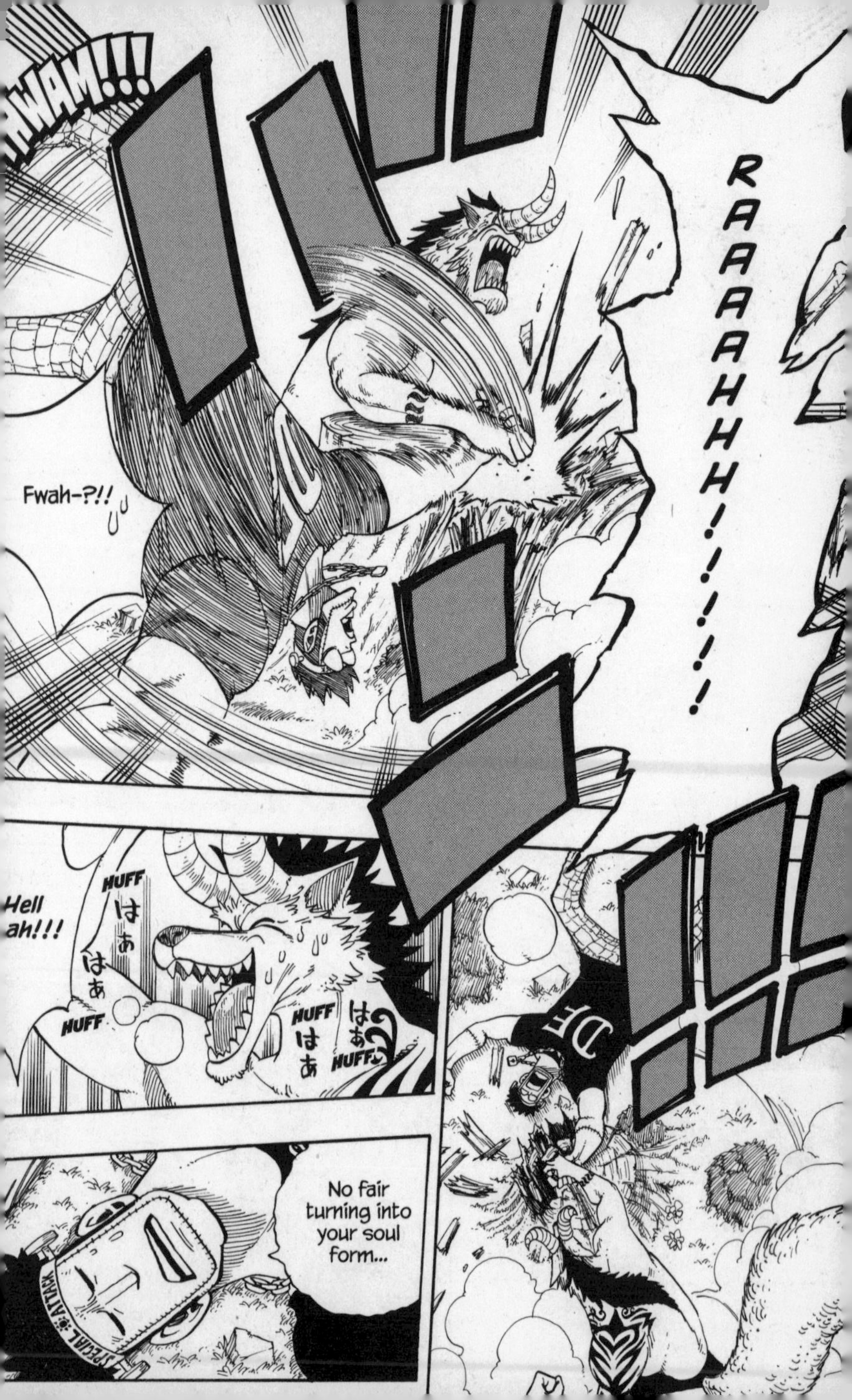

RAAAAHHH!!!!!!
WHAM!!!
Fwah-?!!
Hell
ah!!!
HUFF はぁ
はぁ HUFF
HUFF はぁ
はぁ HUFF
No fair turning into your soul form...
SPECIAL ATTACK

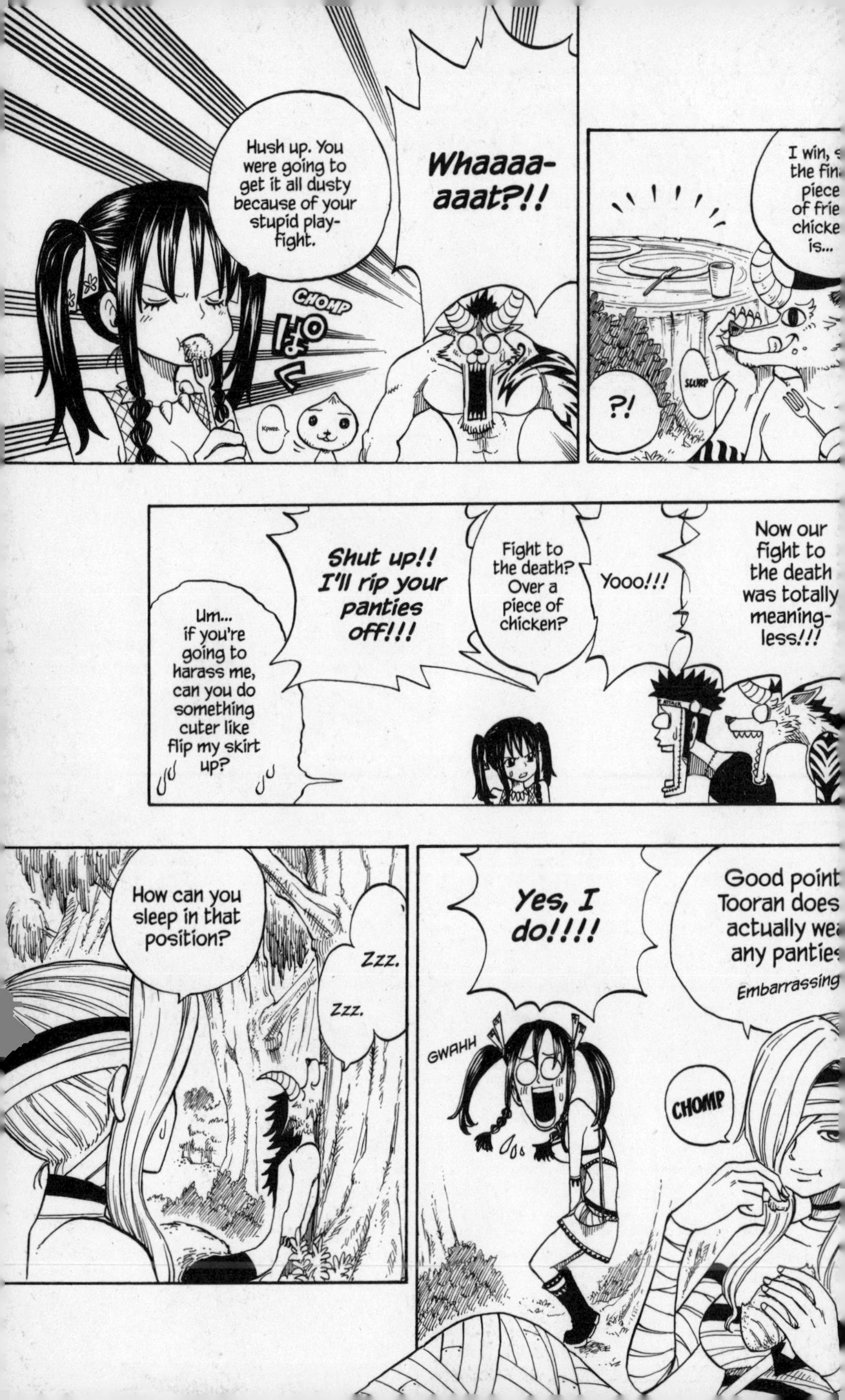

I win, the fin piece of frie chicke is...
SLURP
?!
Whaaaa-aaat?!!
Hush up. You were going to get it all dusty because of your stupid play-fight.
CHOMP
Kpwee.
Now our fight to the death was totally meaning-less!!!
Yooo!!!
Fight to the death? Over a piece of chicken?
Shut up!! I'll rip your panties off!!!
Um... if you're going to harass me, can you do something cuter like flip my skirt up?
Good point Tooran does actually wea any pantie
Embarrassing
Yes, I do!!!!
GWAHH
CHOMP
Zzz.
Zzz.
How can you sleep in that position?

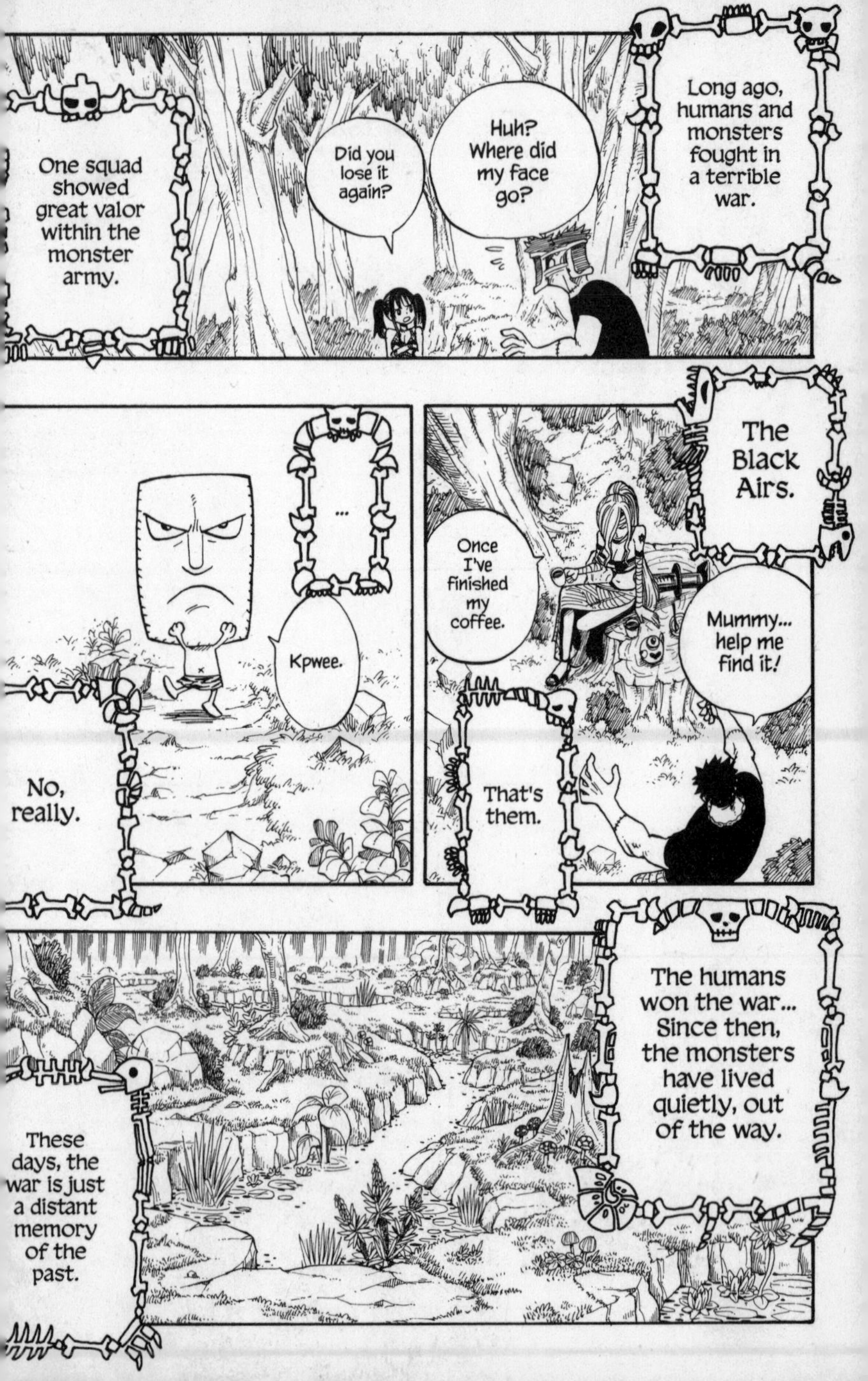
Long ago, humans and monsters fought in a terrible war.
Huh? Where did my face go?
Did you lose it again?
One squad showed great valor within the monster army.
The Black Airs.
Mummy... help me find it!
Once I've finished my coffee.
That's them.
...
Kpwee.
No, really.
The humans won the war... Since then, the monsters have lived quietly, out of the way.
These days, the war is just a distant memory of the past.

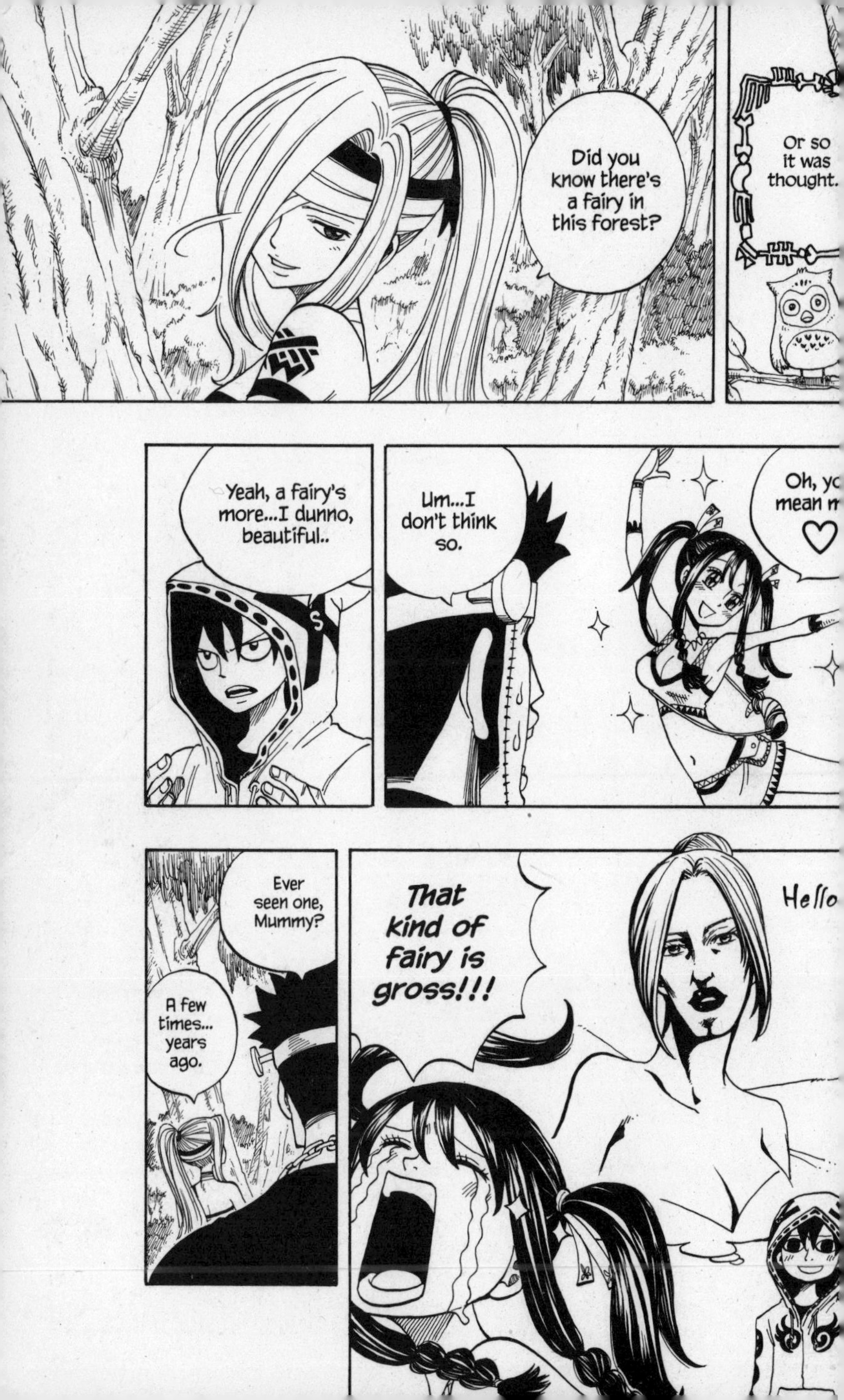
Or so it was thought.
Did you know there's a fairy in this forest?
Oh, yo mean m ♥
Um...I don't think so.
Yeah, a fairy's more...I dunno, beautiful..
Hello
That kind of fairy is gross!!!
Ever seen one, Mummy?
A few times... years ago.

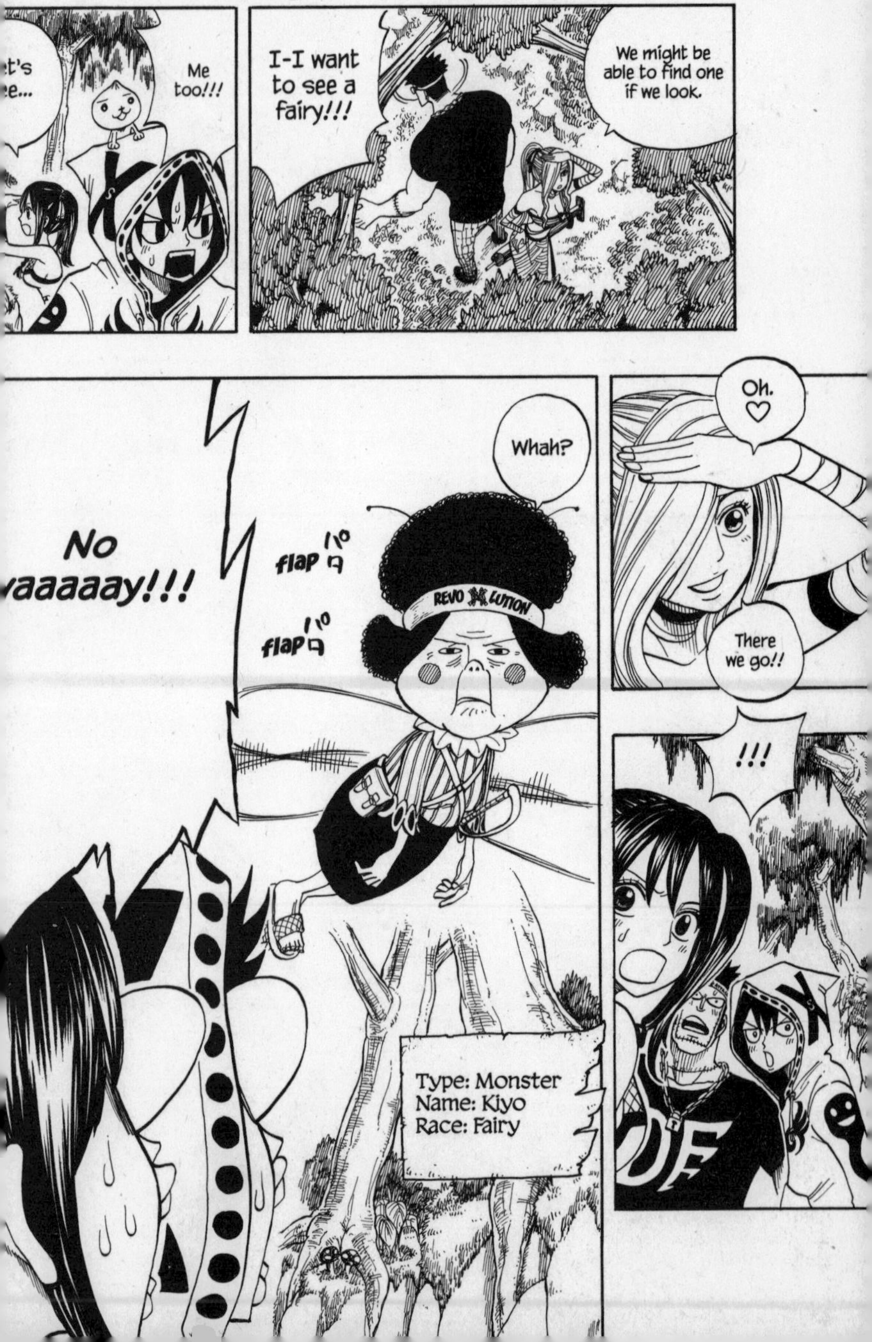
We might be able to find one if we look.
I-I want to see a fairy!!!
Me too!!!
Oh. ♡
There we go!!
!!!
Whah?
flap パタ
flap パタ
REVO LUTION
Type: Monster
Name: Kiyo
Race: Fairy
No aaaaay!!!

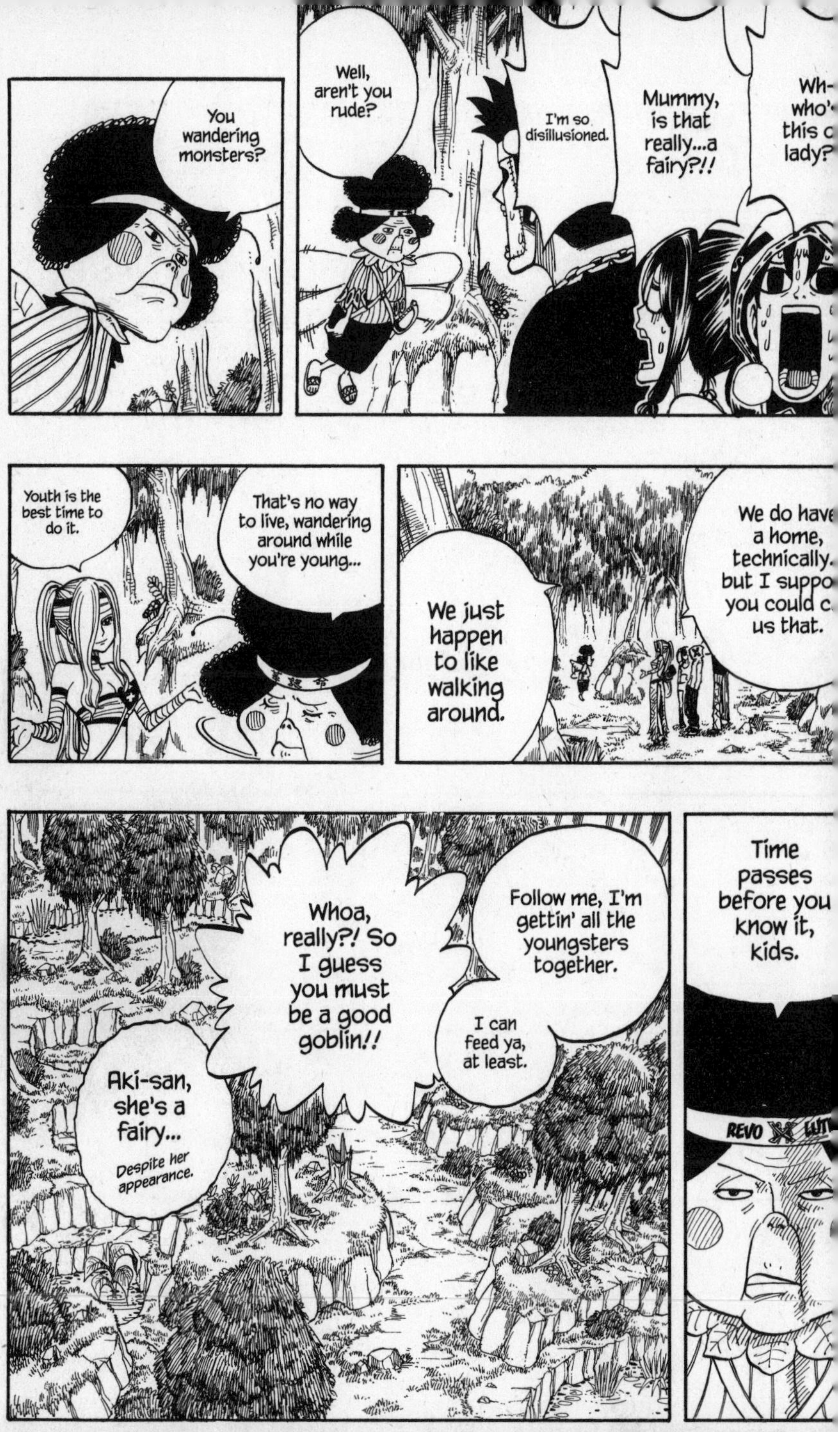
Wh- who' this o lady?
Mummy, is that really...a fairy?!!
I'm so disillusioned.
Well, aren't you rude?
You wandering monsters?
We do have a home, technically.. but I suppo you could c us that.
We just happen to like walking around.
That's no way to live, wandering around while you're young...
Youth is the best time to do it.
Time passes before you know it, kids.
REVO LUTI
Follow me, I'm gettin' all the youngsters together.
I can feed ya, at least.
Whoa, really?! So I guess you must be a good goblin!!
Aki-san, she's a fairy...
Despite her appearance.

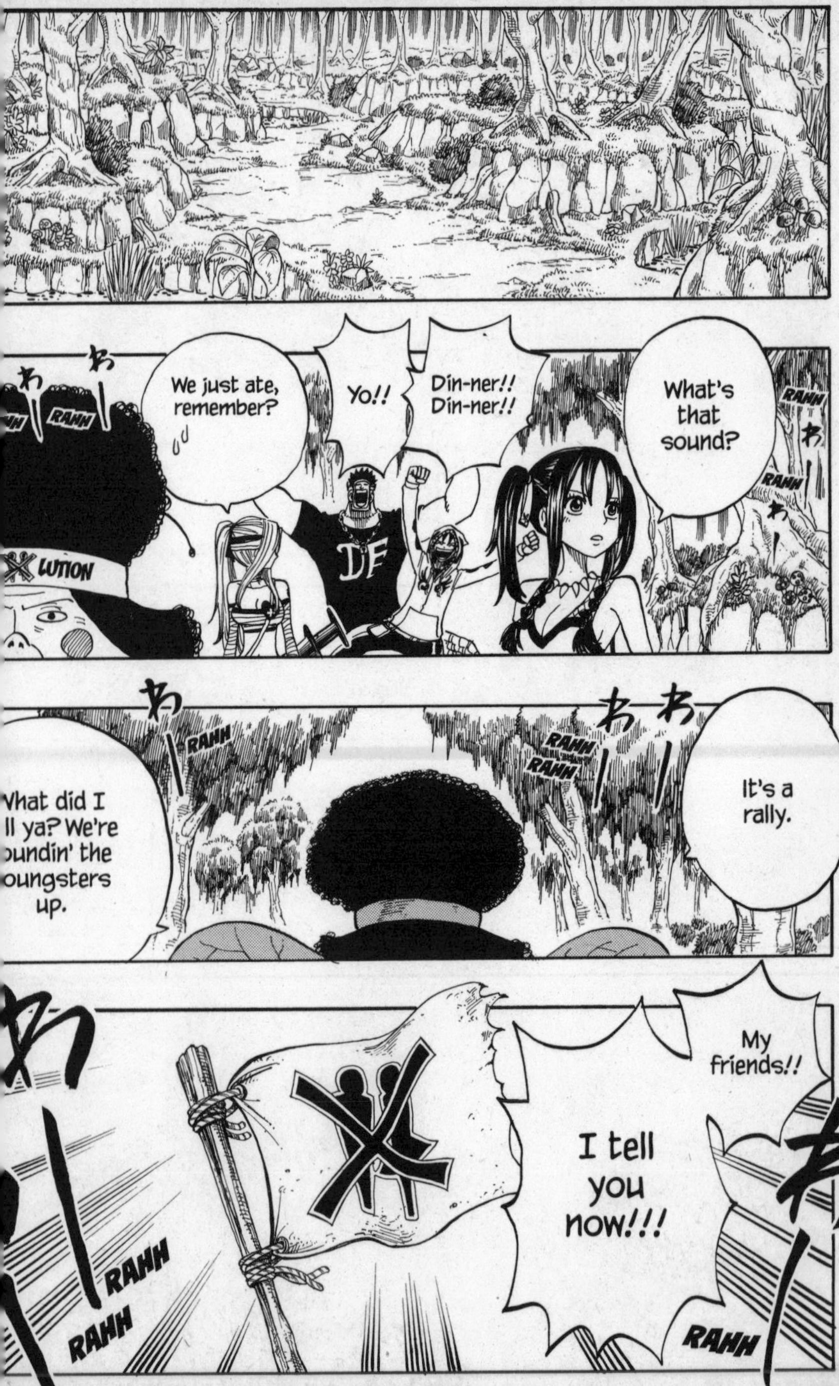
RAHH
わ
What's that sound?
Din-ner!! Din-ner!!
Yo!!
We just ate, remember?
RAHH
わ
LUTION
わ
It's a rally.
RAHH
RAHH
わ
RAHH
Vhat did I ll ya? We're oundin' the oungsters up.
My friends!!
I tell you now!!!
わ
RAHH
わ
RAHH
RAHH

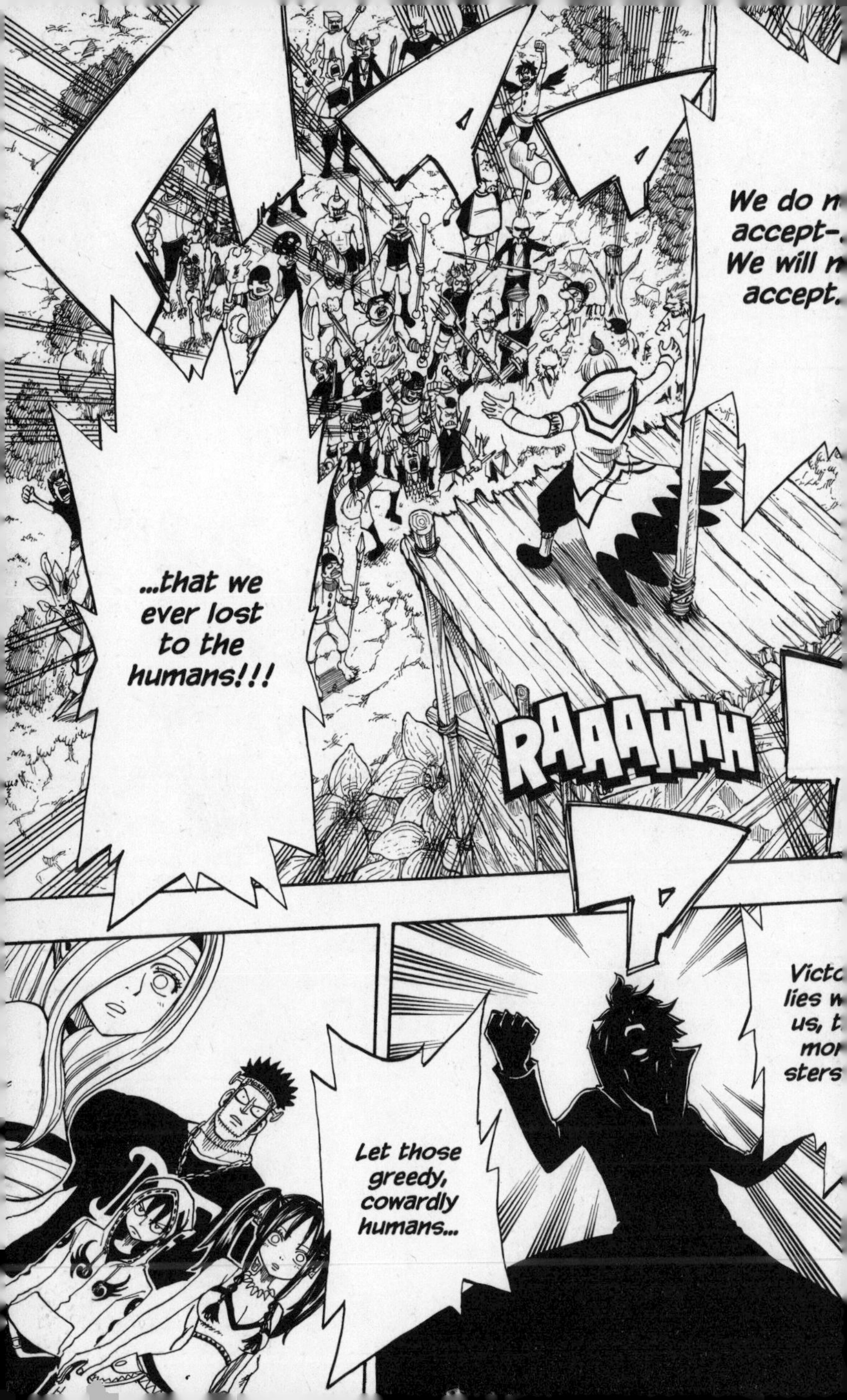
We do n
accept-.
We will n
accept.
...that we ever lost to the humans!!!
RAAAHHH
Victo
lies w
us, t
mon-
sters
Let those greedy, cowardly humans...

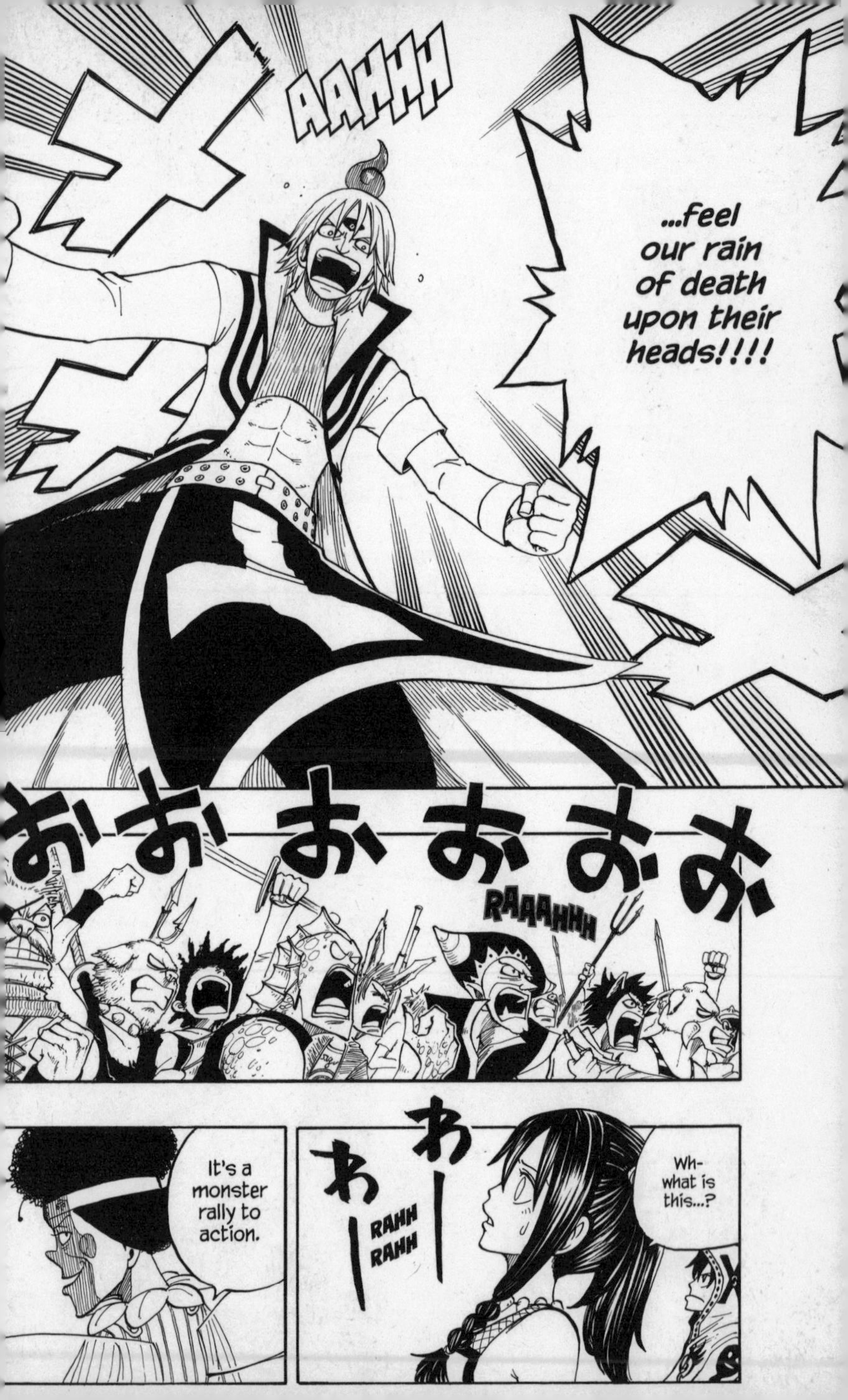
...feel our rain of death upon their heads!!!!
AAHHH
おおおおおお
RAAAHHH
Wh- what is this...?
わーわー
RAHH RAHH
It's a monster rally to action.

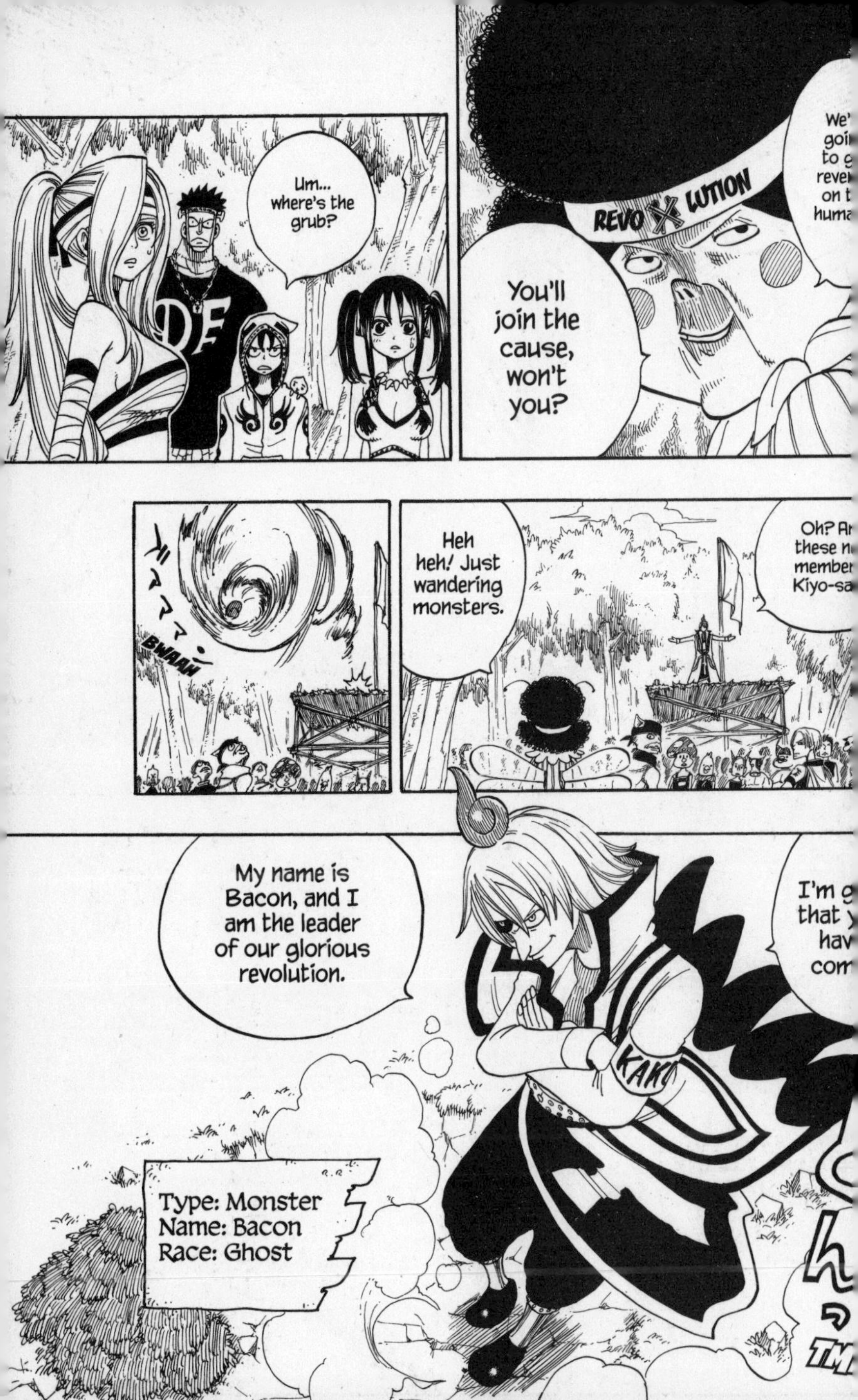
REVO LUTION
You'll join the cause, won't you?
Um... where's the grub?
Heh heh! Just wandering monsters.
BWAAH
My name is Bacon, and I am the leader of our glorious revolution.
Type: Monster
Name: Bacon
Race: Ghost

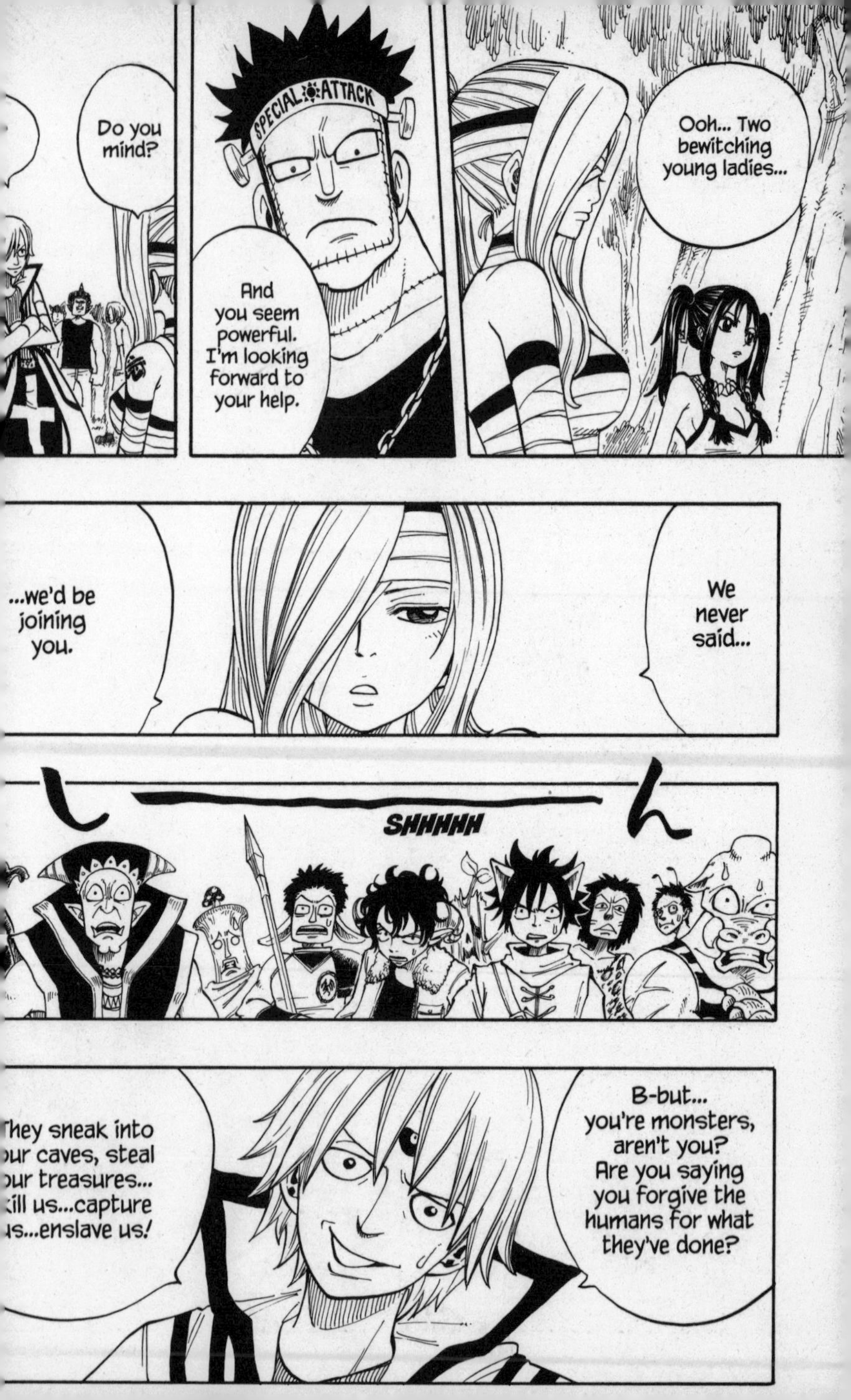
Ooh... Two bewitching young ladies...
And you seem powerful. I'm looking forward to your help.
Do you mind?
We never said...
...we'd be joining you.
しーーーん
SHHHHH
B-but... you're monsters, aren't you? Are you saying you forgive the humans for what they've done?
hey sneak into ur caves, steal ur treasures... ill us...capture s...enslave us!

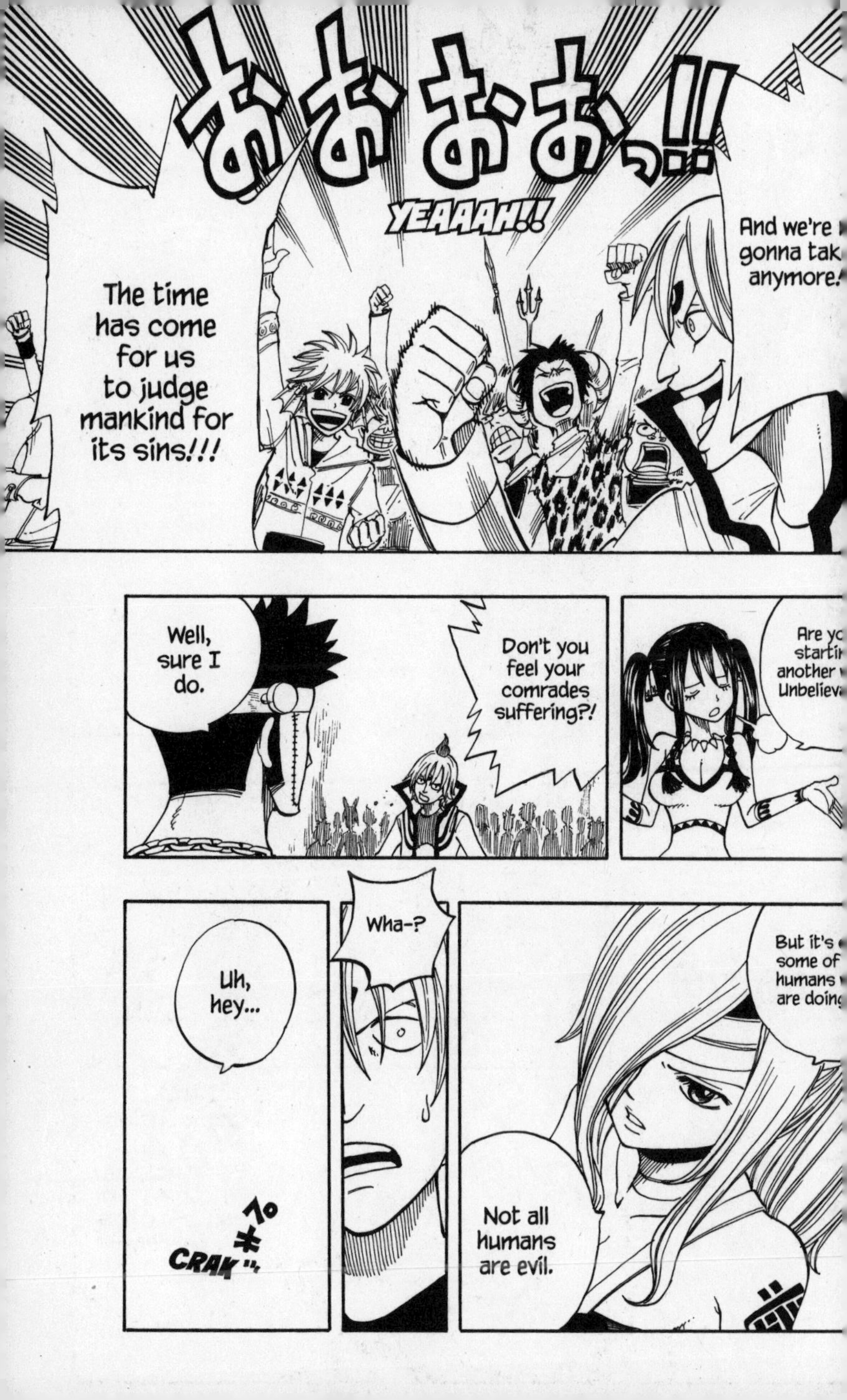
おおおおっ!!
YEAAAH!!
And we're gonna tak anymore!
The time has come for us to judge mankind for its sins!!!
Are yo startir another Unbelieva
Don't you feel your comrades suffering?!
Well, sure I do.
But it's some of humans are doing
Not all humans are evil.
Wha-?
Uh, hey...
CRAK

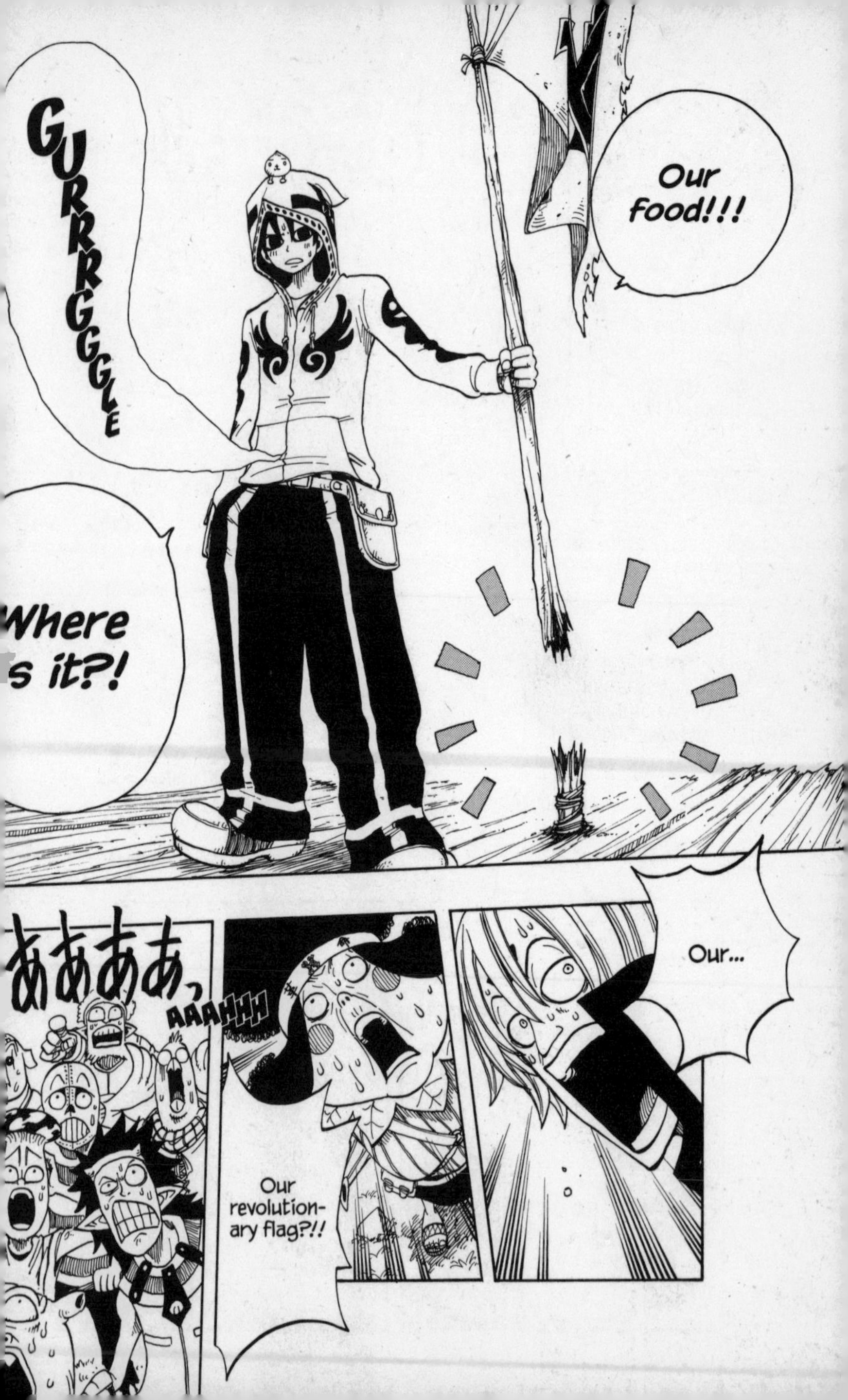

Our food!!!
GURRRGGGLE
Where s it?!
Our...
Our revolution-ary flag?!!
あああああっ
AAAHHH

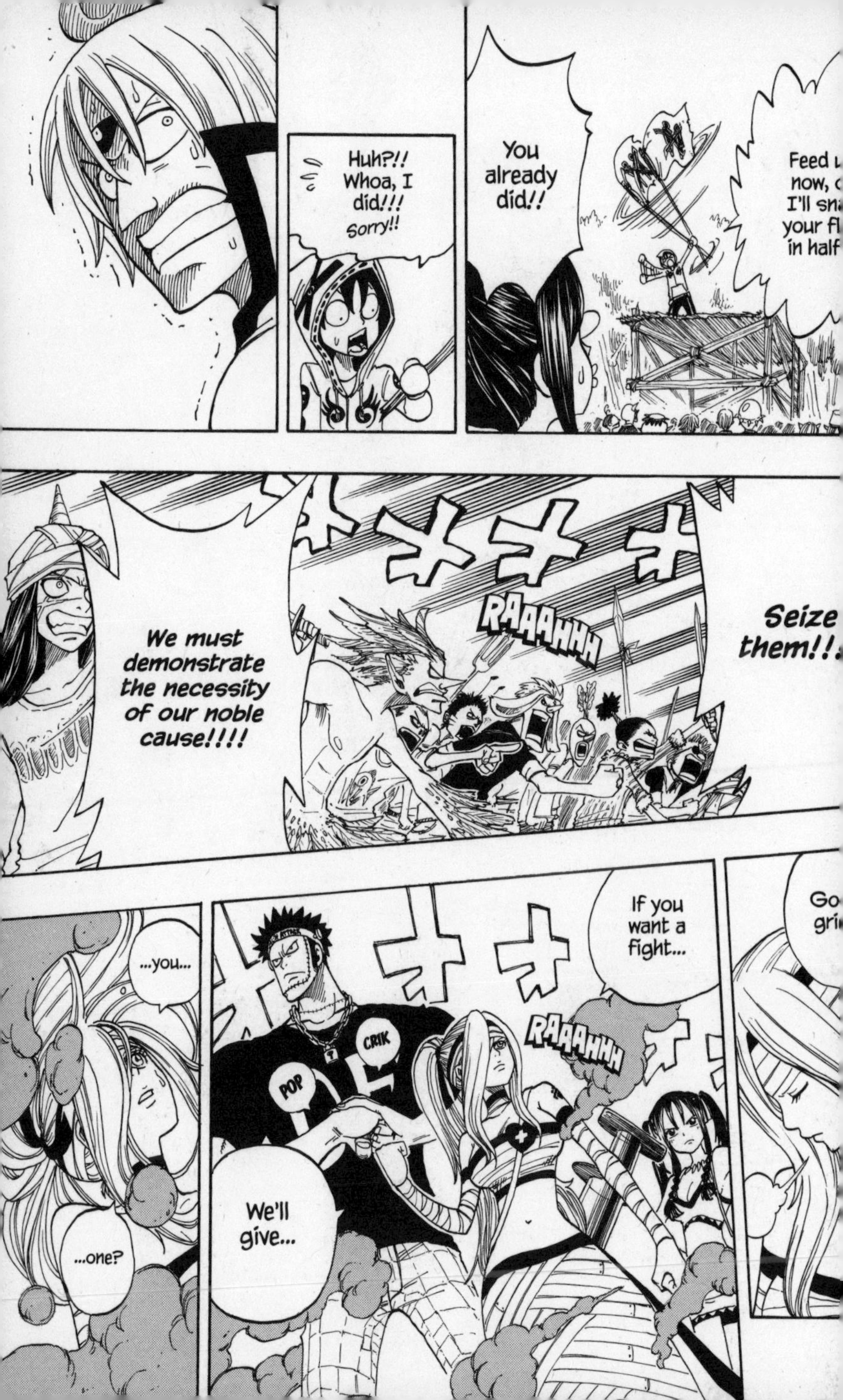

Feed u now, c I'll sn your fl in half
You already did!!
Huh?!! Whoa, I did!!! Sorry!!
Seize them!!
RAAAHHH
We must demonstrate the necessity of our noble cause!!!!
Go gri
If you want a fight...
RAAAHHH
CRIK
POP
We'll give...
...you...
...one?

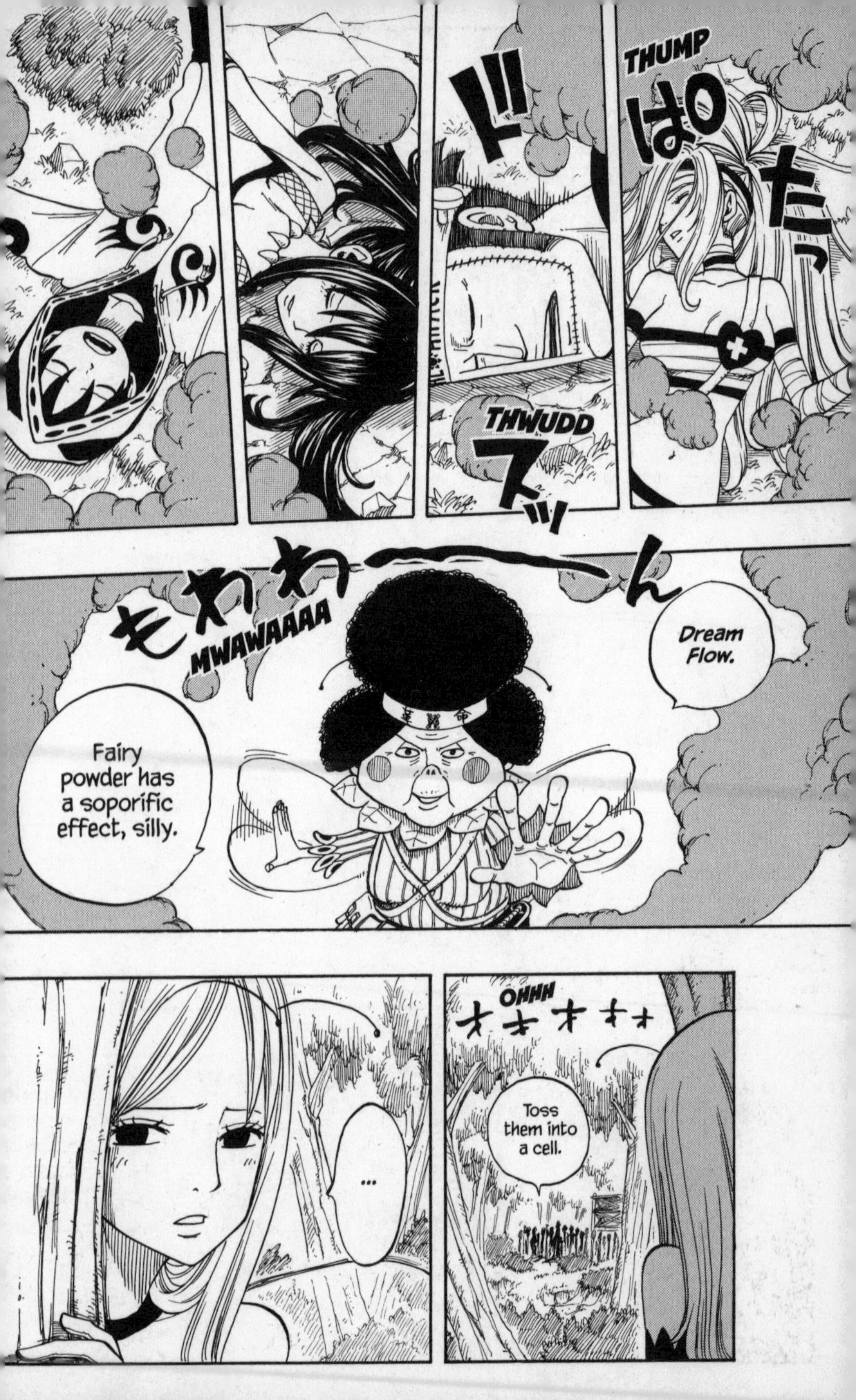
THUMP
はたっ
ド
THWUDD
ドッ
もわわ——ん
MWAWAAAA
Dream Flow.
Fairy powder has a soporific effect, silly.
OHHH
オォオォォ
Toss them into a cell.
...

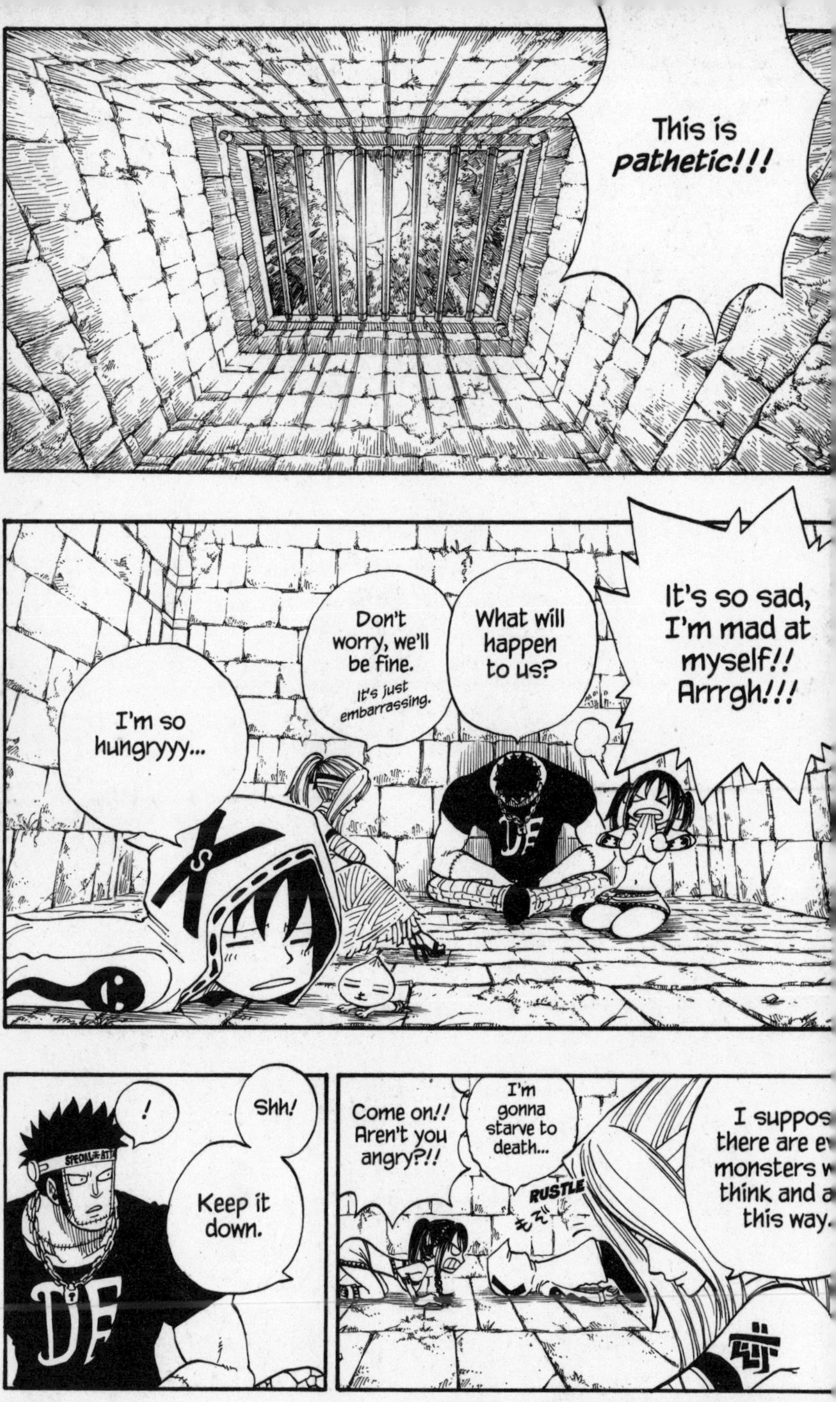
This is *pathetic!!!*
It's so sad, I'm mad at myself!! Arrrgh!!!
What will happen to us?
Don't worry, we'll be fine. It's just embarrassing.
I'm so hungryyy...
I suppos there are ev monsters w think and a this way.
I'm gonna starve to death...
RUSTLE
Come on!! Aren't you angry?!!
Shh!
!
Keep it down.

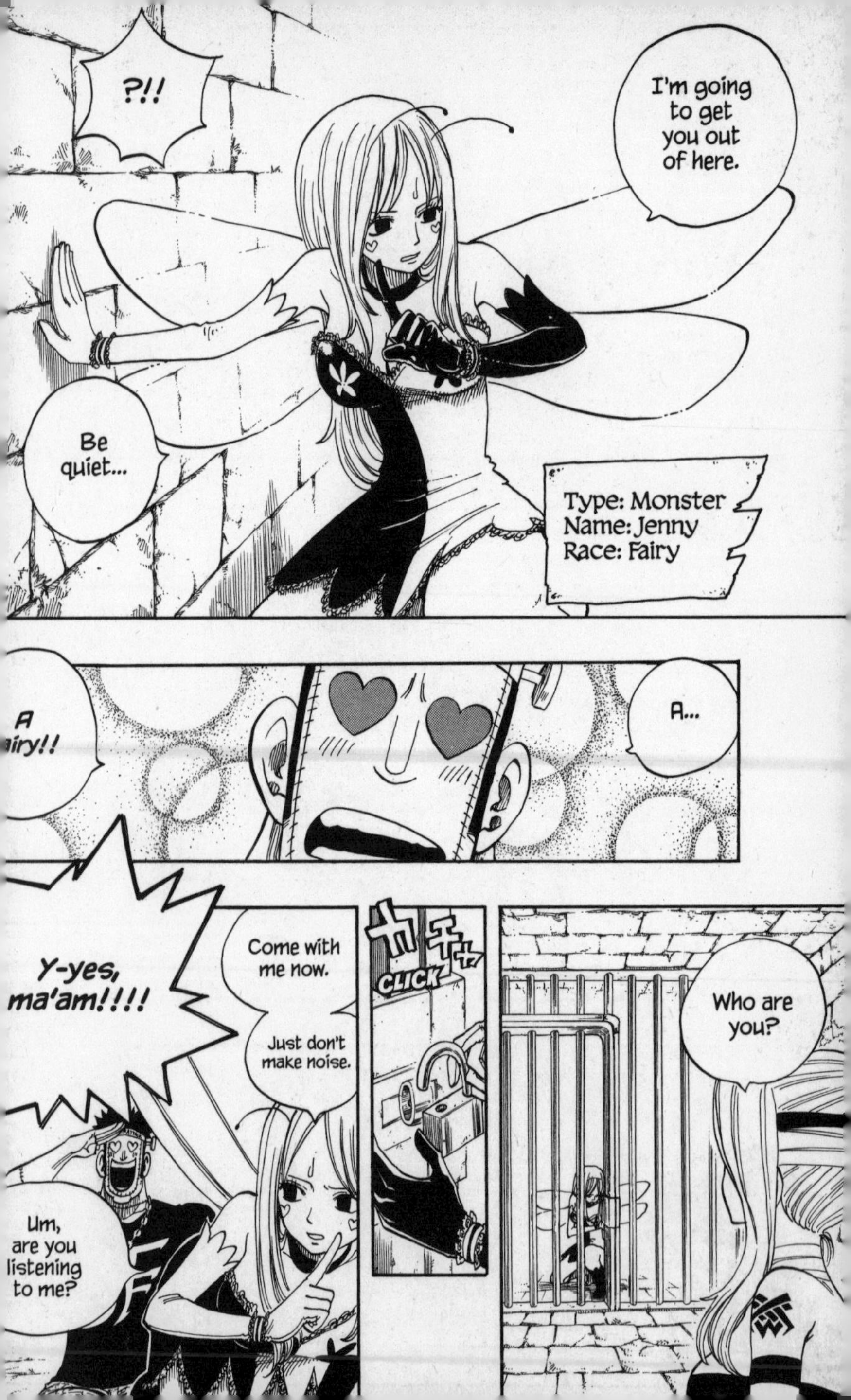
I'm going to get you out of here.
?!!
Type: Monster
Name: Jenny
Race: Fairy
Be quiet...
A...
A airy!!
Who are you?
カチャ
CLICK
Come with me now.
Just don't make noise.
Y-yes, ma'am!!!!
Um, are you listening to me?

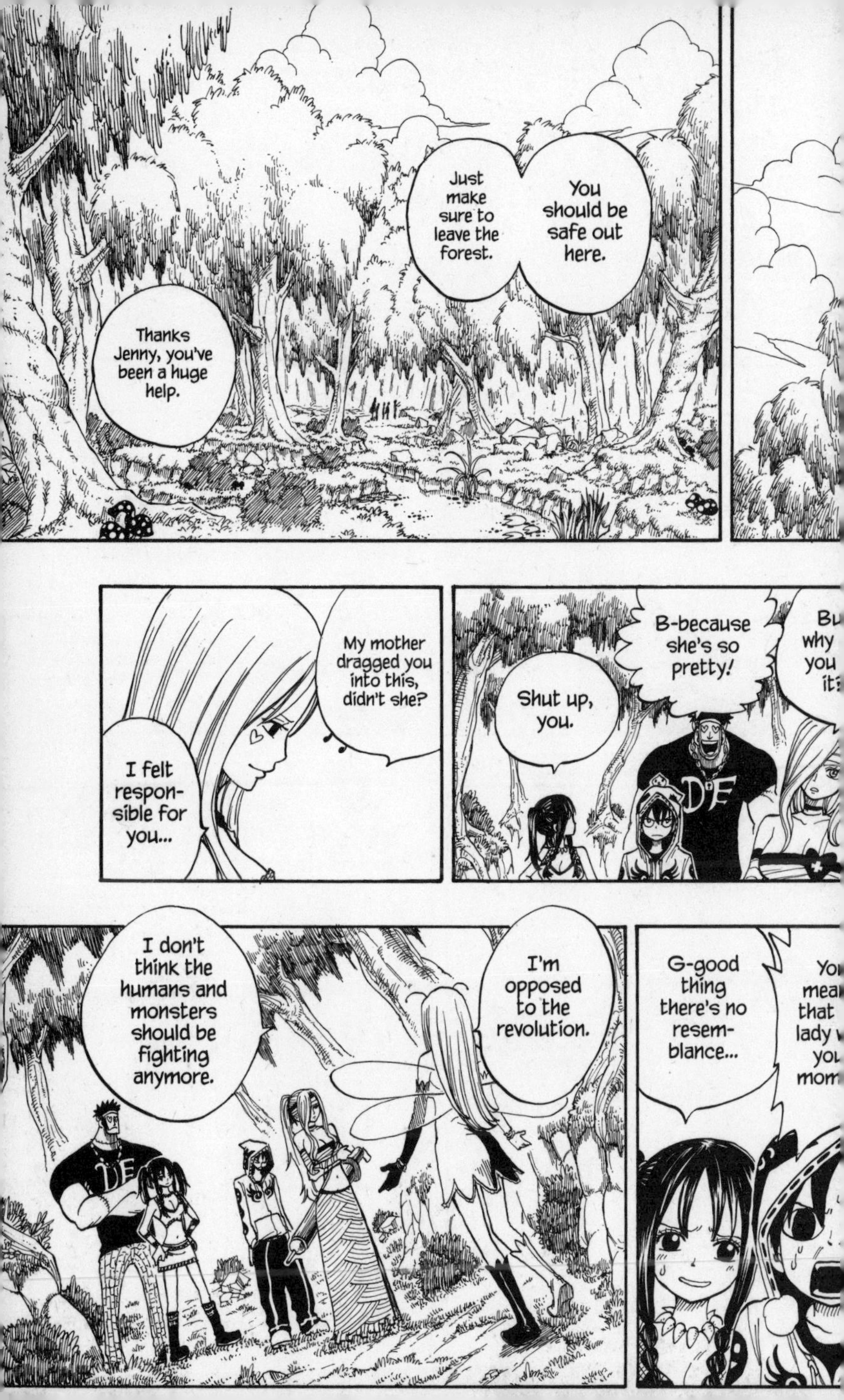
You should be safe out here.
Just make sure to leave the forest.
Thanks Jenny, you've been a huge help.
B-because she's so pretty!
Shut up, you.
My mother dragged you into this, didn't she?
I felt respon-sible for you...
G-good thing there's no resem-blance...
I'm opposed to the revolution.
I don't think the humans and monsters should be fighting anymore.

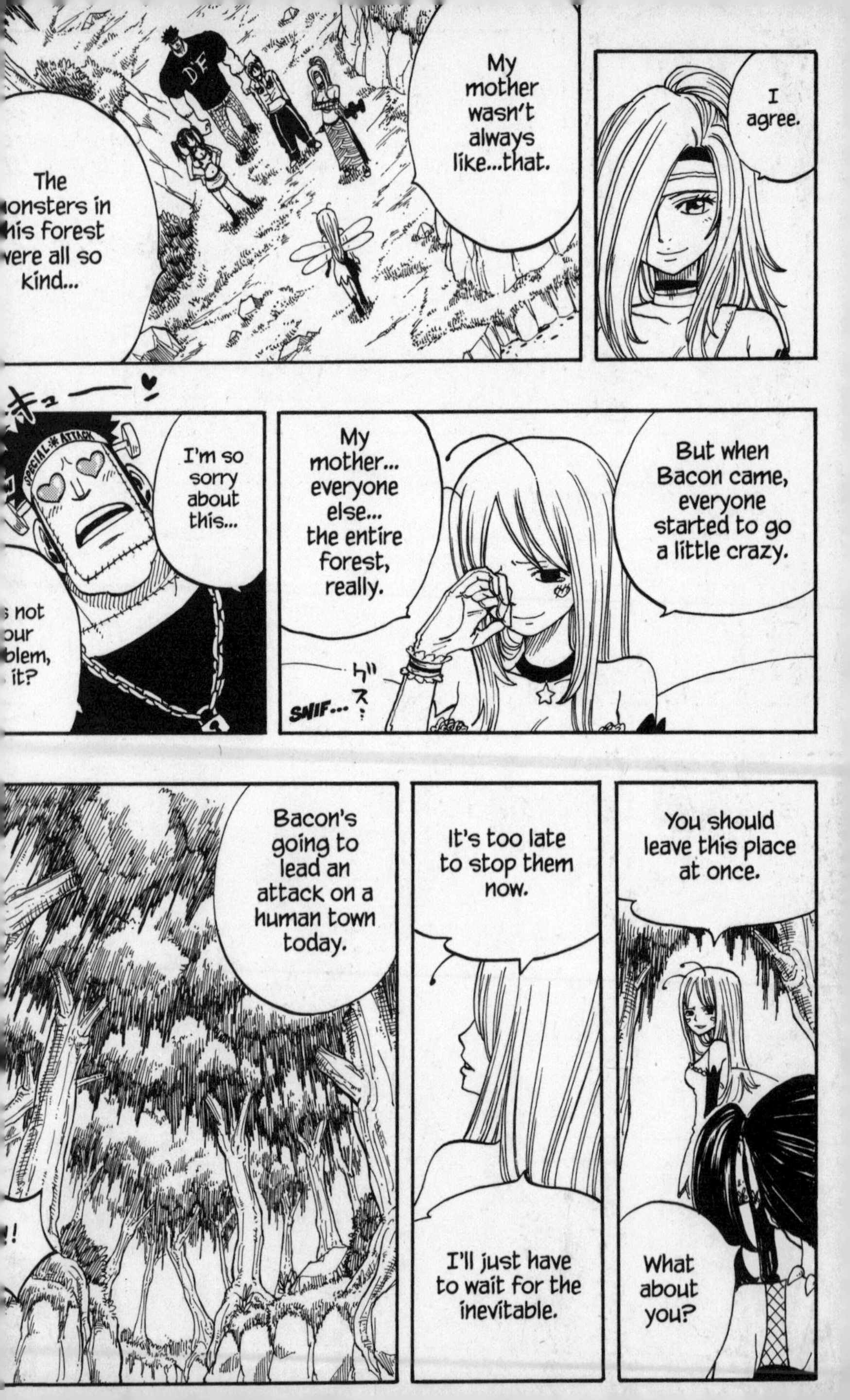

I agree.
My mother wasn't always like...that.
The onsters in his forest vere all so kind...
But when Bacon came, everyone started to go a little crazy.
My mother... everyone else... the entire forest, really.
グス…
SNIF...
キュー♥
I'm so sorry about this...
s not our blem, it?
You should leave this place at once.
What about you?
It's too late to stop them now.
I'll just have to wait for the inevitable.
Bacon's going to lead an attack on a human town today.
!

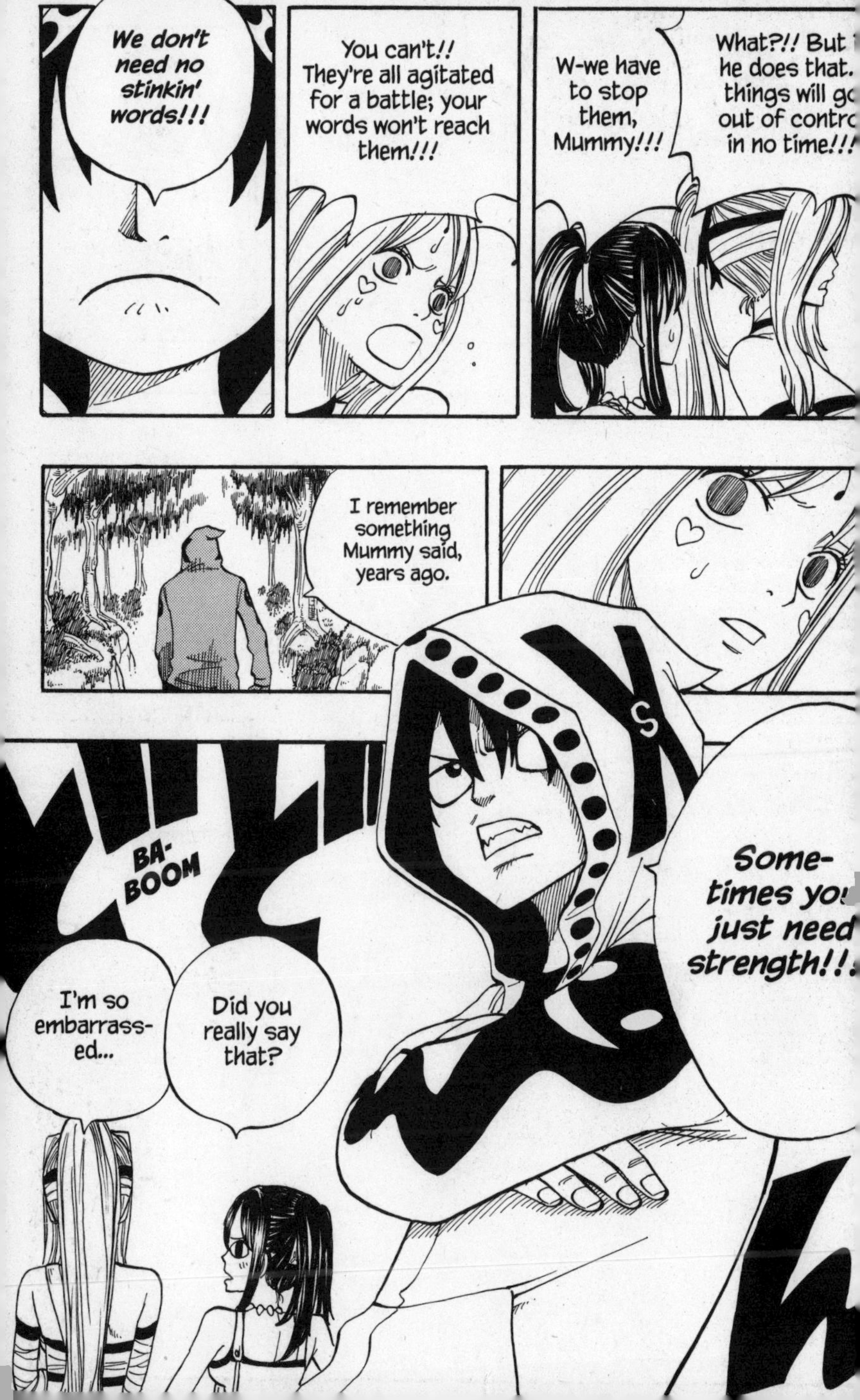
What?!! But
he does that.
things will g
out of contr
in no time!!!
W-we have to stop them, Mummy!!!
You can't!! They're all agitated for a battle; your words won't reach them!!!
We don't need no stinkin' words!!!
I remember something Mummy said, years ago.
Some-times yo
just need
strength!!
BA-BOOM
Did you really say that?
I'm so embarrass-ed...

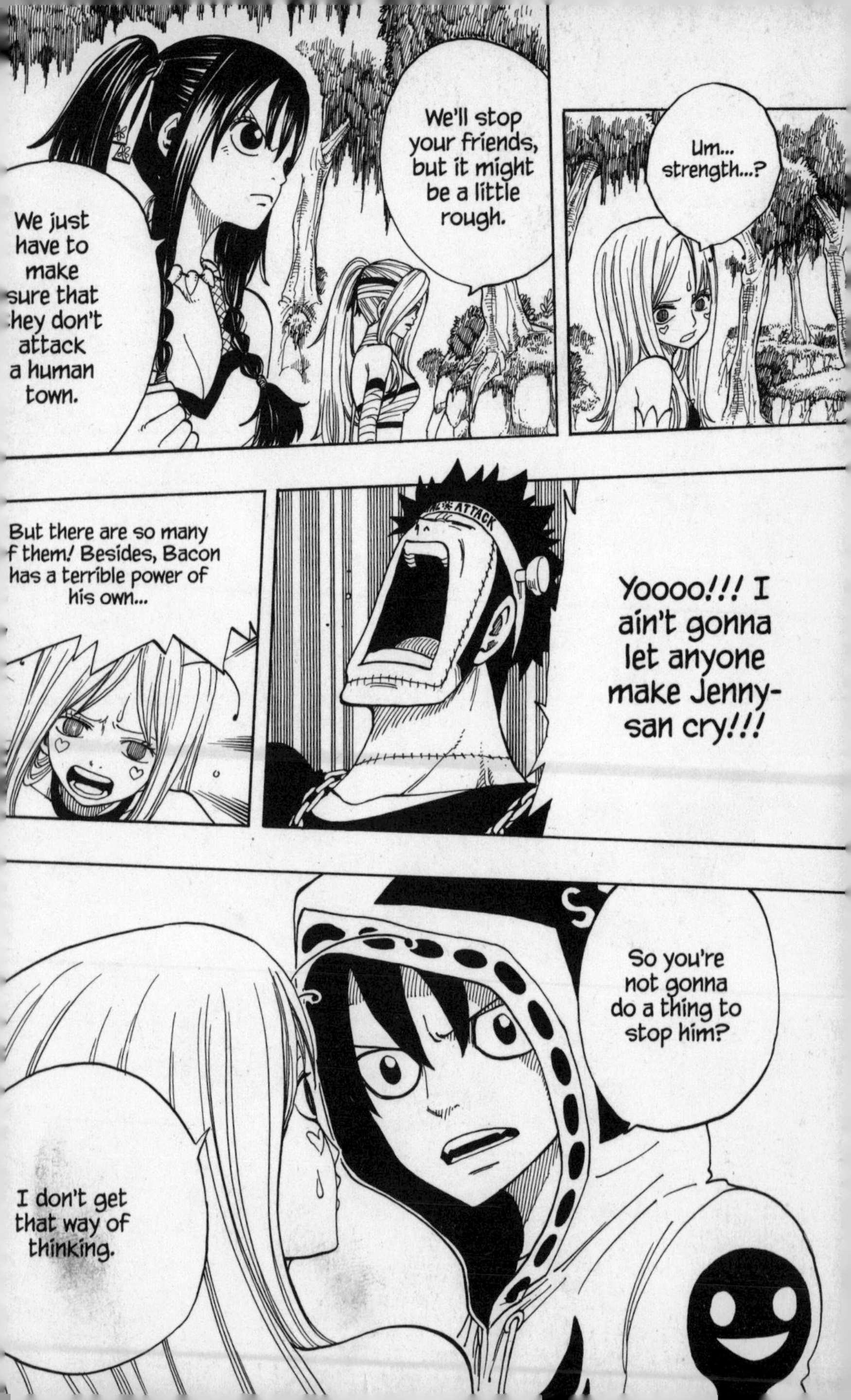
Um... strength...?
We'll stop your friends, but it might be a little rough.
We just have to make sure that hey don't attack a human town.
Yoooo!!! I ain't gonna let anyone make Jenny-san cry!!!
ATTACK
But there are so many f them! Besides, Bacon has a terrible power of his own...
So you're not gonna do a thing to stop him?
I don't get that way of thinking.

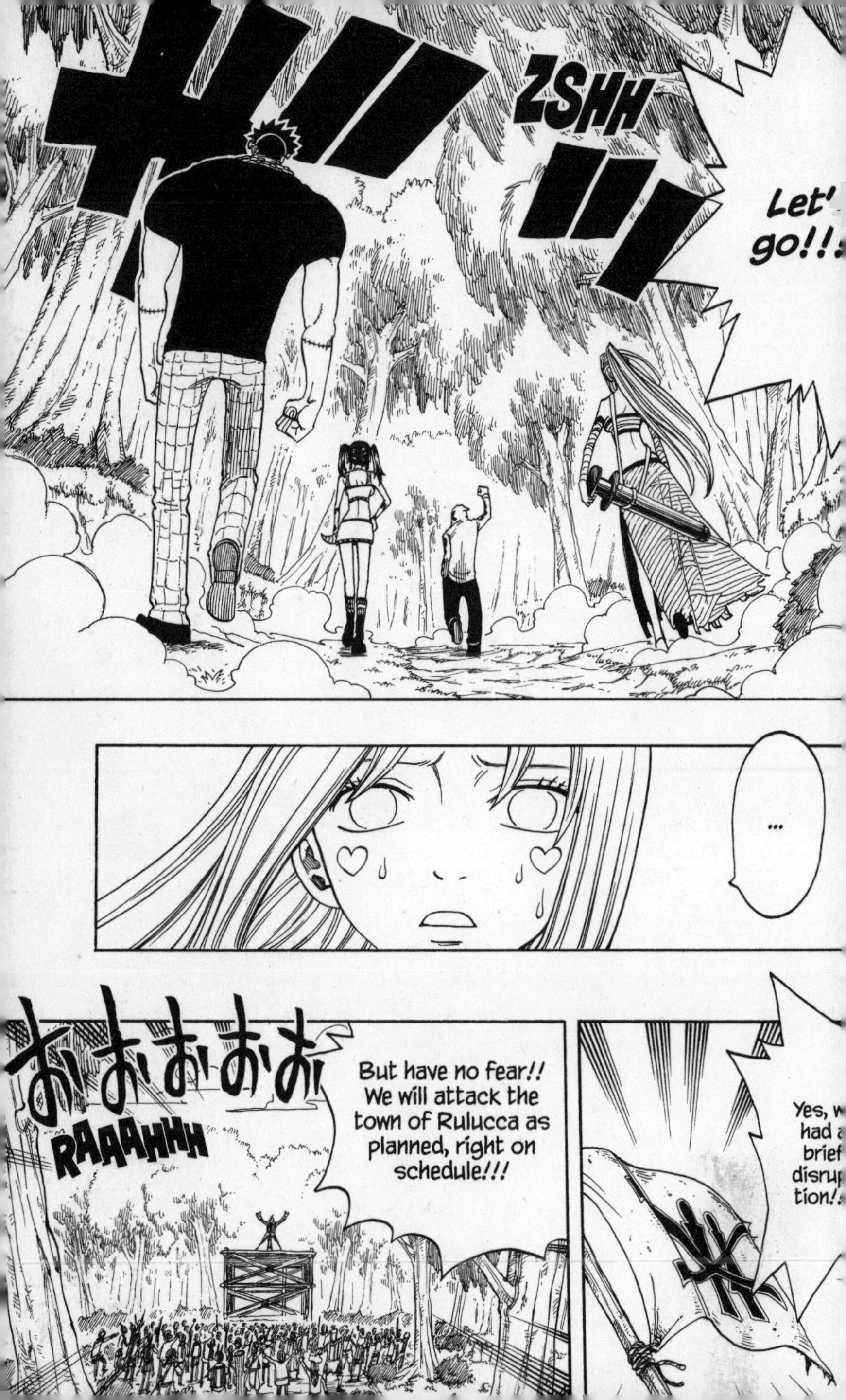
Let's go!!
ZSHH
...
Yes, we had a brief disruption!!
But have no fear!! We will attack the town of Rulucca as planned, right on schedule!!!
おおおおお
RAAAHHH

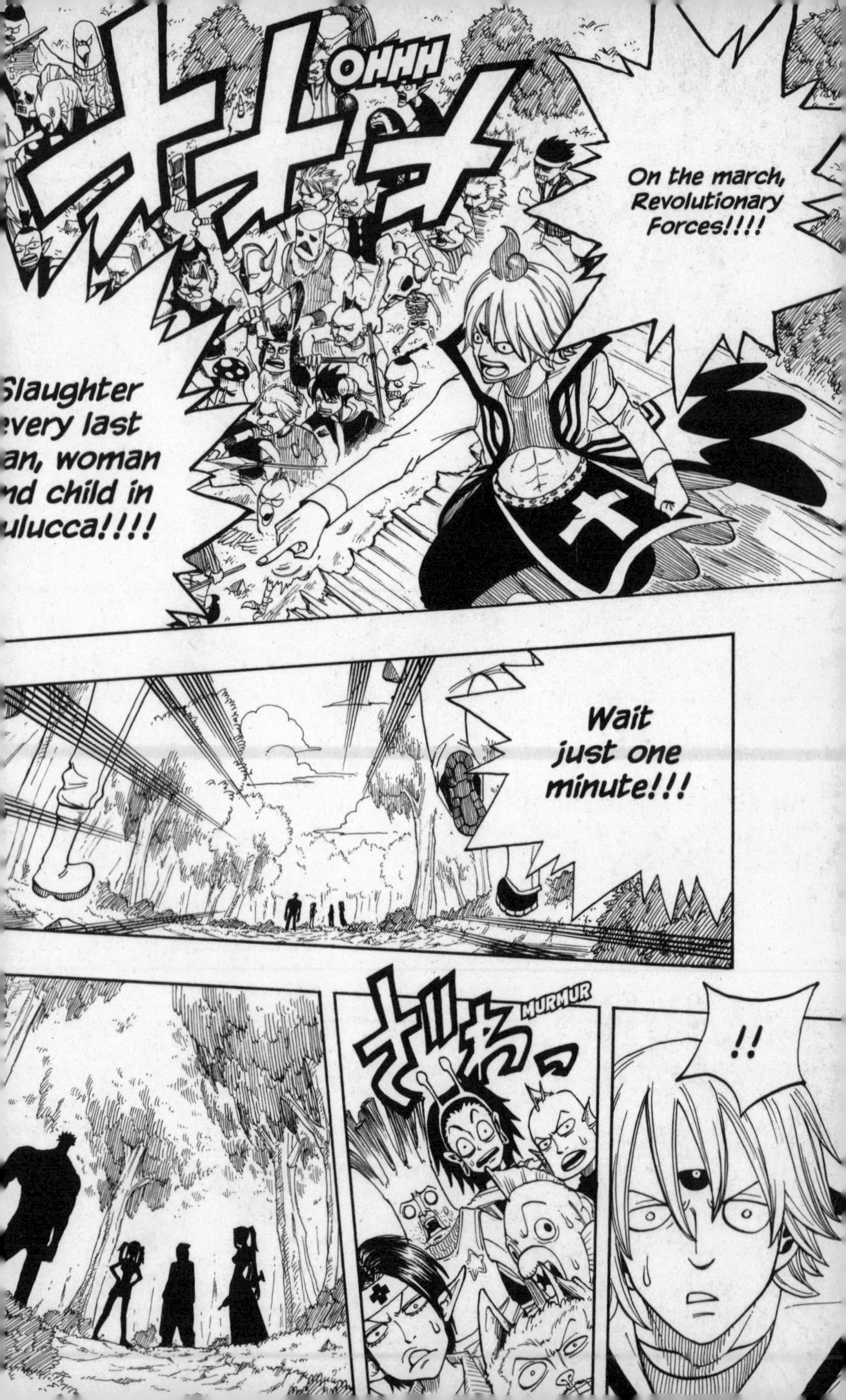
OHHH
On the march, Revolutionary Forces!!!!
Slaughter every last an, woman nd child in ulucca!!!!
Wait just one minute!!!
!!
MURMUR

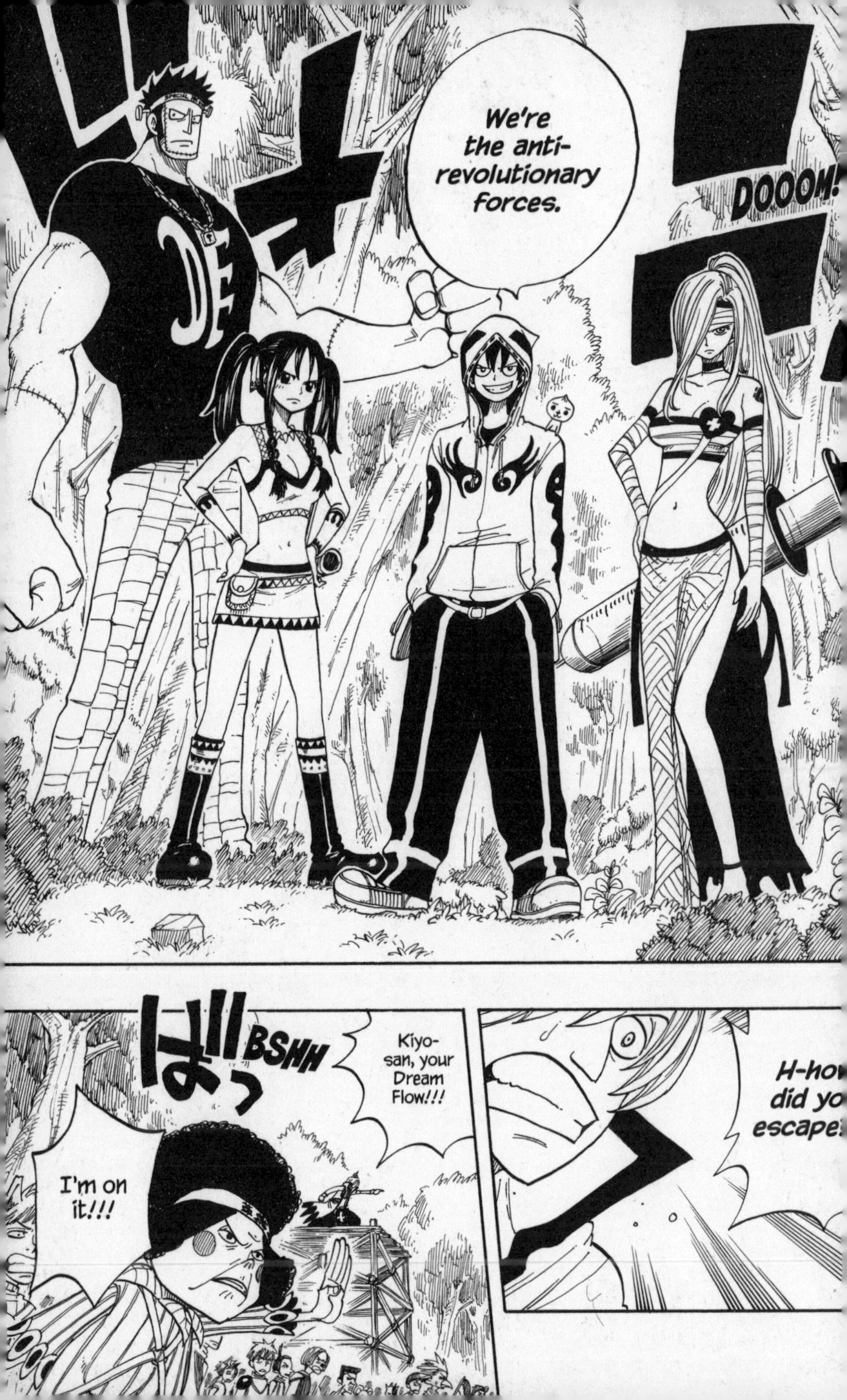

We're the anti-revolutionary forces.
DOOOM!
H-how did yo escape
はっ
BSHH
Kiyo-san, your Dream Flow!!!
I'm on it!!!

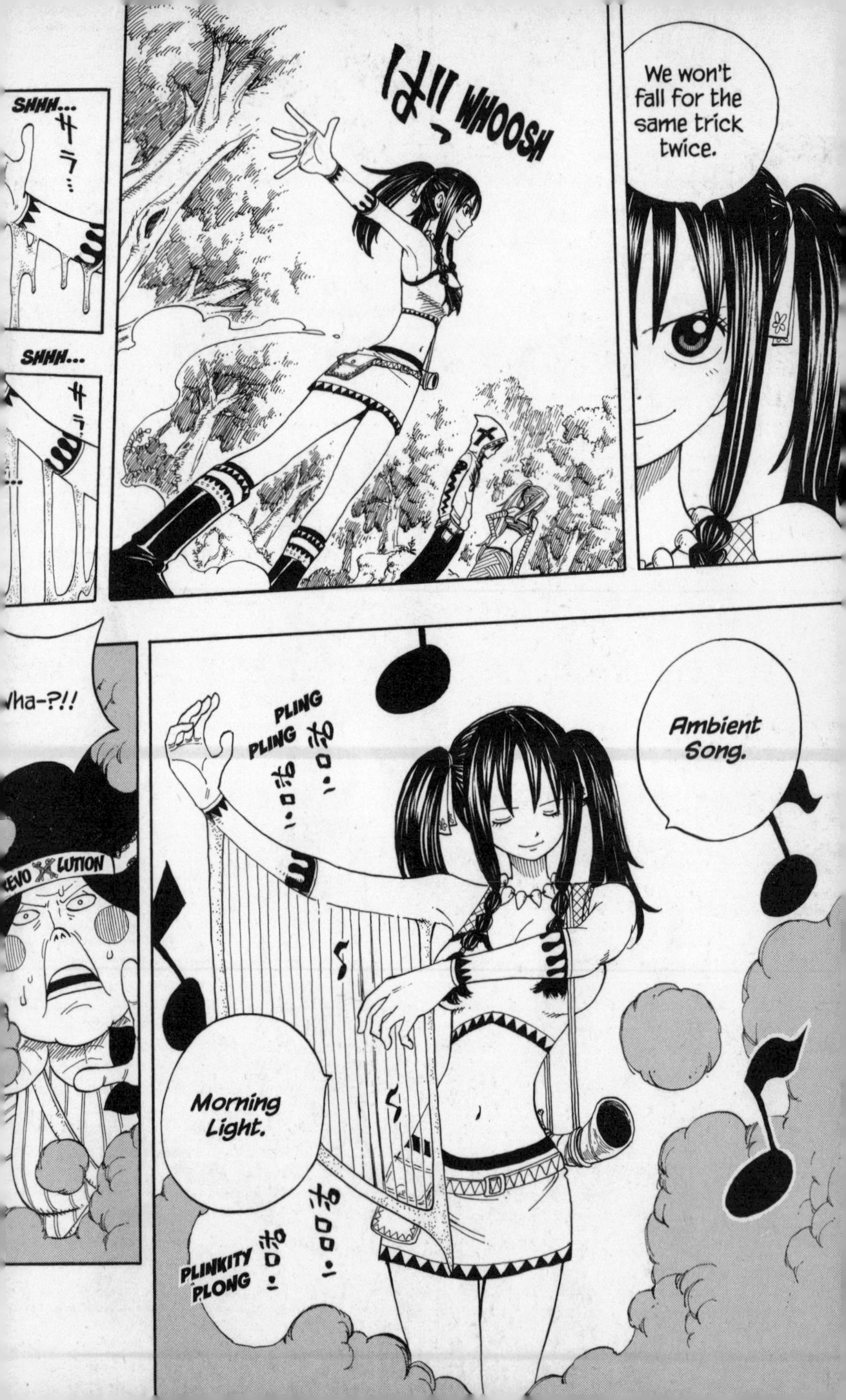

We won't fall for the same trick twice.
WHOOSH
SHHH...
SHHH...
Ambient Song.
PLING PLING
Morning Light.
PLINKITY PLONG
Wha-?!!

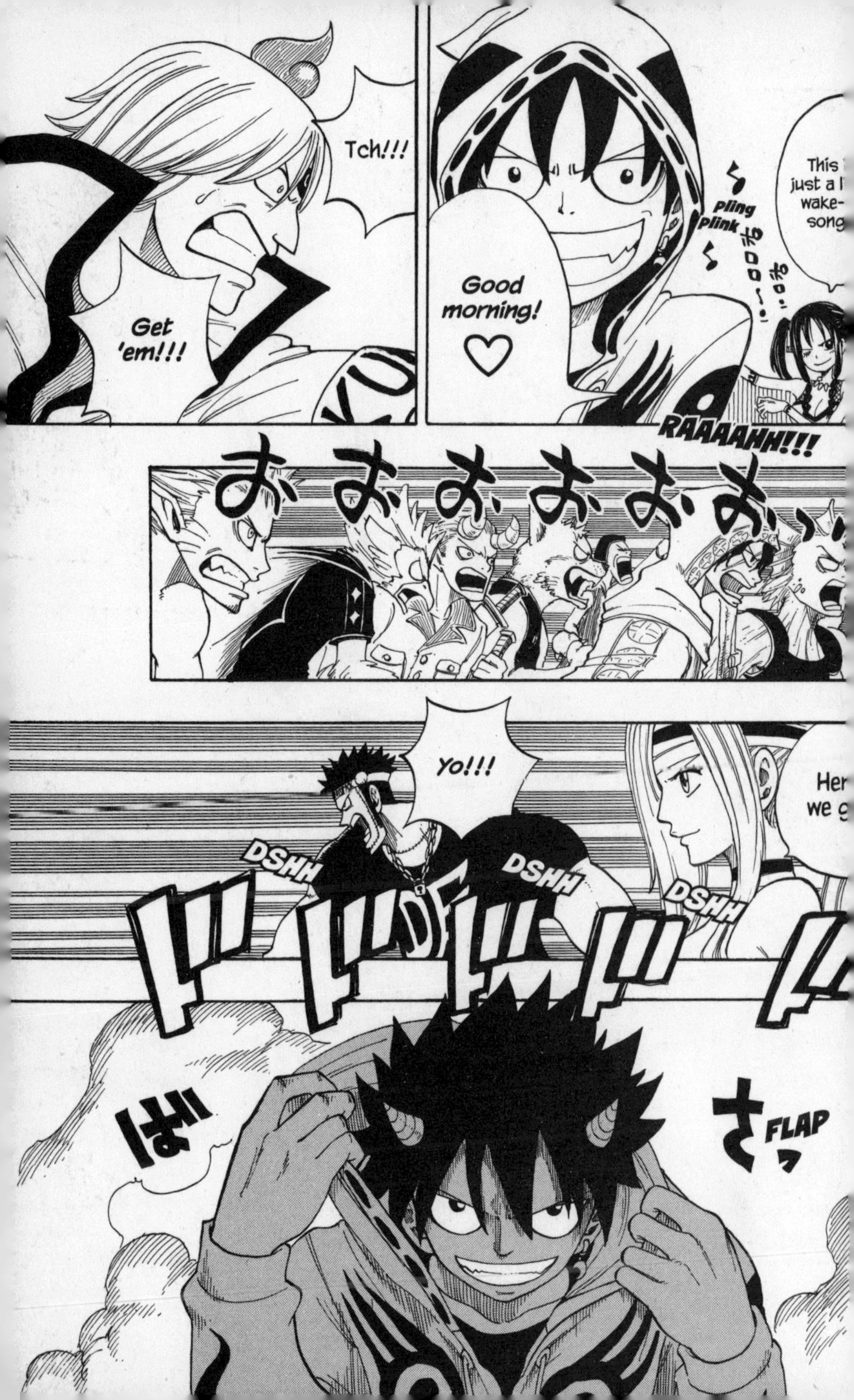

This i just a li wake- song
Pling plink
ホロロ~
ホロ~
Good morning! ♡
Tch!!!
Get 'em!!!
RAAAAHH!!!
おおおおおおっ
Her we g
Yo!!!
DSHH
DSHH
DSHH
ドドドドドド
ばさっ
FLAP

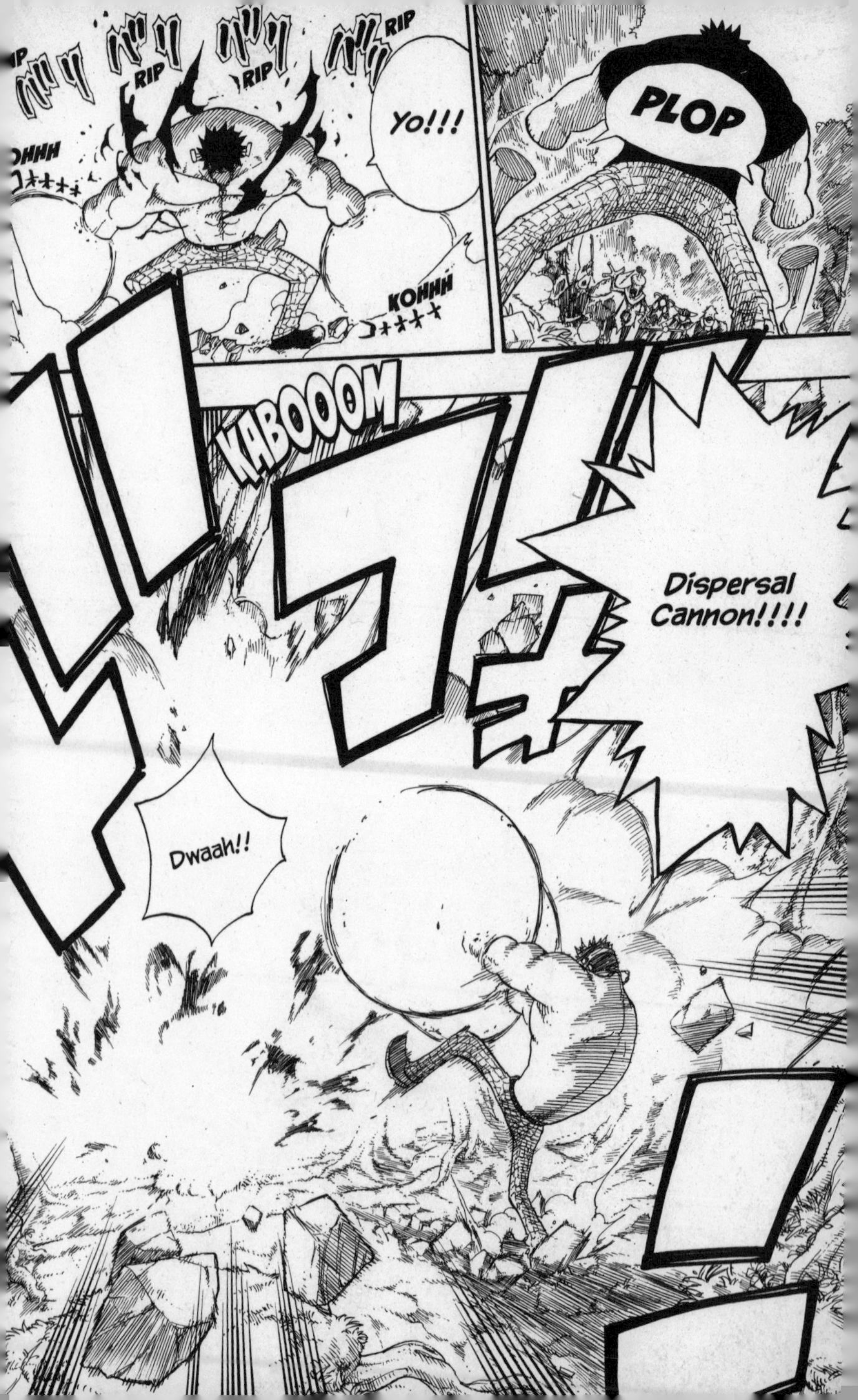
PLOP
Yo!!!
RIP
RIP
RIP
RIP
KOHHH
KOHHH
KABOOOM
Dispersal Cannon!!!!
Dwaah!!

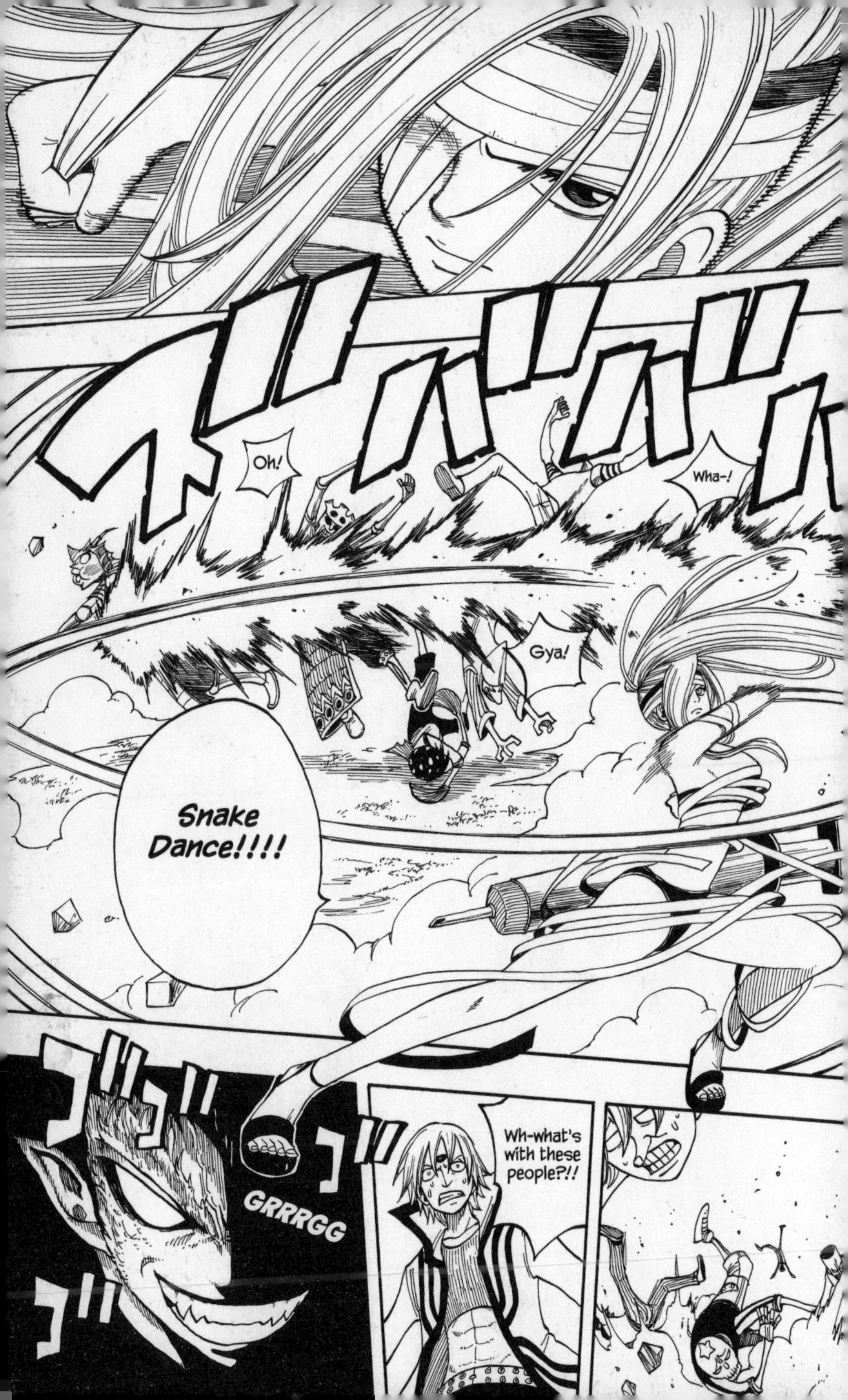
Wha-!
Oh!
Gya!
Snake Dance!!!!
Wh-what's with these people?!!
GRRRGG

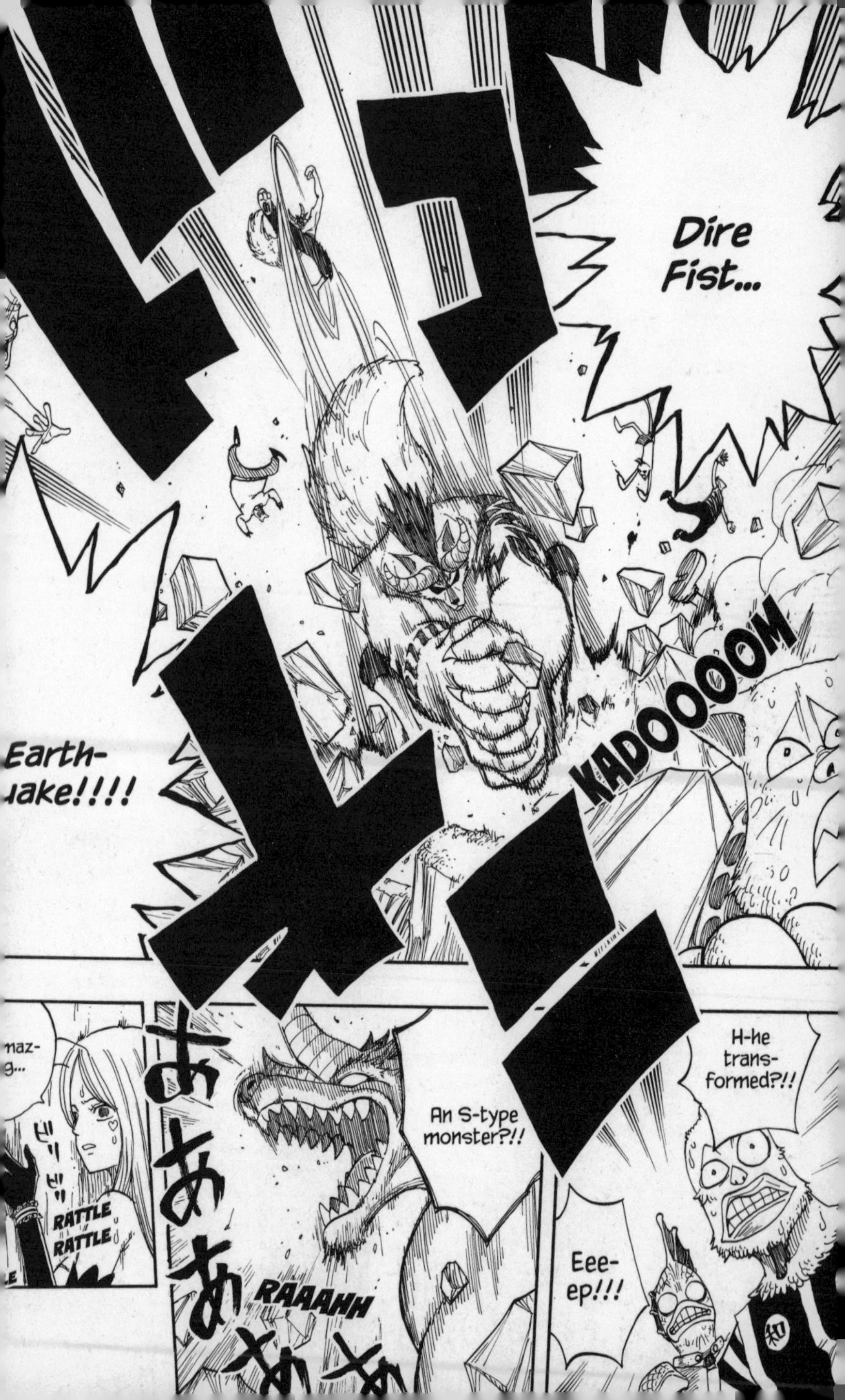
Dire Fist...
Earth-
uake!!!!
KADOOOOOM
H-he transformed?!!
Eee-ep!!!
An S-type monster?!!
あああ
RAAAHH
ビリビリ
RATTLE RATTLE

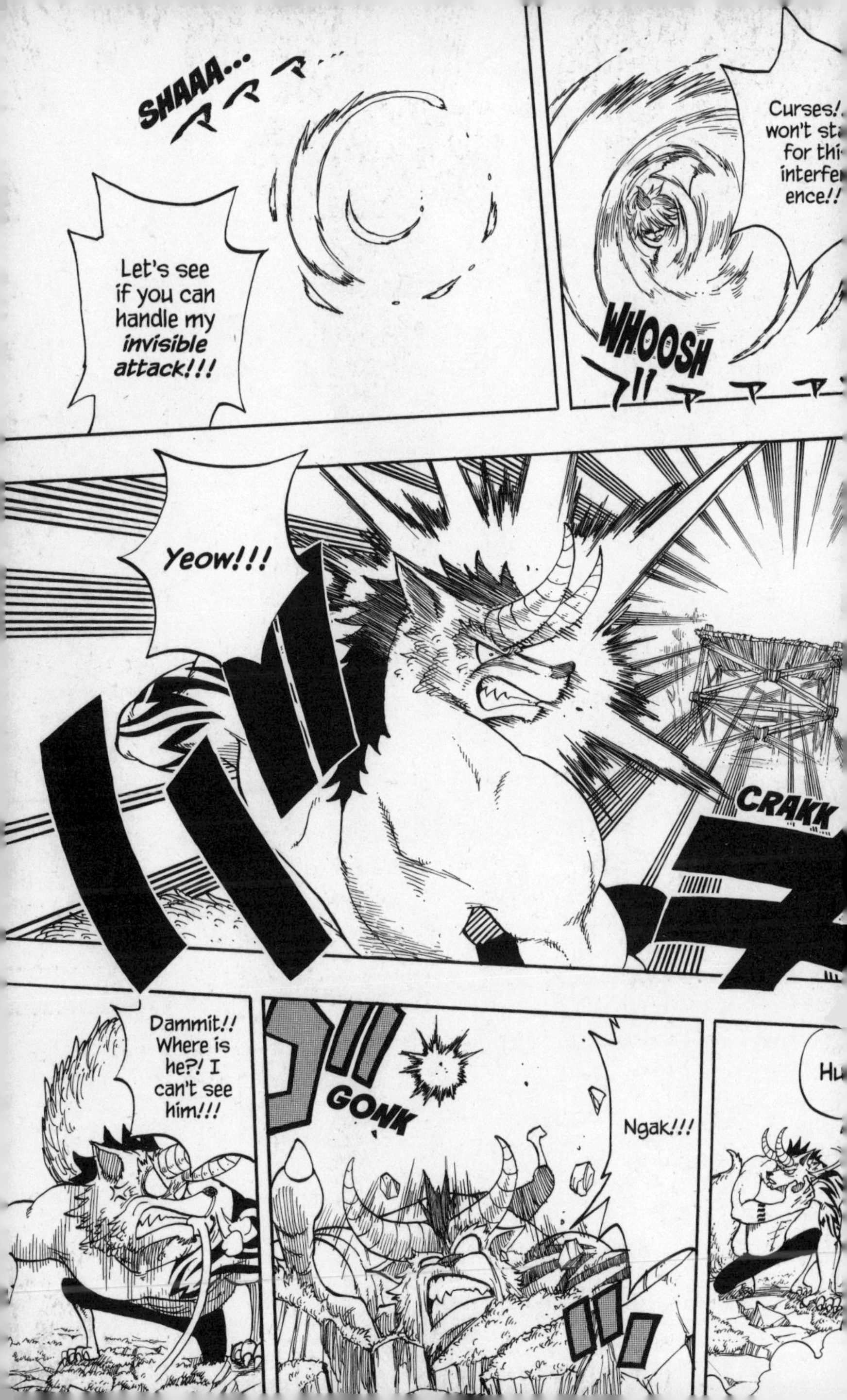

Curses!. won't st for thi interfe ence!!
WHOOSH
SHAAA...
Let's see if you can handle my invisible attack!!!
Yeow!!!
CRAKK
Hu
GONK
Ngak!!!
Dammit!! Where is he?! I can't see him!!!

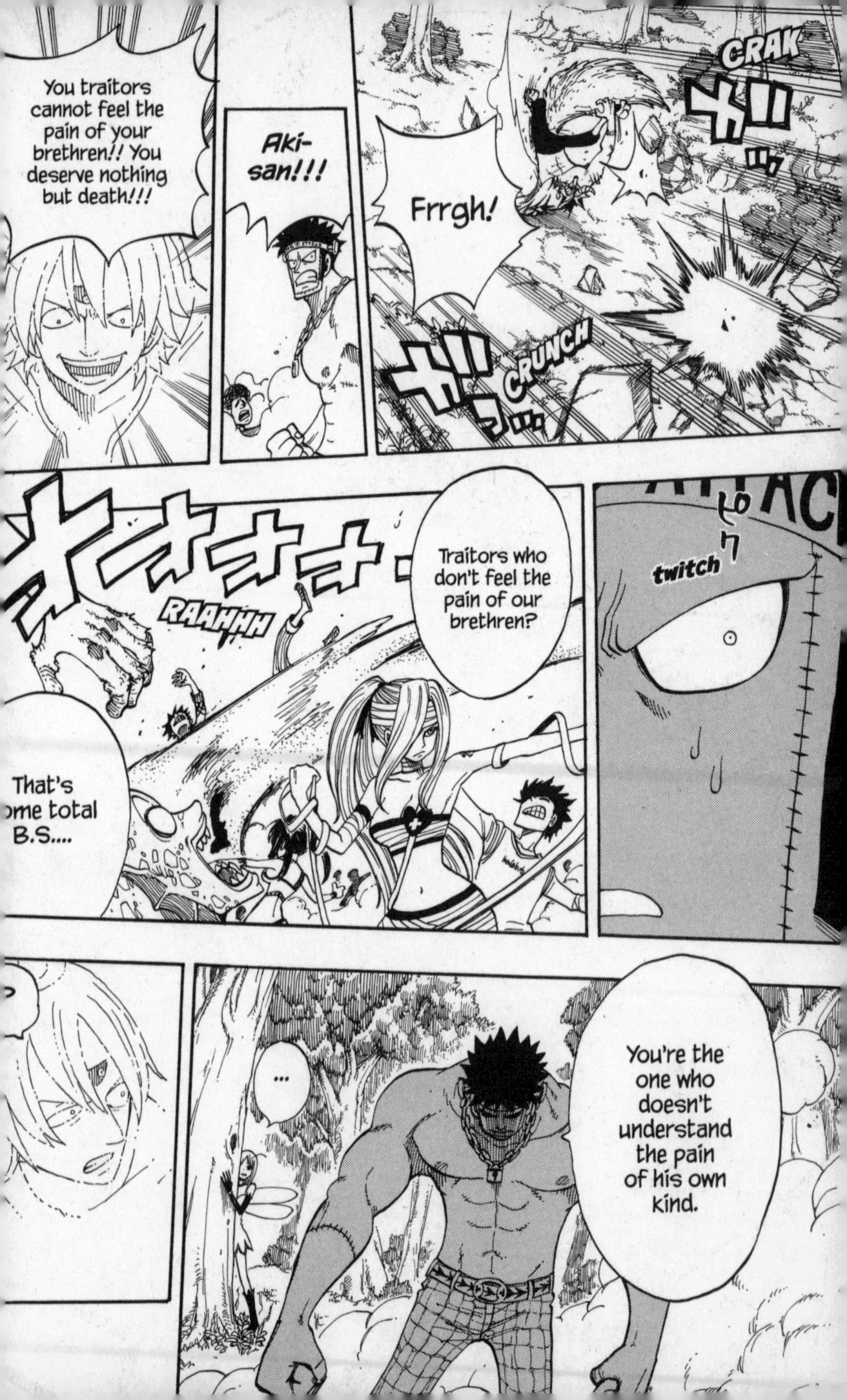
CRAK
ガッ
Frrgh!
ガッ
CRUNCH
Aki-san!!!
You traitors cannot feel the pain of your brethren!! You deserve nothing but death!!!
ピク
twitch
Traitors who don't feel the pain of our brethren?
オオオオ
RAAHHH
That's ome total B.S....
You're the one who doesn't understand the pain of his own kind.
...

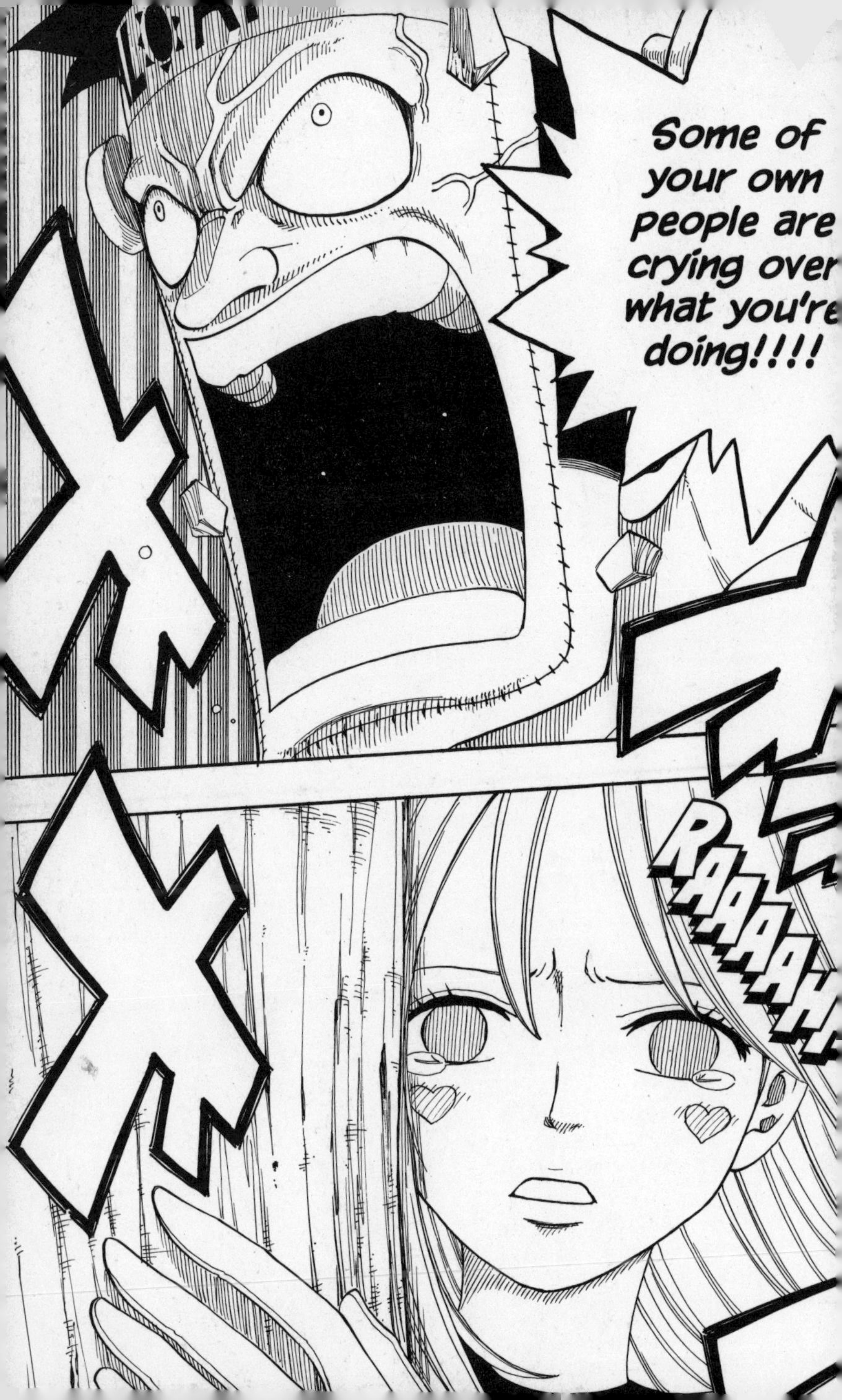
Some of your own people are crying over what you're doing!!!!
RAAAAH!

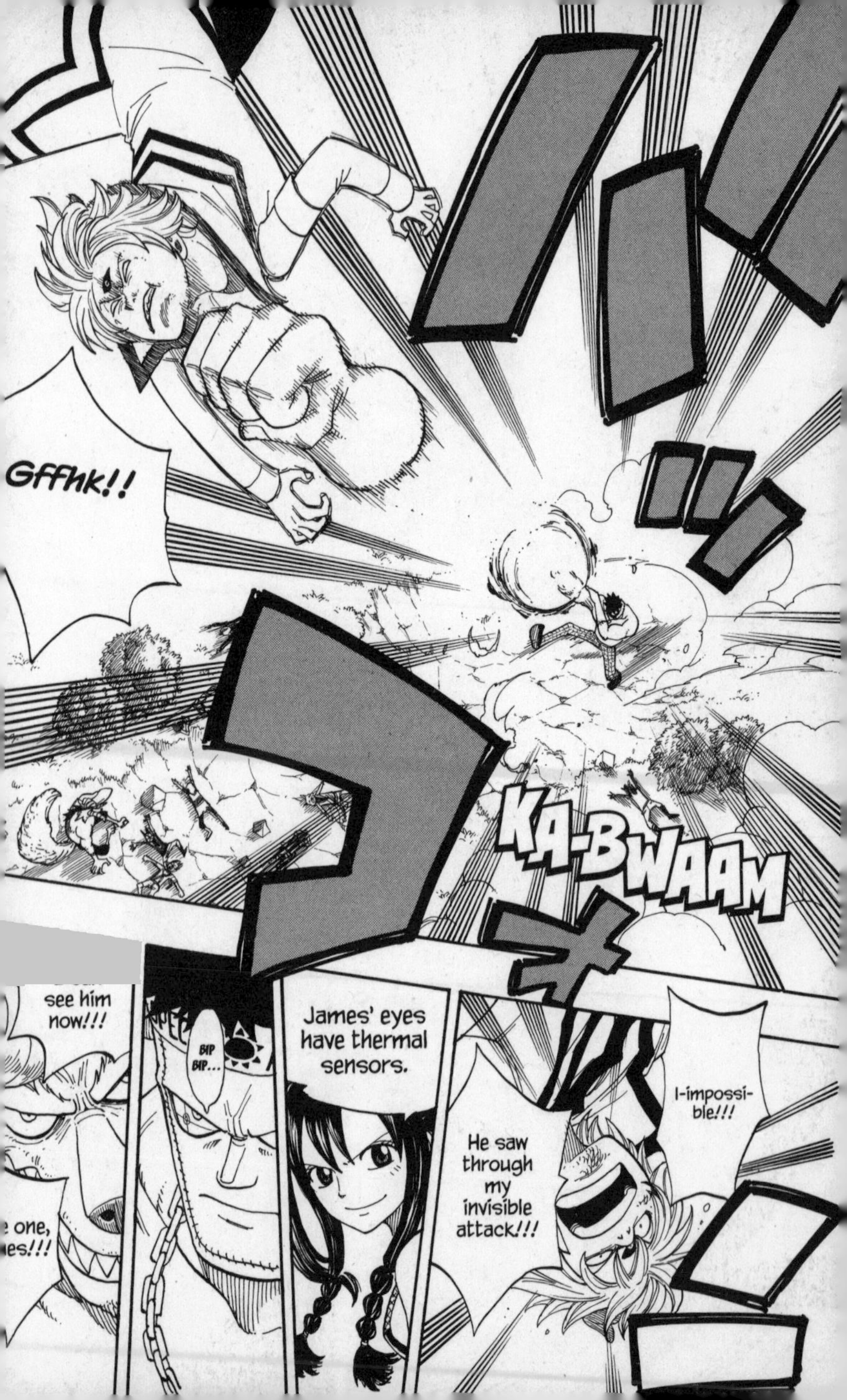
Gffhk!!
KA-BWAAM
I-impossi-
ble!!!
He saw
through
my
invisible
attack!!!
James' eyes
have thermal
sensors.
BIP
BIP...
see him
now!!!

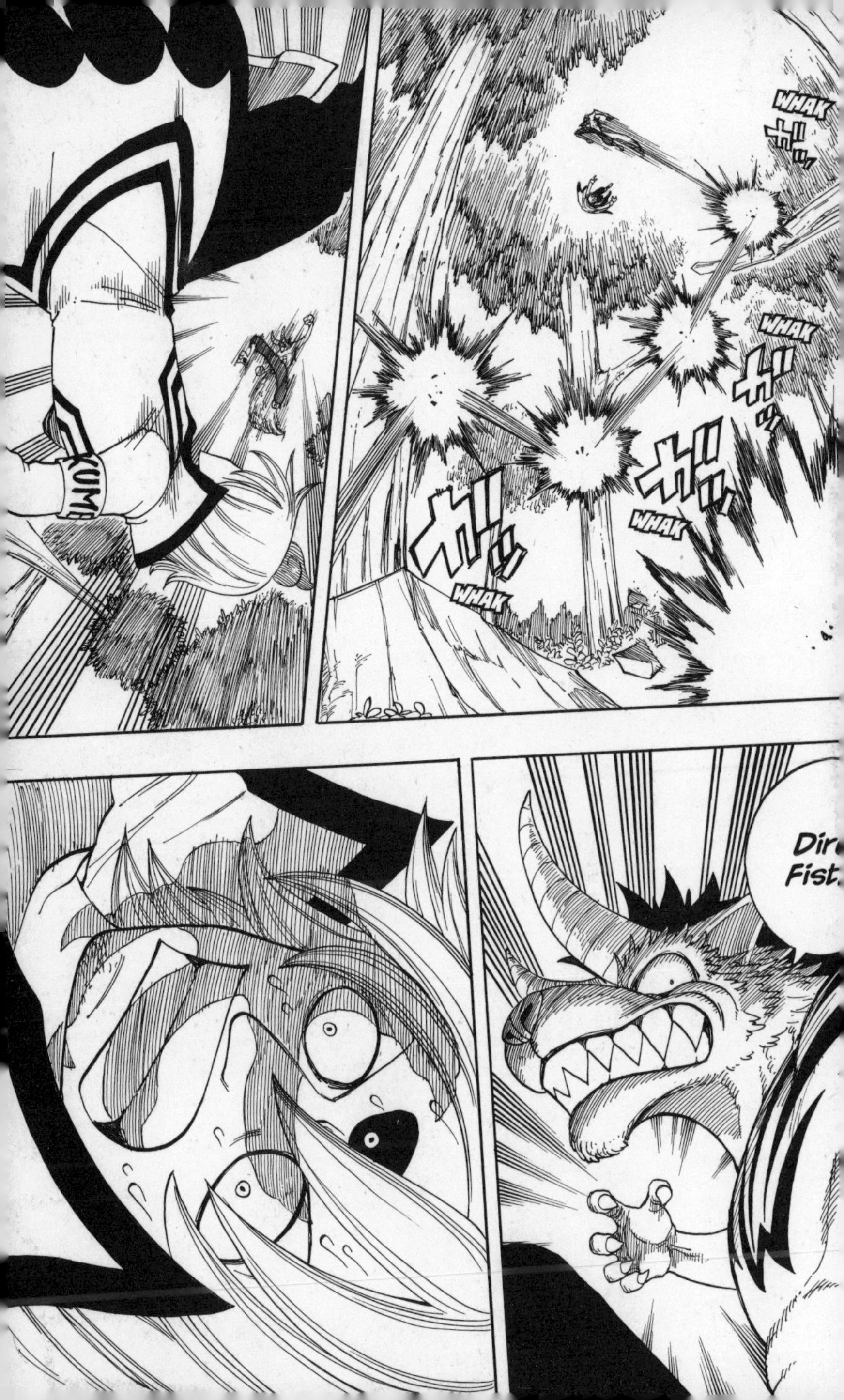
WHAK
WHAK
WHAK
WHAK
Dir
Fist.

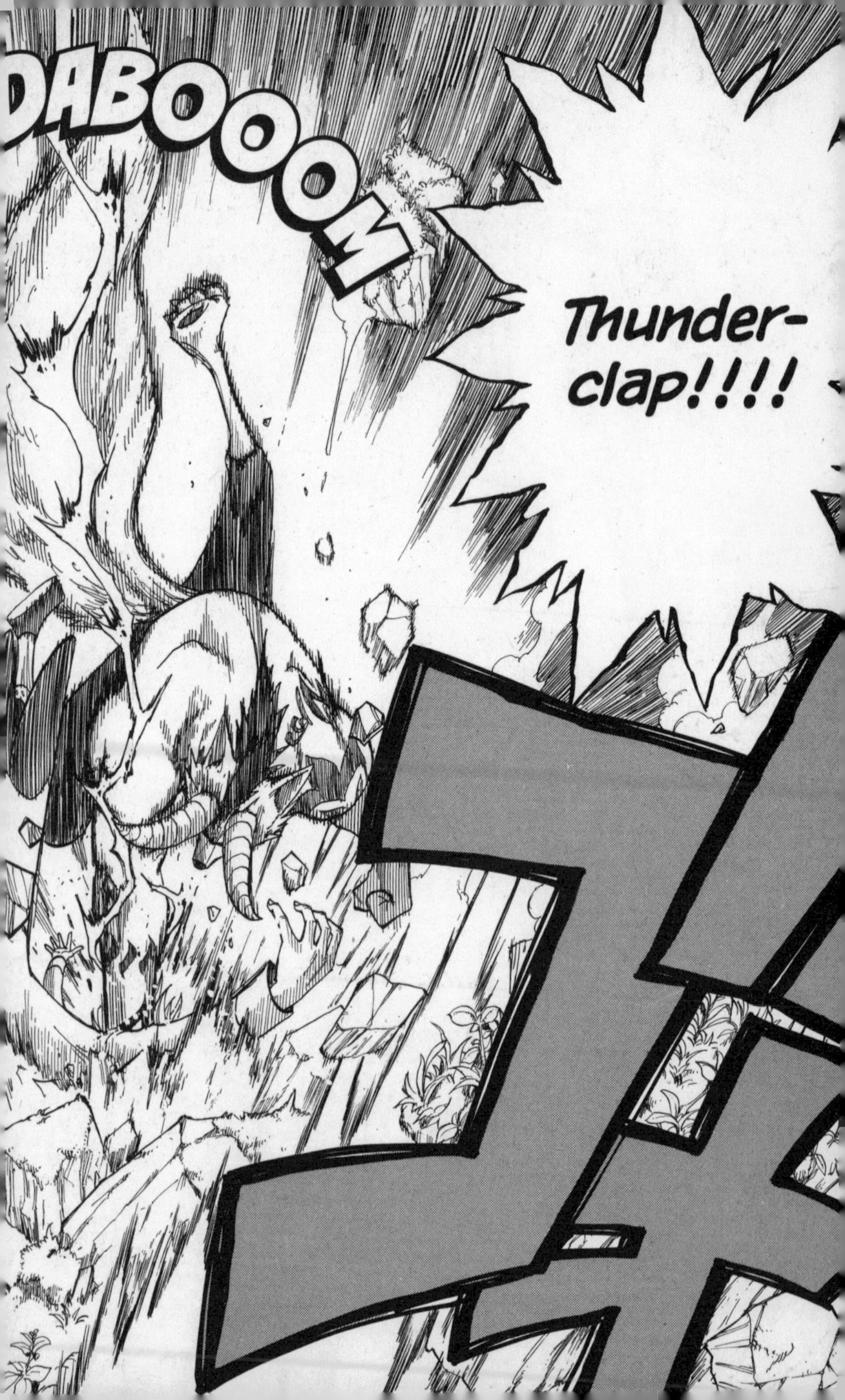
Thunder-
clap!!!!
DABOOOOM

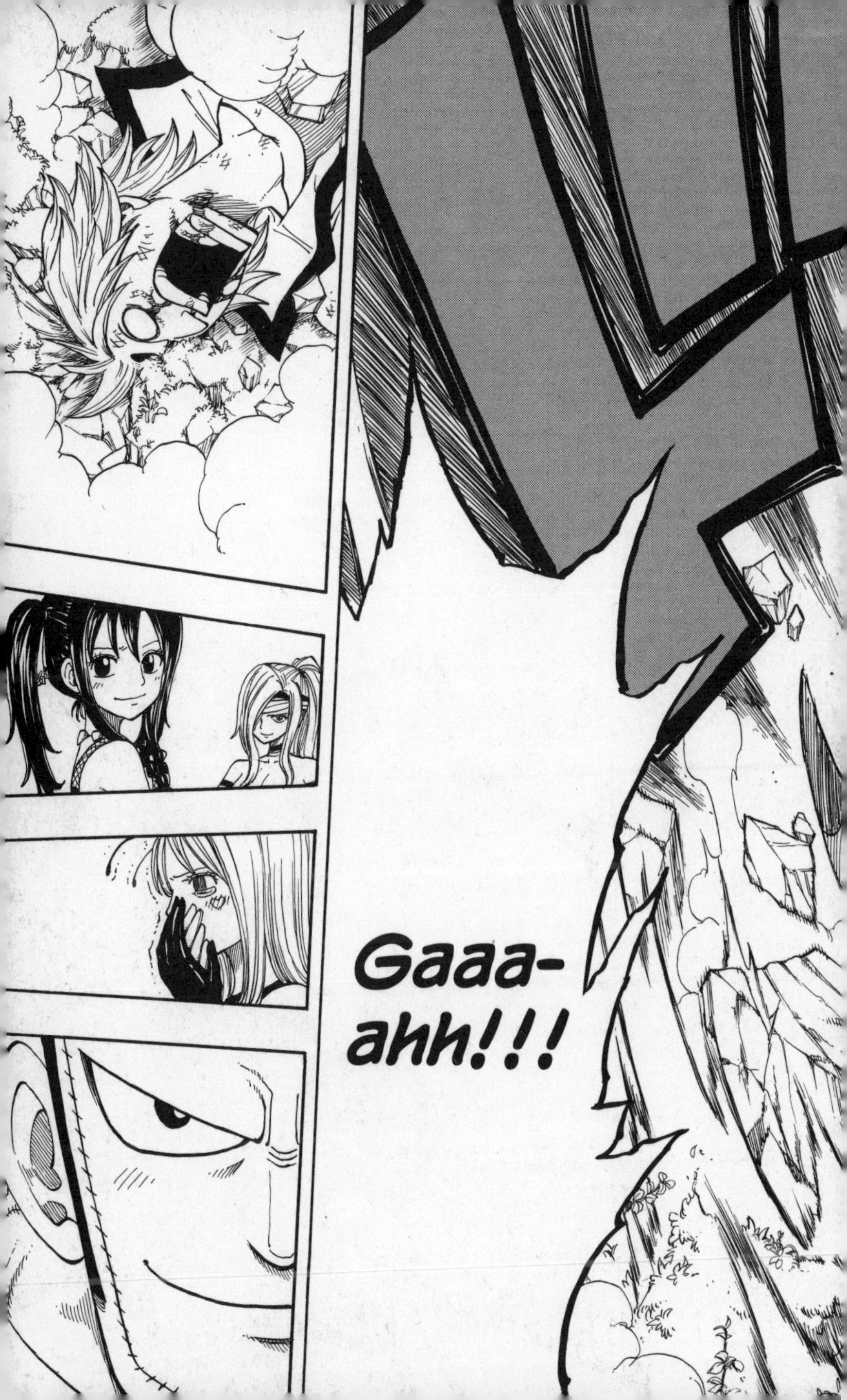
Gaaa-
ahh!!!

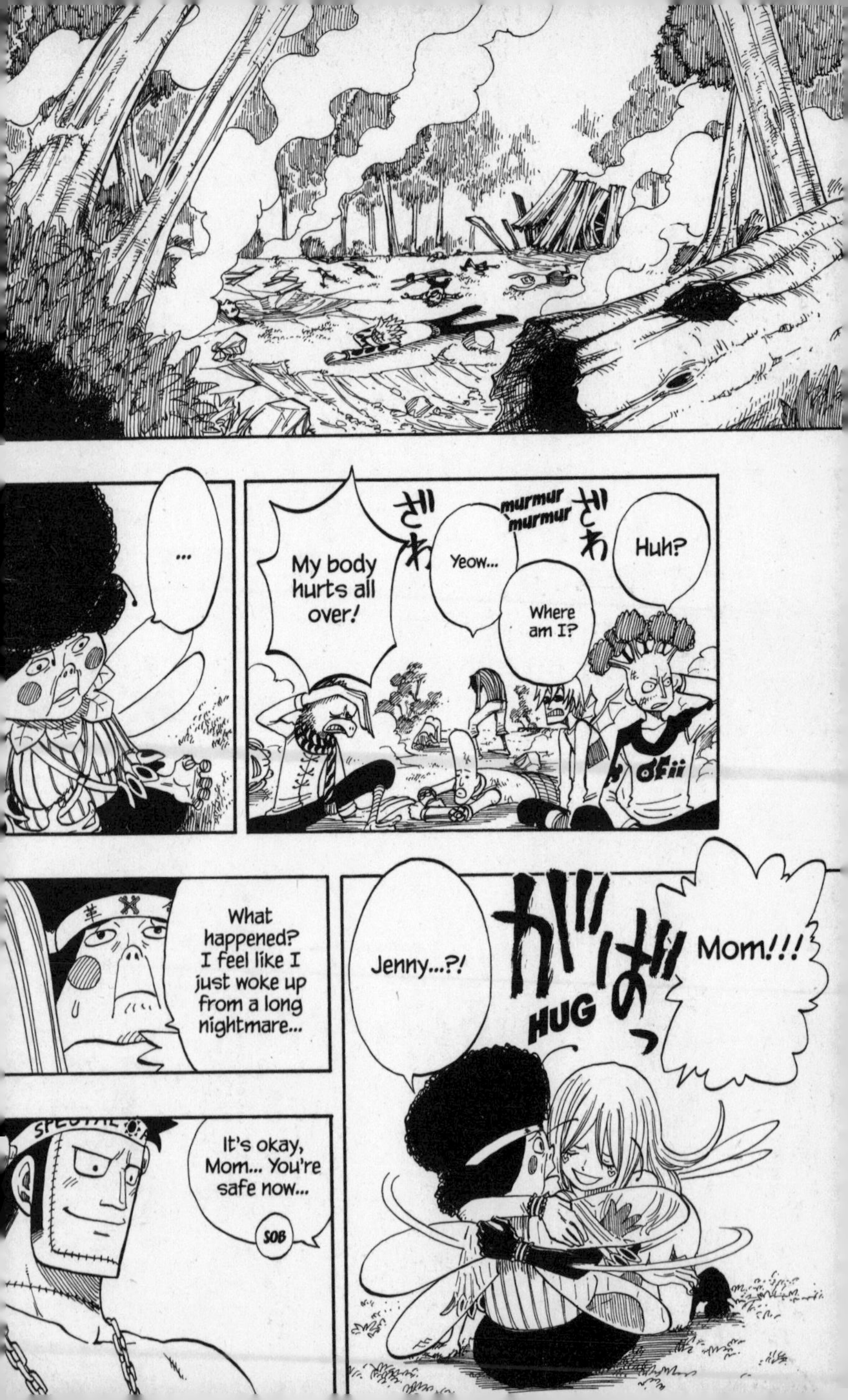
Huh?
murmur murmur
ざわ
Where am I?
Yeow...
ざわ
My body hurts all over!
...
Mom!!!
がばっ
HUG
Jenny...?!
What happened? I feel like I just woke up from a long nightmare...
It's okay, Mom... You're safe now...
SOB

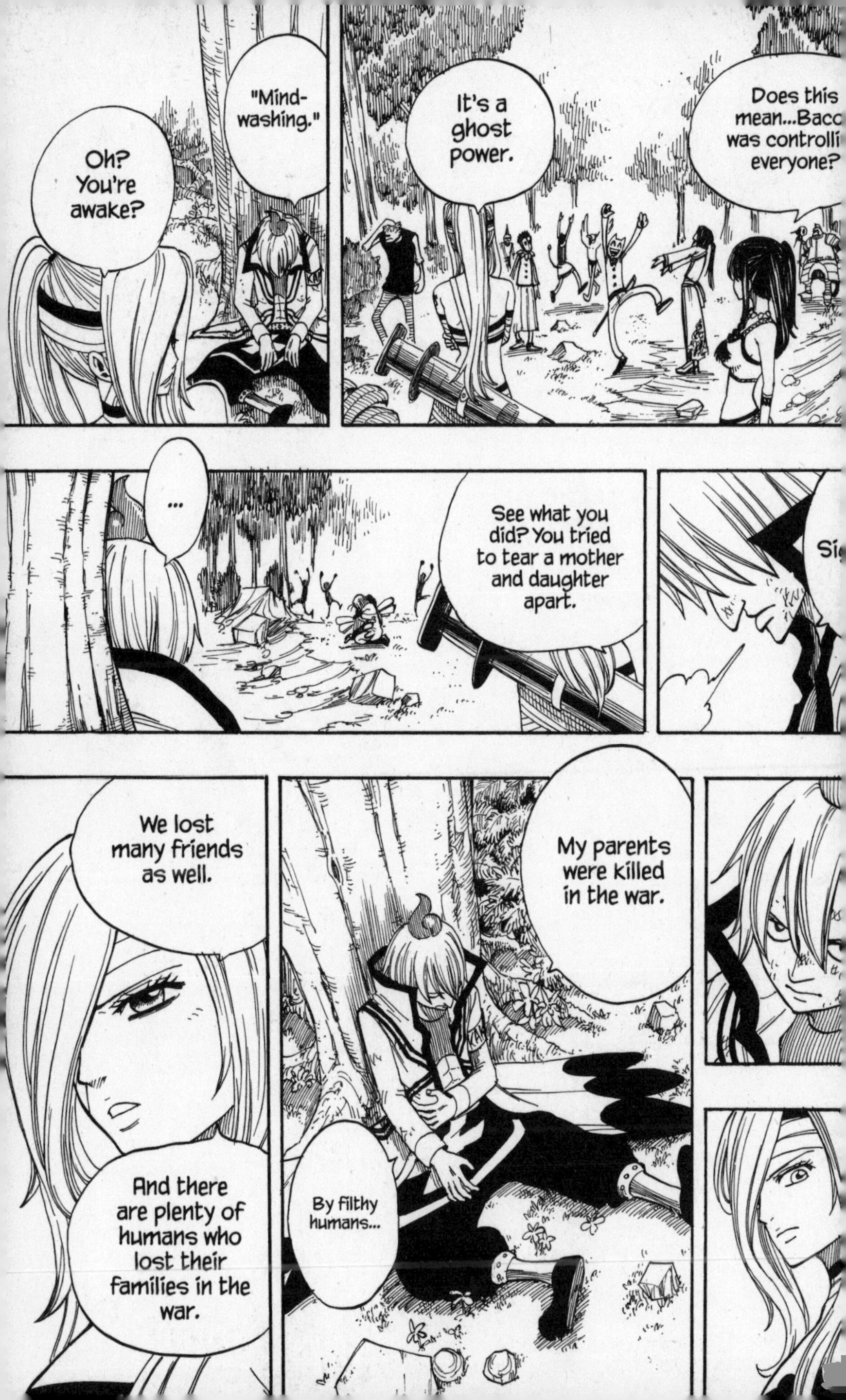
Does this mean...Bacc was controlli everyone?
It's a ghost power.
"Mind-washing."
Oh? You're awake?
See what you did? You tried to tear a mother and daughter apart.
...
My parents were killed in the war.
By filthy humans...
We lost many friends as well.
And there are plenty of humans who lost their families in the war.

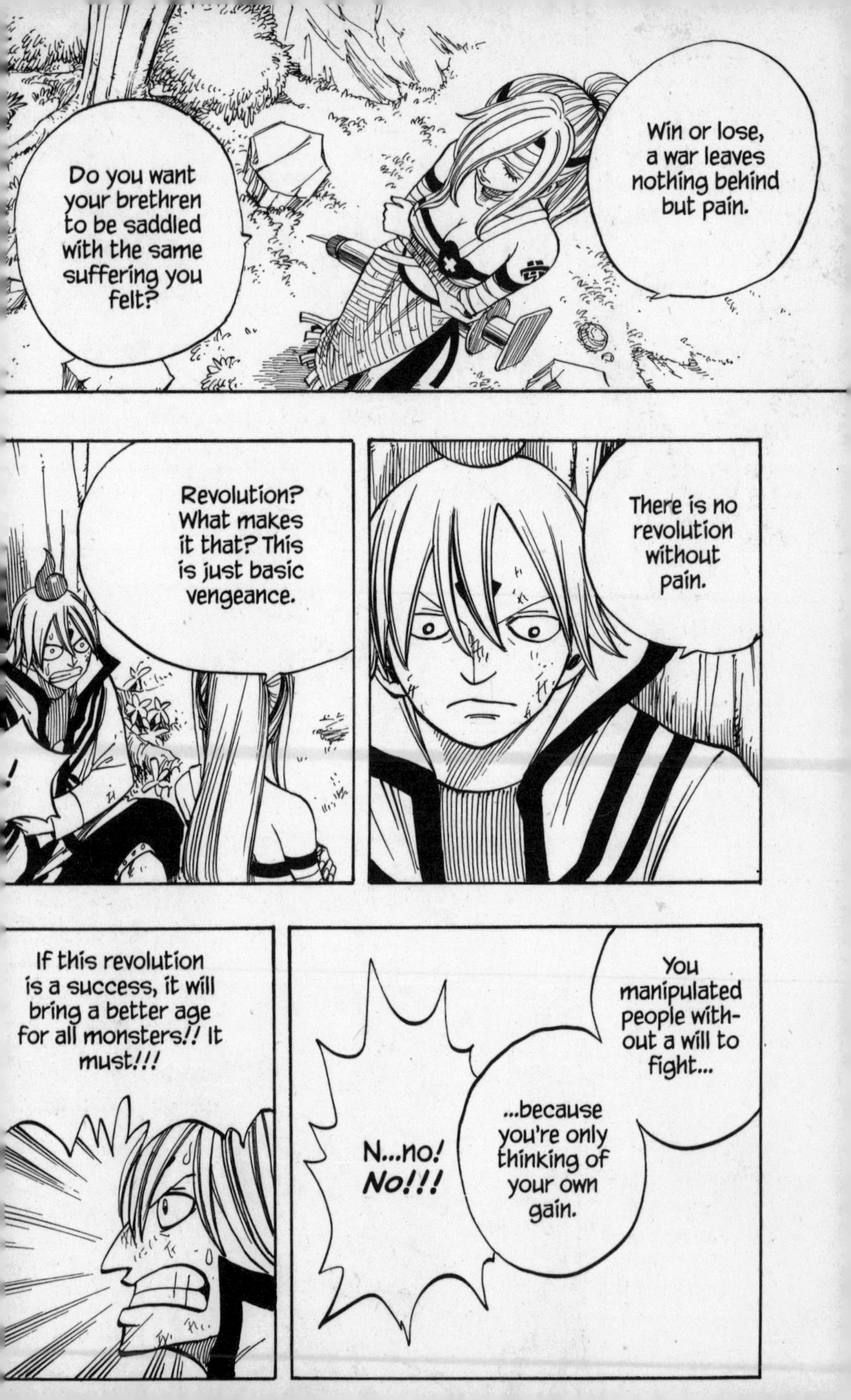
Win or lose, a war leaves nothing behind but pain.
Do you want your brethren to be saddled with the same suffering you felt?
There is no revolution without pain.
Revolution? What makes it that? This is just basic vengeance.
You manipulated people with-out a will to fight...
...because you're only thinking of your own gain.
N...no! *No!!!*
If this revolution is a success, it will bring a better age for all monsters!! It must!!!

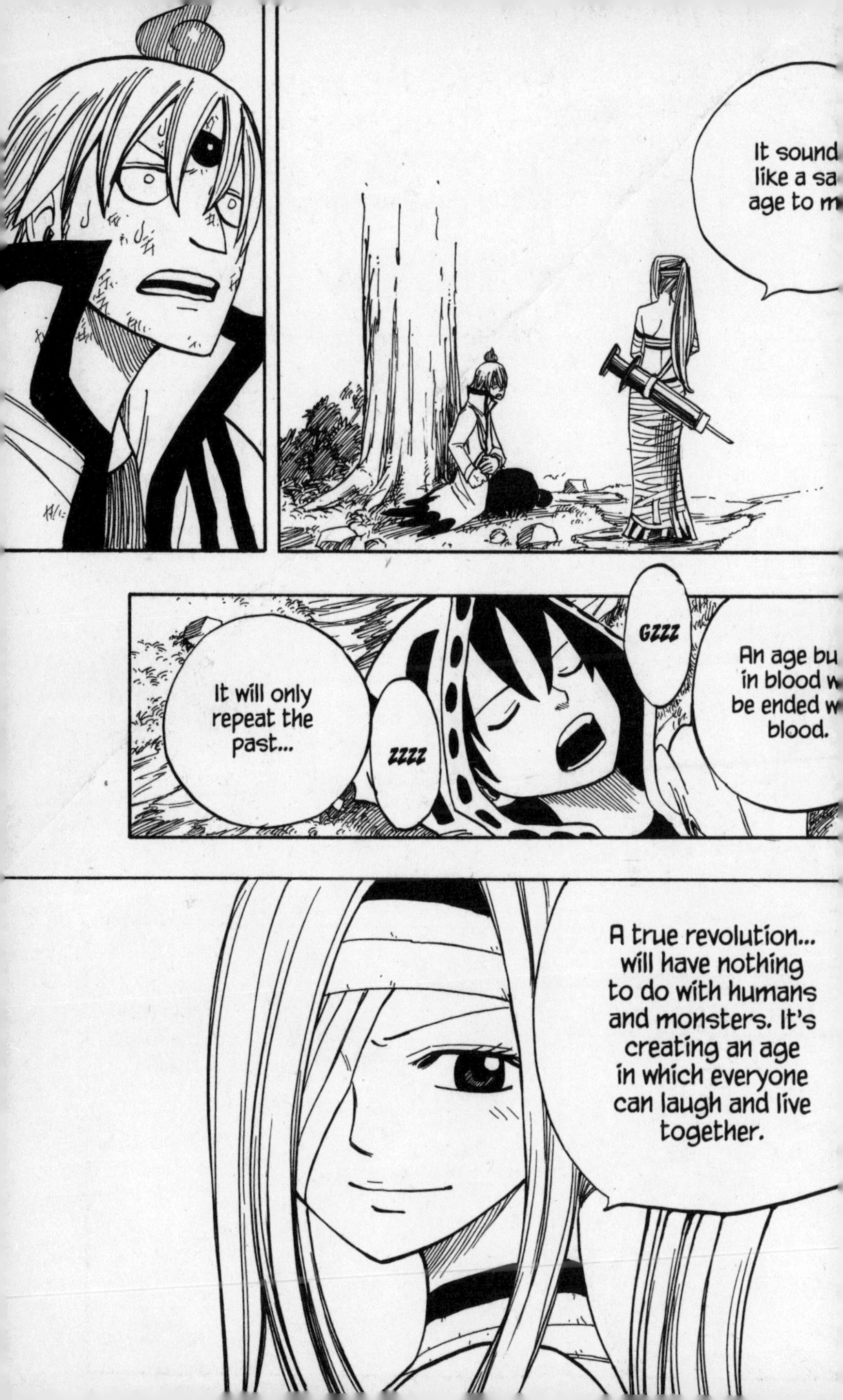

It sound like a sa age to m
An age bu in blood w be ended w blood.
GZZZ
ZZZZ
It will only repeat the past...
A true revolution... will have nothing to do with humans and monsters. It's creating an age in which everyone can laugh and live together.

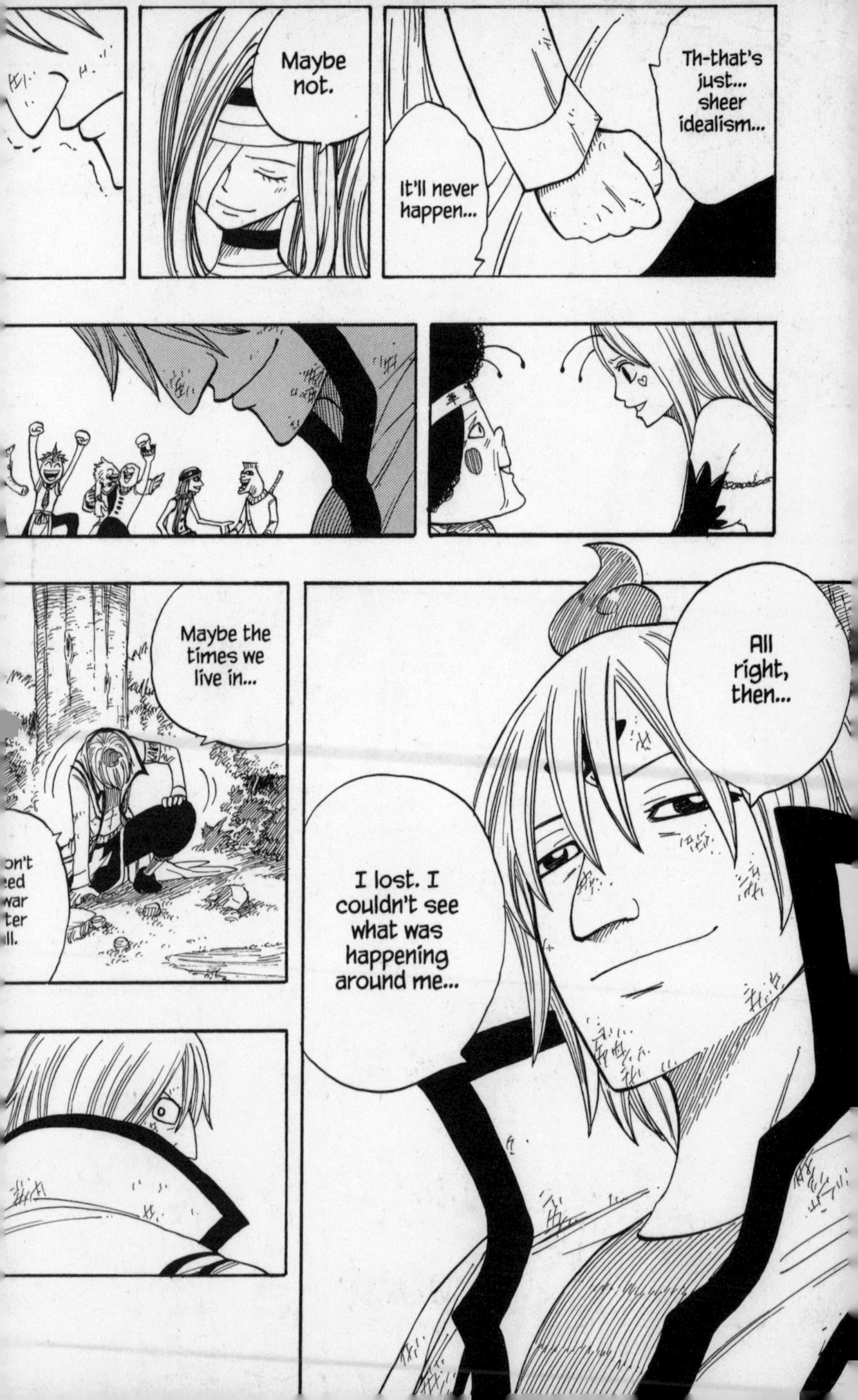
Th-that's just... sheer idealism...
It'll never happen...
Maybe not.
All right, then...
I lost. I couldn't see what was happening around me...
Maybe the times we live in...

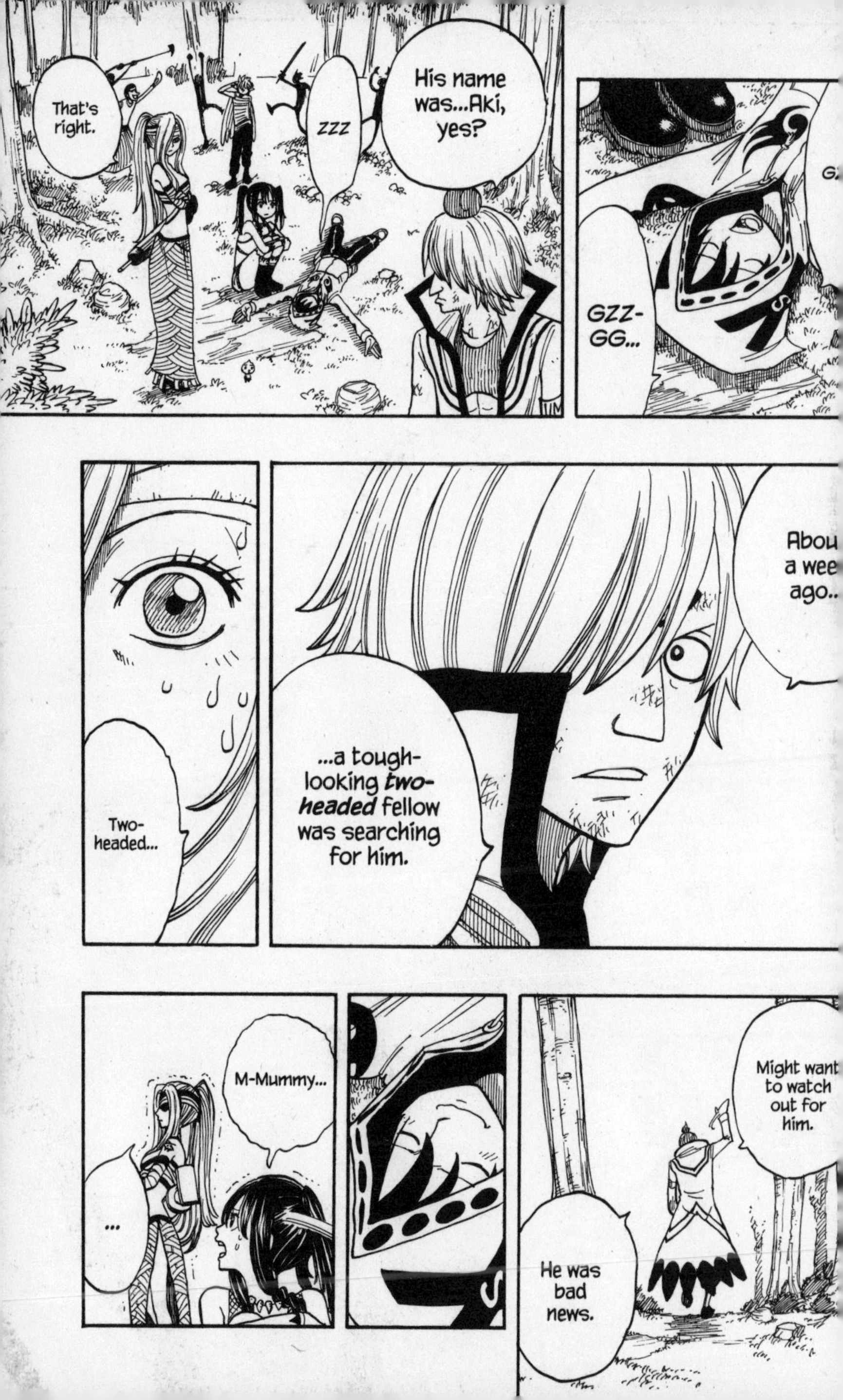
GZZ-GG...
His name was...Aki, yes?
zzz
That's right.
Abou a wee ago..
...a tough-looking *two-headed* fellow was searching for him.
Two-headed...
Might want to watch out for him.
He was bad news.
M-Mummy...
...

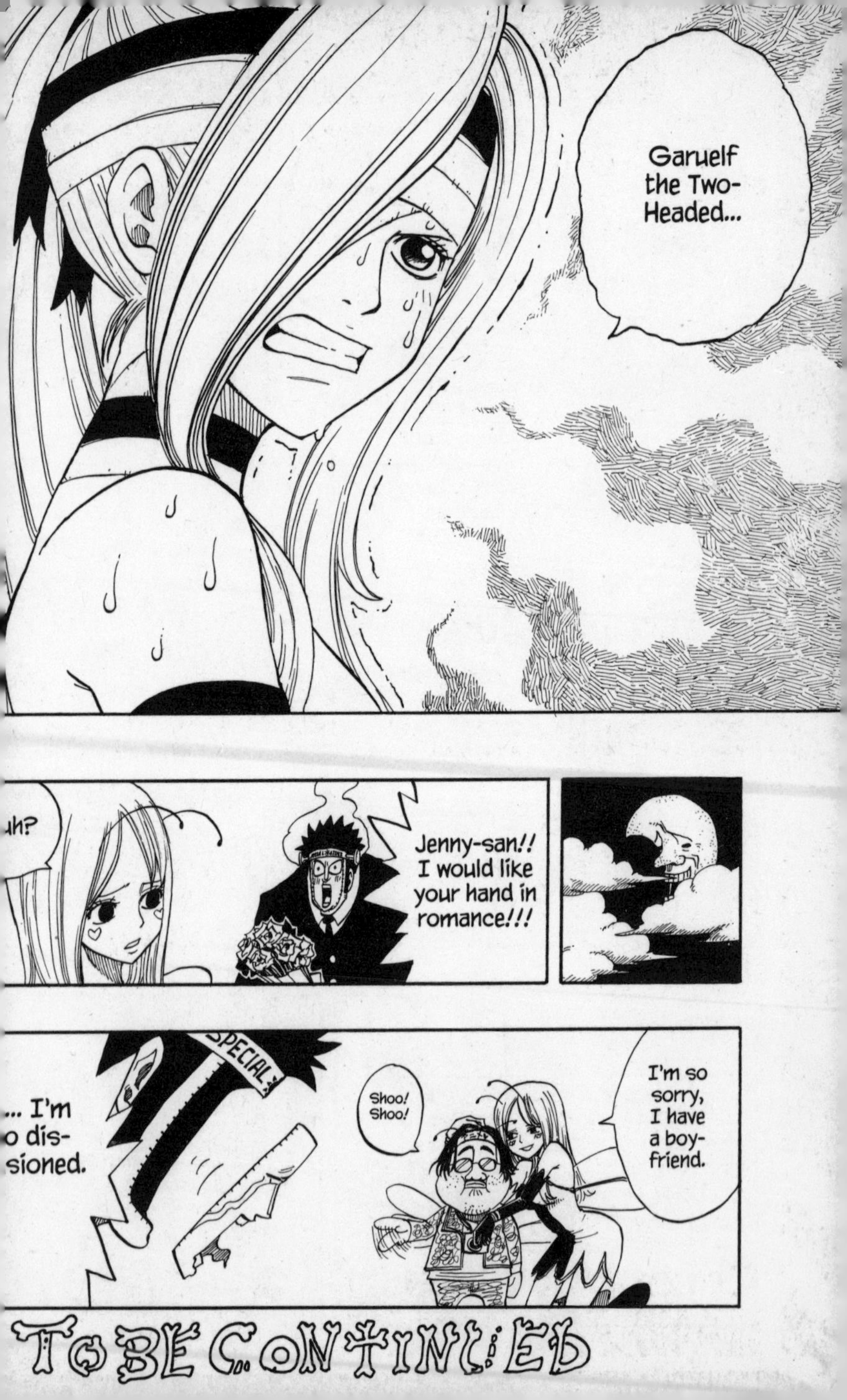
Garuelf the Two-Headed...
Jenny-san!! I would like your hand in romance!!!
uh?
I'm so sorry, I have a boyfriend.
Shoo! Shoo!
SPECIAL
... I'm o dis- sioned.
TO BE CONTINUED

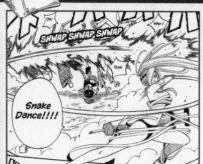

Oh!
Wha-!
SHWAP SHWAP SHWAP
Gya!
Snake Dance!!!!

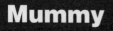

Mummy

Race: Mummy-Woman Type: Monster

She whips around the bandages that cover her body at will. Rumors abound about the syringe she keeps on her back, but its use is still a mystery. One theory says she draws the blood of her victims to turn them into mummies...

Bounty: 4000000

Danger Lvl: ★★★★★★

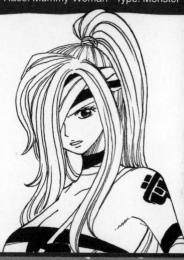

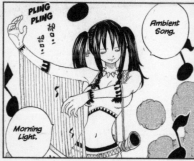

PLING PLING
Ambient Song.
Morning Light.

Tooran

Race: Golem Type: Monster

Her body is made of sand, which she can control at will. Not only can she attack with her sand, she can also play a harp of sand to aid her friends. It's said that she has dozens of types of sand in her body.

Bounty: 2000000

Danger Lvl: ★★★☆☆☆

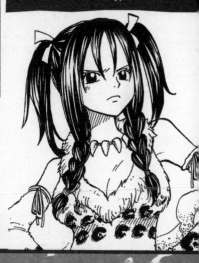

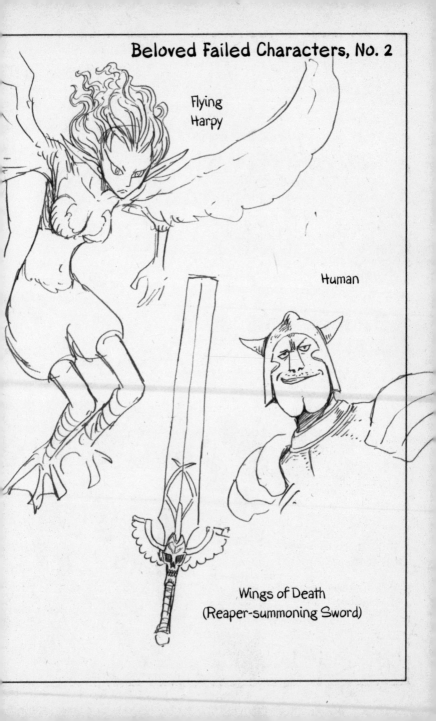

Beloved Failed Characters, No. 2

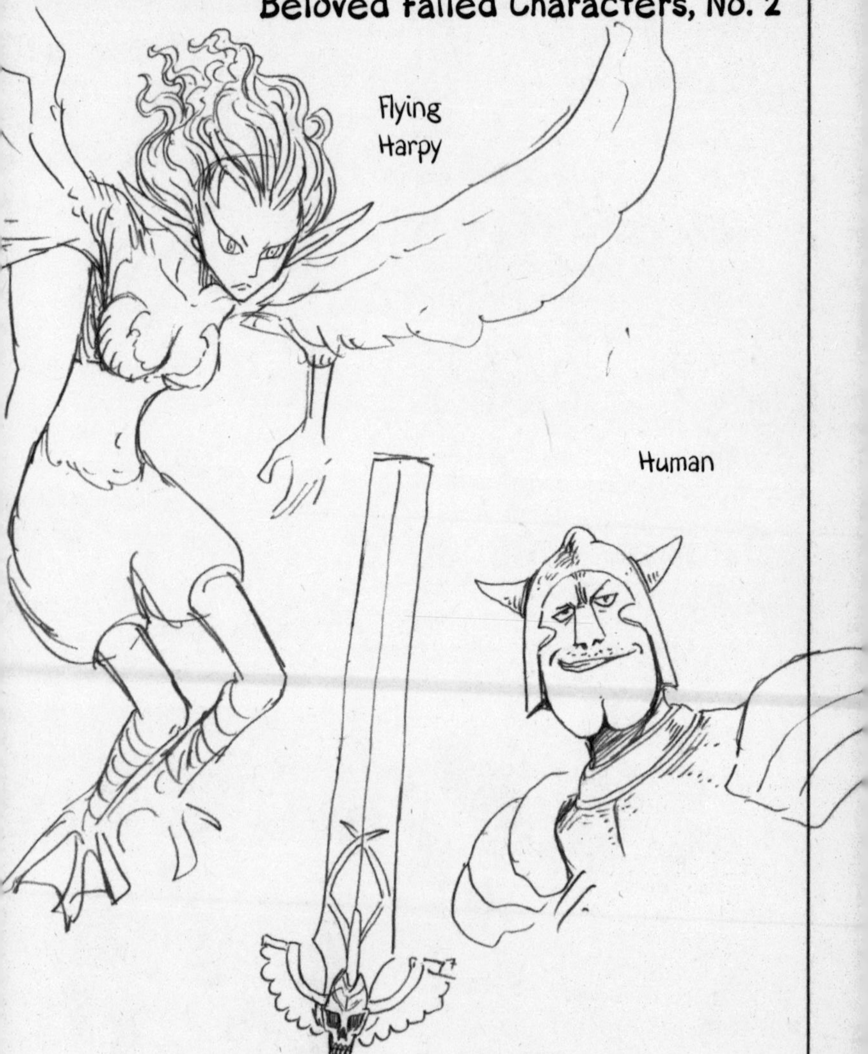
Flying Harpy
Human
Wings of Death
(Reaper-summoning Sword)

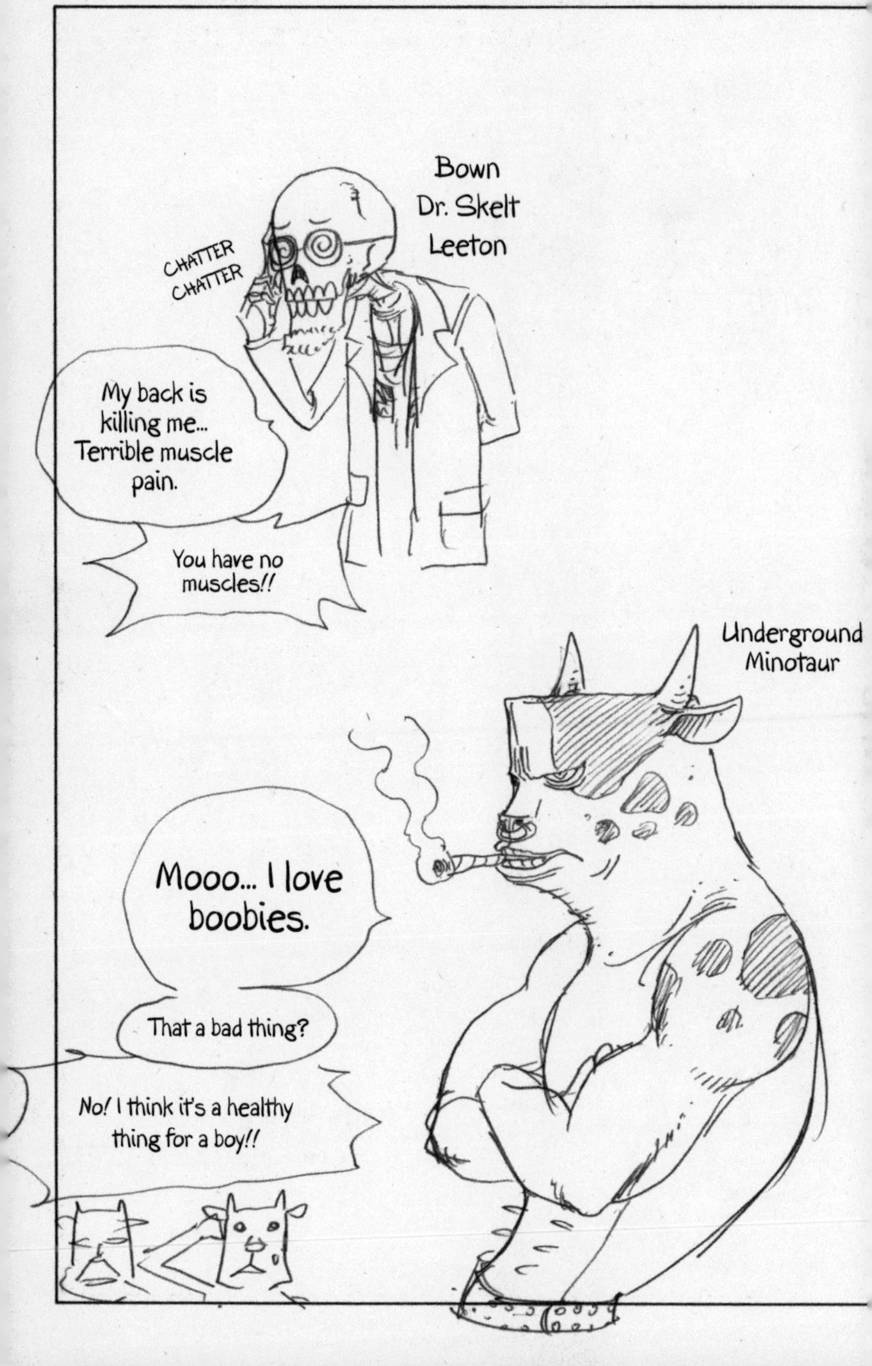
Bown Dr. Skelt Leeton
CHATTER CHATTER
My back is killing me... Terrible muscle pain.
You have no muscles!!
Underground Minotaur
Mooo... I love boobies.
That a bad thing?
No! I think it's a healthy thing for a boy!!

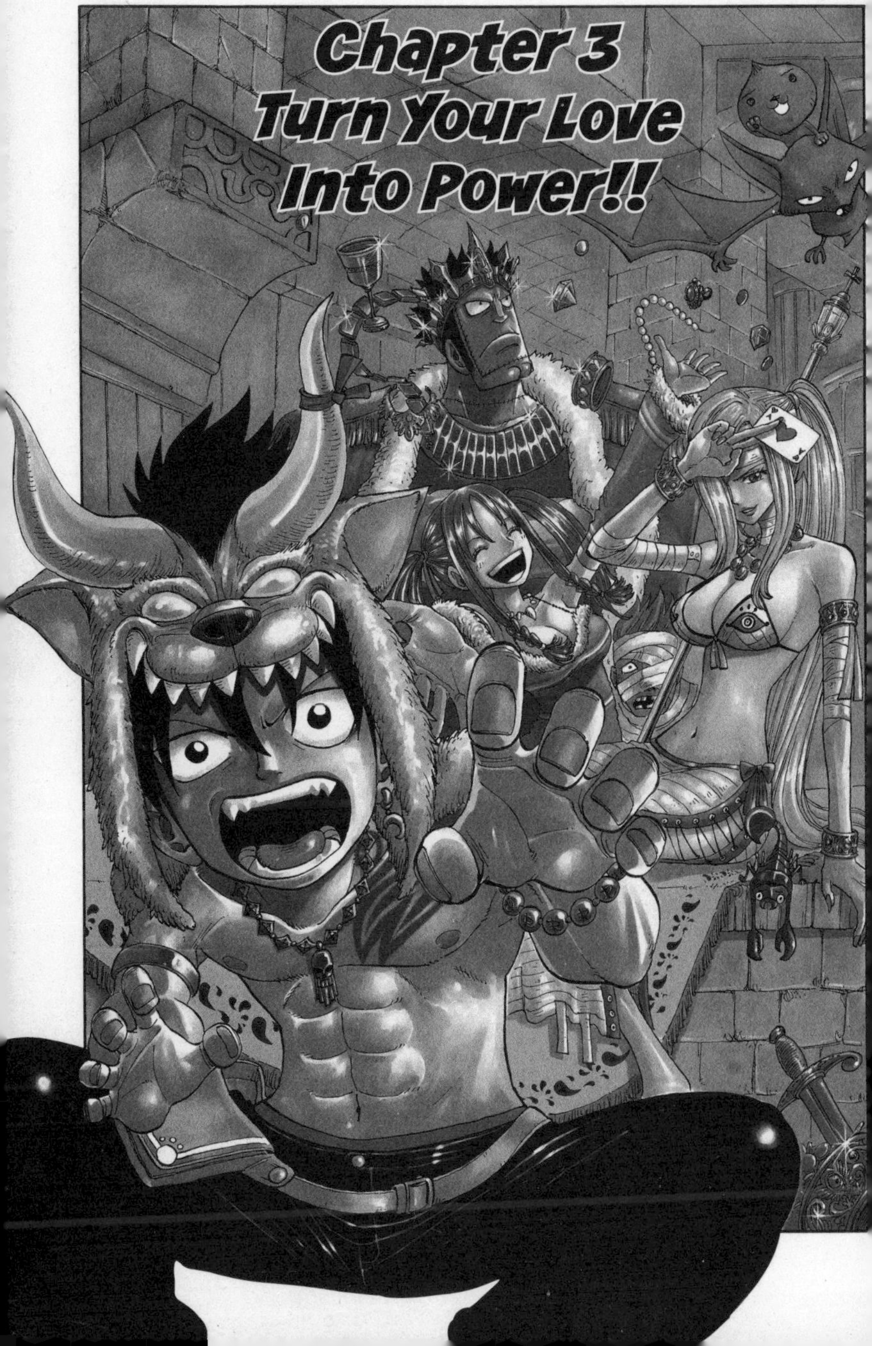
Chapter 3
Turn Your Love Into Power!!

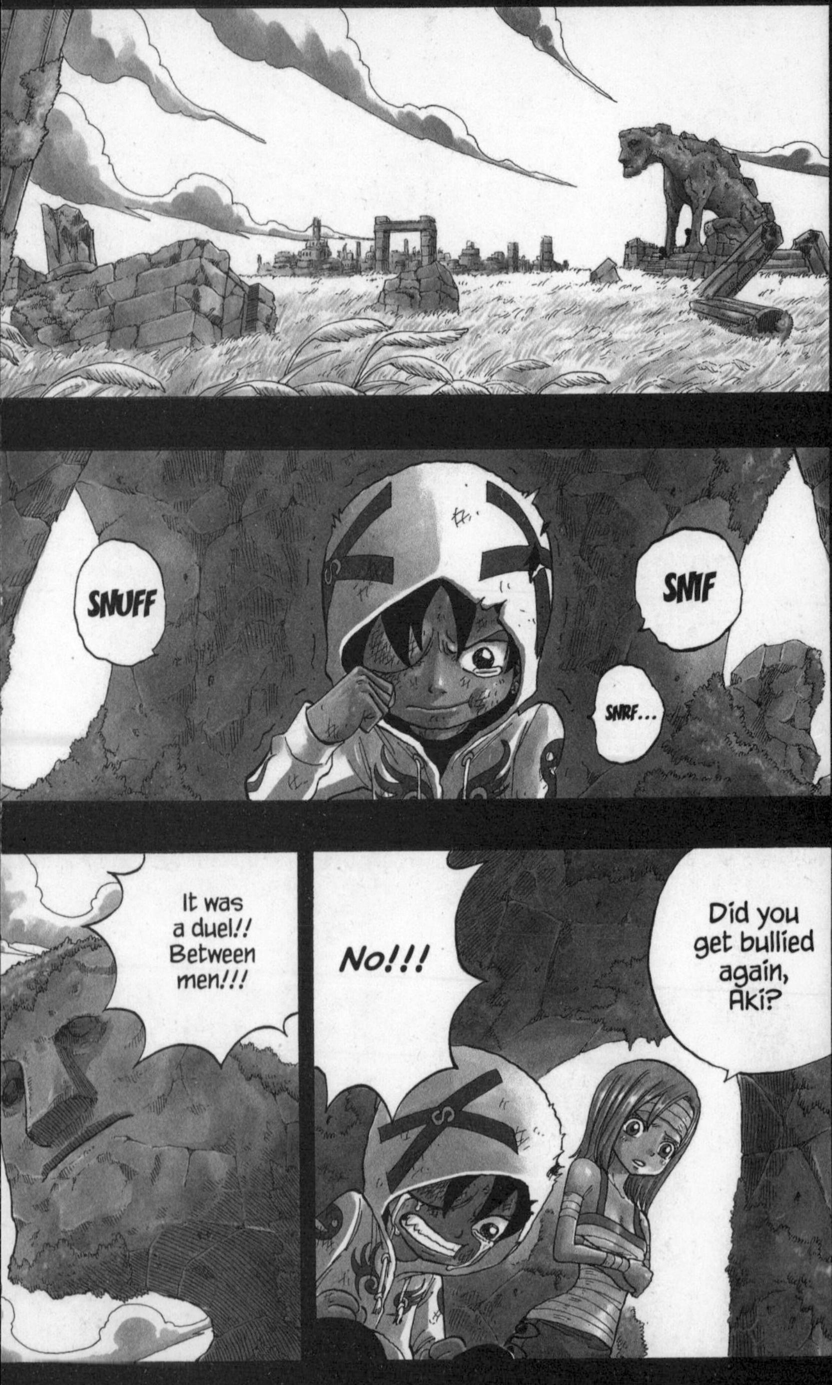
SNIF
SNRF...
SNUFF
Did you get bullied again, Aki?
No!!!
It was a duel!! Between men!!!

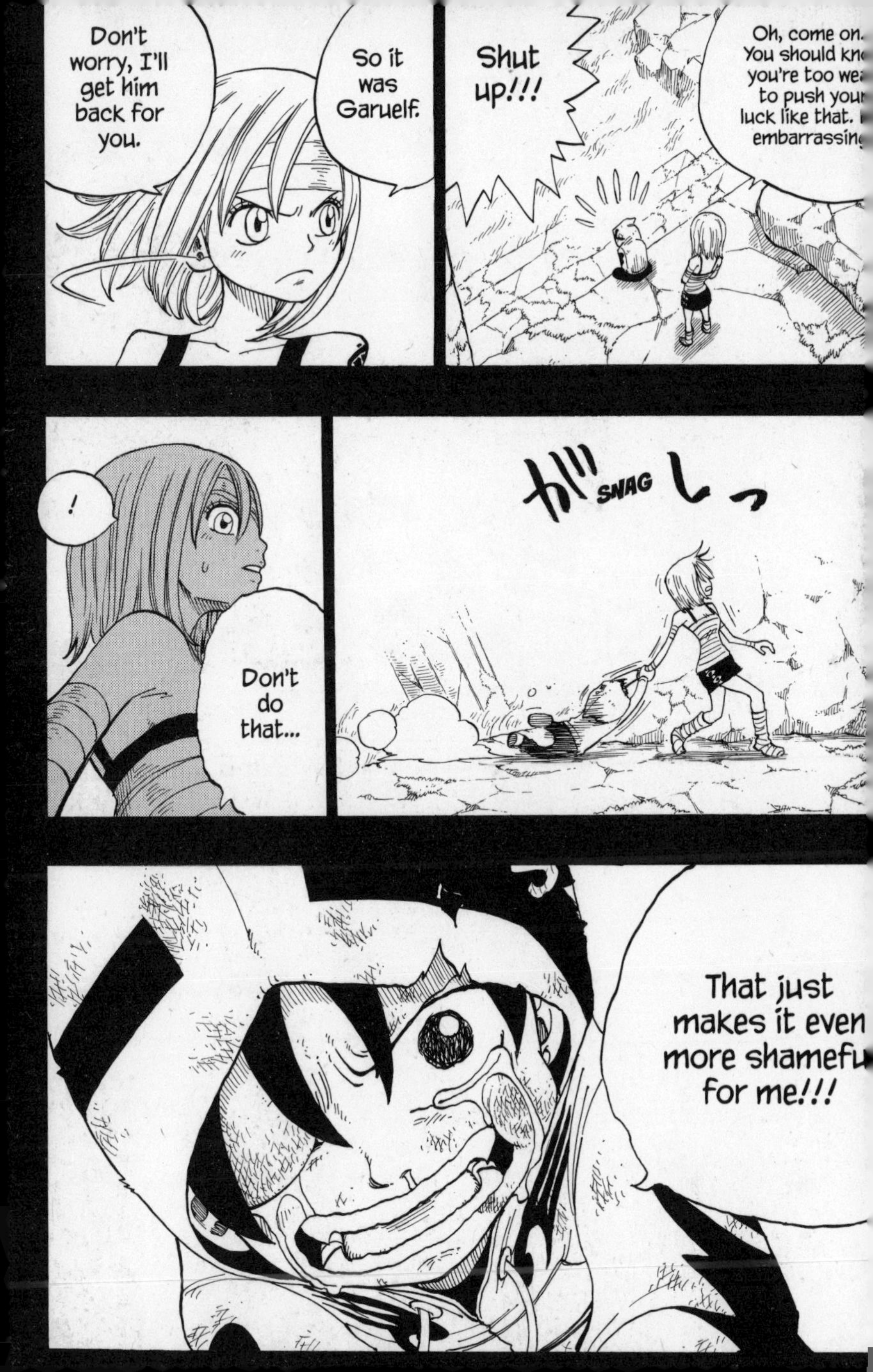
Oh, come on. You should kn you're too wea to push your luck like that. embarrassin
Shut up!!!
So it was Garuelf.
Don't worry, I'll get him back for you.
SNAG
!
Don't do that...
That just makes it even more shamefu for me!!!

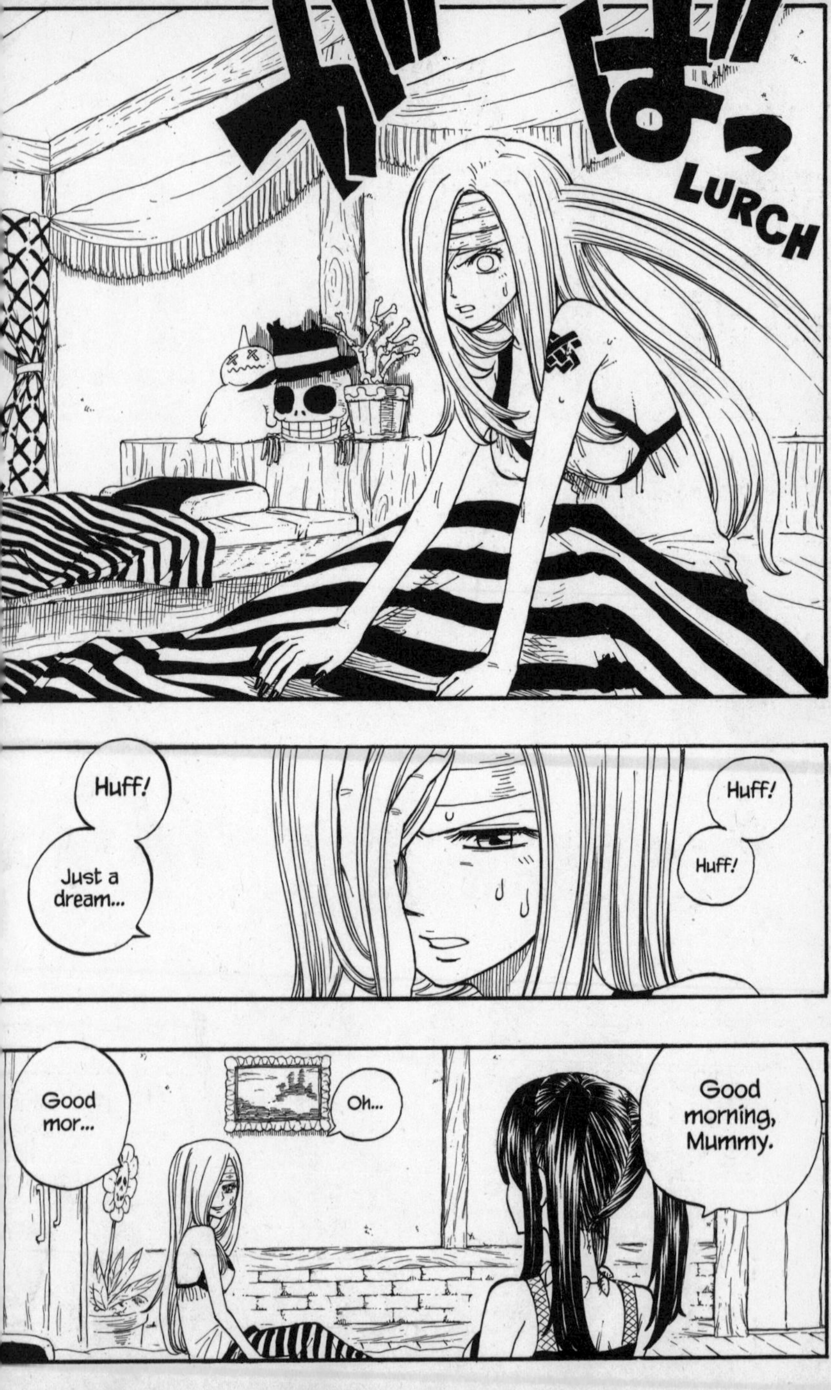
LURCH
Huff!
Huff!
Huff!
Just a dream...
Good morning, Mummy.
Oh...
Good mor...

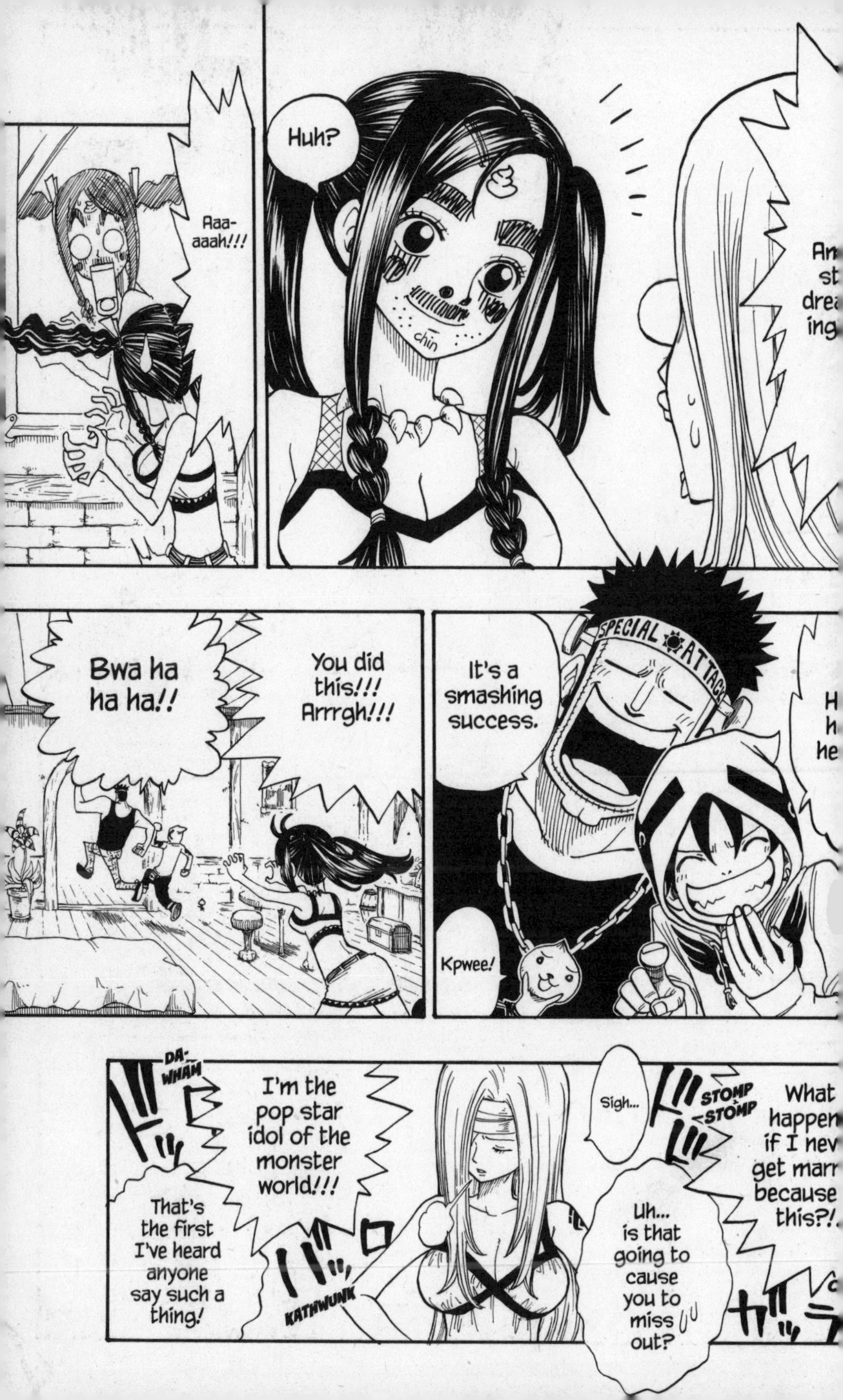
An
st
drea
ing
Huh?
chin
Aaa-aaah!!!
H
h
he
It's a smashing success.
Kpwee!
You did this!!! Arrrgh!!!
Bwa ha ha ha!!
What happen
if I nev
get marr
because
this?!.
STOMP STOMP
Sigh...
Uh... is that going to cause you to miss out?
I'm the pop star idol of the monster world!!!
KATHWUNK
DA-WHAM
That's the first I've heard anyone say such a thing!

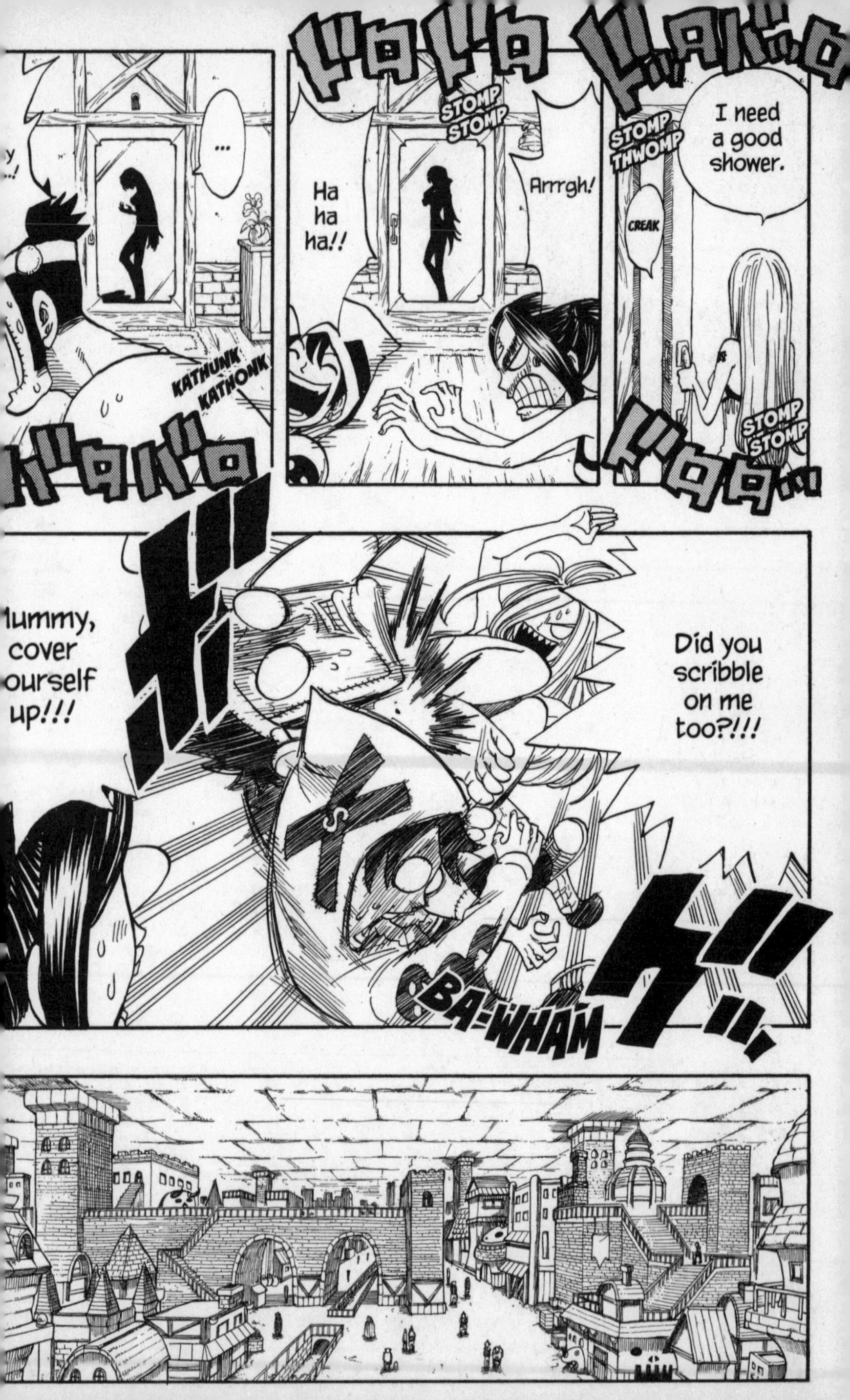
STOMP THWOMP
I need a good shower.
CREAK
STOMP STOMP
STOMP STOMP
Arrrgh!
Ha ha ha!!
...
KATHUNK KATHONK
Did you scribble on me too?!!!
BA-WHAM
lummy, cover ourself up!!!

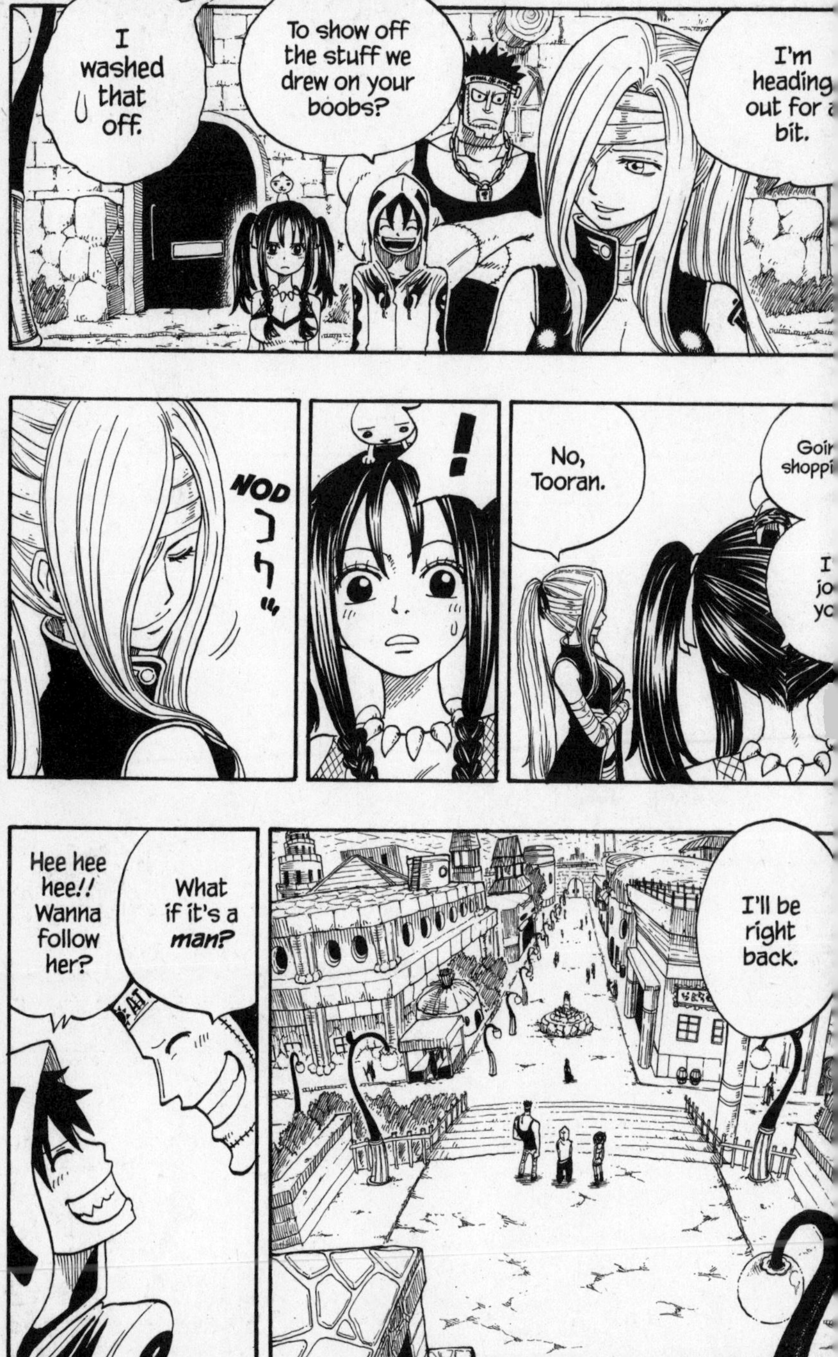

I'm heading out for a bit.
To show off the stuff we drew on your boobs?
I washed that off.
No, Tooran.
!
NOD
コク
I'll be right back.
What if it's a *man?*
Hee hee hee!! Wanna follow her?

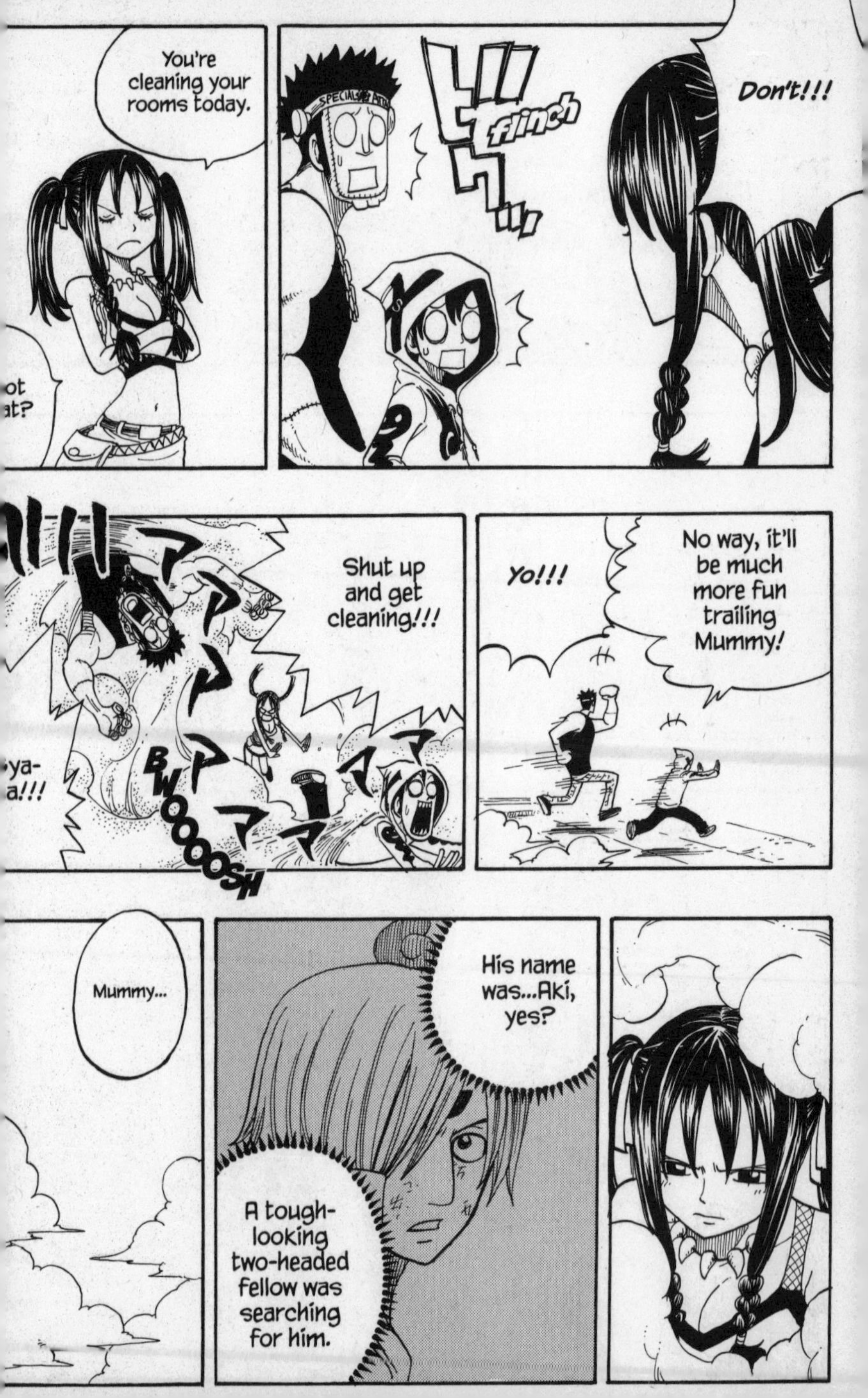
Don't!!!
flinch
You're cleaning your rooms today.
No way, it'll be much more fun trailing Mummy!
Yo!!!
Shut up and get cleaning!!!
BWOOOOOSH
His name was...Aki, yes?
A tough-looking two-headed fellow was searching for him.
Mummy...

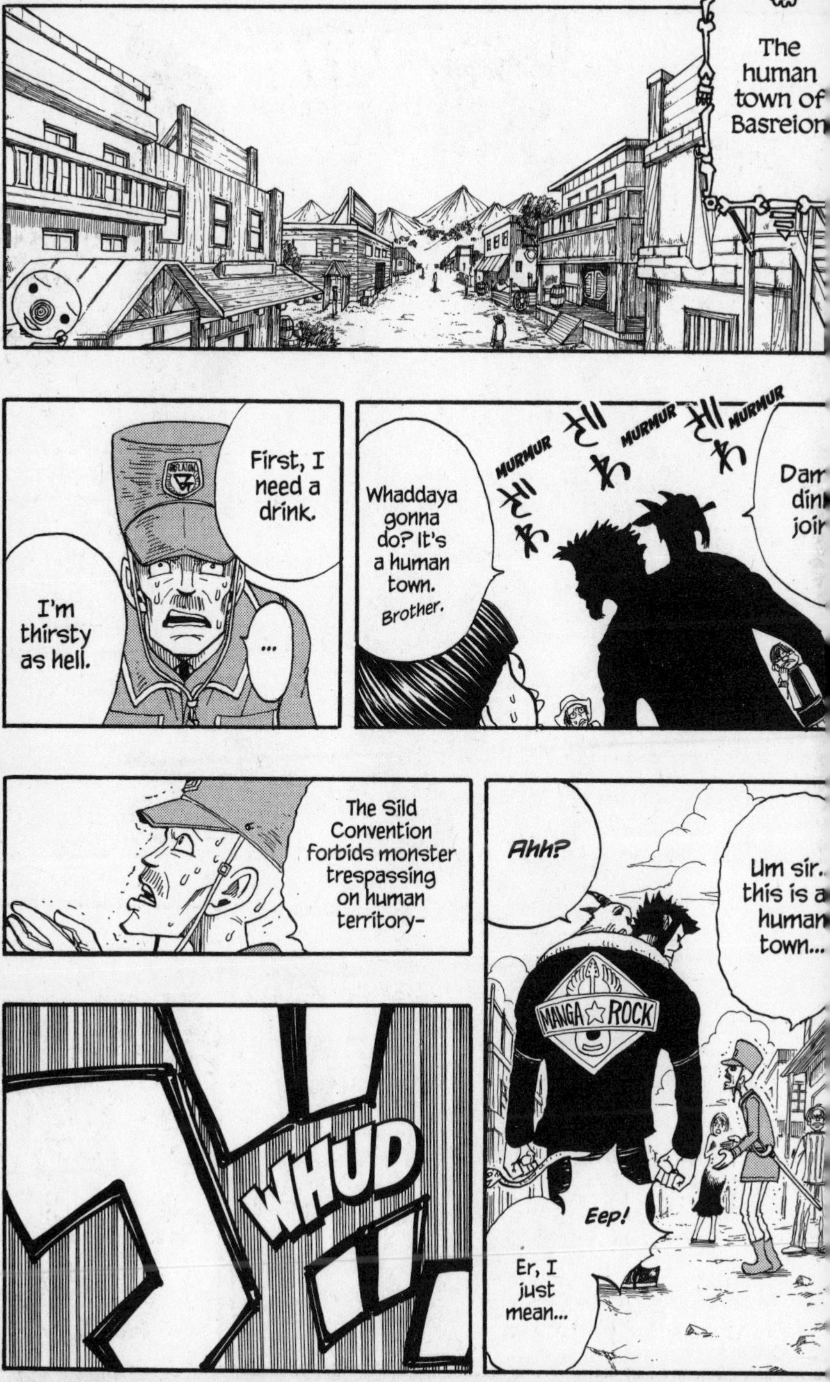

The human town of Basreion
MURMUR
ざわ
MURMUR
ざわ
MURMUR
ざわ
Whaddaya gonna do? It's a human town. Brother.
First, I need a drink.
...
I'm thirsty as hell.
Um sir... this is a human town...
Ahh?
MANGA ROCK
Eep!
Er, I just mean...
The Sild Convention forbids monster trespassing on human territory-
WHUD

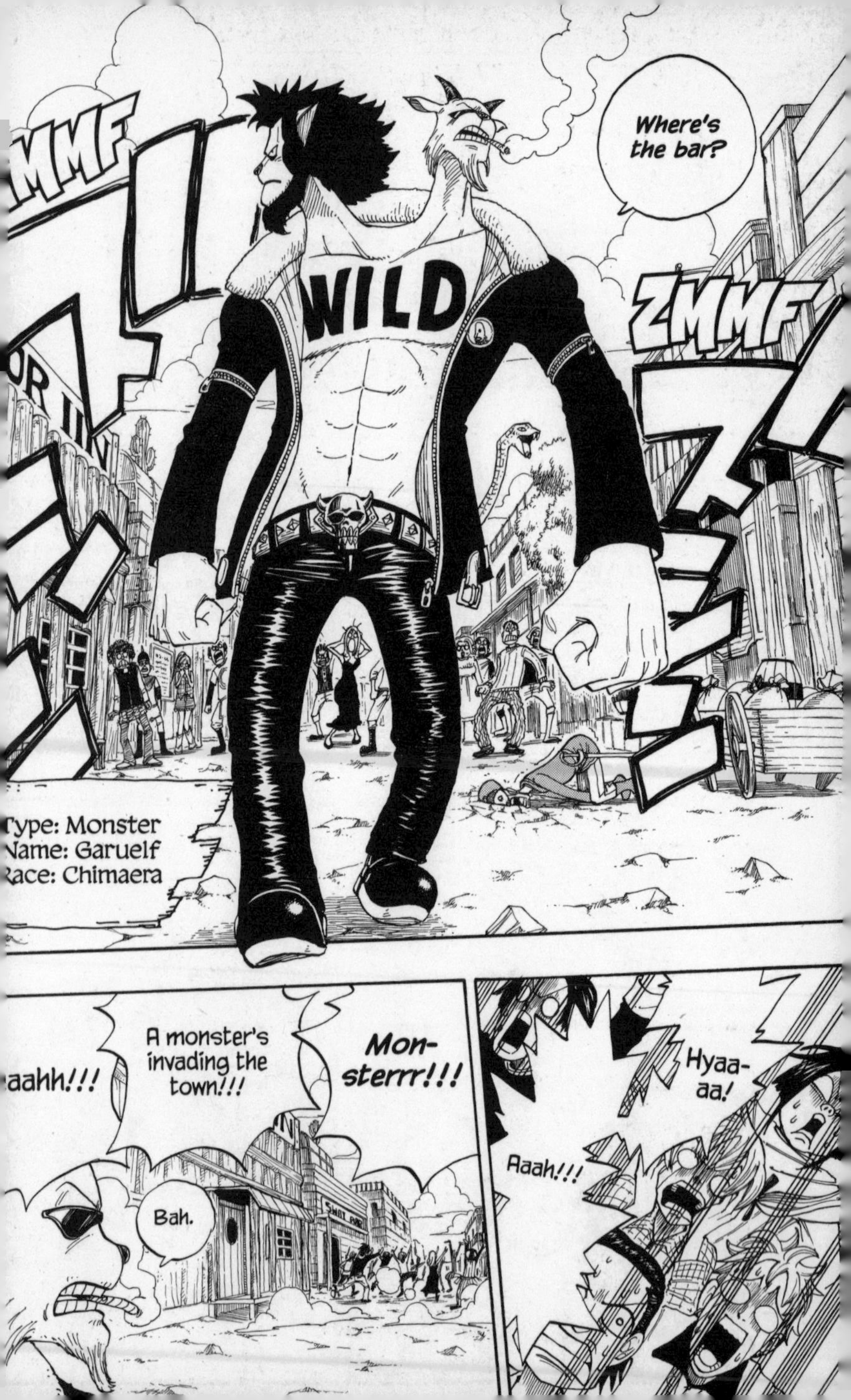
Where's the bar?
ZMMF
MMF
WILD
Type: Monster
Name: Garuelf
Race: Chimaera
Hyaa-aa!
Aaah!!!
Mon-sterrr!!!
A monster's invading the town!!!
aahh!!!
Bah.

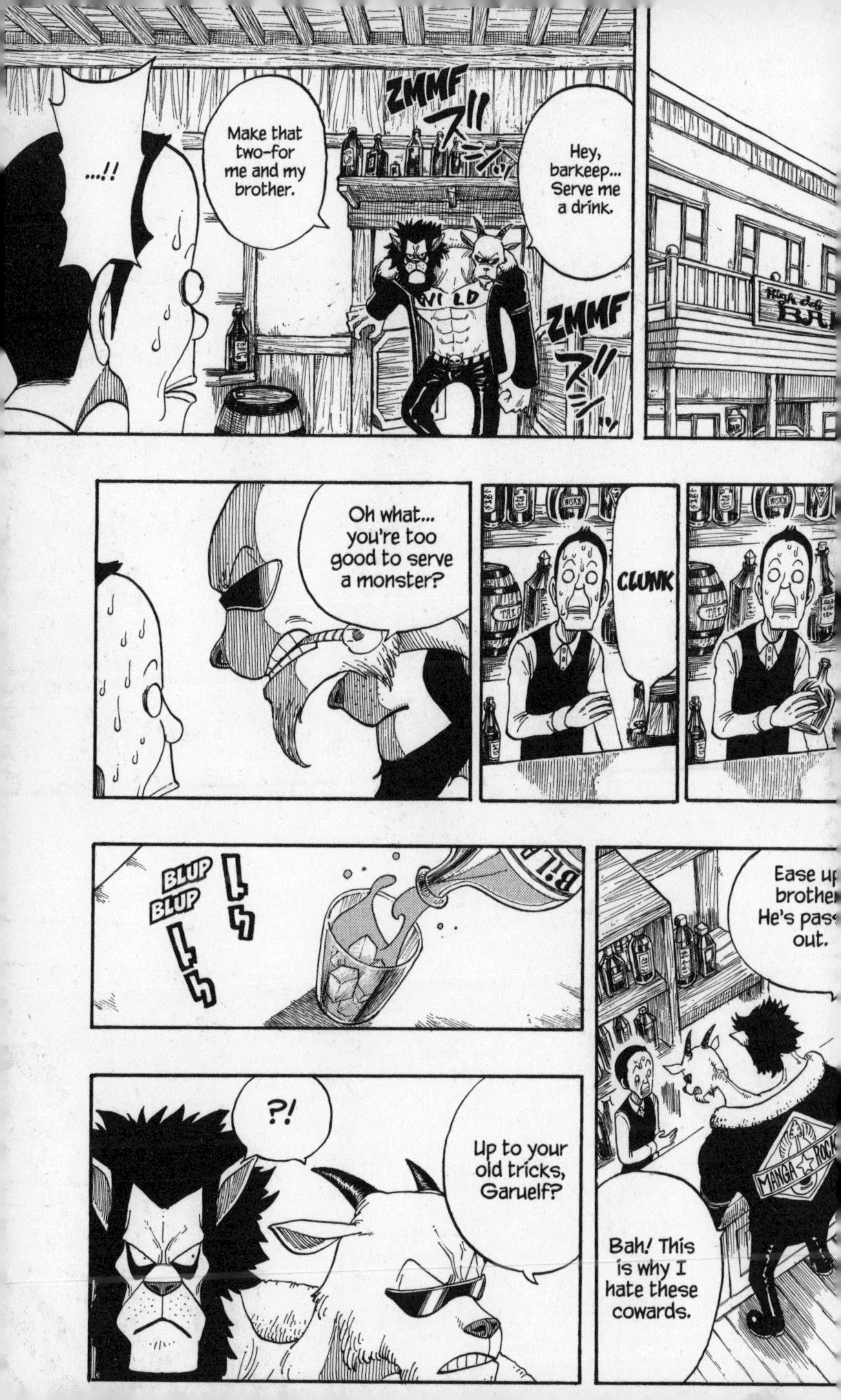
ZMMF
Hey, barkeep... Serve me a drink.
ZMMF
Make that two-for me and my brother.
...!!
CLUNK
Oh what... you're too good to serve a monster?
Ease up brothe He's pas out.
Bah! This is why I hate these cowards.
BLUP BLUP
?!
Up to your old tricks, Garuelf?

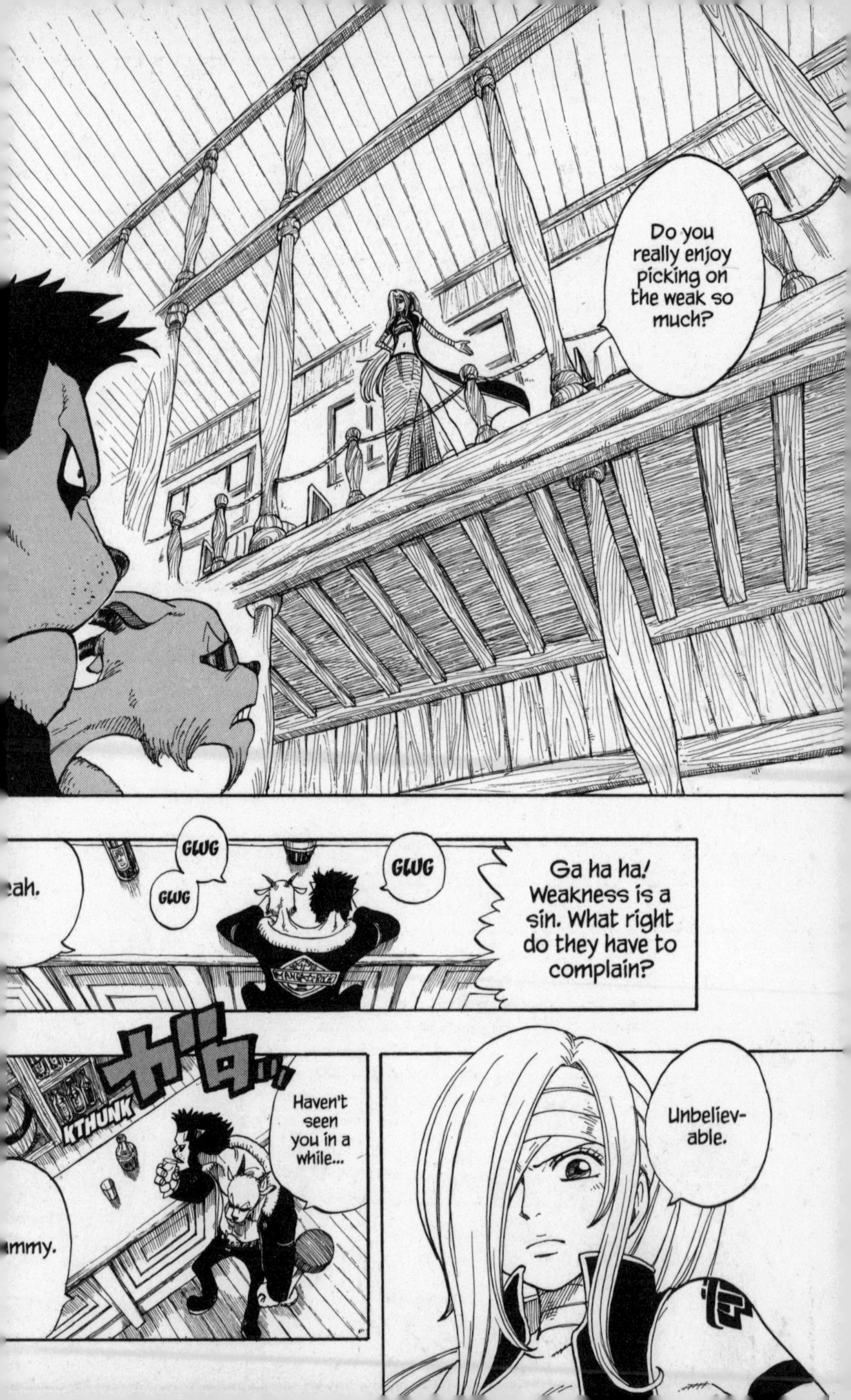
Do you really enjoy picking on the weak so much?
Ga ha ha! Weakness is a sin. What right do they have to complain?
GLUG
GLUG
GLUG
eah.
Unbeliev-able.
Haven't seen you in a while...
KTHUNK
mmy.

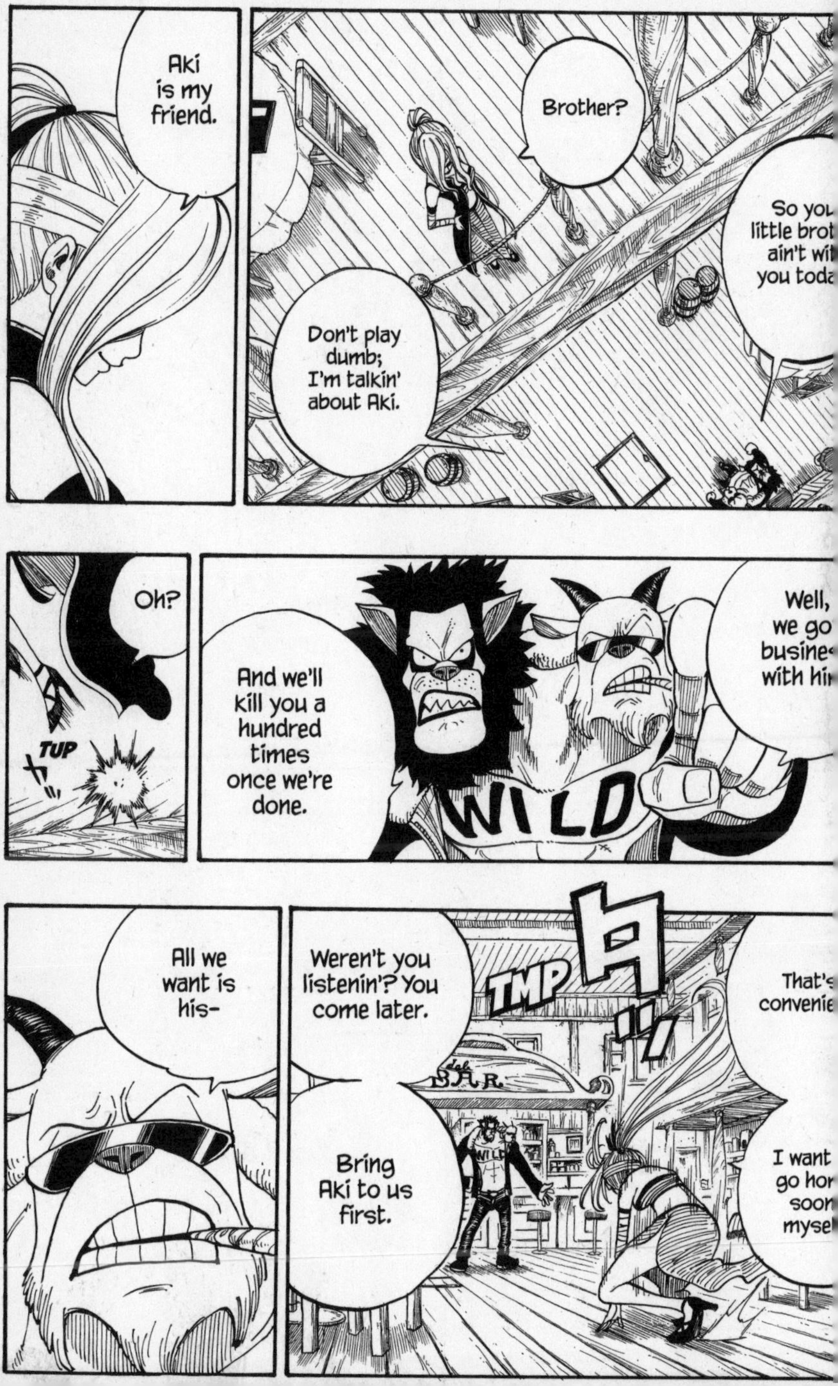

So you
little brot
ain't wi
you toda
Brother?
Don't play dumb; I'm talkin' about Aki.
Aki is my friend.
Well, we go busine with hi
And we'll kill you a hundred times once we're done.
Oh?
TUP
That's convenie
TMP
Weren't you listenin'? You come later.
I want go hon soon mysel
Bring Aki to us first.
BAR
All we want is his-

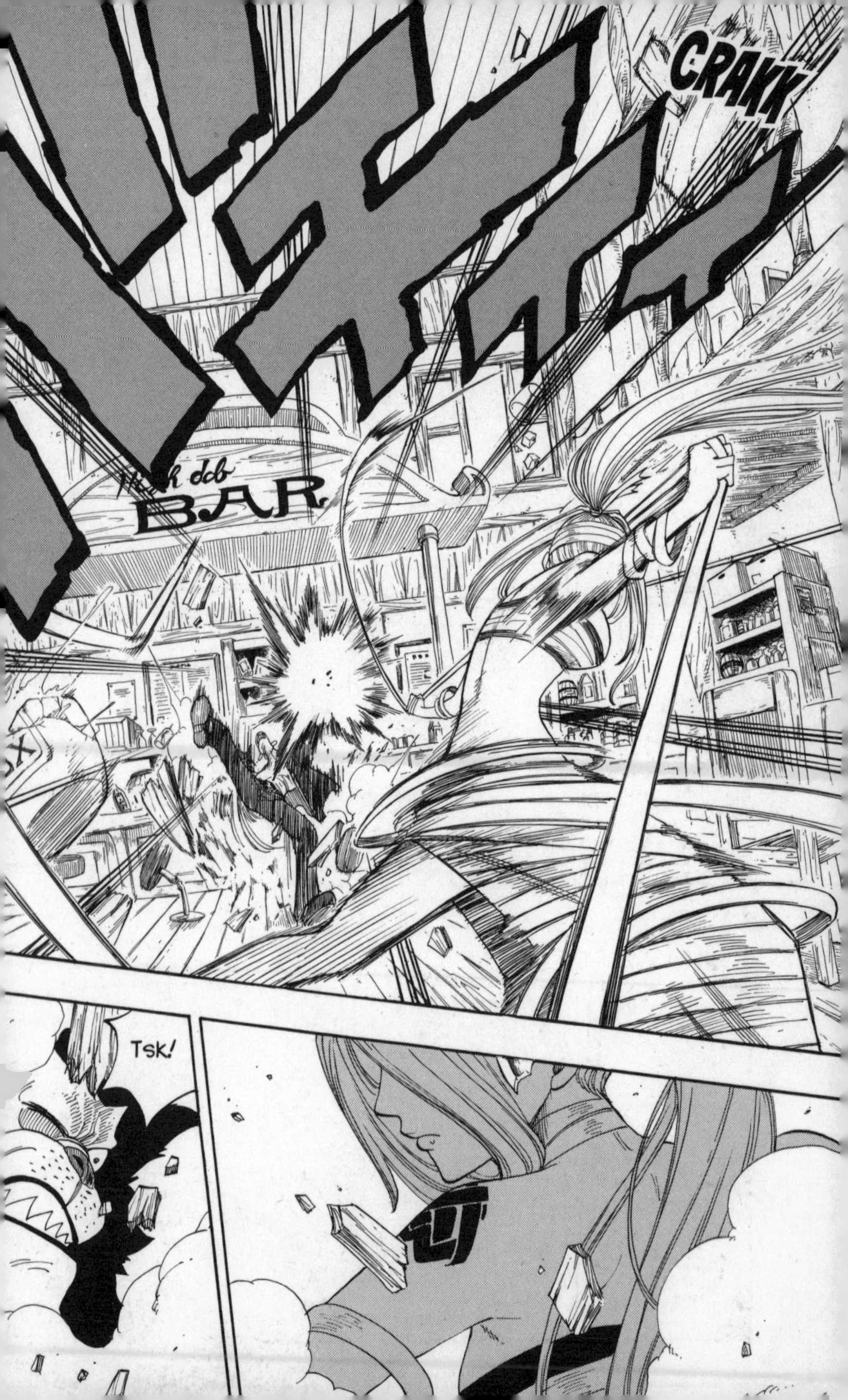
CRAKK
BAR
TSK!

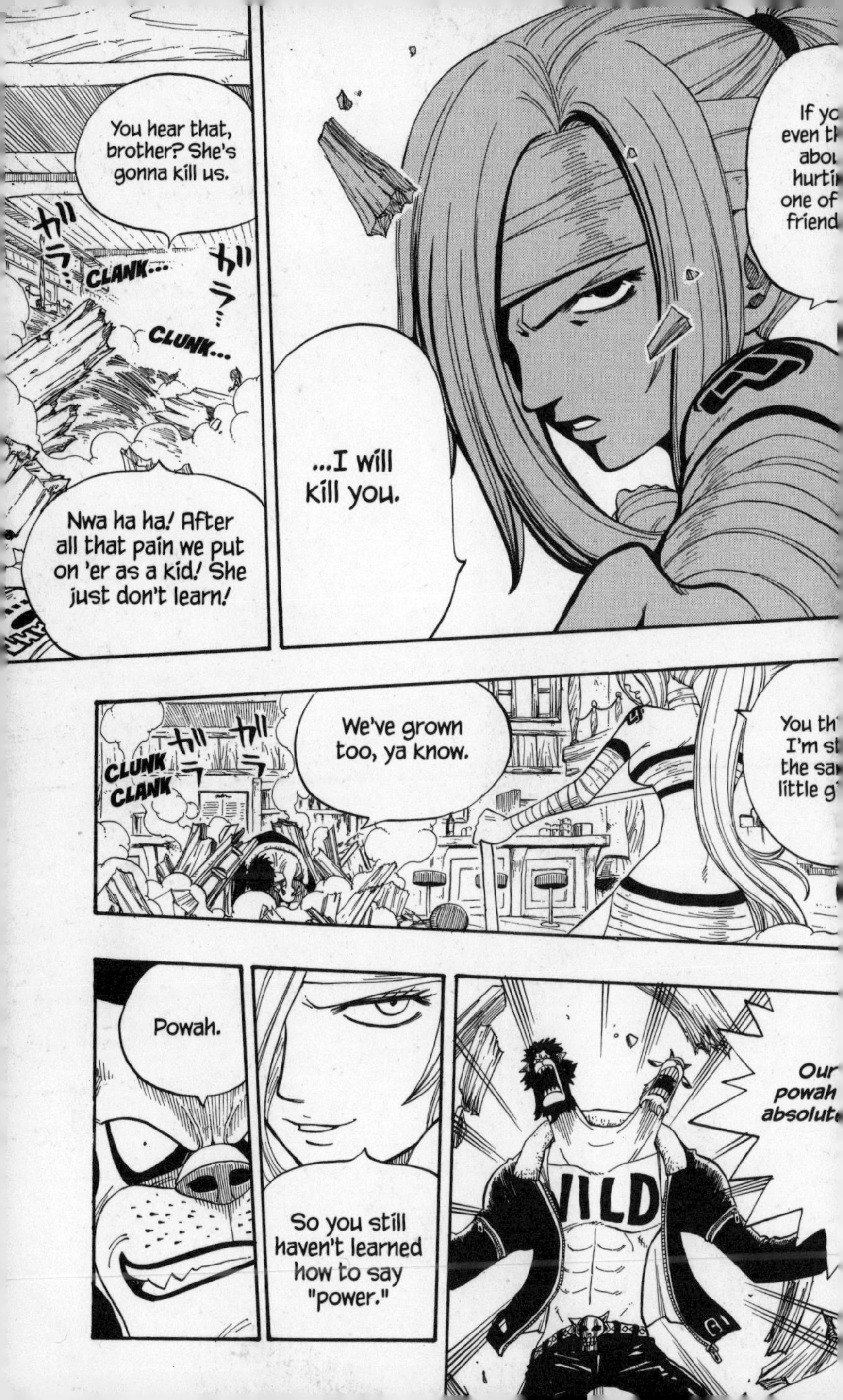

If yo even tl abou hurti one of friend
...I will kill you.
You hear that, brother? She's gonna kill us.
CLANK...
CLUNK...
Nwa ha ha! After all that pain we put on 'er as a kid! She just don't learn!
You th I'm st the sa little g
We've grown too, ya know.
CLUNK CLANK
Our powah absolut
So you still haven't learned how to say "power."
Powah.

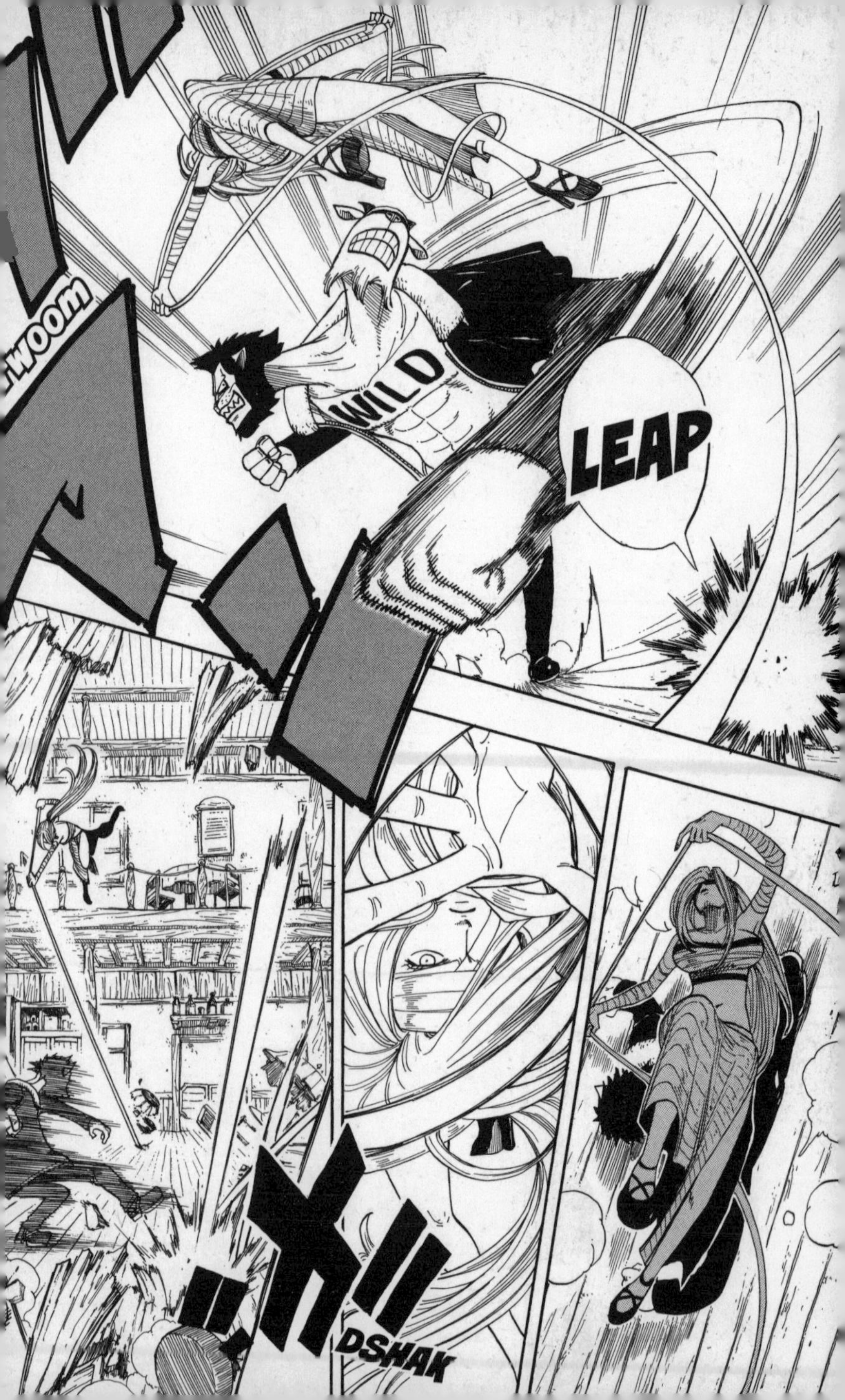
LEAP
WILD
woom
DSHAK

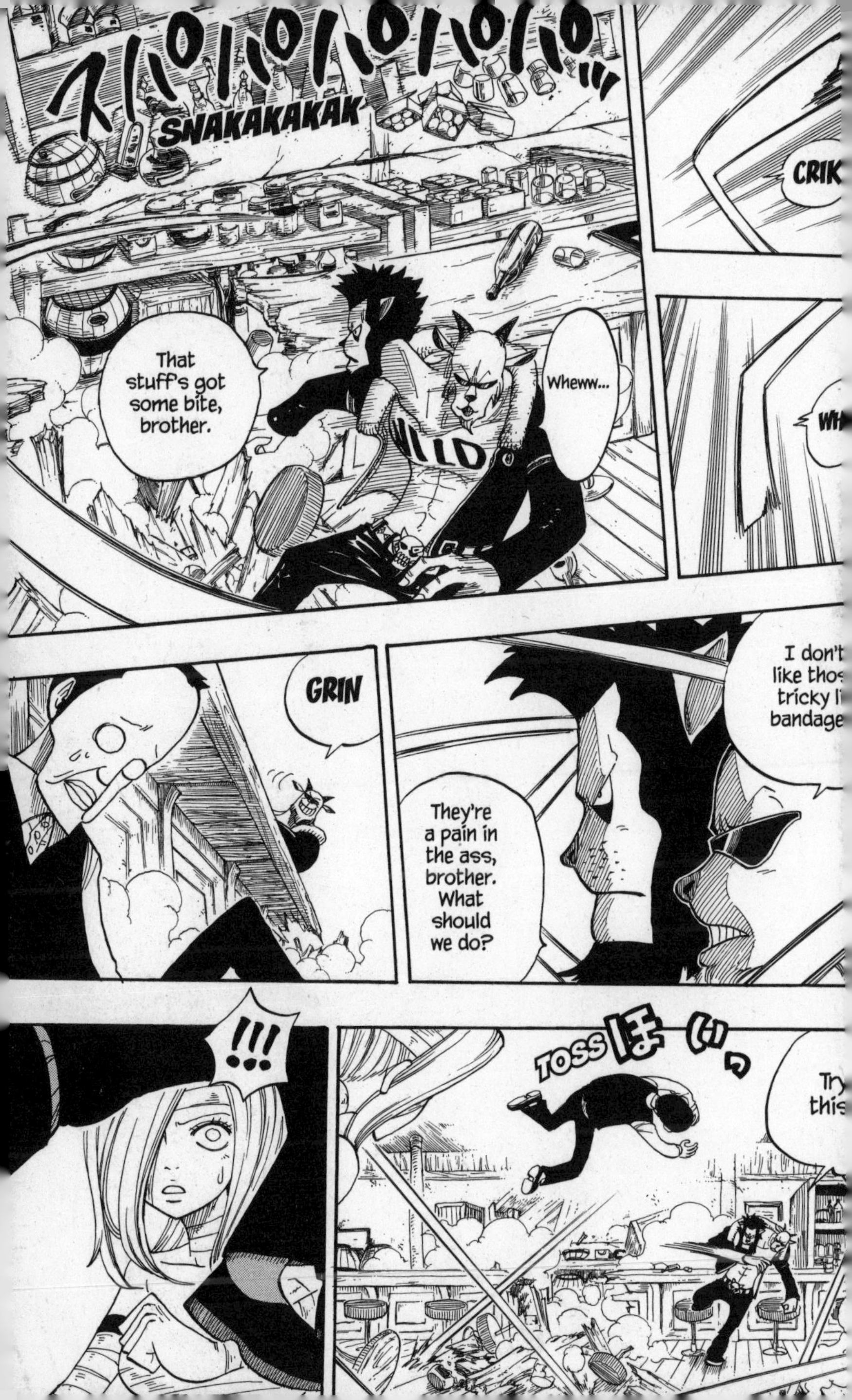
CRIK
Wh
SNAKAKAKAK
Wheww...
That stuff's got some bite, brother.
I don't like thos tricky li bandage
They're a pain in the ass, brother. What should we do?
GRIN
TOSS
Try this
!!!

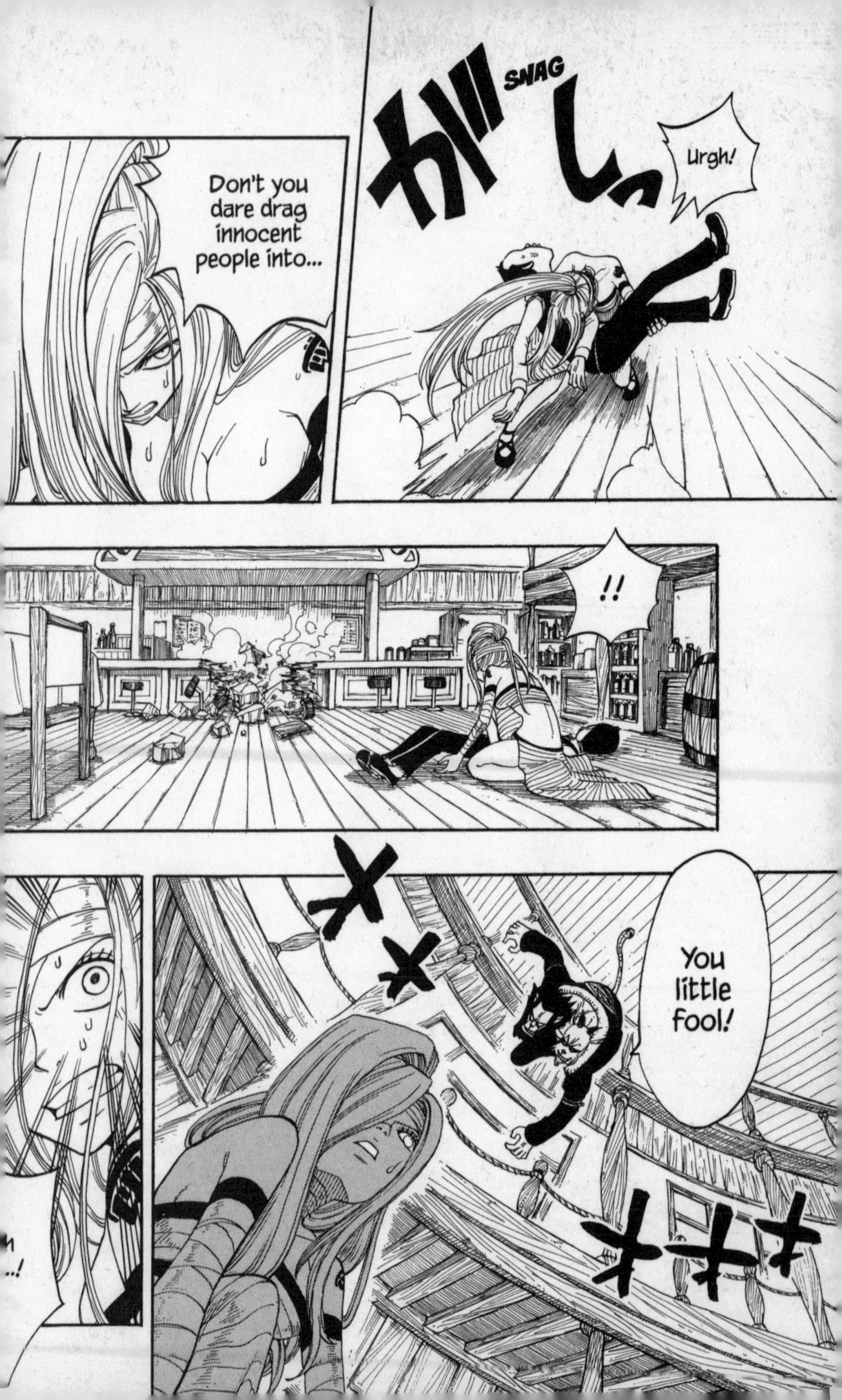

SNAG
Urgh!
Don't you dare drag innocent people into...
!!
You little fool!

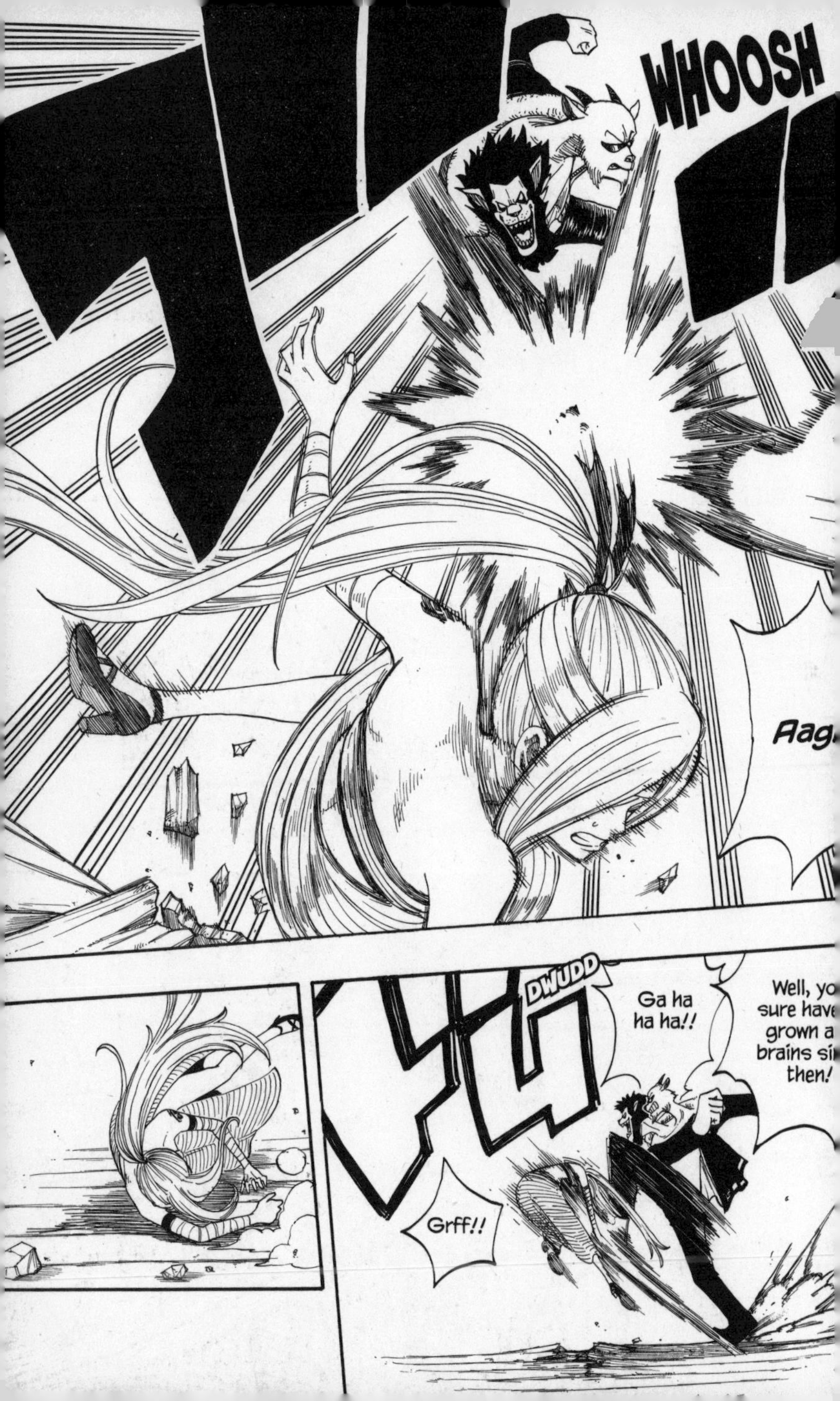
WHOOSH
Aag..
DWUDD
Well, yo sure have grown a brains si then!
Ga ha ha ha!!
Grff!!

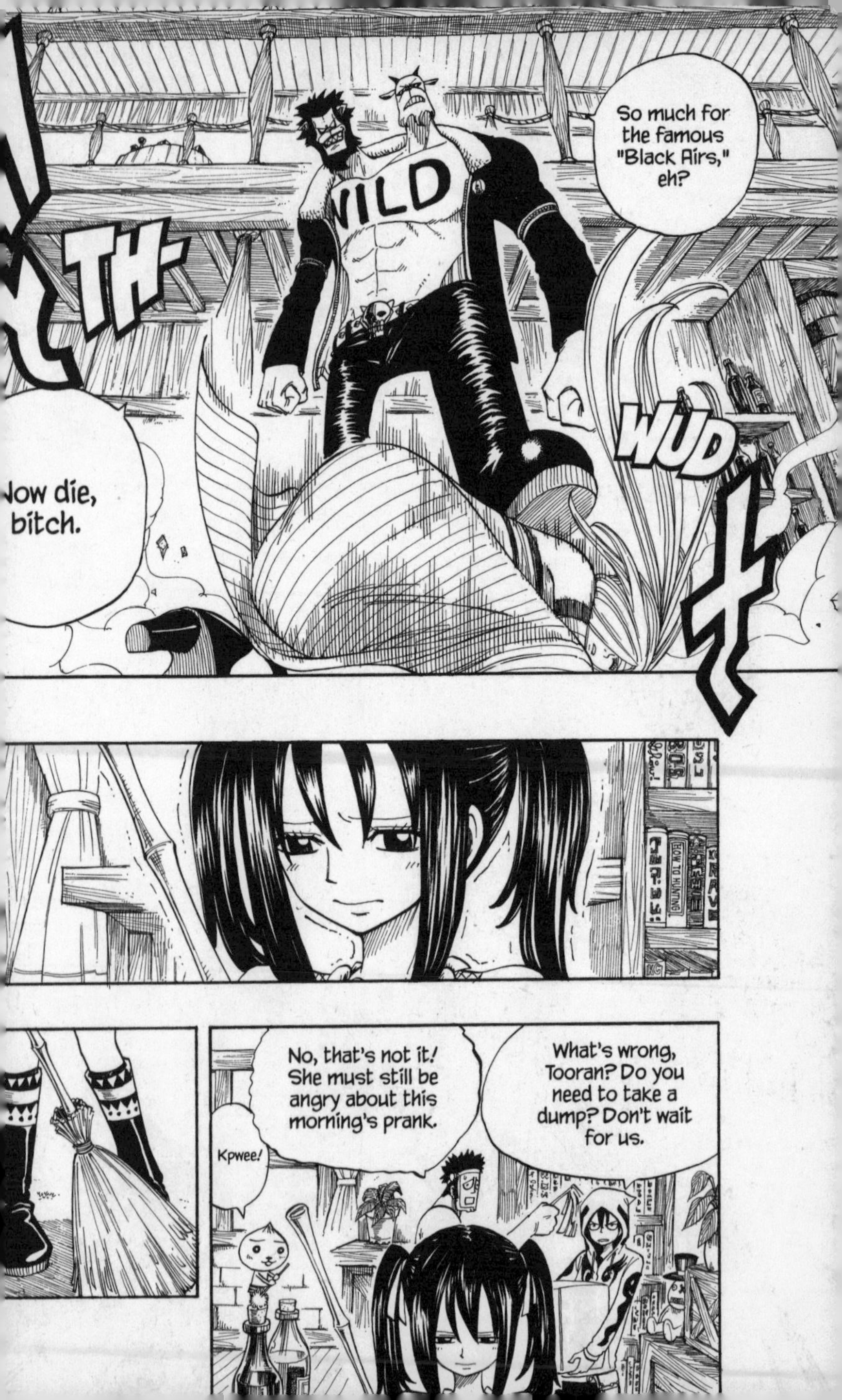
So much for the famous "Black Airs," eh?
WUD
TH-
Now die, bitch.
What's wrong, Tooran? Do you need to take a dump? Don't wait for us.
No, that's not it! She must still be angry about this morning's prank.
Kpwee!

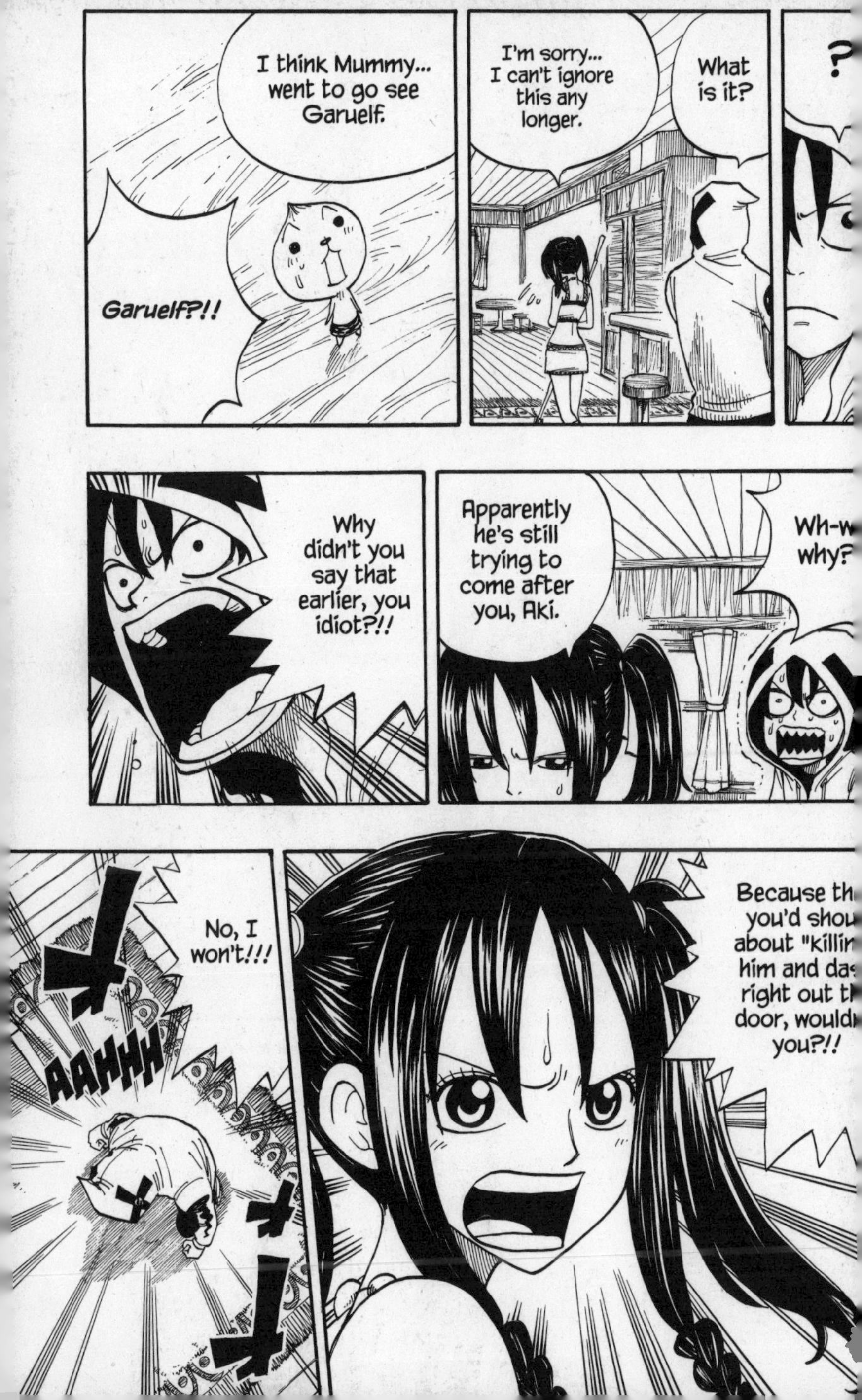
?
What is it?
I'm sorry... I can't ignore this any longer.
I think Mummy... went to go see Garuelf.
Garuelf?!!
Wh-w why?
Apparently he's still trying to come after you, Aki.
Why didn't you say that earlier, you idiot?!!
Because th you'd shou about "killin him and das right out t door, wouldn you?!!
No, I won't!!!
AAHHH

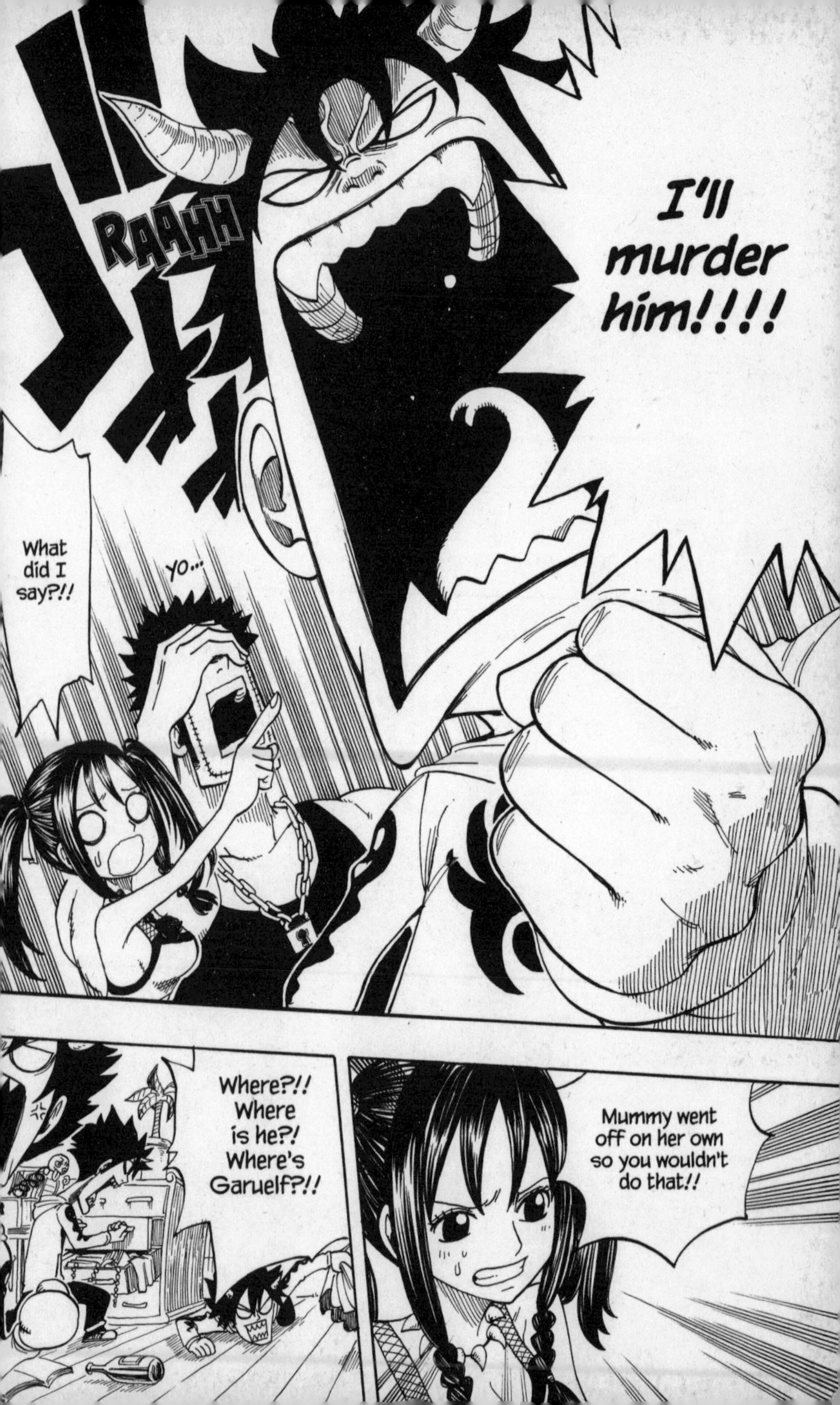
I'll murder him!!!!
RAAHH
Yo...
What did I say?!!
Mummy went off on her own so you wouldn't do that!!
Where?!! Where is he?! Where's Garuelf?!!

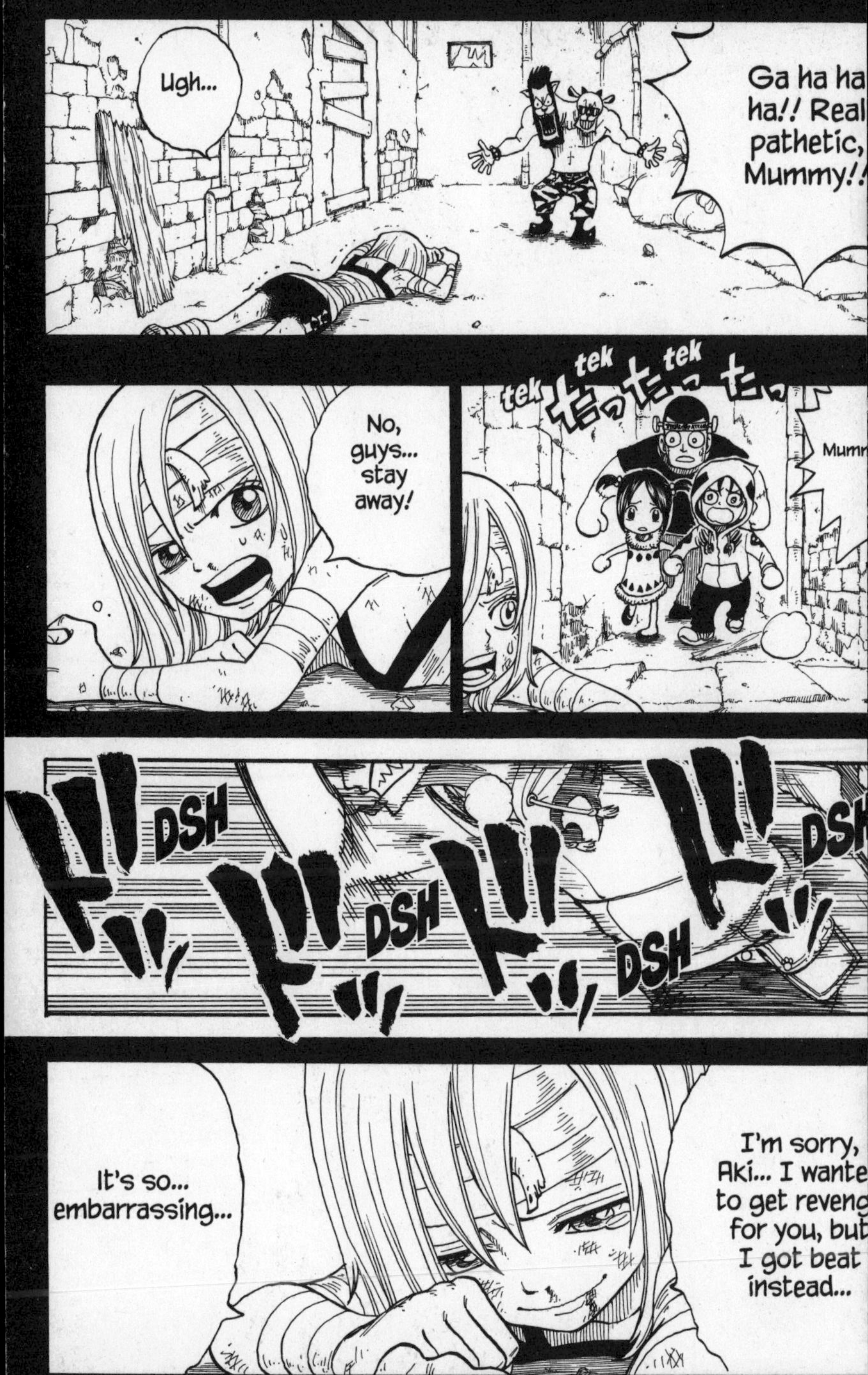
Ga ha ha ha!! Real pathetic, Mummy!!
Ugh...
tek tek tek
Mumm
No, guys... stay away!
DSH
DSH
DSH
DSH
I'm sorry, Aki... I wante to get reveng for you, but I got beat instead...
It's so... embarrassing...

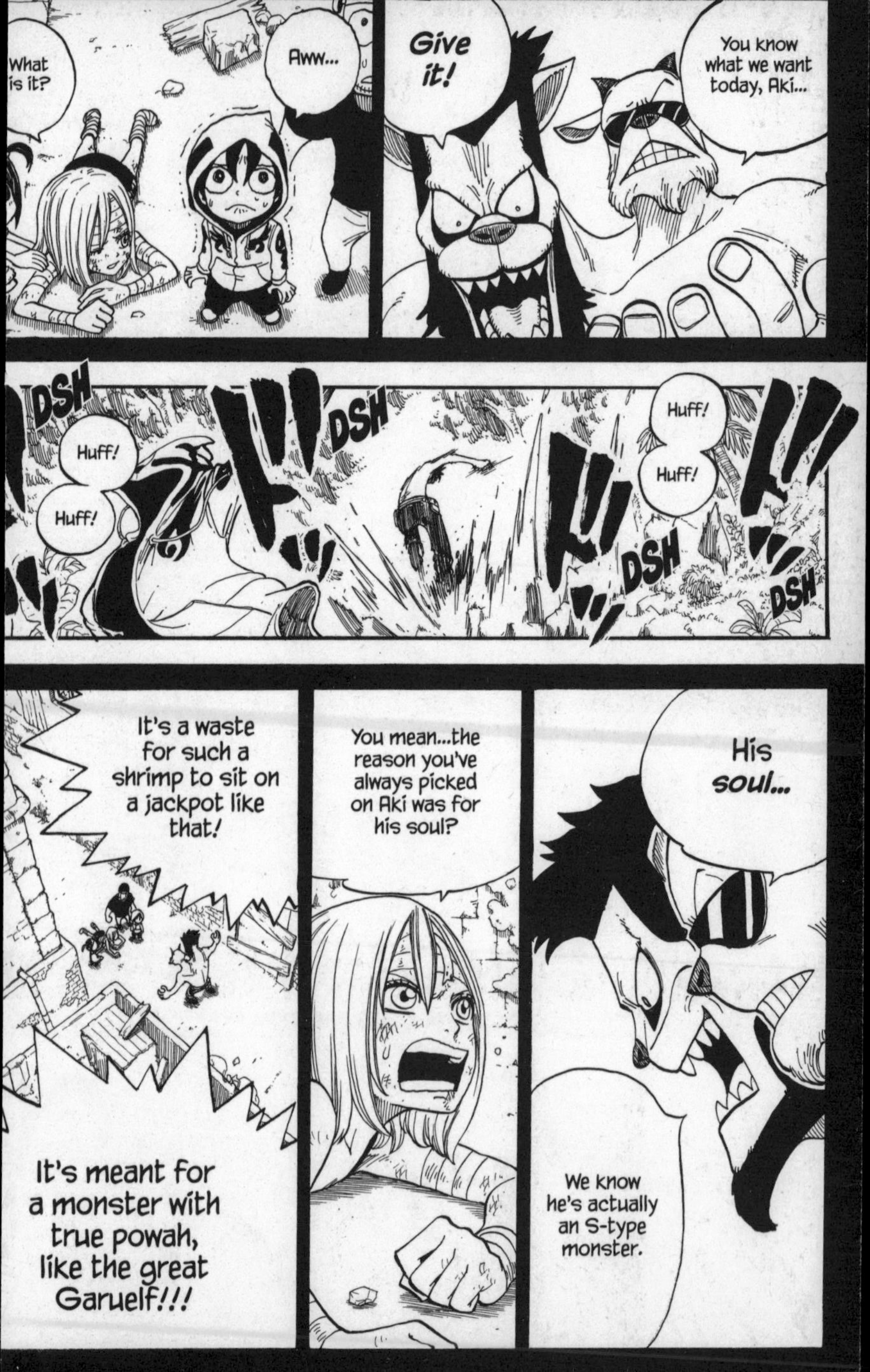
You know what we want today, Aki...
Give it!
Aww...
What is it?
Huff!
Huff!
DSH
DSH
DSH
DSH
Huff!
Huff!
DSH
His soul...
We know he's actually an S-type monster.
You mean...the reason you've always picked on Aki was for his soul?
It's a waste for such a shrimp to sit on a jackpot like that!
It's meant for a monster with true powah, like the great Garuelf!!!

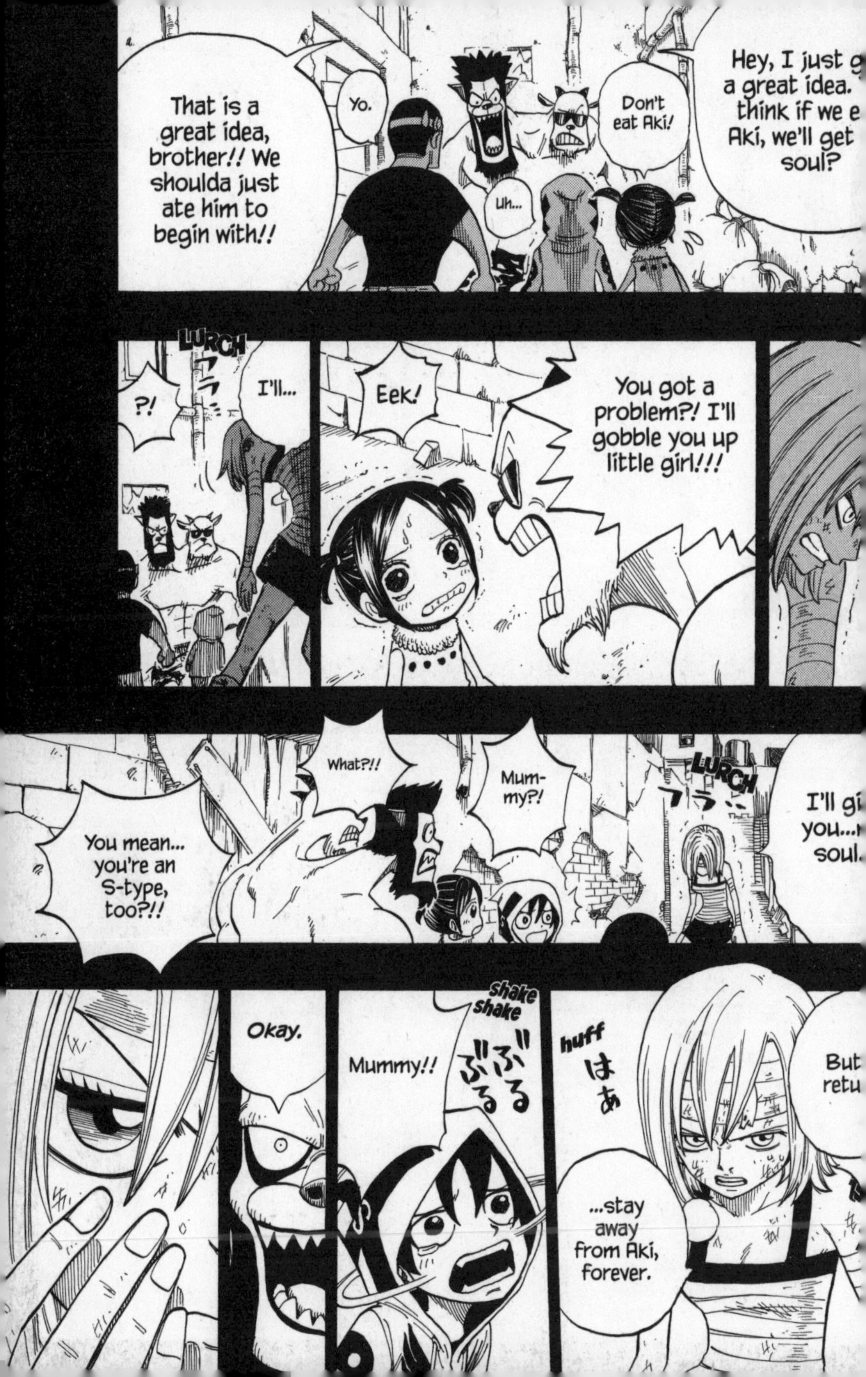
Hey, I just g
a great idea.
think if we e
Aki, we'll get
soul?
Don't eat Aki!
Yo.
Uh...
That is a great idea, brother!! We shoulda just ate him to begin with!!
You got a problem?! I'll gobble you up little girl!!!
Eek!
I'll...
LURCH
フラ
?!
I'll gi
you...
soul.
LURCH
フラ
Mum-my?!
What?!!
You mean... you're an S-type, too?!!
But
retu
...stay away from Aki, forever.
huff
はぁ
shake shake
ぶるぶる
Mummy!!
Okay.

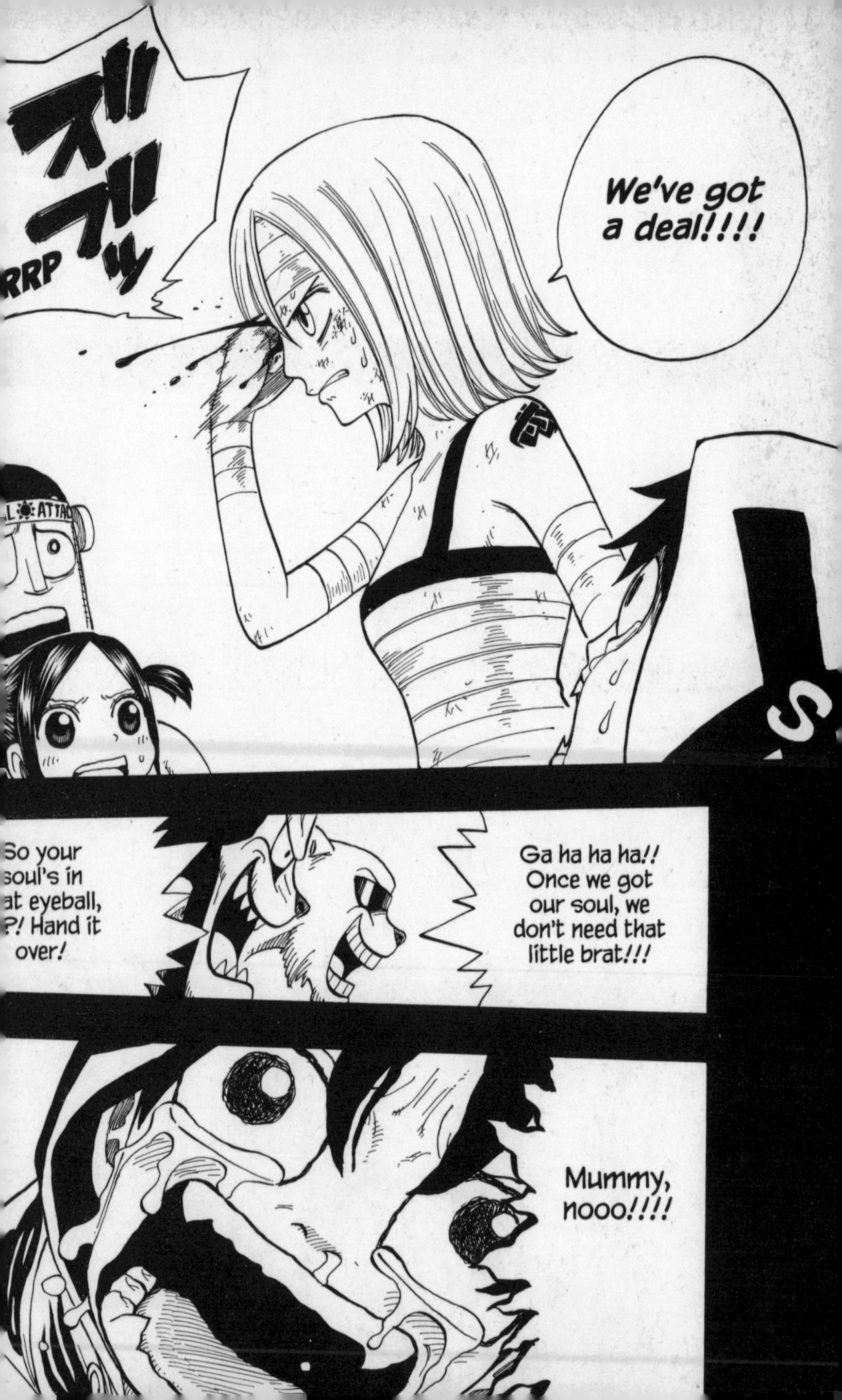
We've got a deal!!!!
ズブッ
RRP
Ga ha ha ha!! Once we got our soul, we don't need that little brat!!!
So your soul's in at eyeball, ?! Hand it over!
Mummy, nooo!!!!

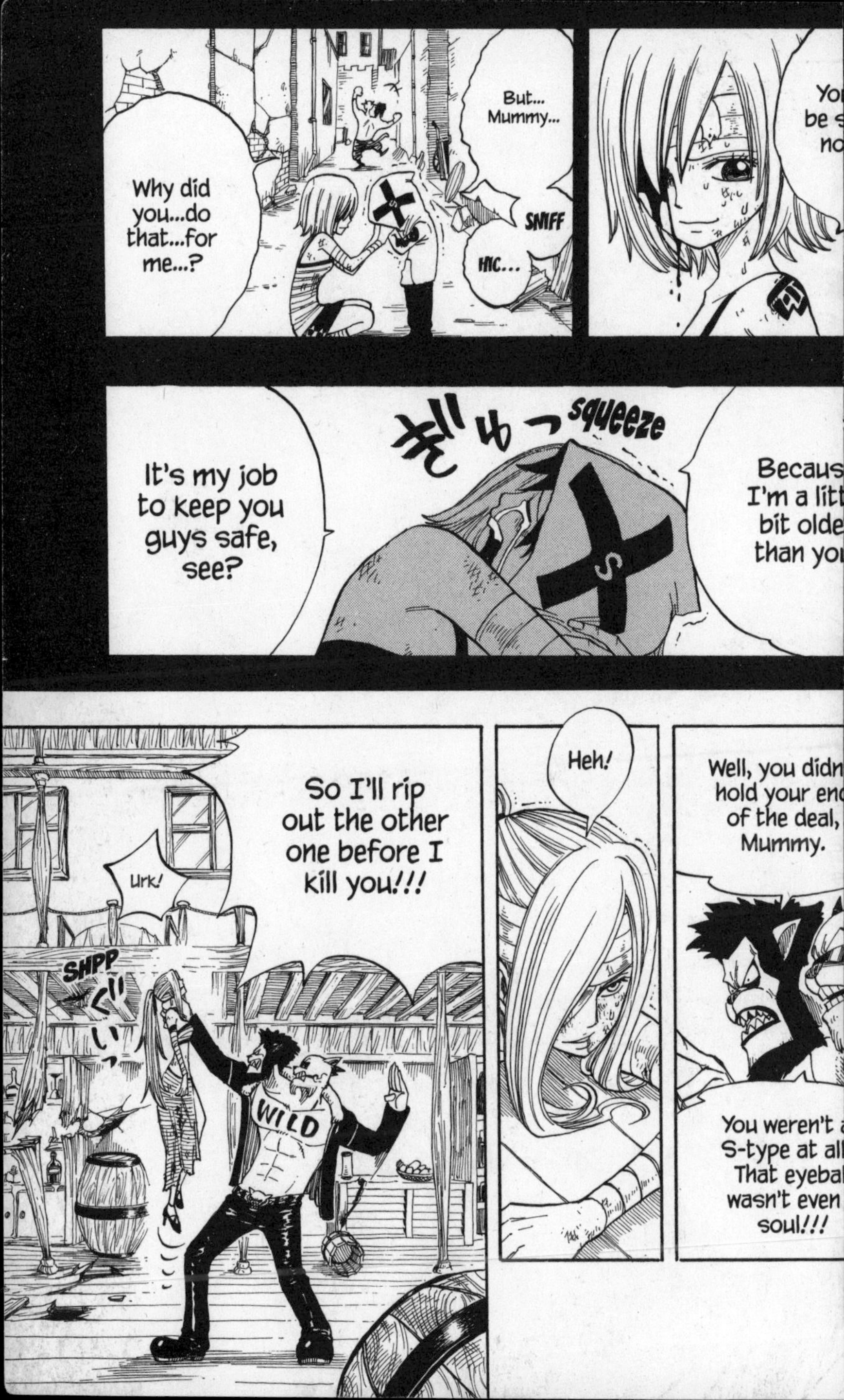
Yo
be s
no
But... Mummy...
SNIFF
HIC...
Why did you...do that...for me...?
Becaus
I'm a litt
bit olde
than yo
ぎゅっ squeeze
It's my job to keep you guys safe, see?
Well, you didn
hold your en
of the deal,
Mummy.
You weren't a
S-type at all
That eyebal
wasn't even
soul!!!
Heh!
So I'll rip out the other one before I kill you!!!
Urk!
SHPP ぐいっ

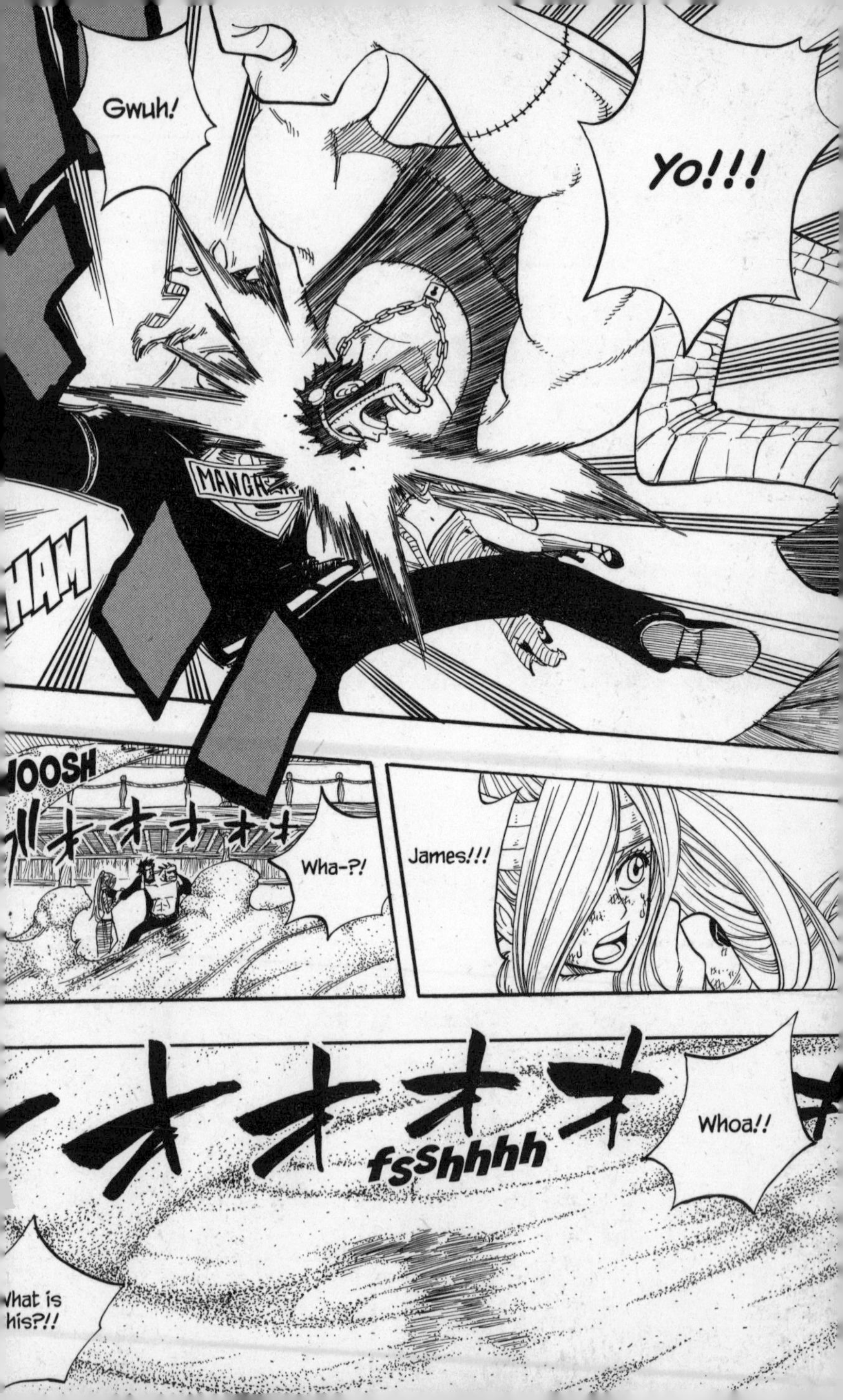

Yo!!!
Gwuh!
HAM
James!!!
Wha-?!
OOSH
Whoa!!
fsshhhh
hat is
his?!!

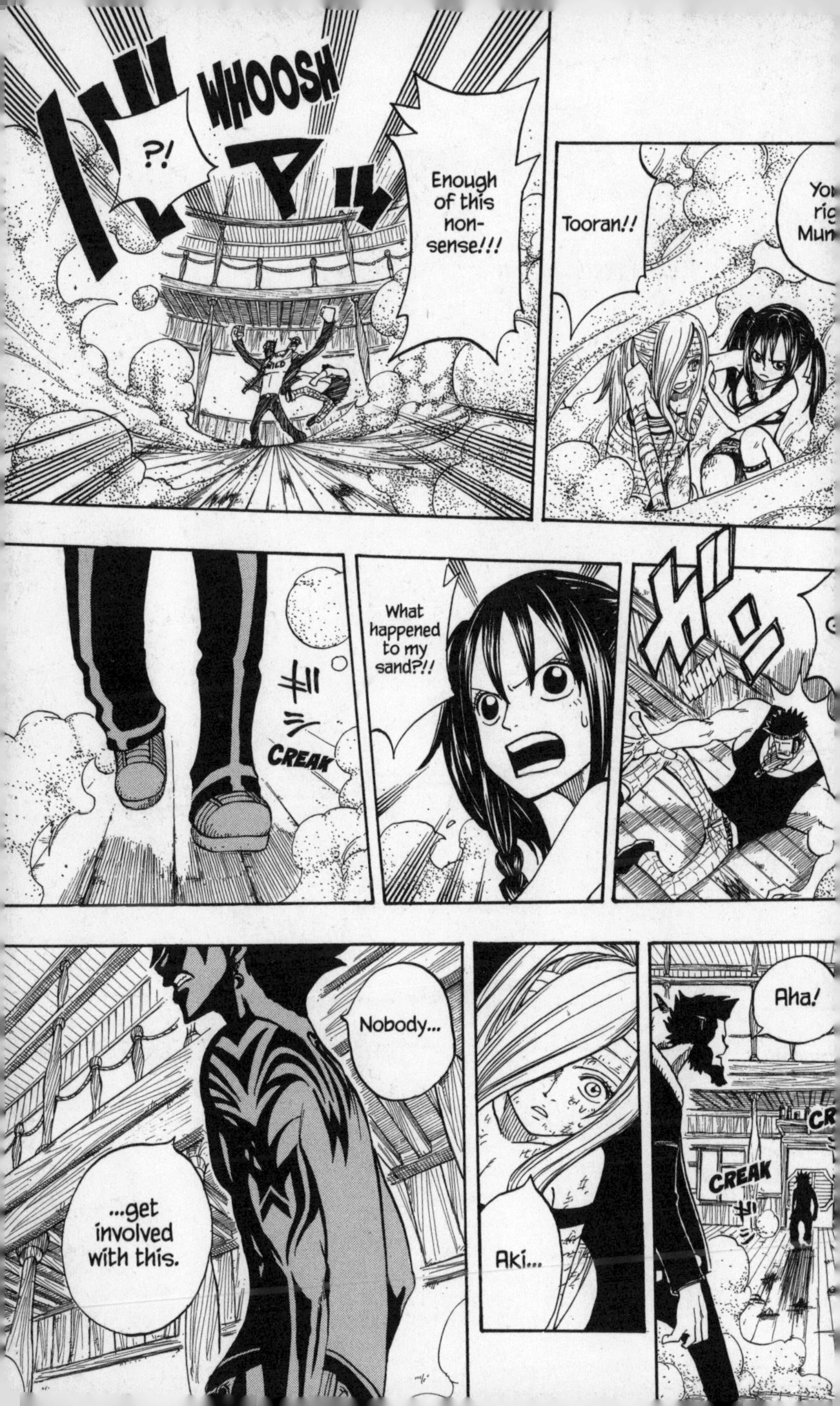

Tooran!!
Enough of this non-sense!!!
WHOOSH
?!
WHAM
What happened to my sand?!!
CREAK
Aha!
CREAK
Aki...
Nobody...
...get involved with this.

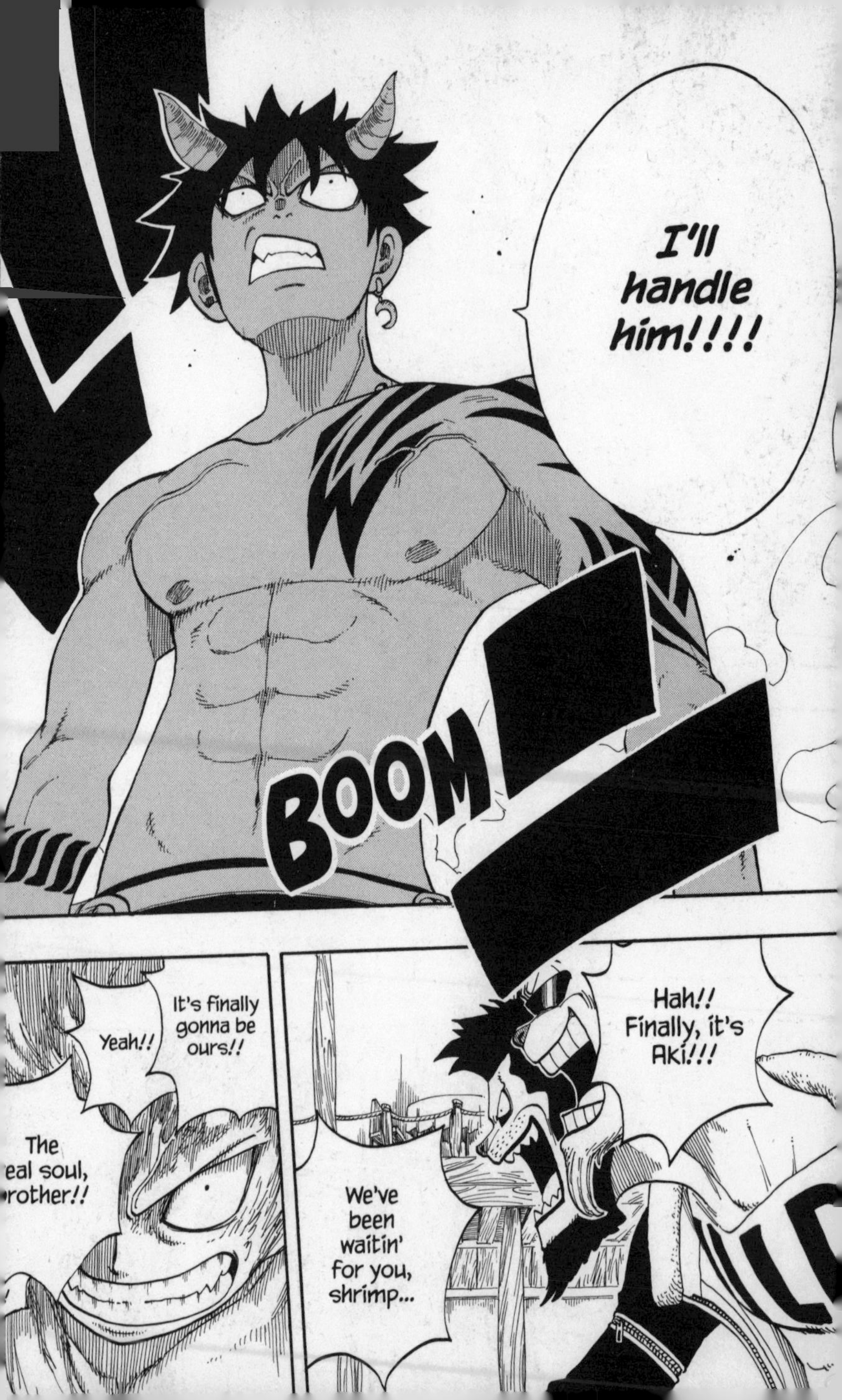
I'll handle him!!!!
BOOM
Hah!! Finally, it's Aki!!!
We've been waitin' for you, shrimp...
It's finally gonna be ours!!
Yeah!!
The eal soul, rother!!

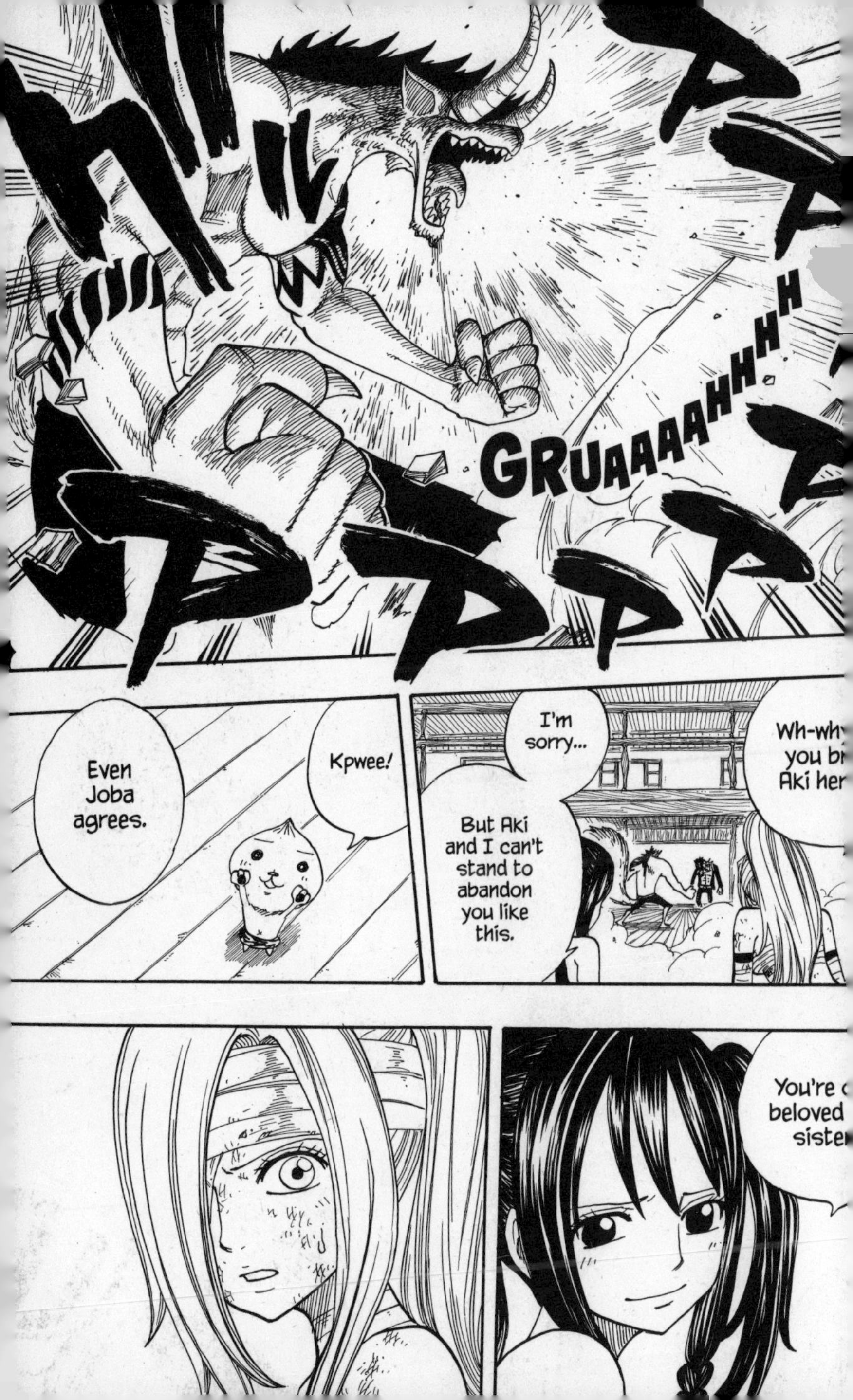
GRUAAAAHHHH
Wh-why you bi Aki her
I'm sorry...
But Aki and I can't stand to abandon you like this.
Kpwee!
Even Joba agrees.
You're beloved siste

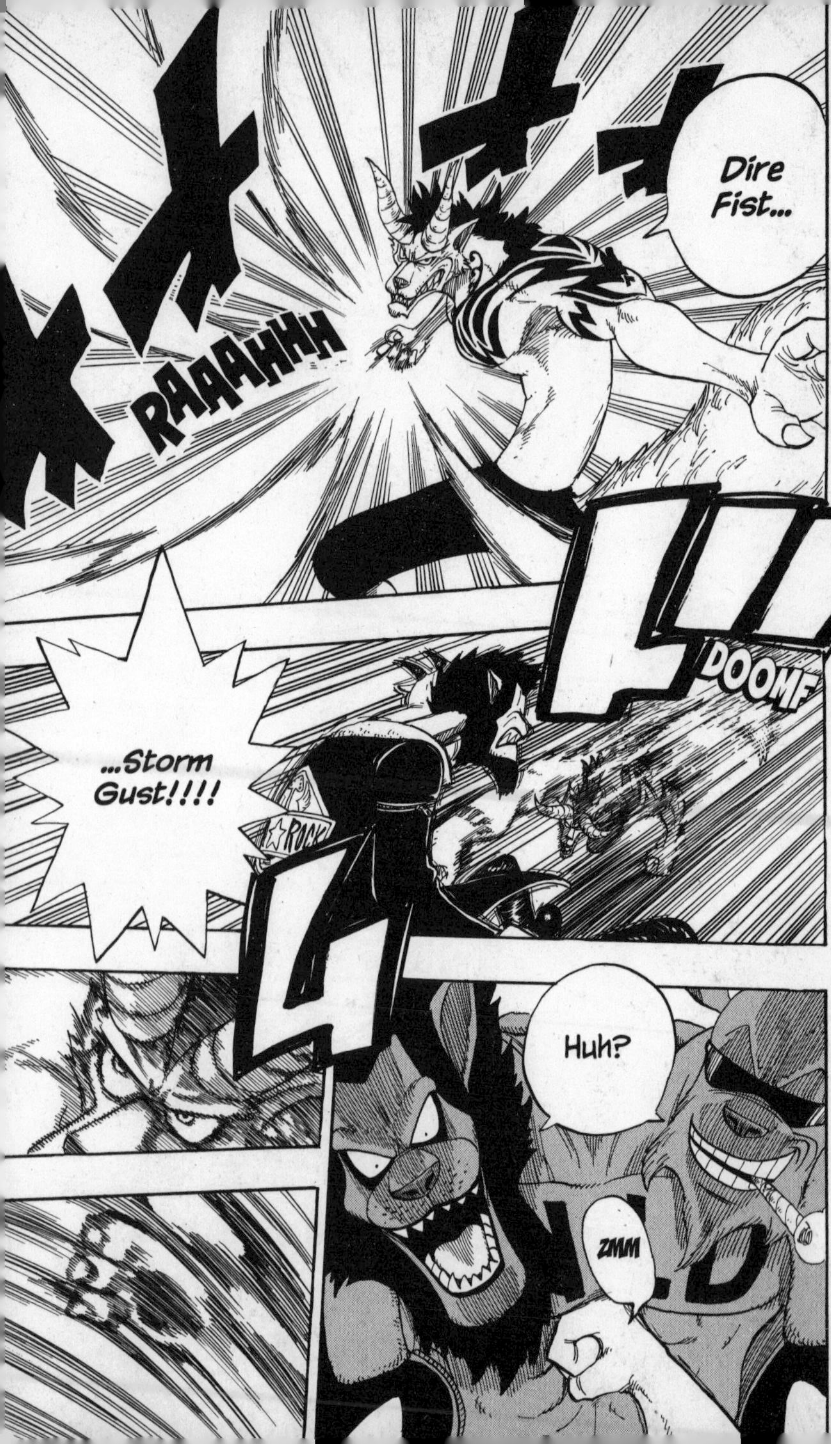
Dire Fist...
RAAAAHHH
DOOMF
...Storm Gust!!!!
Huh?
ZMM

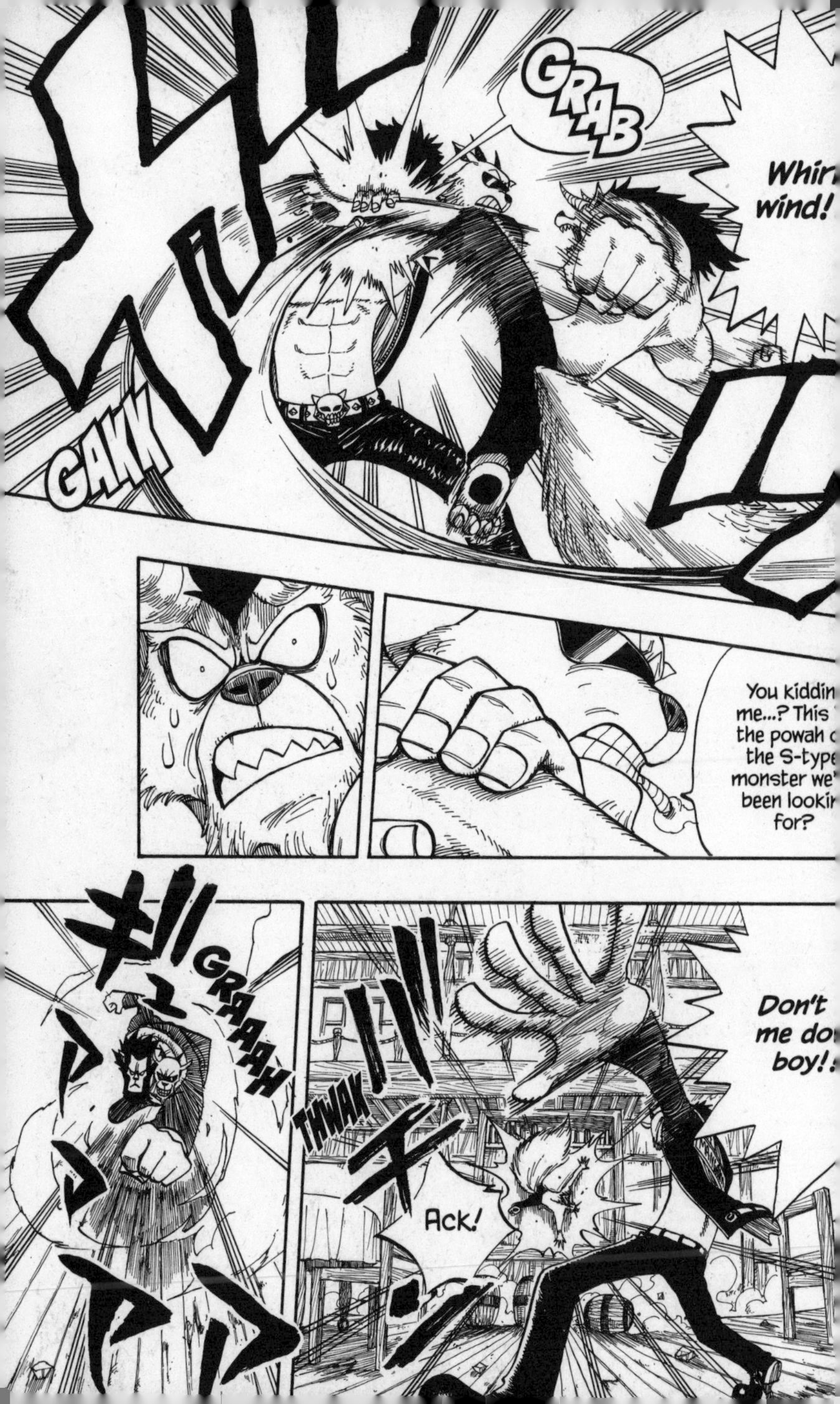

Whir
wind!
GRAB
GAKK
You kiddin
me...? This
the powah
the S-type
monster we'
been lookin
for?
Don't
me do
boy!!
Ack!
THWAK
GRAAAH

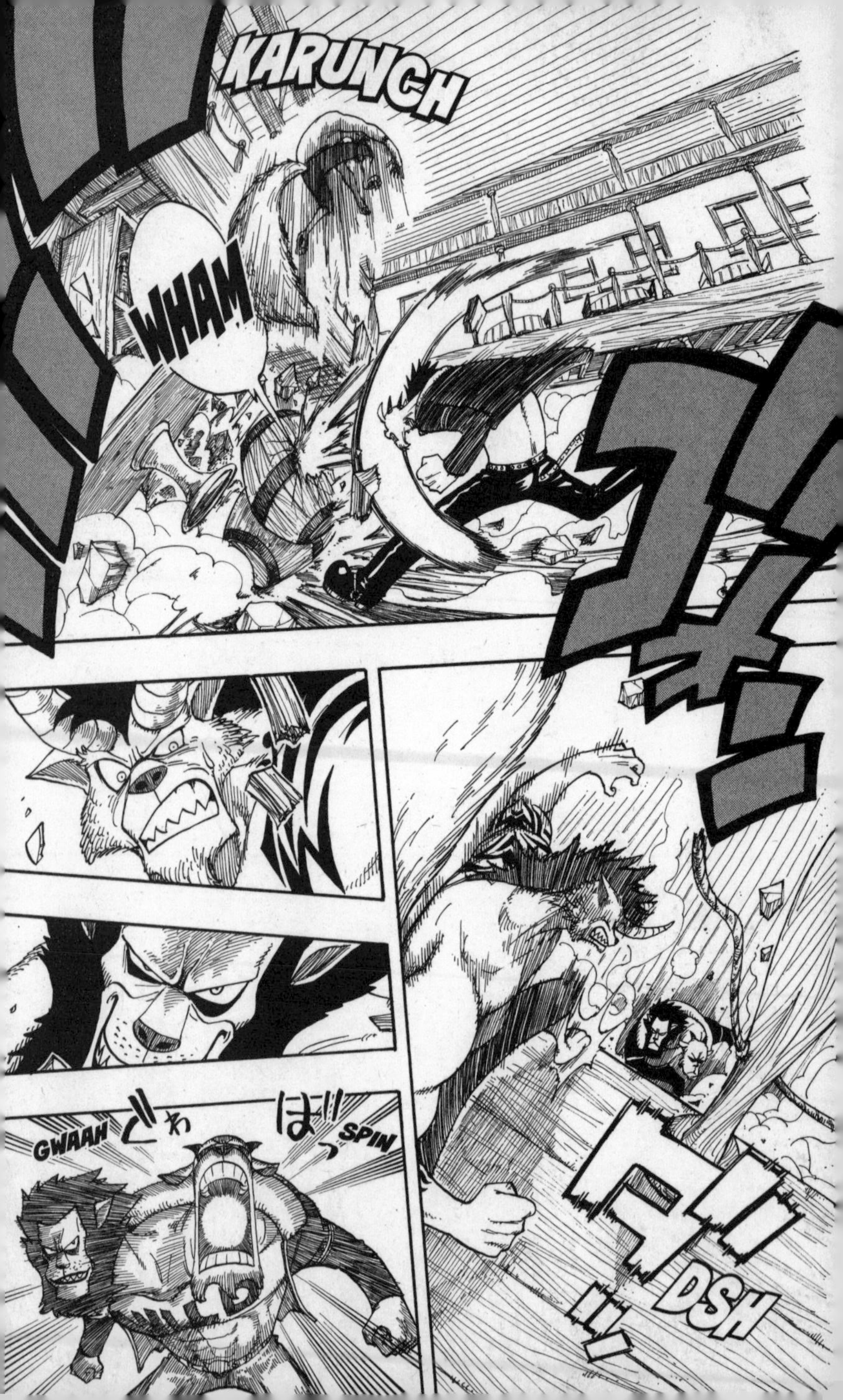

KARUNCH
WHAM
DSH
GWAAH
SPIN

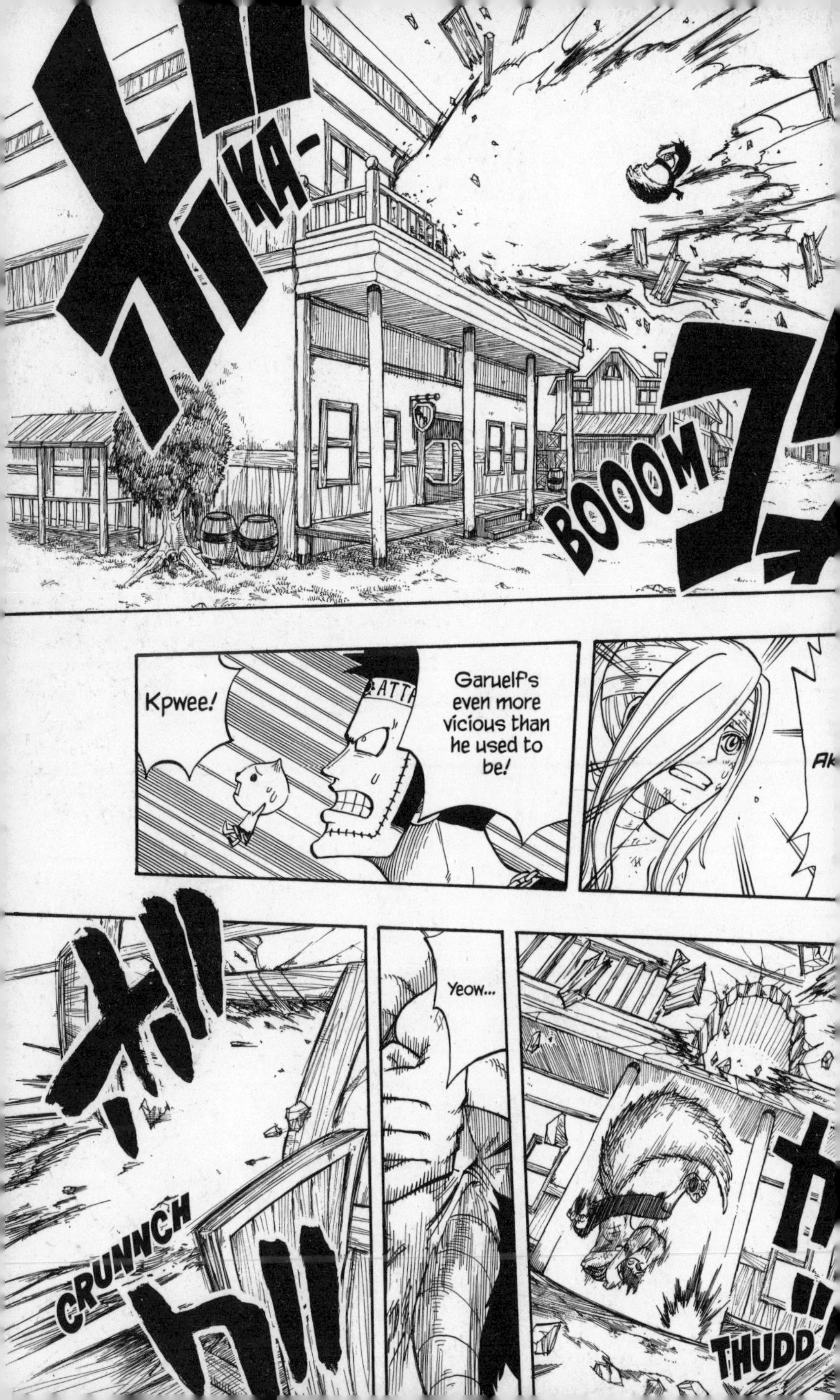

KA-
BOOOM
Ak
Garuelf's even more vicious than he used to be!
Kpwee!
THUDD
Yeow...
CRUNNCH

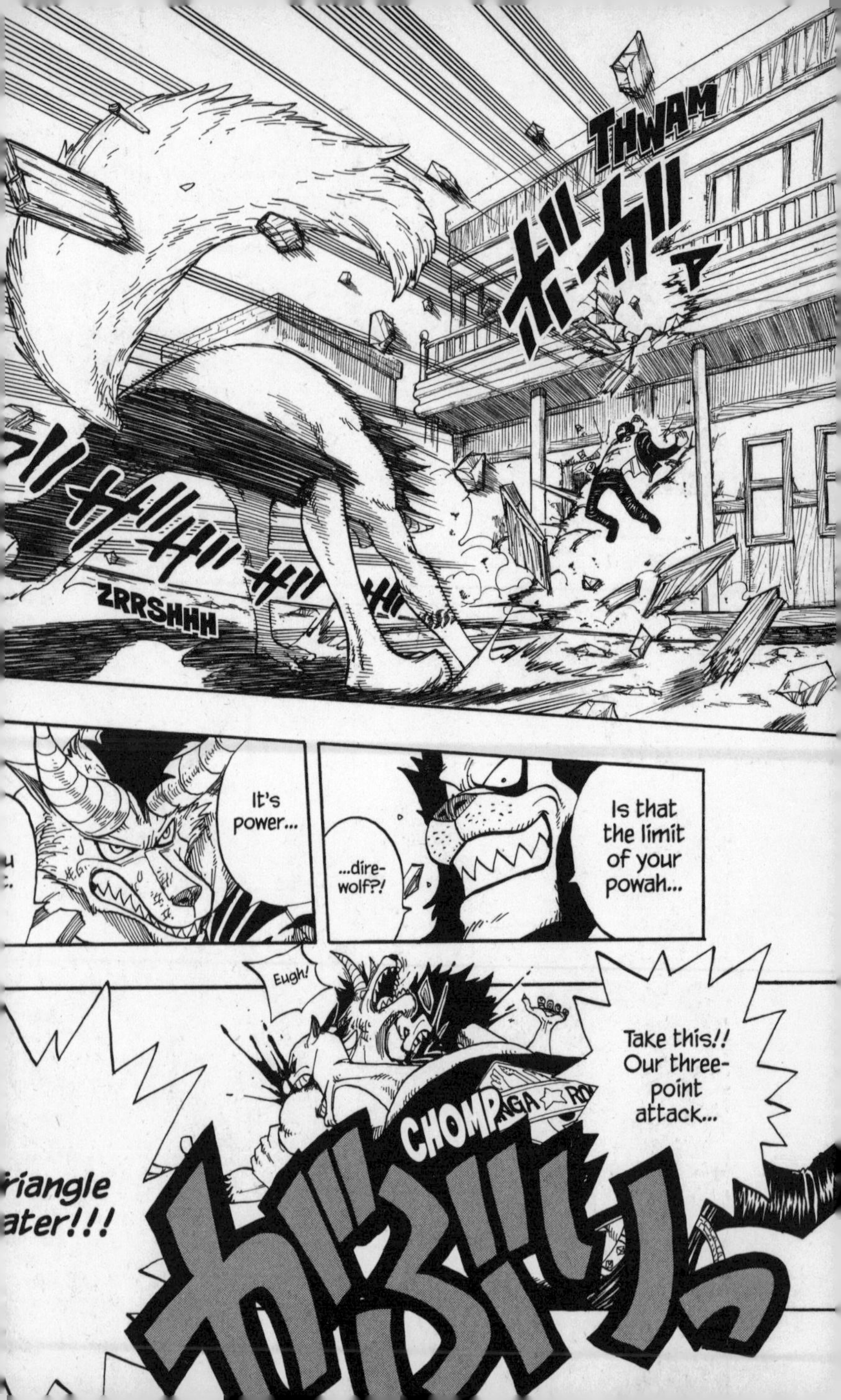
THWAM
ZRRSHHH
Is that the limit of your powah...
...dire-wolf?!
It's power...
Take this!! Our three-point attack...
Eugh!
CHOMP
riangle
ater!!!

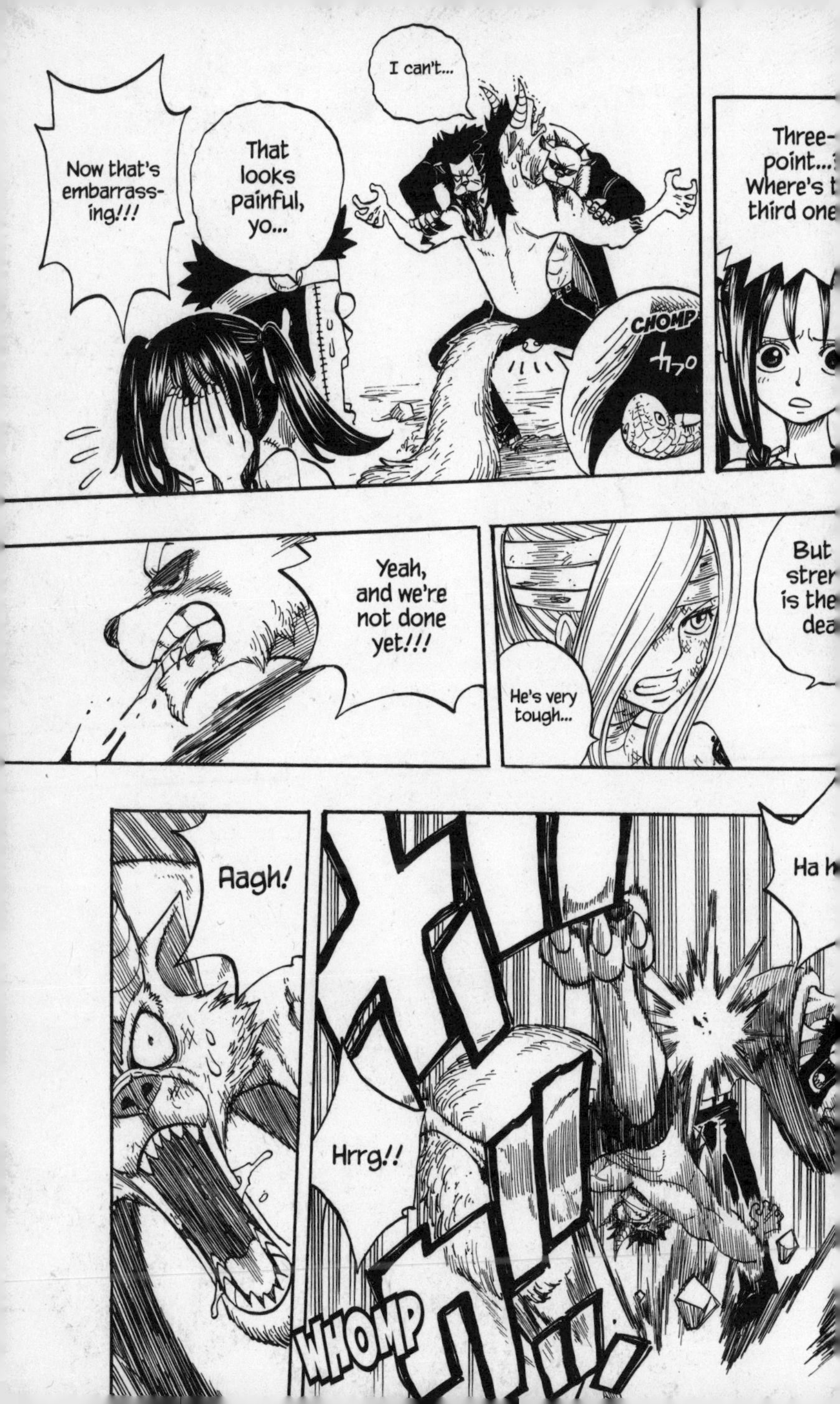
Three-
point...!?
Where's t
third one
I can't...
That looks painful, yo...
Now that's embarrassing!!!
CHOMP
But
strer
is the
dea
He's very tough...
Yeah, and we're not done yet!!!
Ha h
Hrrg!!
WHOMP
Aagh!

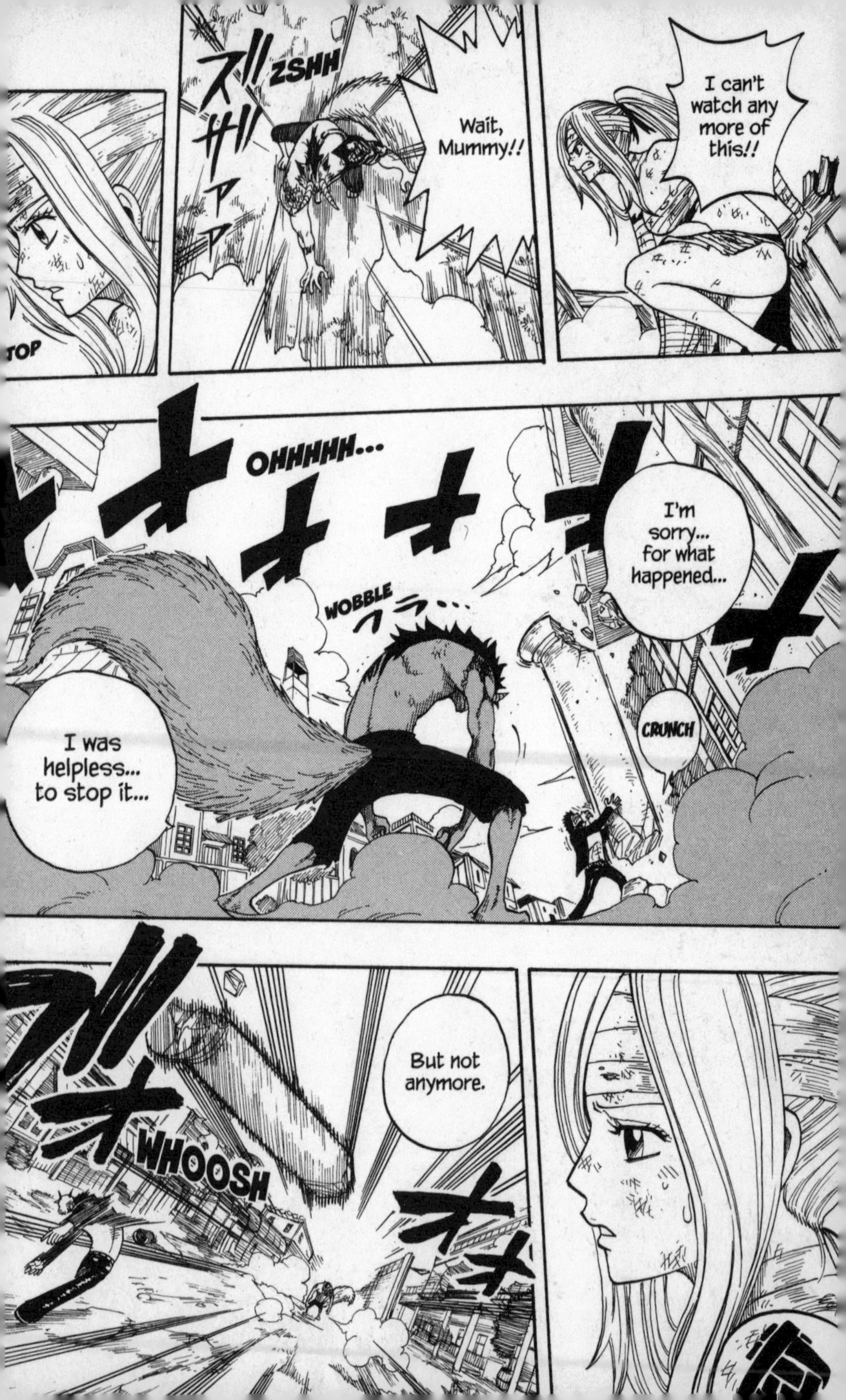
I can't watch any more of this!!
ZSHH
Wait, Mummy!!
TOP
I'm sorry... for what happened...
OHHHHH...
WOBBLE
CRUNCH
I was helpless... to stop it...
But not anymore.
WHOOSH

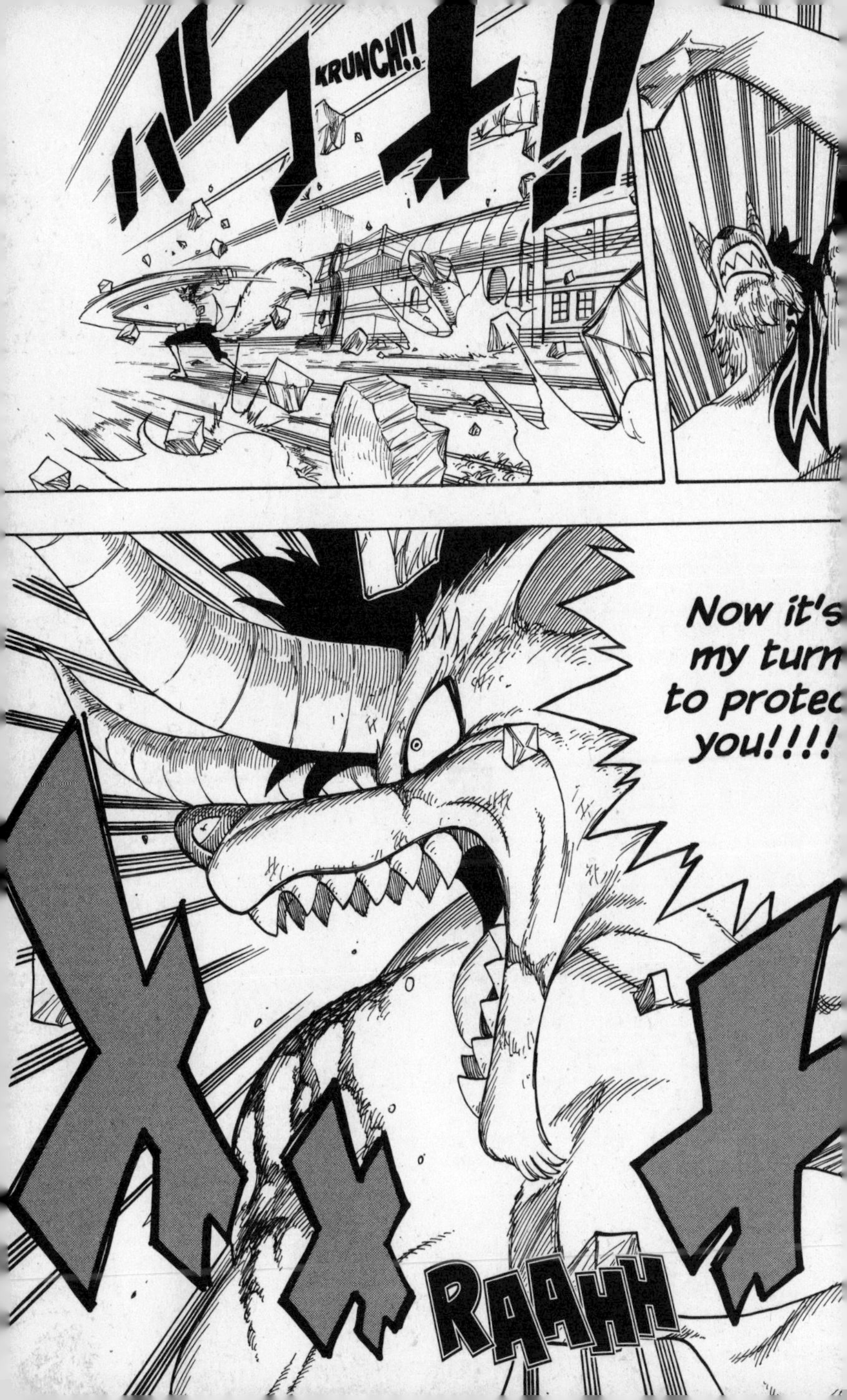
KRUNCH!!
Now it's my turn to protec you!!!!
RAAHH

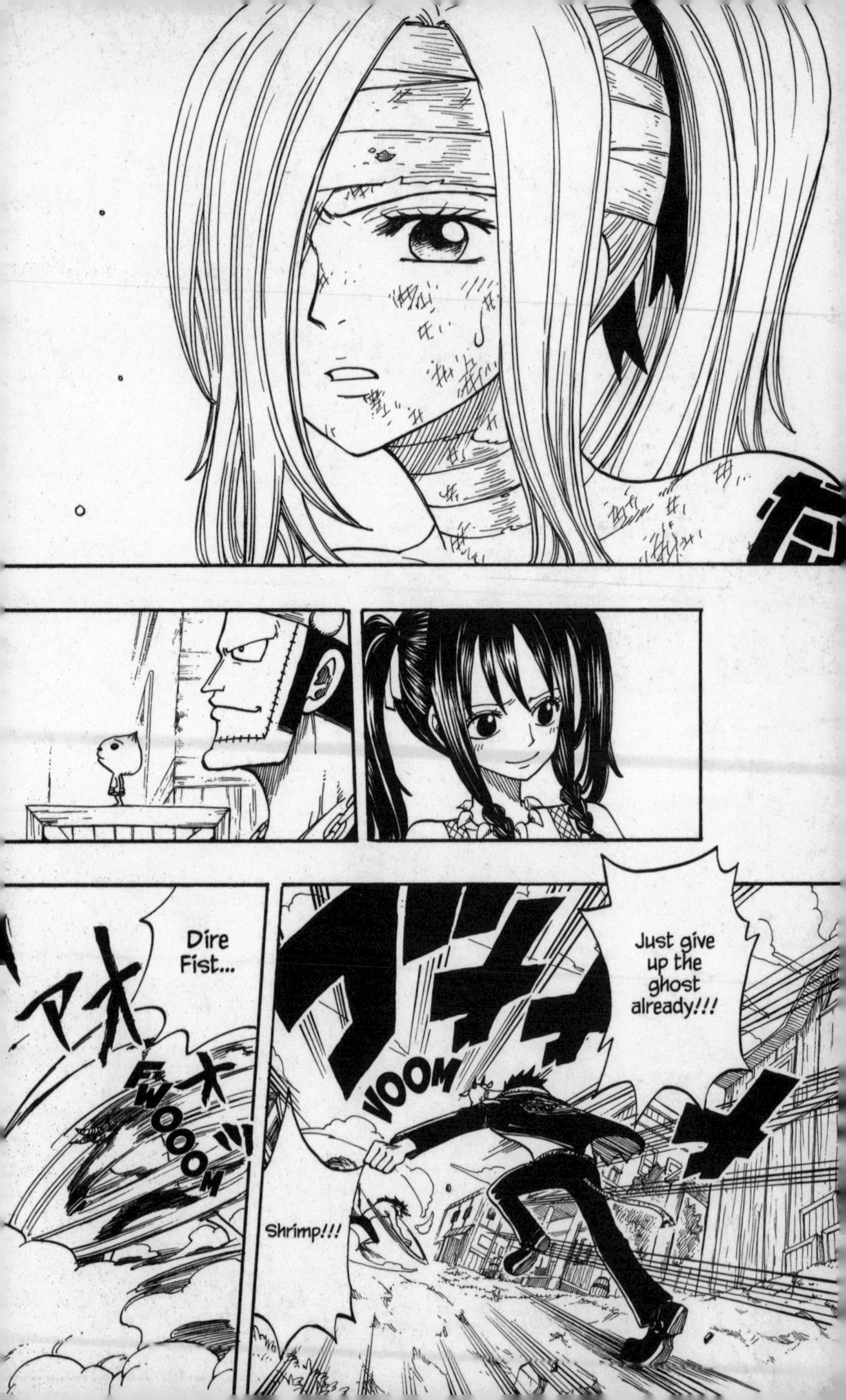
Just give up the ghost already!!!
VOOM
Shrimp!!!
Dire Fist...
FWOOOM

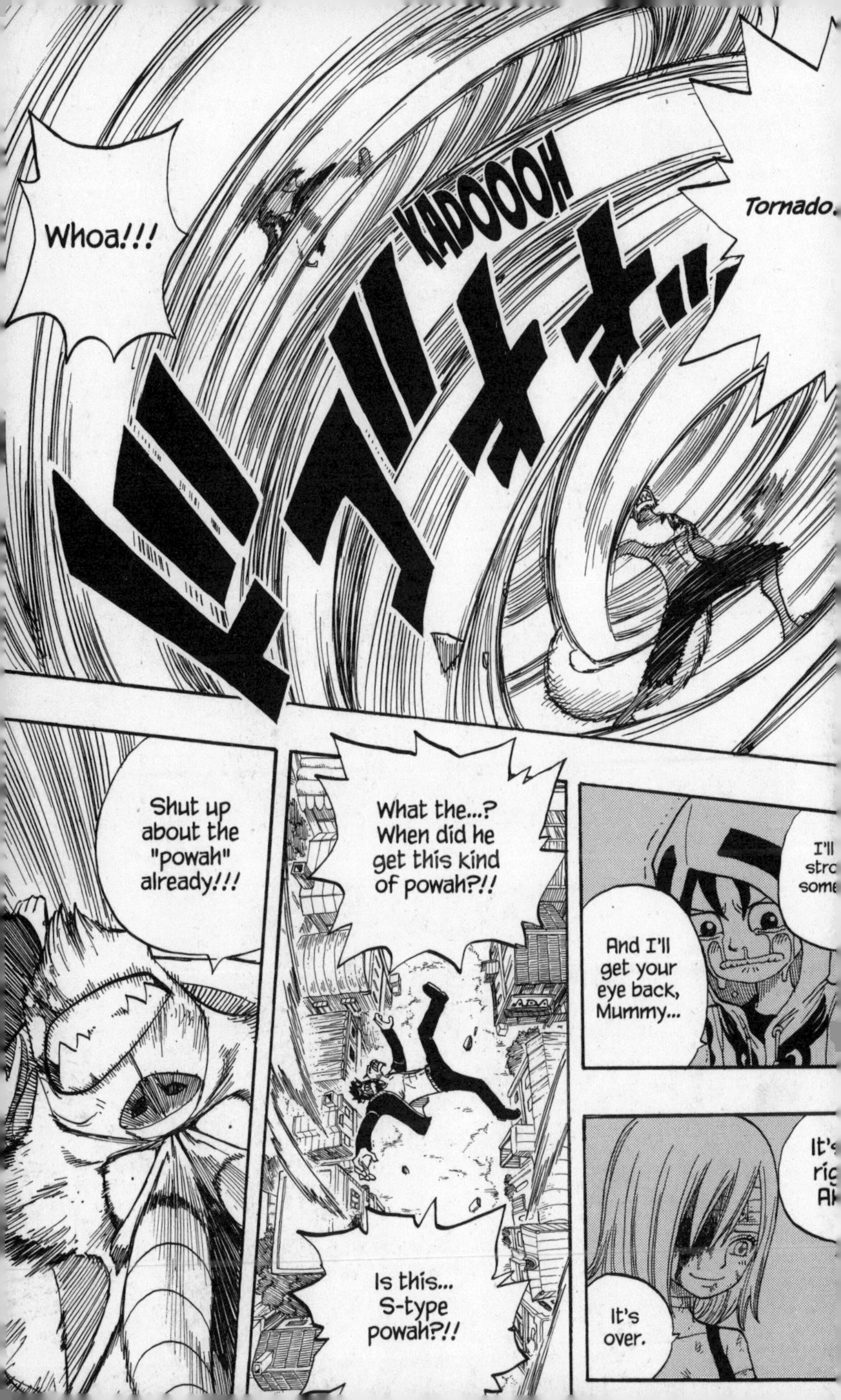

Tornado...
KADOOOH
Whoa!!!
I'll stro some
And I'll get your eye back, Mummy...
It's rig Al
It's over.
What the...? When did he get this kind of powah?!!
Is this... S-type powah?!!
Shut up about the "powah" already!!!

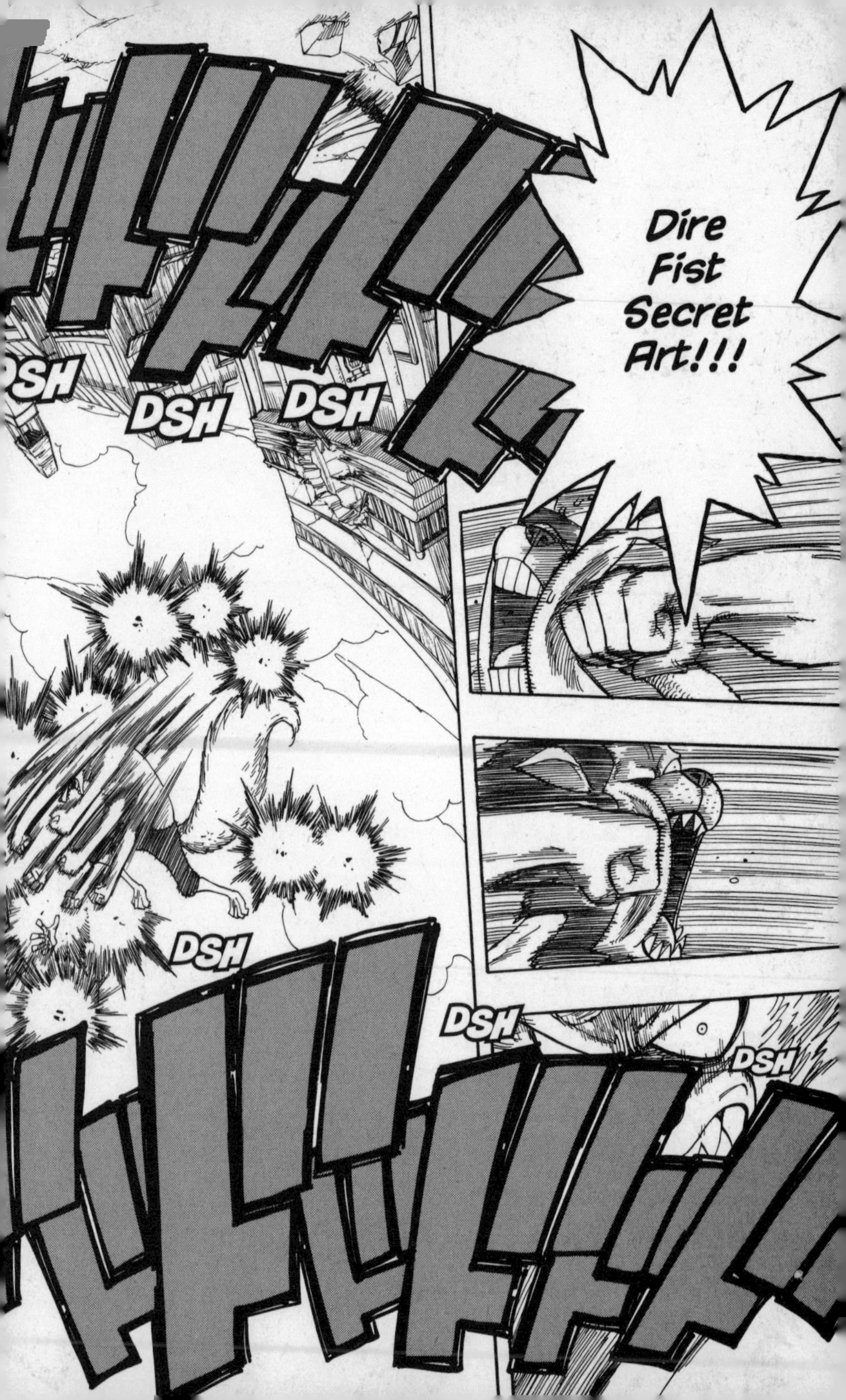

Dire Fist Secret Art!!!
DSH
DSH
DSH
DSH
DSH
DSH

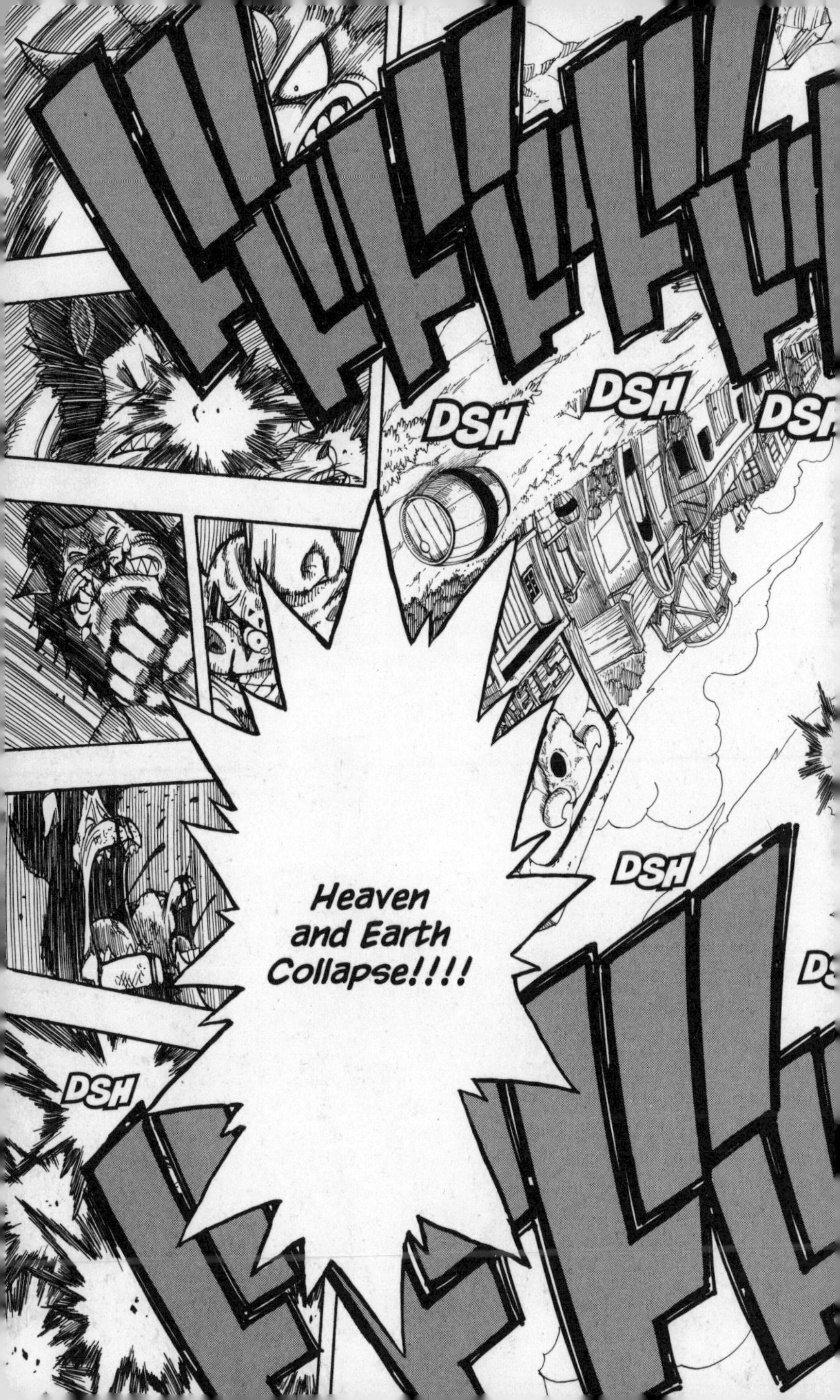
DSH
DSH
DSH
Heaven and Earth Collapse!!!!
DSH

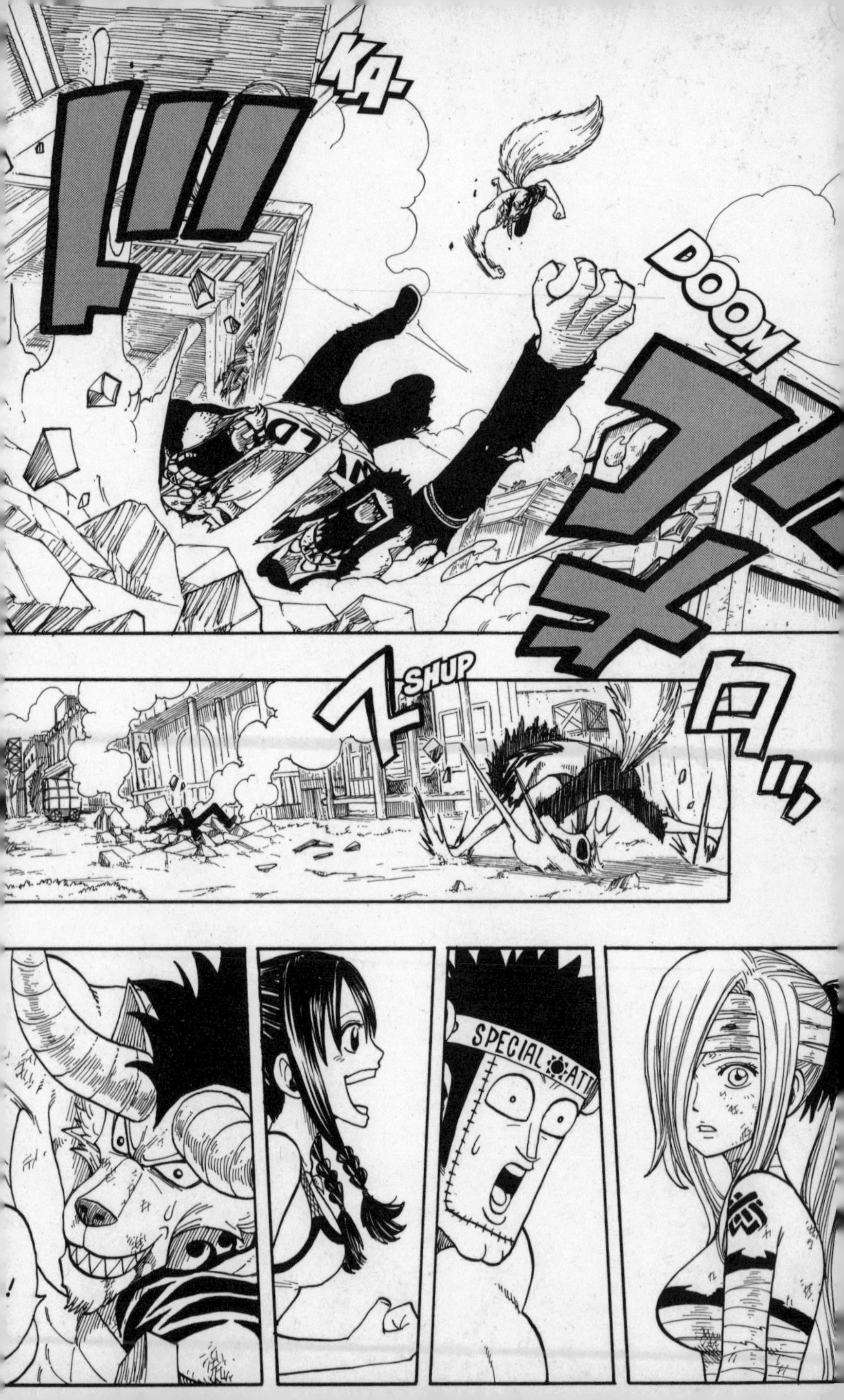
KA-
DOOM
SHUP
SPECIAL

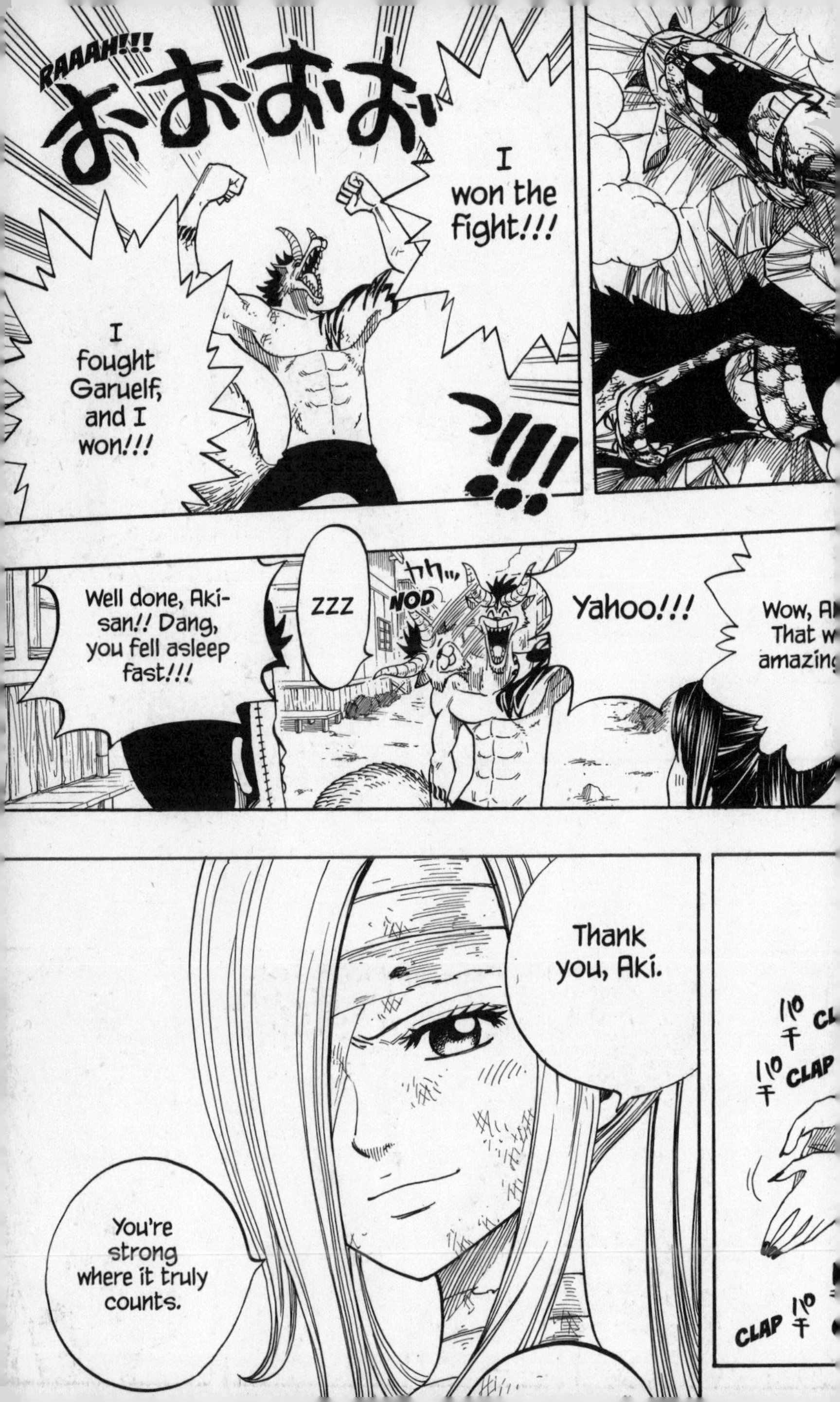

RAAAH!!!
おおおお
I won the fight!!!
I fought Garuelf, and I won!!!
っ!!!
Wow, A
That w
amazing
Yahoo!!!
NOD
ZZZ
Well done, Aki-san!! Dang, you fell asleep fast!!!
パチ CLAP
パチ CLAP
パチ CLAP
Thank you, Aki.
You're strong where it truly counts.

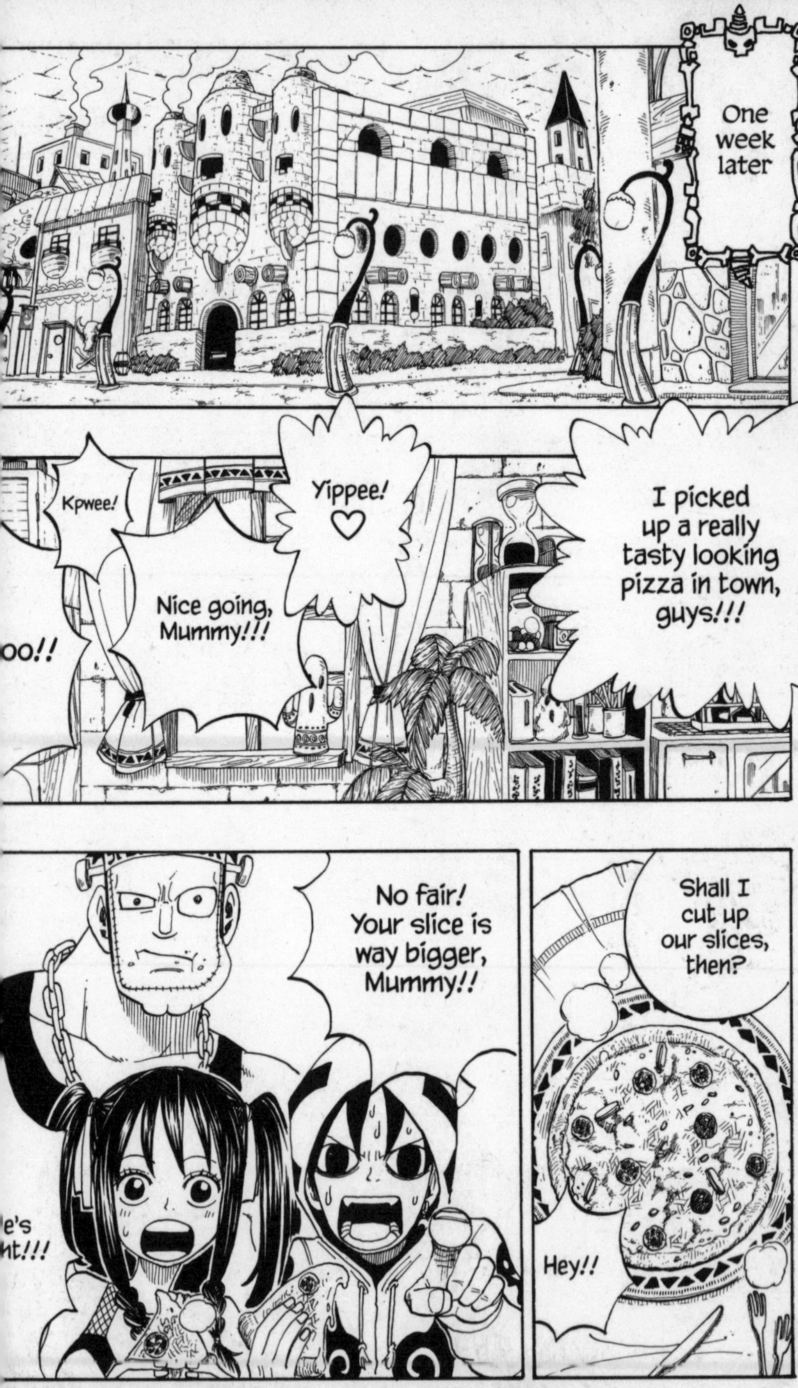
One week later
I picked up a really tasty looking pizza in town, guys!!!
Yippee! ♡
Kpwee!
Nice going, Mummy!!!
Shall I cut up our slices, then?
Hey!!
No fair! Your slice is way bigger, Mummy!!

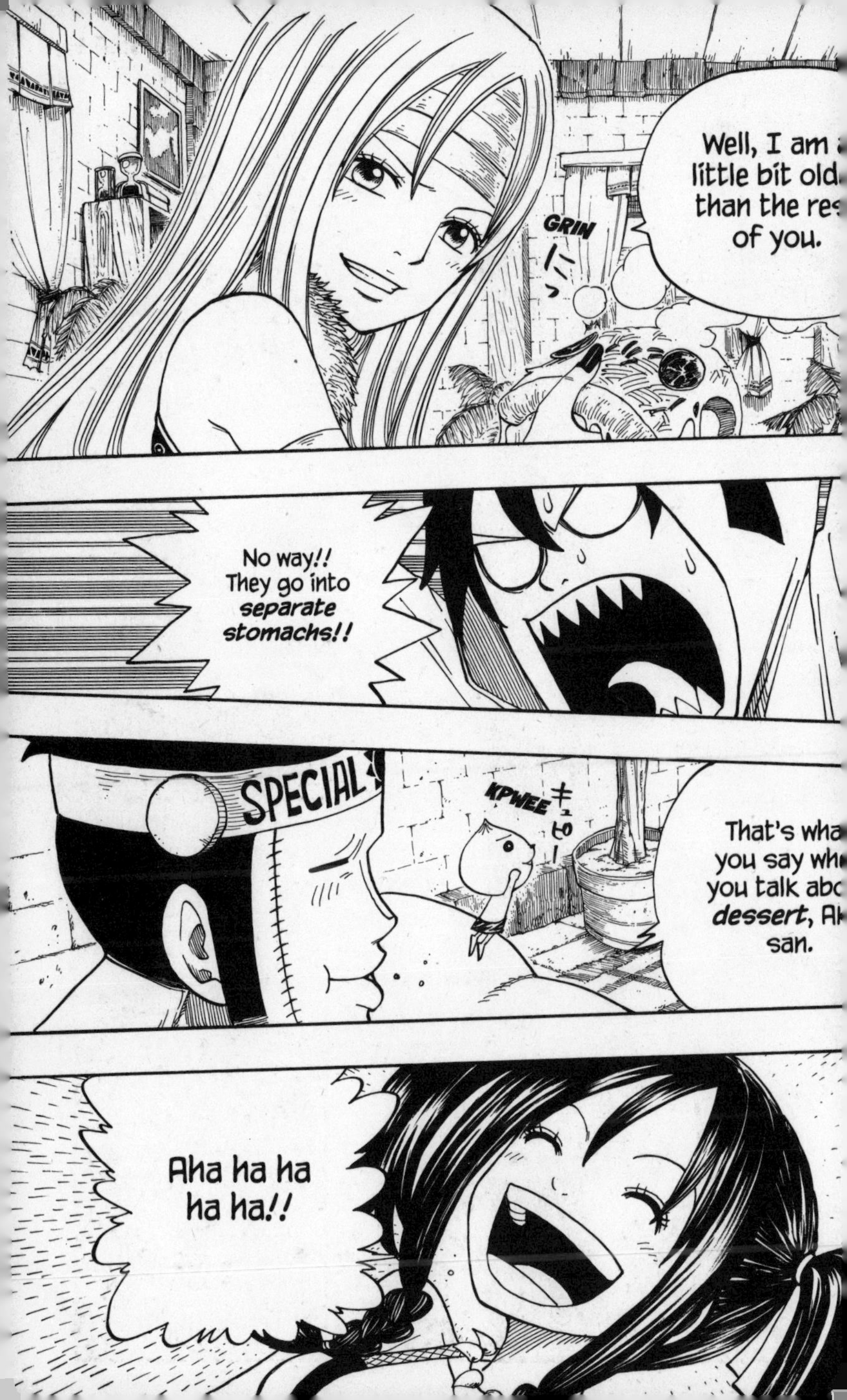

Well, I am a little bit old than the res of you.
GRIN
No way!! They go into *separate stomachs!!*
That's wha you say wh you talk abo *dessert*, Ak san.
KPWEE
SPECIAL
Aha ha ha ha ha!!

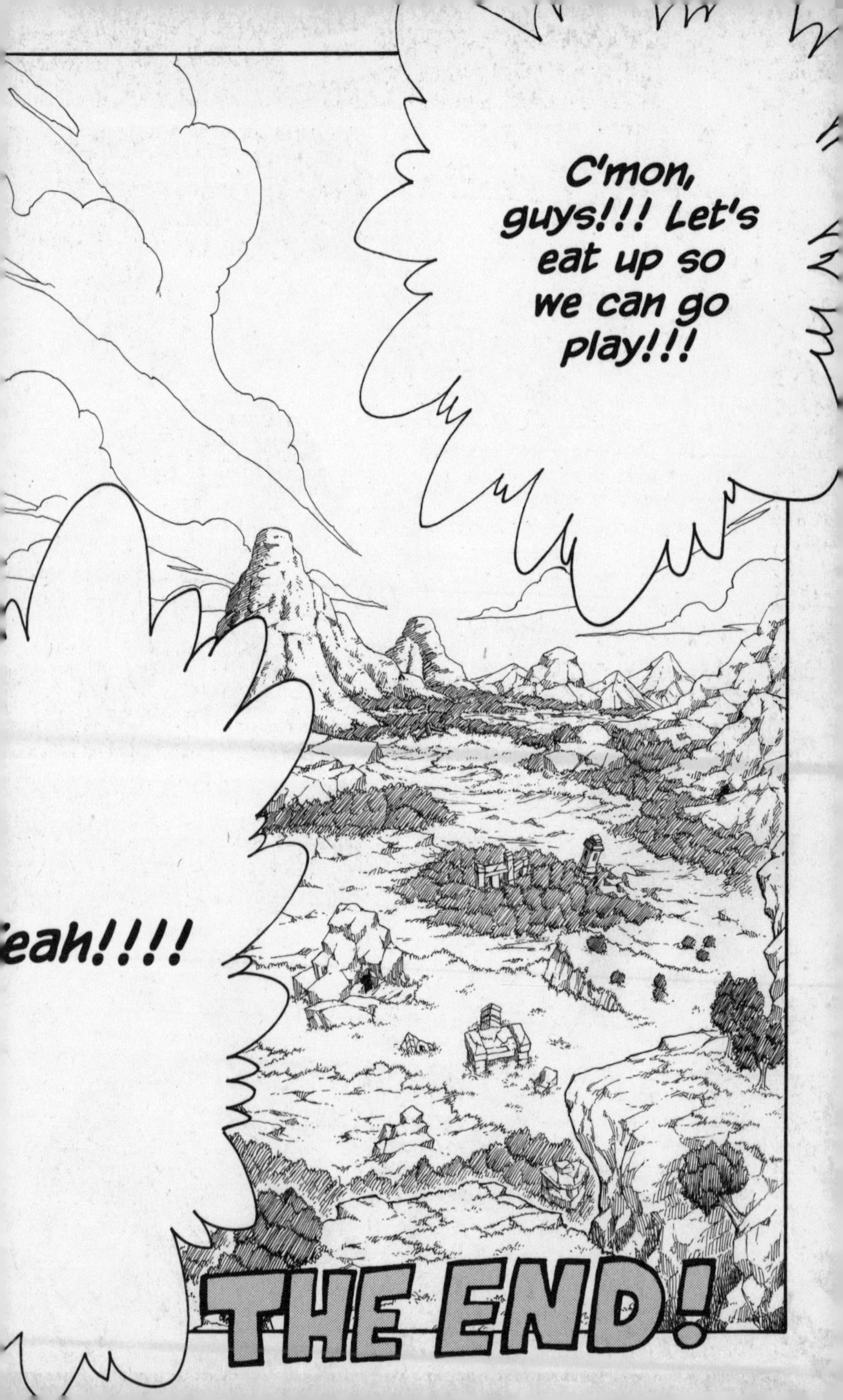
C'mon, guys!!! Let's eat up so we can go play!!!
eah!!!!
THE END!

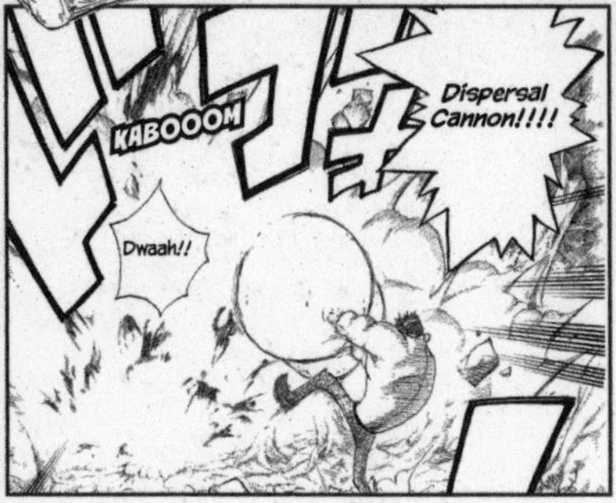
KABOOOM
Dispersal Cannon!!!!
Dwaah!!

James

Race: Frankenstein Type: Monster

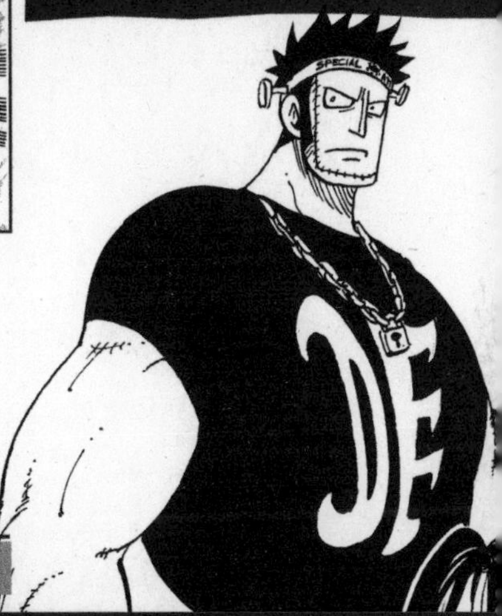

A manmade monster with weapons built all over his body. He can even detect enemies in the dark, as he has heat sensors inside his eyes. Powerful cannons are built into his elbows that shoot his forearms as ammo.

Bounty: 3500000

Danger Lvl: ★★★★☆☆

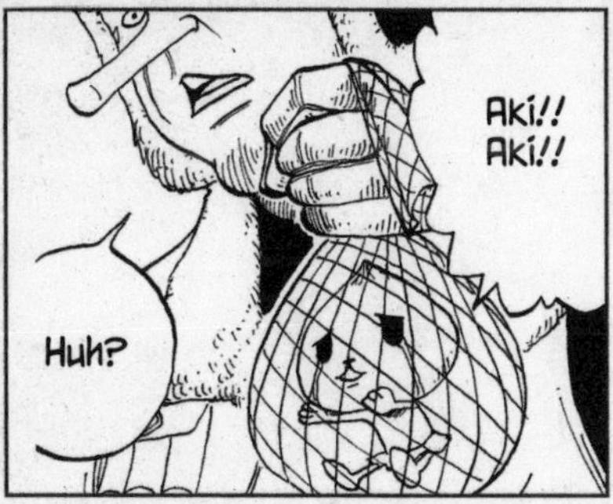
Aki!!
Aki!!
Huh?

Joba

Race: Onion Imp Type: Monster

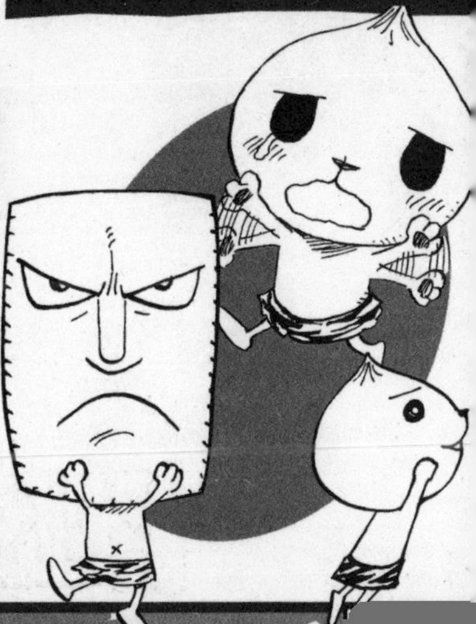

A monster whose head is shaped like an onion. Everything about him is a mystery, as no other onion imps have been sighted in several centuries. He hasn't taken part in any battles so far, but what if he did?

Bounty: Varies

Cute Lvl: ★★★★★★

Jenny

Race: Fairy   Type: Monster

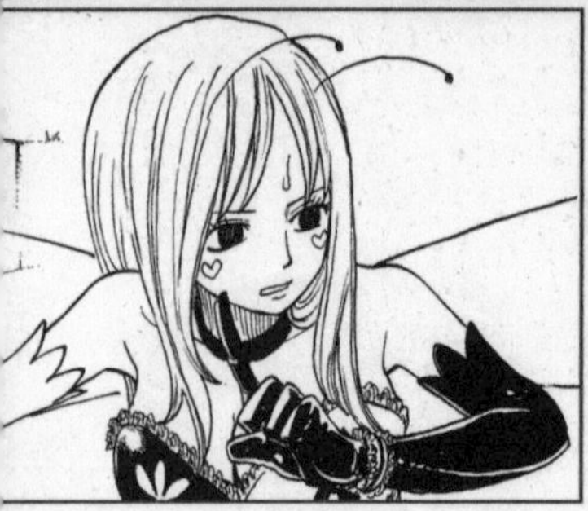

Fairies are only said to appear before those who are pure of soul. They hate conflict and live quietly, deep within the forest.

Babe Lvl: ★★★★★★

Bacon

Race: Ghost   Type: Monster

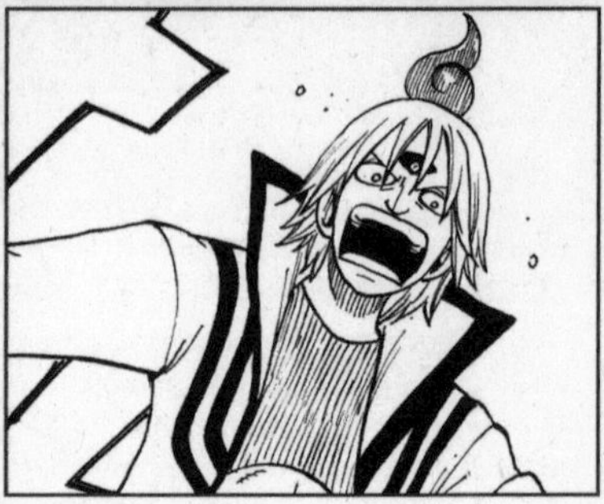

A monster with the ability to control human beings and monsters alike. His special attack involves turning invisible.

Danger Lvl: ★★★☆☆☆

Kiyo

Race: Fairy   Type: Monster

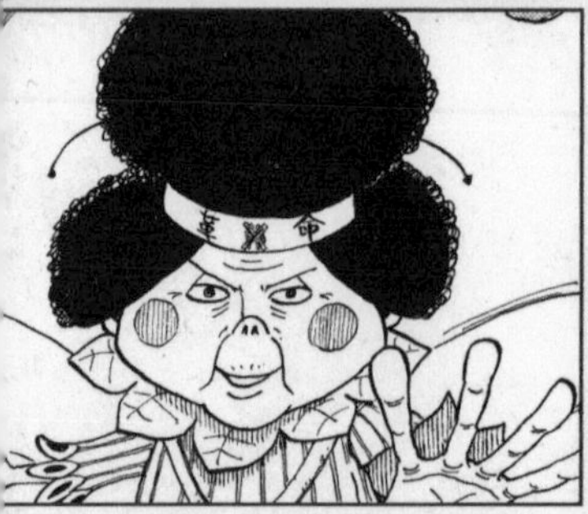

Impossible as it is to believe, she is Jenny's mother. Fairy powder has a sleep effect, which makes her "Dream Flow" attack very potent.

etdown Lvl: ★★★★★★

Garuelf

Race: Chimaera   Type: Monster

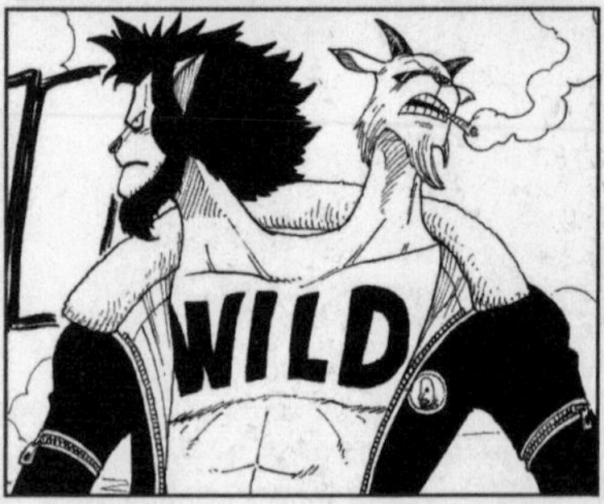
WILD

He's famed for having two heads, but there's actually a third on his tail. Garuelf's special move is "Triangle Eater," a bite attack with all three heads.

Danger Lvl: ★★★★★★

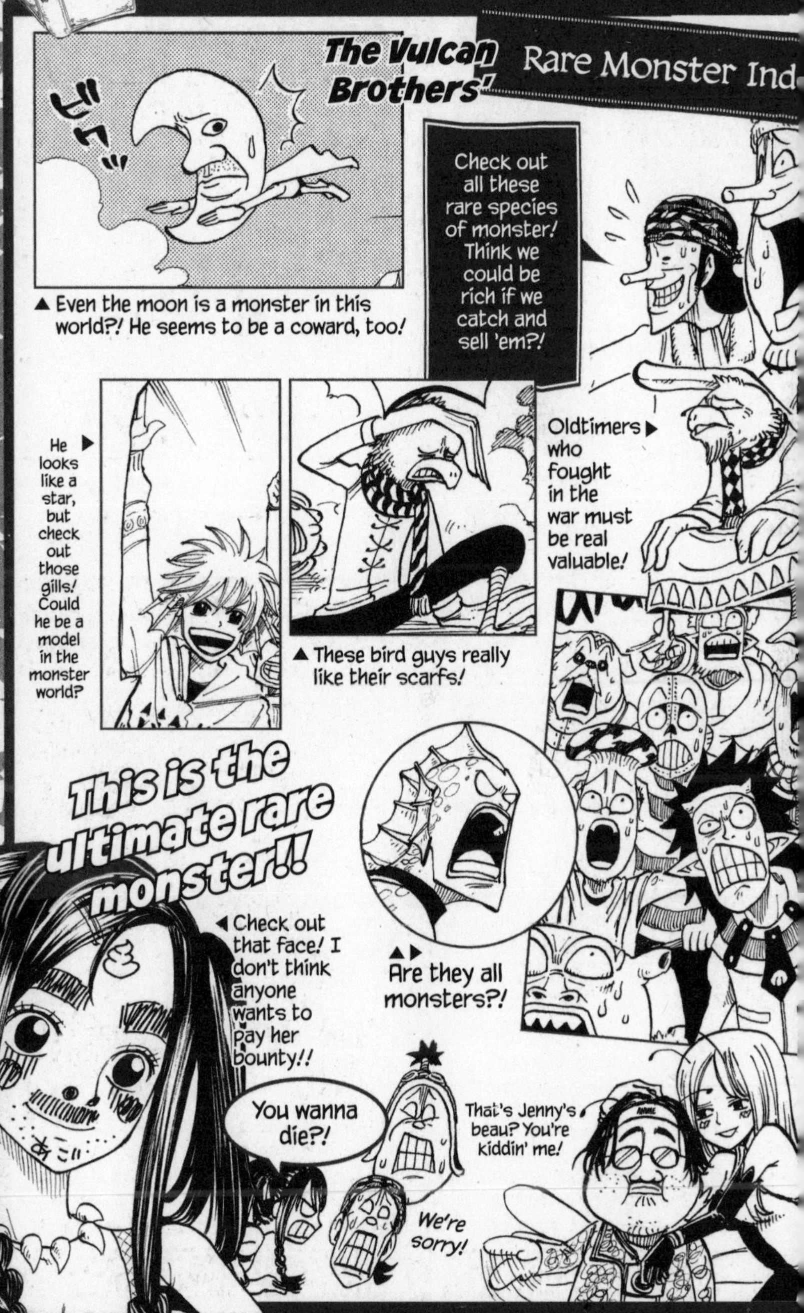
The Vulcan Brothers' Rare Monster Ind
Check out all these rare species of monster! Think we could be rich if we catch and sell 'em?!
▲ Even the moon is a monster in this world?! He seems to be a coward, too!
Oldtimers ▶ who fought in the war must be real valuable!
▲ These bird guys really like their scarfs!
He ▶ looks like a star, but check out those gills! Could he be a model in the monster world?
This is the ultimate rare monster!!
▲▶ Are they all monsters?!
◀ Check out that face! I don't think anyone wants to pay her bounty!!
That's Jenny's beau? You're kiddin' me!
You wanna die?!
We're sorry!

Beloved Failed Characters, No. 3

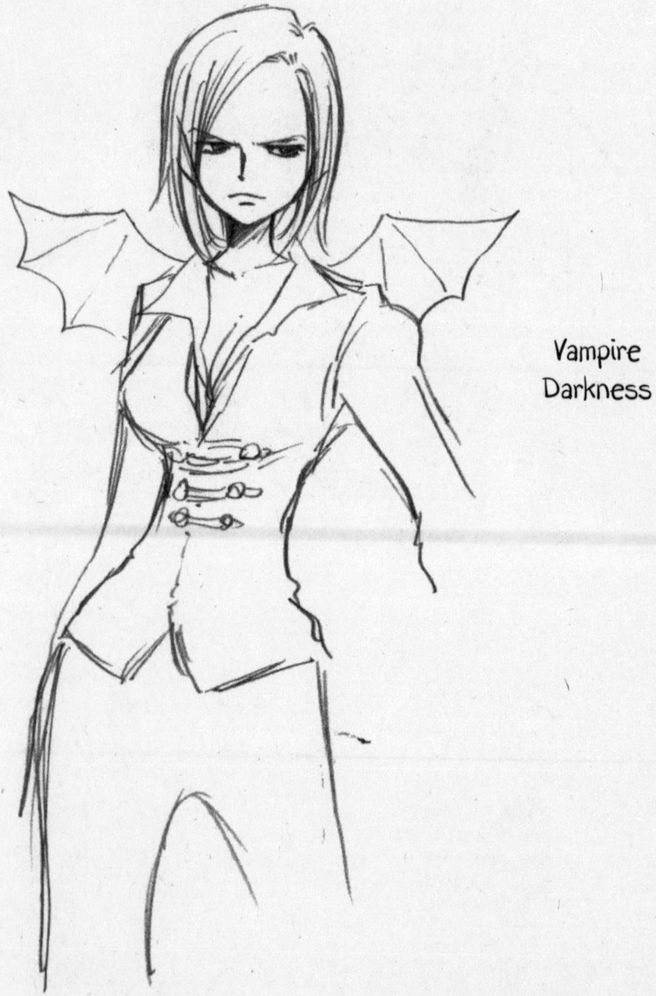
Vampire
Darkness

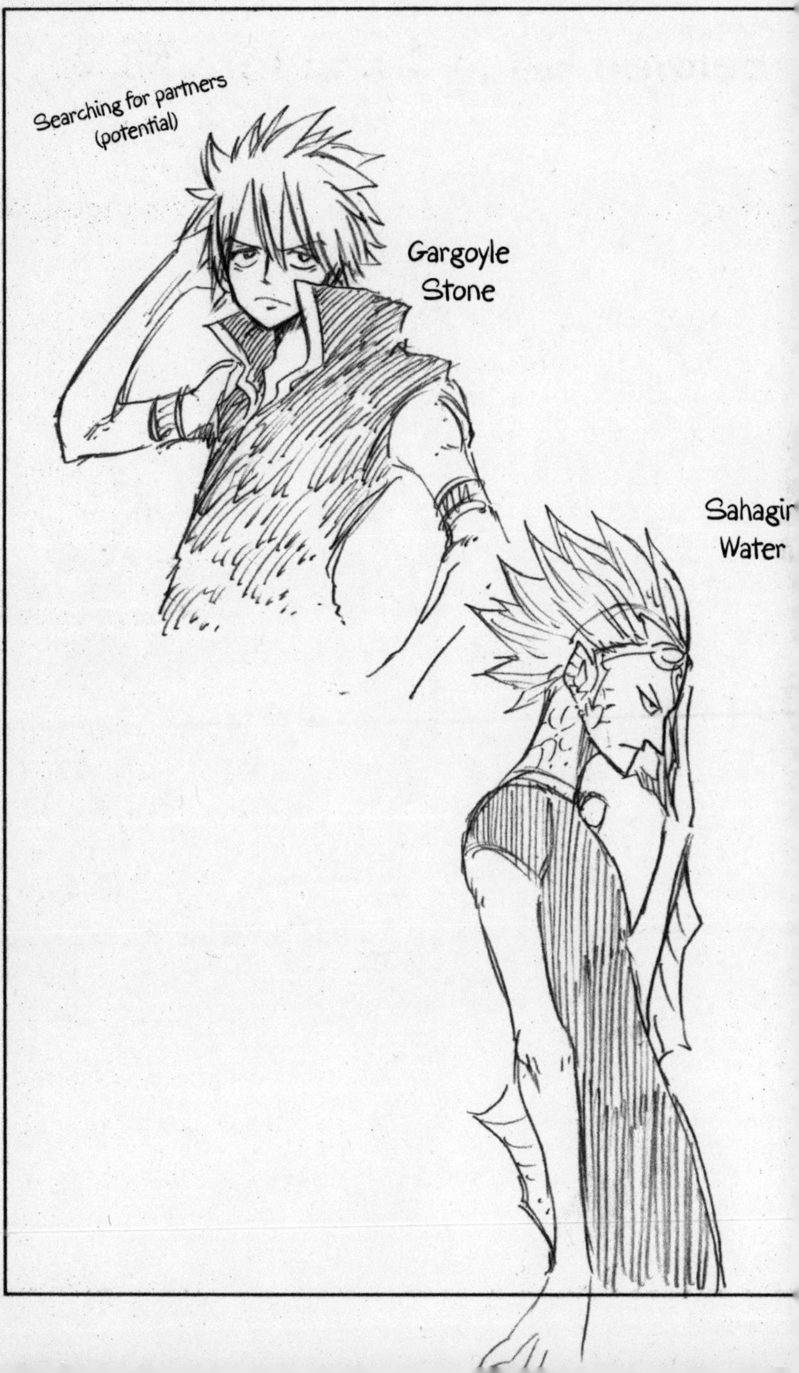
Searching for partners
(potential)
Gargoyle
Stone
Sahagin
Water

Welcome! MONSTER's Gallery★

Art Gallery

by Hiro's Staff

Shinya, Ue-chan & Bobby

Presenting work by Hiro Mashima's assistant staff!!

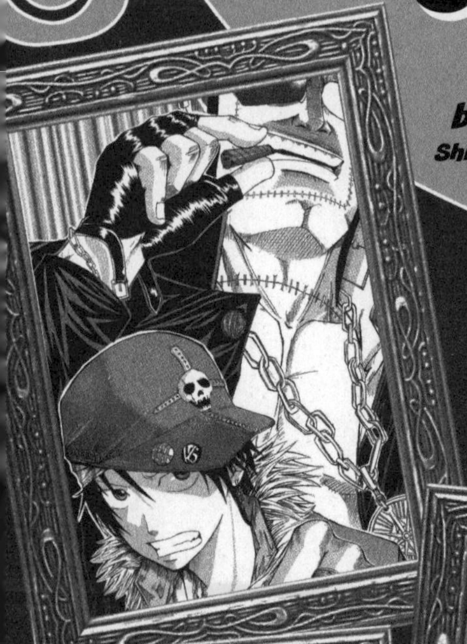

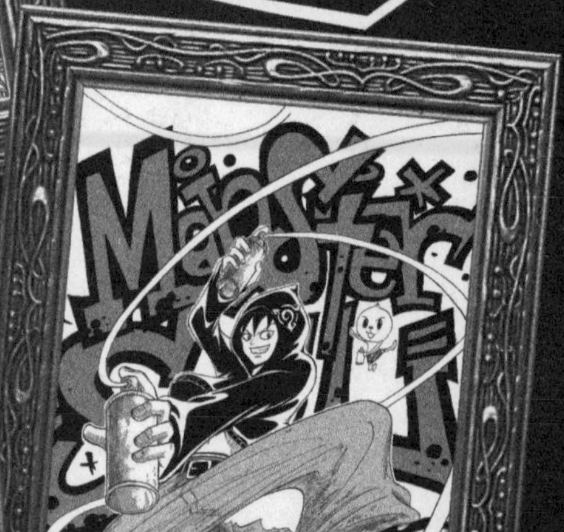

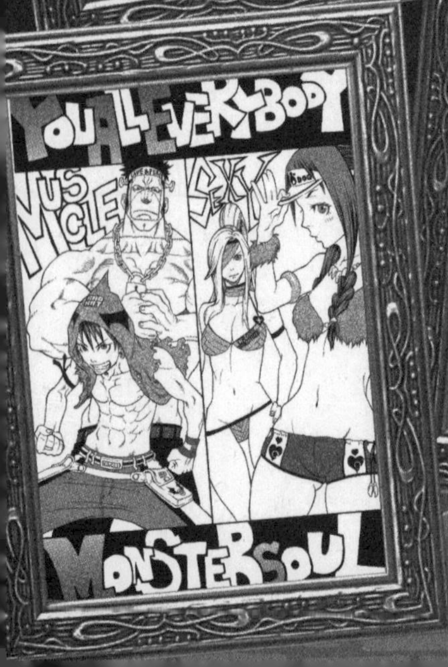
YOU ALL EVERYBODY
MUSCLE
SEXY
MONSTER SOUL

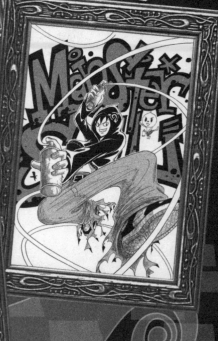

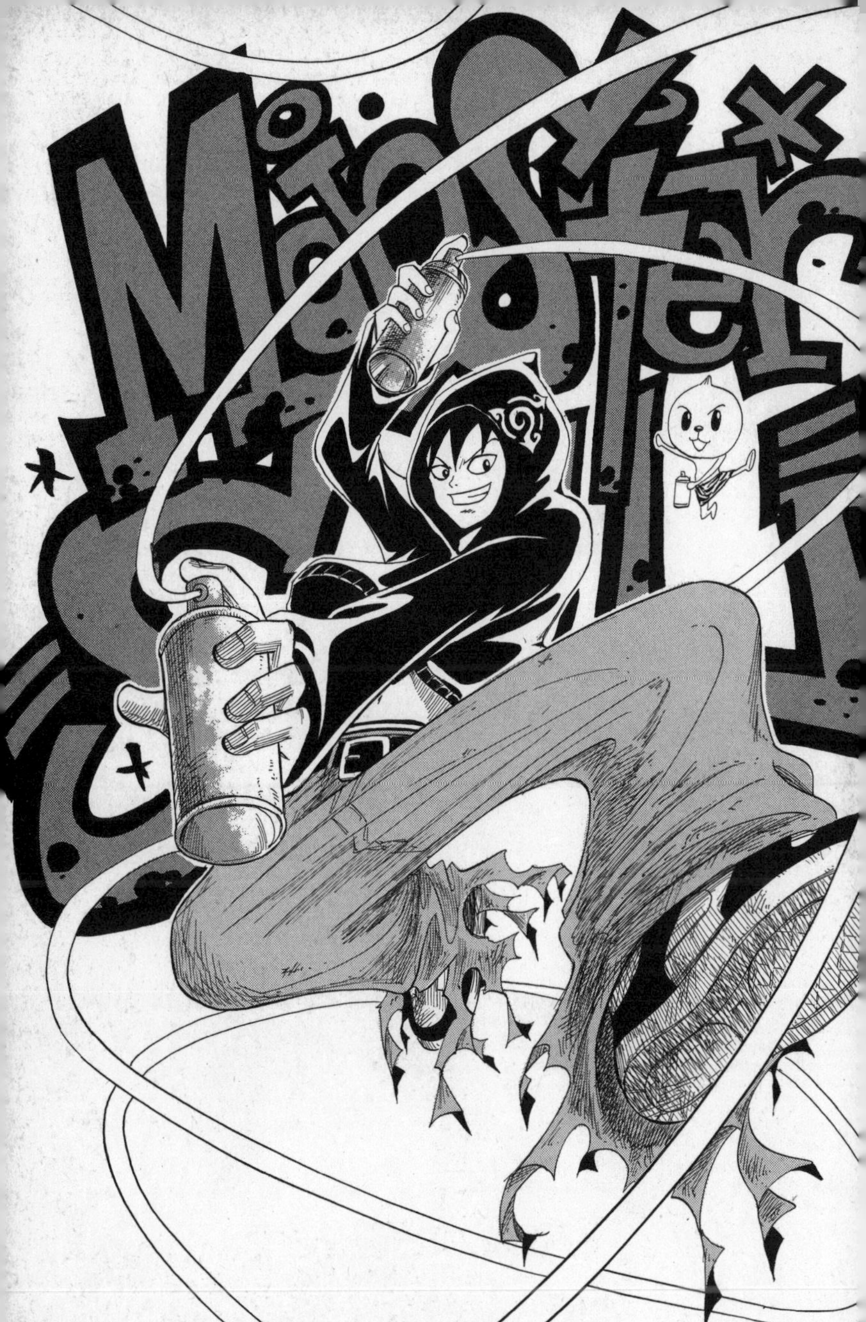

by Shinya Toda

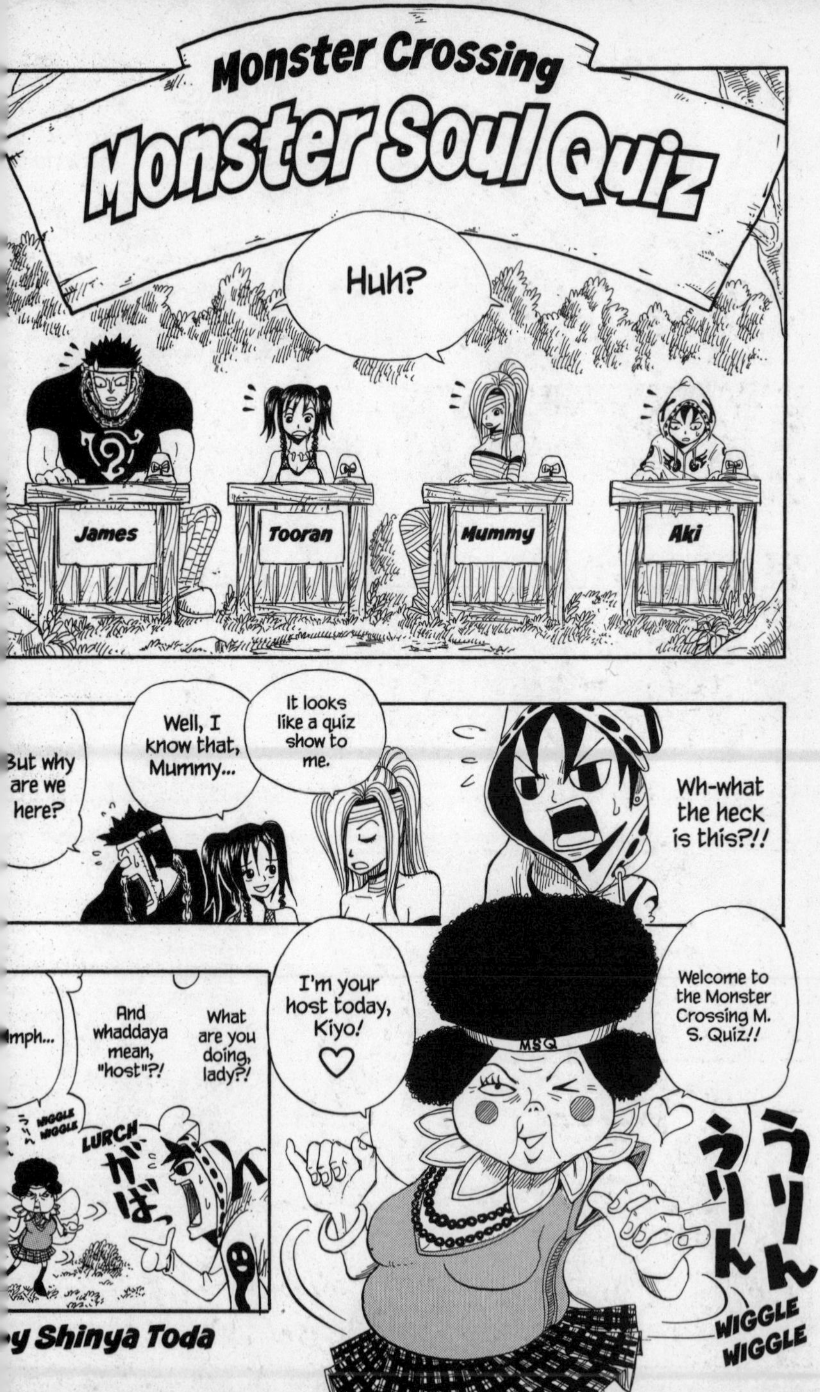
Monster Crossing
Monster Soul Quiz
Huh?
James
Tooran
Mummy
Aki
Wh-what the heck is this?!!
It looks like a quiz show to me.
Well, I know that, Mummy...
ut why are we here?
Welcome to the Monster Crossing M. S. Quiz!!
うりんうりん
WIGGLE WIGGLE
I'm your host today, Kiyo! ♡
What are you doing, lady?!
And whaddaya mean, "host"?!
mph...
がばっ
LURCH
うりん
WIGGLE WIGGLE
y Shinya Toda

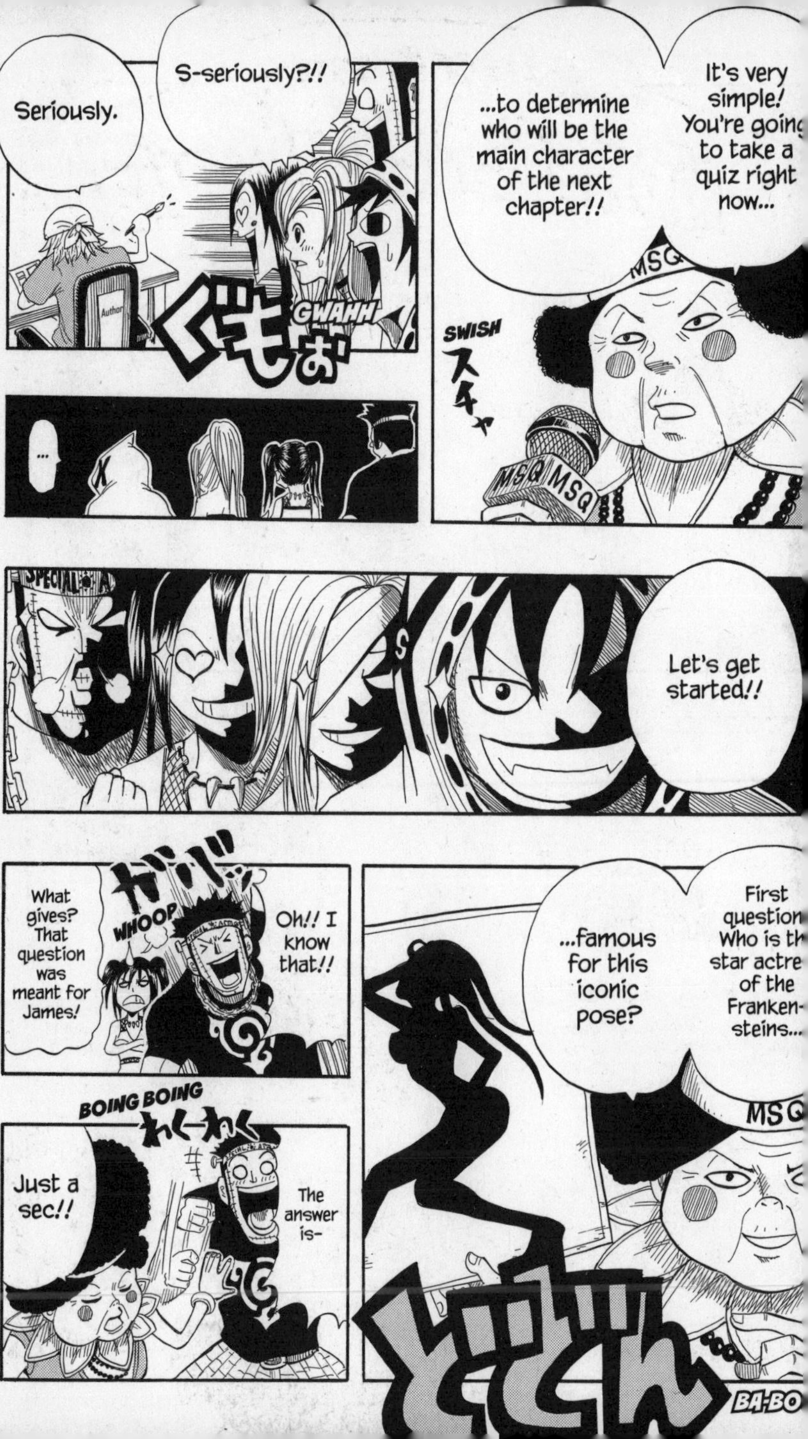

It's very simple! You're goin to take a quiz right now...
...to determine who will be the main character of the next chapter!!
SWISH
スキャ
S-seriously?!!
Seriously.
GWAHH
ぐもぉ
...
Let's get started!!
First questio Who is th star actre of the Franken-steins...
...famous for this iconic pose?
BA-BO
どーん
Oh!! I know that!!
WHOOP
ガバッ
What gives? That question was meant for James!
BOING BOING
わくわく
The answer is-
Just a sec!!

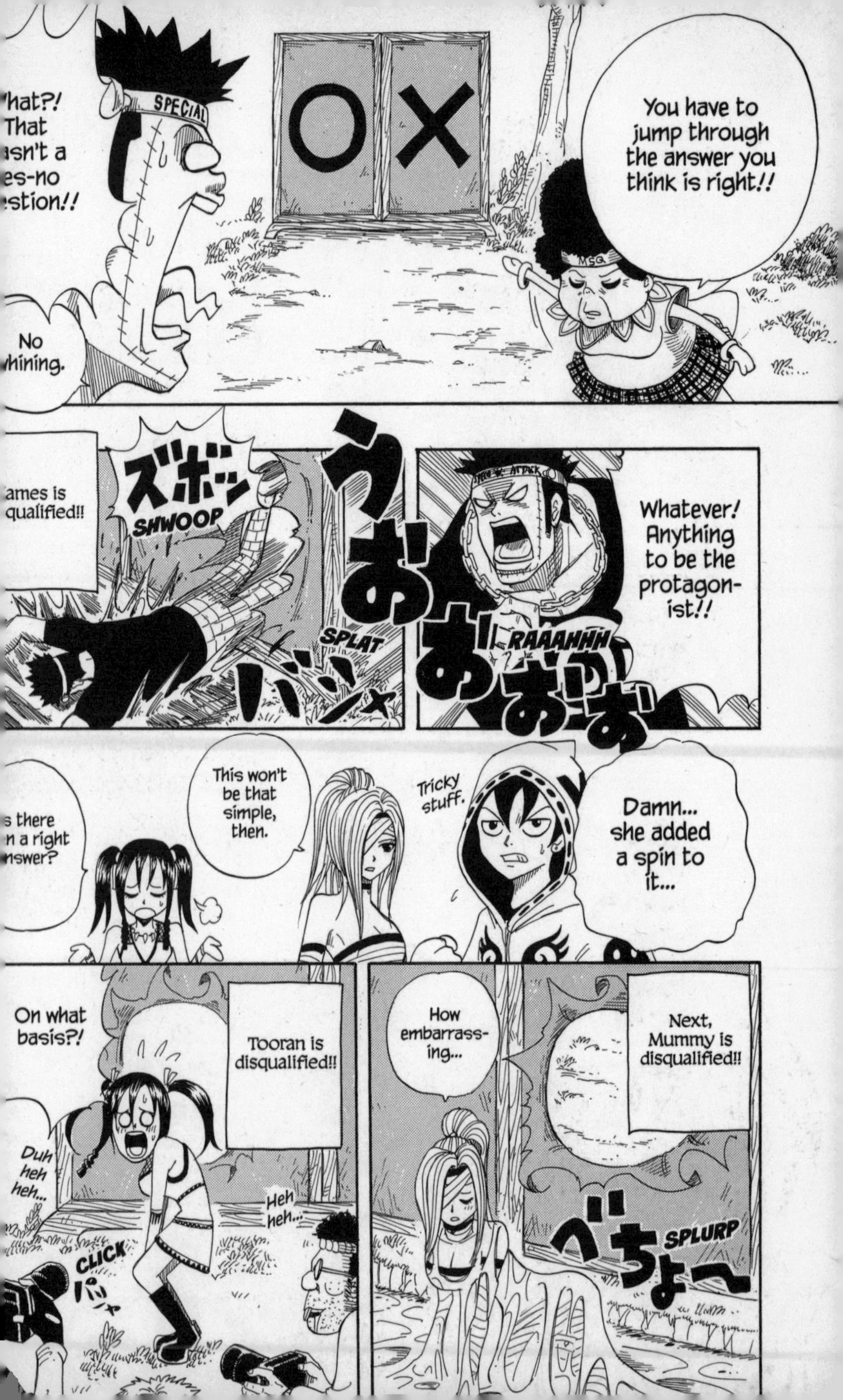
You have to jump through the answer you think is right!!
hat?! That asn't a es-no estion!!
No hining.
Whatever! Anything to be the protagonist!!
うおおおおお
RAAAHHH
ズボッ
SHWOOP
ames is qualified!!
SPLAT
バシャ
Damn... she added a spin to it...
Tricky stuff.
This won't be that simple, then.
s there n a right nswer?
Next, Mummy is disqualified!!
How embarrassing...
べちょ
SPLURP
Tooran is disqualified!!
On what basis?!
Heh heh...
Duh heh heh...
CLICK
パシャ

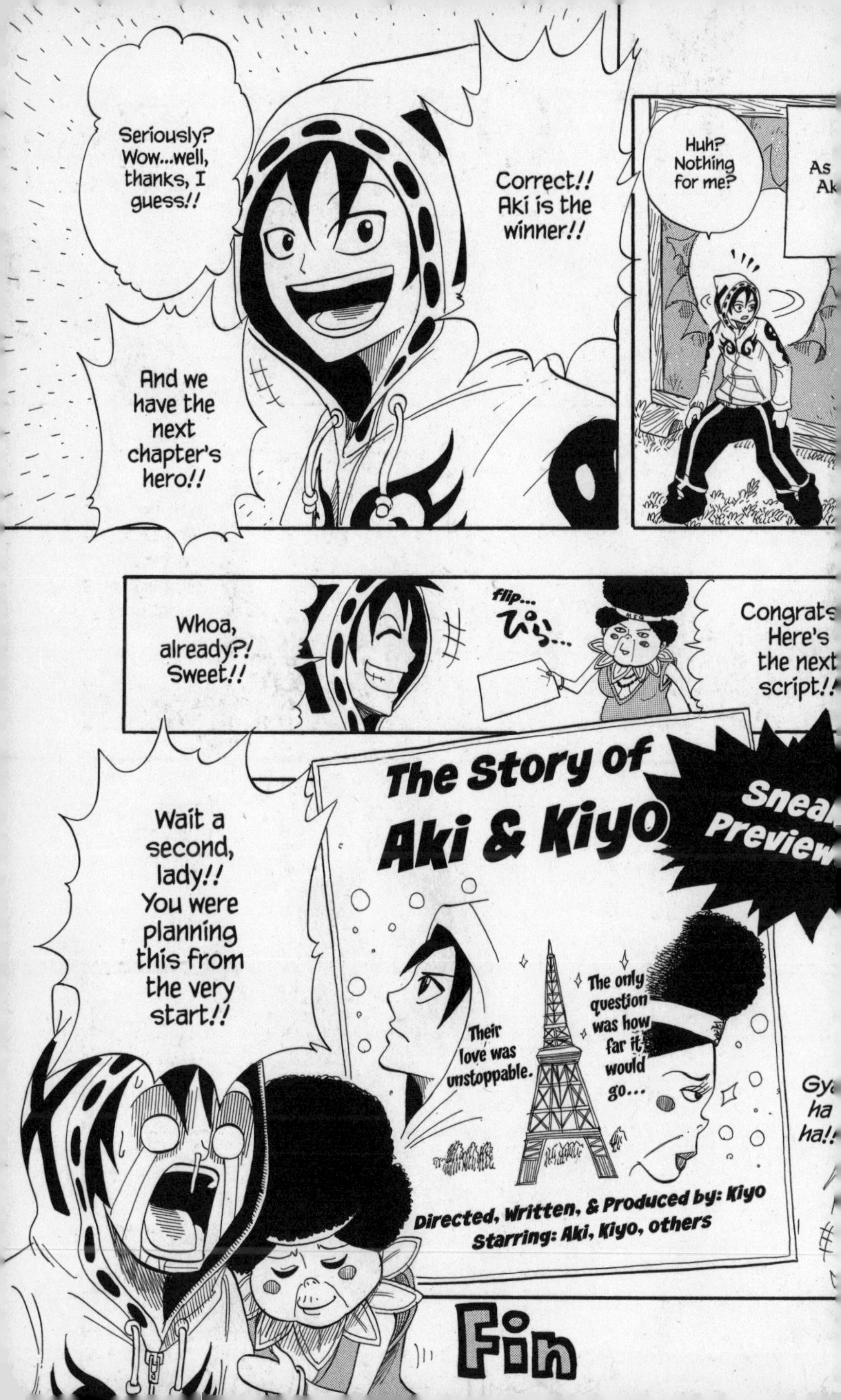
Huh? Nothing for me?
Correct!! Aki is the winner!!
Seriously? Wow...well, thanks, I guess!!
And we have the next chapter's hero!!
Congrats Here's the next script!!
flip...
ぴら...
Whoa, already?! Sweet!!
The Story of Aki & Kiyo
Their love was unstoppable.
The only question was how far it would go...
Directed, Written, & Produced by: Kiyo
Starring: Aki, Kiyo, others
Wait a second, lady!! You were planning this from the very start!!
Fin

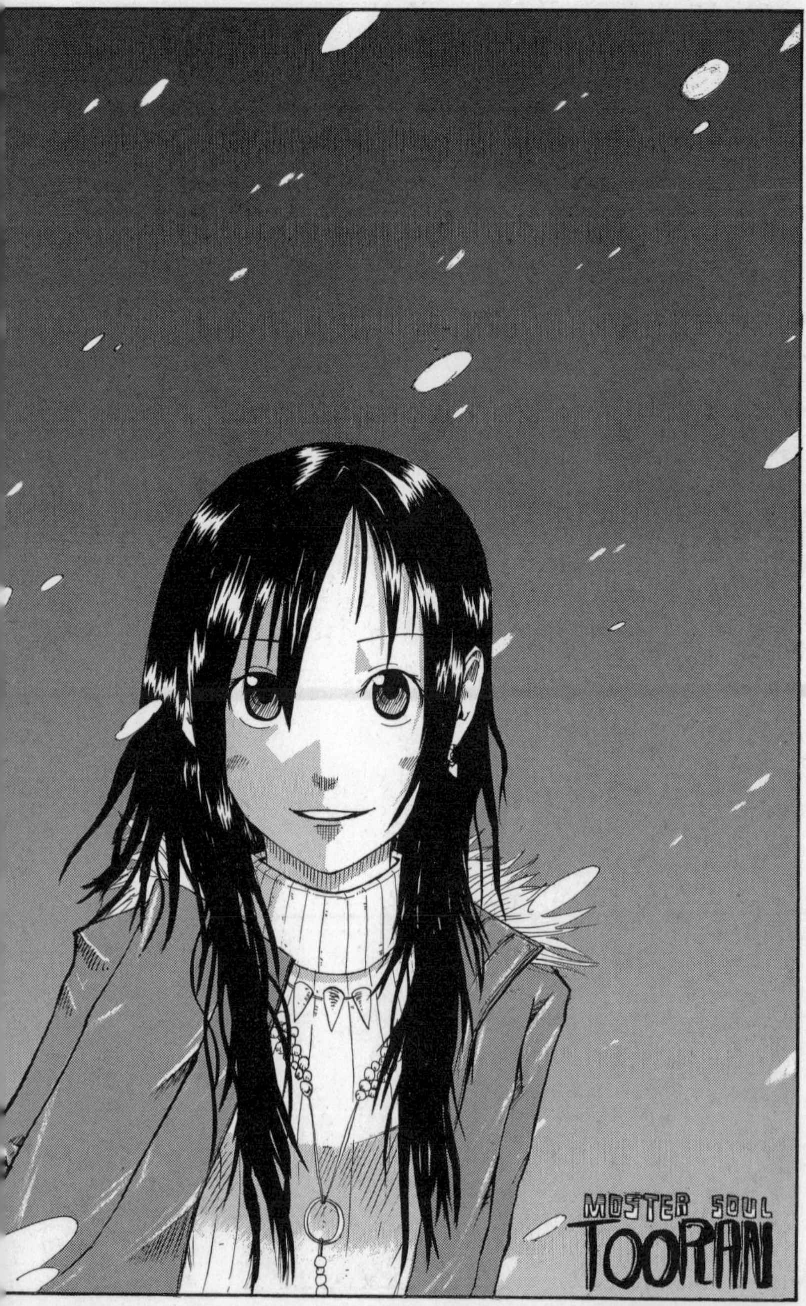
MOSTER SOUL
TOORAN
Ue-chan

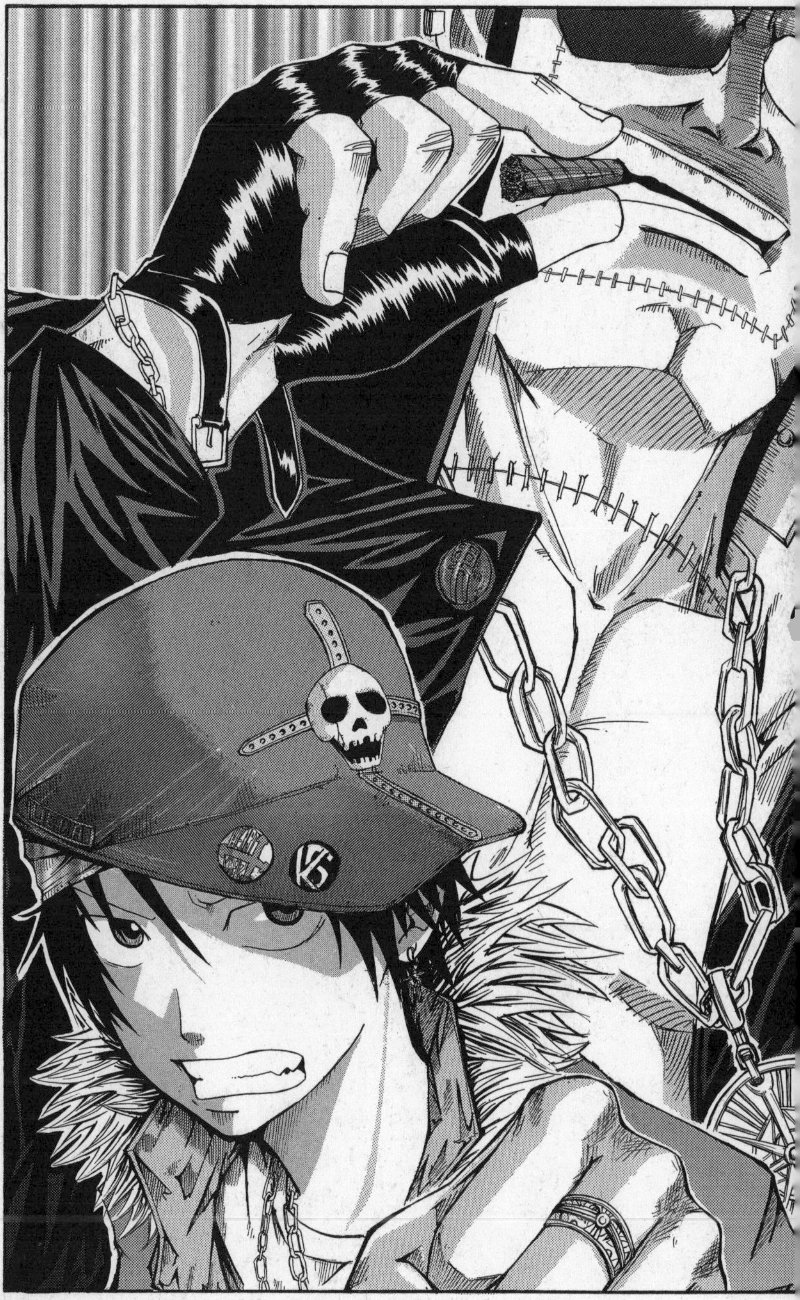

by Ue-chan

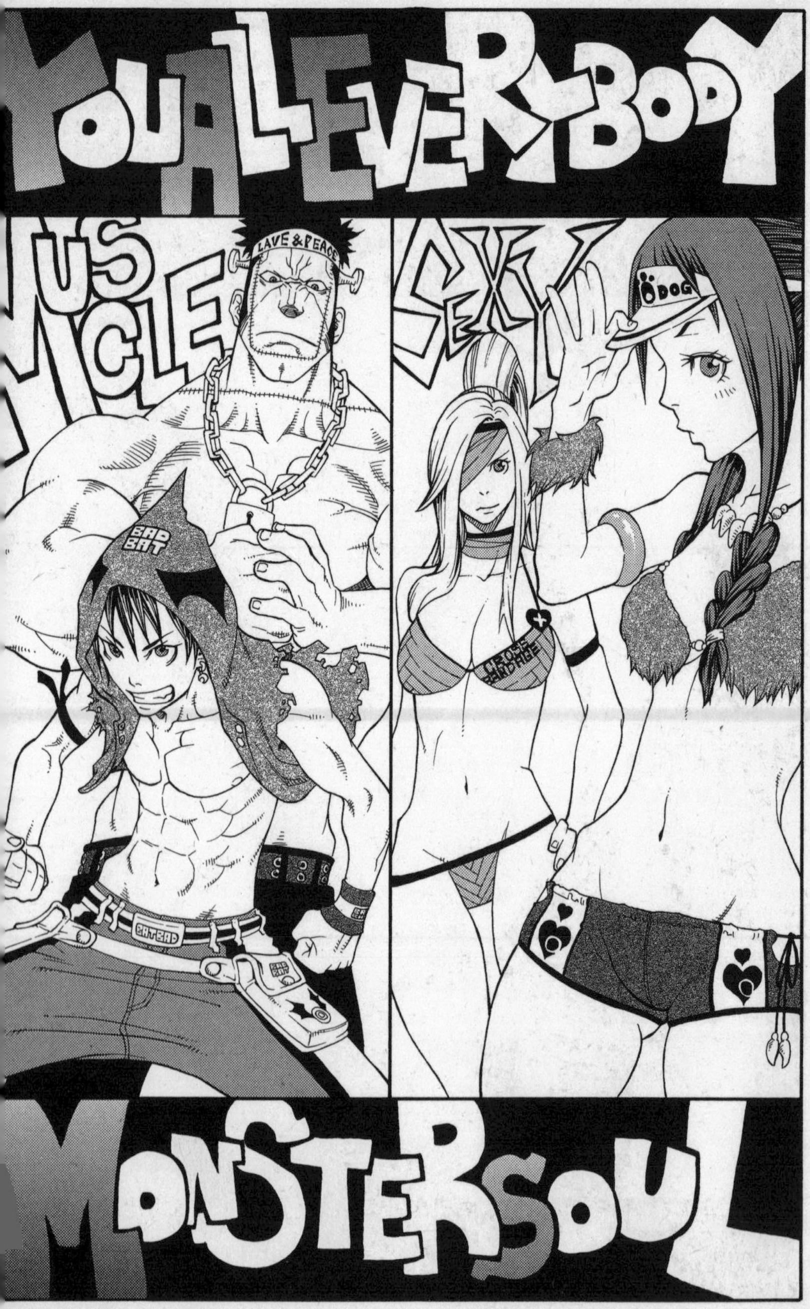
YOU ALL EVERYBODY
LAVE & PEACE
BAD BAT
SEXY
DOG
CROSS BANDAGE
MONSTER SOUL

y Bobby

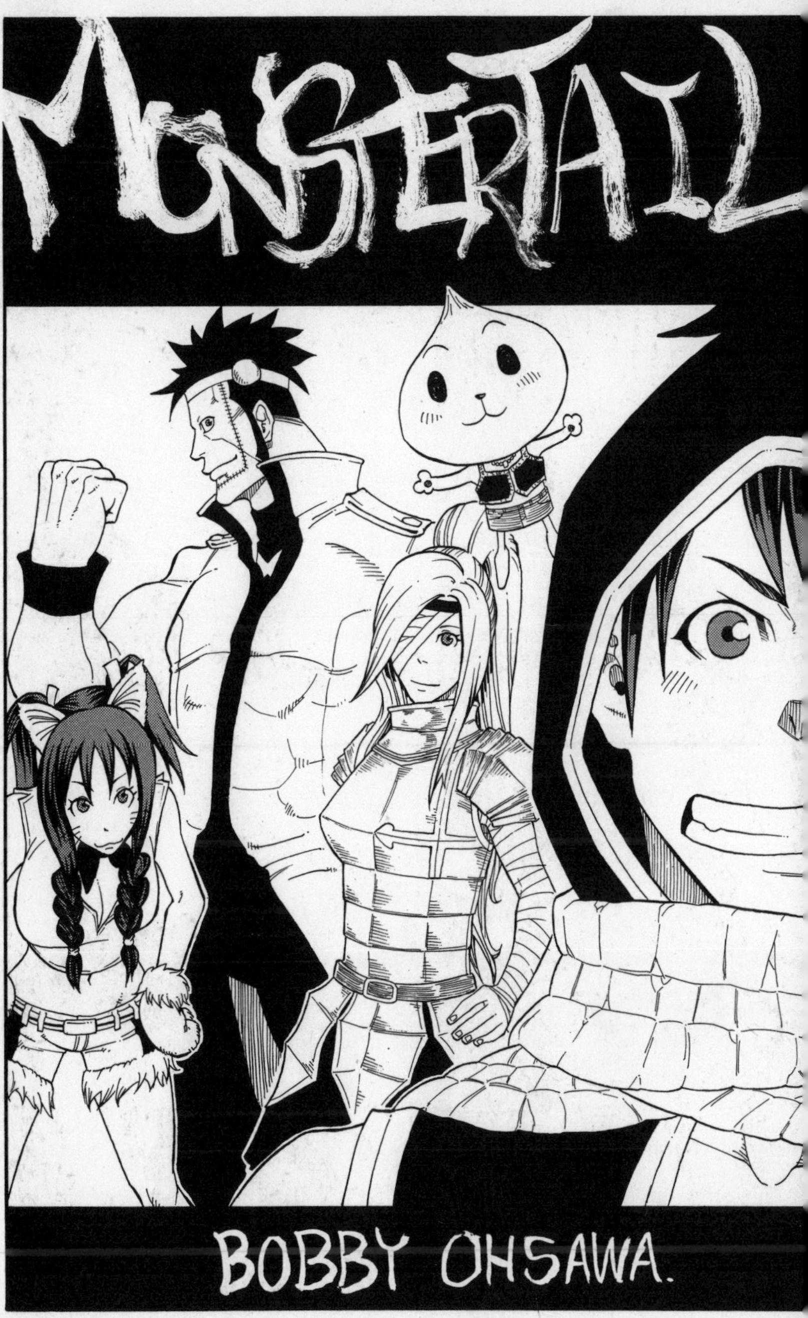
MONSTERTAIL
BOBBY OHSAWA.

by Bobby

Sketches

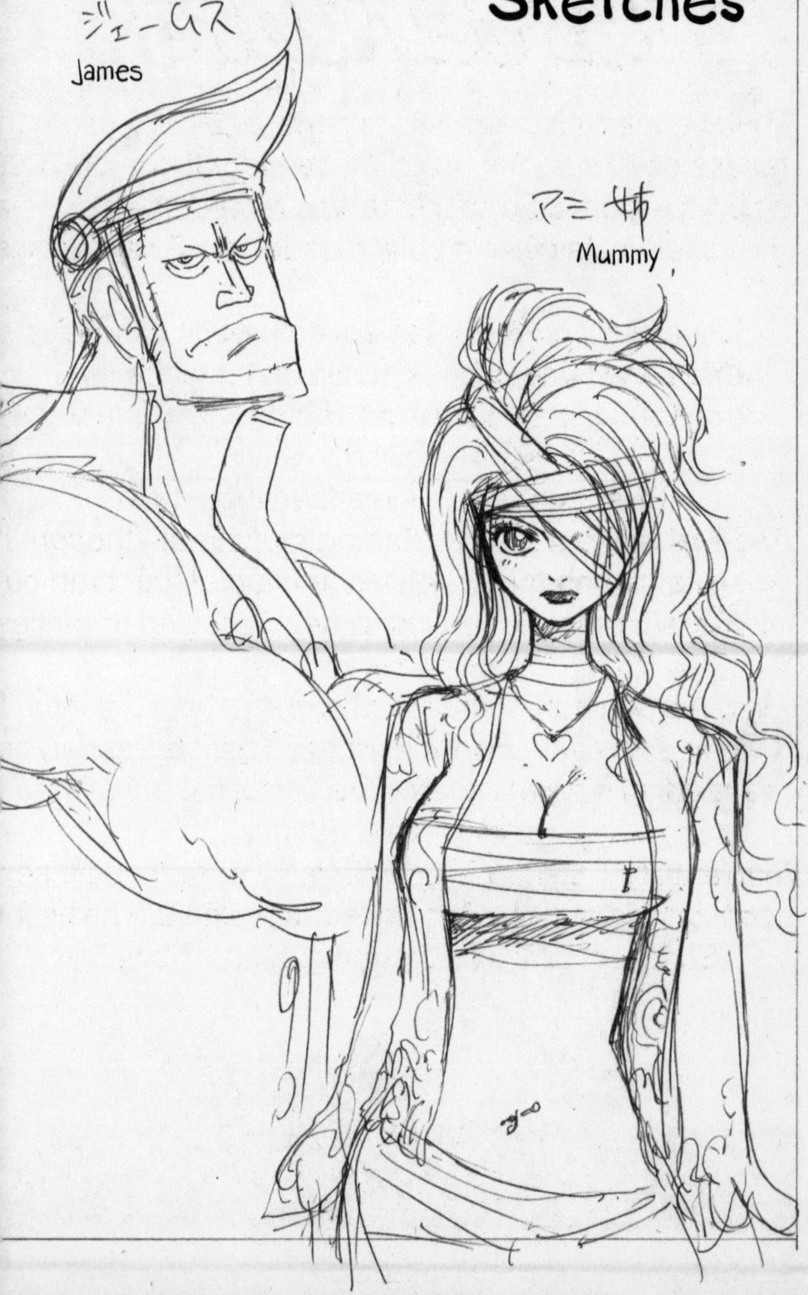
ジェームス
James
Mummy

Afterword

This manga was a short-term serial originally run in th
magazine Comic Bonbon from January to March 200(
When the Comic Bonbon line was retired, the story wa
reprinted in its current edition under the Rival Comics
line.

I love playing RPGs. I've adventured in countless
worlds and vanquished countless monsters for their
experience, gold and items. But one day, a thought
popped into my head.

"How do the monsters feel about this?"

And that led to a manga starring monsters! I thought I
make a human the enemy each chapter, but I ran ou
of ideas by the second installment. That led to battles
between monsters.

In consideration of the magazine's target audience, I
tried to skew this one for a slightly younger reader, bu
re-reading it now, it seems like the same old manga I
always draw. (laughs)

Incidentally, I really like how Mummy turned out: a sex
cool big sister type. She ended up being the basis for
Erza, a character in my next series, Fairy Tail.

anslation Notes

anese is a tricky language for most Westerners, and translation is often more than science. For your edification and reading pleasure, here are notes on ne of the places where we could have gone in a different direction on our nslation, or where a Japanese cultural reference is used.

ıe, page 22

: spikey-nosed mascot character of author Hiro Mashima's first hit series, *ve Master!* Plue has made cameos here and there throughout Mashima's ious works. He's technically a dog... kind of.

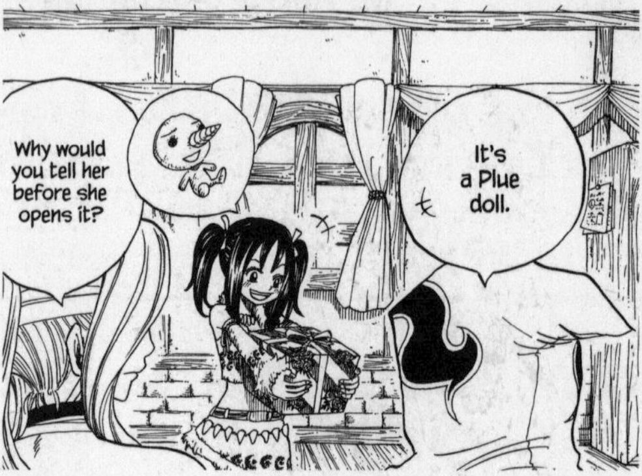

It's a Plue doll.
Why would you tell her before she opens it?

's me" scam, page 22

ype of phone scam that was notable in Japan in the past. Scammers would call elderly and pretend to be their grandchildren by saying, "It's me, it's me!" (In anese this was called the *ore-ore* scam after the masculine self-pronoun *ore.*) : grandparents, unable to tell the difference based on the voice alone, would n be tricked into wiring the scammers money due to some kind of disaster. example, "I hit someone's car and need to pay insurance! Can you send me ne money?"

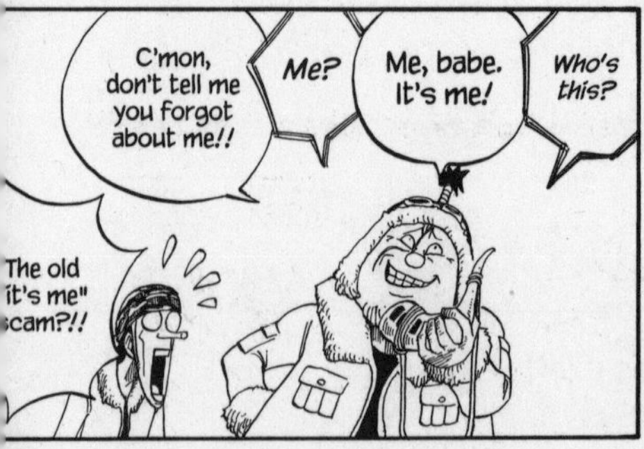

Who's this?
Me, babe. It's me!
Me?
C'mon, don't tell me you forgot about me!!
The old it's me" scam?!!

SHERLOCK BONES

DEDUCTIVE DOG DETECTIVE

When Takeru adopts a new pet, he's in for a surprise—the dog is none other than the reincarnation of Sherlock Holmes. With no one else able to communicate with Holmes, Takeru is roped into becoming Sherdog's assistant, John Watson. Using his sleuthing skills, Holmes uncovers clues to solve the trickiest crimes. 🐾

A KODANSHA COMICS TRADE PAPERBACK ORIGINAL.

PUBLISHED IN THE UNITED STATES BY KODANSHA COMICS, AN IMPRINT OF KODANSHA USA PUBLISHING, LLC, NEW YORK.

PUBLICATION RIGHTS FOR THIS ENGLISH EDITION ARRANGED THROUGH KODANSHA LTD., TOKYO.

FIRST PUBLISHED IN JAPAN IN 2007 BY KODANSHA LTD., TOKYO.

ISBN 978-1-61262-589-8

PRINTED IN THE UNITED STATES OF AMERICA.

WWW.KODANSHACOMICS.COM

9 8 7 6 5 4 3 2 1

TRANSLATOR: STEPHEN PAUL
LETTERING: PAIGE PUMPHREY

TOMARE!
STOP

You're going the wrong way!

Manga is a completely different type of reading experience.

To start at the beginning,
Go to the end!

That's right! Authentic manga is read the traditional Japanese way—from right to left, exactly the opposite of how American books are read. It's easy to follow: Just go to the other end of the book and read each page—and each panel—from right side to left side, starting at the top right. Now you're experiencing manga as it was meant to be!